THE GREAT DIRIGIBLES

THEIR TRIUMPHS AND DISASTERS

THE GREAT DIRIGIBLES

THEIR TRIUMPHS AND DISASTERS

(formerly titled: *Ships in the Sky:
The Story of the Great Dirigibles*)

BY JOHN TOLAND

DOVER PUBLICATIONS, INC., NEW YORK

Published in Canada by General Publishing Company, Ltd., 30 Lesmill Road, Don Mills, Toronto, Ontario.
Published in the United Kingdom by Constable and Company, Ltd., 10 Orange Street, London WC 2.

This Dover edition, first published in 1972, is an unabridged republication of the work originally published as *Ships in the Sky: The Story of the Great Dirigibles* by Henry Holt and Company, New York, in 1957. A new footnote (on page 339) has been written by the author specially for the present edition. A few minor errata have been rectified.

International Standard Book Number: 0-486-21397-8
Library of Congress Catalog Card Number: 72-81284

Manufactured in the United States of America
Dover Publications, Inc.
180 Varick Street
New York, N.Y. 10014

For Marcia and Diana

CONTENTS

Picture section follows page 64

PROLOGUE

When the huge air-liner, the *Hindenburg*, approached Lakehurst Naval Air Station at 5:10 P.M., October 9, 1936, there wasn't a passenger aboard who doubted that the airship, long held to be a dangerous and impractical invention, was the final answer to those who wanted to travel in luxury, in the shortest time, to the farthest points of the world.

Never before, or since, had so many famous names been collected in one aircraft. This human cargo was collectively worth more than four times as much as all the wealthy passengers on the ill-starred maiden voyage of the *Titanic*. Seventy-three leaders of industry and government were aboard at the joint invitation of Dr. Hugo Eckener, head of the German Zeppelin Transport Company, and the Esso Marketers. Although the ostensible purpose of the ten-hour trip was to enjoy the scenery of New England, brilliant now in its fall foliage, the real purpose was to convince these hard-headed industrialists that commercial airship service was the next logical step in man's constant effort to improve his means of transportation.

In 1936 the *Hindenburg* had inaugurated a new transatlantic passenger service. In that brief time the big dirigible had flown with unfailing regularity, in rain, fog, and storm, and had done much to allay the public distrust inspired by the terrible airship disasters of the early thirties. Not even the devastating hurricane that had uprooted so much of New England earlier that fall had stopped the *Hindenburg*. So calm was the trip that most of the passengers weren't aware they were passing over scenes of violent destruction. In fact, no one was even slightly seasick. It seemed that Dr. Eckener, the visionary with the goatee, was well on the way to vindicating himself.

The season had also been a revelation to investors. The ship, twice the size of the *Graf Zeppelin* and more than three city blocks long, was as cheap to run as a Ford car. A scant 300 dollars' worth of crude oil was needed to carry a trip payload of seventy passengers at 400 dollars each, plus 26,000 pounds of freight at a dollar a pound. Air flight, reduced from the 2250 dollars charged per passenger by the *Graf Zeppelin*, was now no longer for the rich alone but well within the budget of the average traveler.

The luxury of the *Hindenburg* was another inducement. The ship boasted seventy modernistic private cabins, six toilets, a shower bath, a spacious dining room, an ornate lounge furnished with special lightweight easy chairs and grand piano, and two long observation decks for those who liked to walk while sailing.

The *Hindenburg's* larder was stocked with turkeys, live lobsters, gallons of ice cream, crates of all kinds of fruits, cases of American whisky, and hundreds of bottles of German beer. Its freight manifests were weird, ranging from two antelopes bound for a German zoo and a circus equestrienne's trained horse to automobiles and airplanes. Only one item had ever been turned down, and that with deep regrets—a full-grown elephant.

And its flights were so comfortable that one socialite said enthusiastically as she landed at Lakehurst, "Traveling this way is a wonderful beauty asset. It is so absolutely calm and effortless. There is no nervous strain. Now any woman knows what that does for your appearance."

Besides comfort, the ship offered by far the fastest transatlantic passage of its day. Only nine days before, reporter Dorothy Kilgallen had chosen the *Hindenburg* for the first leg of a spectacular round-the-world race with two male rivals from the *Telegram* and *Times*. One evening she inspected the control car and the Watch Officer offered to let her pilot the great ship. She was amazed to discover that it steered as easily as an automobile.

The ship had already established too many "firsts" to be listed, including the first mass ever celebrated in the skies. Till then, because of the risk of spilling the consecrated wine, the mass in the air had been forbidden; but when it was proved that a fountain pen had been balanced on end for many hours of flight, the Pope gave his permission. Father Paul Schulte conducted services over the ocean on the Feast of the Apparition of St. Michael, the patron saint of mariners.

More than a billion dollars were riding the *Hindenburg* on that beautiful October 9 in 1936. Nelson Rockefeller, Winthrop Aldrich, and Thomas McCarter were aboard. Also on hand were three admirals, a general, well-known newsmen, a former governor, assorted government officials, and aviation leaders including the ubiquitous Eddie Rickenbacker. As John B. Kennedy, the noted announcer, told his NBC Blue Network listeners, "We've got enough notables aboard to make the *Who's Who* say what's what."

On boarding the ship, almost everyone had felt an unwilling
sense of danger. A series of spectacular airship accidents, played up
melodramatically by the press, had given most people an instinctive
fear of dirigibles. The passengers were not notably relieved when
the German officers confiscated lighters and matches and warned of
the dangers of fire. Hydrogen gas was still being used, explained an
officer in a matter-of-fact tone, and one match in the wrong place
would blow them all out of the sky. Then the man in the midnight-
blue uniform added reassuringly that there hadn't ever been an
accident in a commercial Zeppelin. All one had to do was obey
safety regulations.

However a few minutes in the air dispelled everyone's fears. The
ride was so smooth and quiet and peaceful—and the Germans
were so capable and confident. At first Winthrop Aldrich was
keenly aware of the sixteen huge cells full of flammable hydrogen,
but soon he felt "a sense of great security." Kennedy expressed the
general feeling when he told his radio audience that ". . . it seems
no more exciting than a ride in a trolley car and it's a thousand
times more comfortable."

The day was one continuous triumph for the airship that German Ambassador Hans Luther, also aboard, had called "our second
ambassador to America."

Early that morning the streets of Elizabeth and Newark were
jammed with the curious. At 8:53 A.M. the shouts of children on
their way to school in Yonkers could be heard by passengers looking out the windows of the lounges. The ship passed over the colorful Danbury Fair, wound through the Housatonic Valley, and on
toward Boston. Below, millions stopped their work to cheer, and
all along the route factory whistles blasted out a welcome.

Shortly after noon the guests enjoyed the most sumptuous meal
ever served in the air. There was Indian swallow nest soup, cold
Rhine salmon, tenderloin steak, chateau potatoes, beans à la Prin-
cesse, Carmen salad, iced California melon, Turkish coffee, French
pastry, liqueurs, and the finest wines and beer, including 1934er
Piesporter Goldtröpfchen and 1928er Feist Brut.

After lunch the famous guests hung out the big, slanted windows of the two promenades, entranced by the panorama below
them. As the ship wheeled over Boston, Paul Litchfield, president
of Goodyear, proudly pointed out his alma mater, M.I.T. And a
few moments later Winthrop Aldrich, chairman of the board of
the Chase National Bank, just as proudly pointed out the landmarks of his old school, Harvard.

Several hours later, as the *Hindenburg* headed in confidently for
the Lakehurst mooring mast, everyone agreed that it had been a

delightful and instructive trip. Even now Medley Whelpley recalls the great comfort of the ship. Byron Foy, head of De Soto Motors, won't forget the smoothness of the voyage. Joseph Ripley, president of Brown, Harriman and Company, was impressed by the wonderful food and wine. John Royal, then vice-president of NBC, admired the heavy glassware so much he resolved to commandeer a set as a souvenir. And to Jim Kilgallen of INS, whose young daughter Dorothy was just then in the middle of her race around the world, it was like a gracious party on a yacht. "They had good German beer," he remembers with a smile, "and plenty of it." It was, as announcer Kennedy said, "the end of a perfect day in the air."

At 5:17 P.M. the "Millionaires' Flight" ended safely. It had been even more successful than Eckener had hoped. American capital had been "sold" on airship travel, and the government officials aboard were so impressed they promised to recommend that the United States help subsidize an American airship company. It was proposed that two American commercial airships, larger than the *Hindenburg,* be built. Baltimore and Alexandria, Virginia, were selected as tentative airship ports.

That October day in 1936 the future of the dirigible seemed assured; Dr. Eckener's great dream, inherited from Count Zeppelin, seemed within an ace of final realization. Everyone, from the man in the street to the infallible New York *Times,* was convinced the *Hindenburg* would become even more famous and spectacular in 1937.

They were right.

1

THE AMAZING
DR. SOLOMON ANDREWS

On September 5, 1862, Washington was in a feverish state of excitement. There were rumors that Stonewall Jackson had crossed the Potomac and was only a few miles from the city. The coffee houses and hotels buzzed with stories of treason by Union generals. Some accused Pope and McDowell. Others had "positive" information that Fitz-John Porter had sold out his country to General Lee.

Then a rumor of a different nature began spreading among high government officials: a "madman from New Jersey," had just submitted an invention to Lincoln and Secretary of War Stanton that might turn the tide of battle overnight. The "madman" was Solomon Andrews, a fifty-six-year-old physician from Perth Amboy, New Jersey. He claimed that he could build an airship that would easily sail "5 to 10 miles into Secessia and back again." Andrews was so confident that he agreed to forfeit real estate valued at more than 50,000 dollars if his airship failed.

Ever since the Montgolfier Brothers had sent up the first balloon on June 5, 1783, inventors all over the world had been struggling to produce a dirigible—that is, a self-propelled balloon that could be steered. The Frenchman Giffard had come the closest in 1852 with a 104-foot-long, cigar-shaped gas bag driven by a steam engine. But although this airship actually could go forward at six and a half miles an hour, the slightest breeze brought it to a standstill in midair.

In spite of the long line of failures that had preceded him, Dr. Andrews was positive that his flying machine, the *Aereon*, could master the stiffest wind; and he was so persuasive that Stanton turned him over to the Bureau of Topographical Engineers.

"What will it cost?" asked Captain Lee, one of the assistants to the chief of the Bureau.

"Not over five thousand dollars," answered the inventor, a big, handsome man with a magnetic personality. "And," he added without hesitation, "I'll guarantee its success or no pay."

Lee was impressed in spite of his natural skepticism and the ap-

parent wildness of the project. He knew that Andrews was no hum-
bug but a highly respected citizen. In fact, he had been mayor of
Perth Amboy three times and president of the Board of Health for
many years. And there was no doubting Andrews' inventive genius.
He was already credited with twenty-four successful inventions, including a sewing machine, a barrel-making machine, fumigators,
forging presses, a kitchen range, a gas lamp, and a padlock used by
the United States Post Office since 1842.

At the age of twenty-six he had put 1000 dollars in cash in an
iron chest chained to a lamp post at the corner of Broad and Wall
streets in New York City. He then secured the chest with a combination lock of his invention, announcing that anyone who could pick
the lock could take the money. The crooks and experts of New
York tried for a month to open the chest. All failed. On this one
lock he made a tidy fortune, 30,000 dollars.

Dr. Andrews had also had time to build up a successful medical
practice, get married, construct the first sewer in Perth Amboy, be
Port Collector, save his town from cholera and yellow-fever epidem-
ics, and sire five daughters and two sons. He was an active man.

Lee told the doctor to come back the next day. He wanted a high
official of the Bureau to hear the incredible story of the airship.

That night Dr. Andrews was so excited that he found it difficult
to sleep. Never had he been so close to the realization of his fondest
hope. He had been dreaming of flying ever since a hot Sunday afternoon at the Perth Amboy Presbyterian Church when he was trying
to stay awake during one of his father's sermons. He was seventeen
then. He looked out of a church window and saw an eagle swooping.
"Not till I have the wings of a bird," he promised himself, "will I be
at rest!"

Years later, in 1849, he and his colleagues of "The Inventor's
Institute"—a cooperative organization of inventors that he had
set up in the old British barracks of Perth Amboy—built an airship.
Although it never left the big balloon house, Andrews learned so
much by his mistakes that now he was positive he could fly. He was
so positive that he was willing to gamble his reputation, his fortune
—and his life.

Next morning, by the time Andrews got to the Bureau of Topographical Engineers, the city was in a fright. Enemy gunboats were
in sight of the Capitol. General Pope resigned his command so he
could prefer charges against Fitz-John Porter and two other generals.

At the Bureau a nervous little man listened for a few minutes
while Andrews described the flying machine that was going to save
the tottering Union. The little man, whose name Andrews never

learned, grew excited when he learned of the doctor's past successes But he frowned over the plans. They showed no visible means of propulsion. "But what motive power will you use, Dr. Andrews?" he asked.

Andrews leaned forward. "Gravitation," he said mysteriously.

The official sniffed in disgust, turned on his heel, and left the room without saying another word.

Several days later the Bureau reported that "the device appears to be ingenious in a high degree but we are not fully convinced of its practical utility."

When Andrews learned of the rebuff he was indignant but undiscouraged. He decided to build the airship himself and present it to the government "in the hope that it may shorten the war."

He hastened to Perth Amboy and began work on the *Aereon* (a portmanteau word of his own invention meaning "age of air"). Andrews' theory was that an airship should be shaped to offer the least forward resistance and the maximum vertical resistance. His revolutionary dirigible was made of three parallel cigar-shaped balloons, each eighty feet long and thirteen feet wide. Inside these cylinders were twenty-one cells to prevent movement of the gas. Slung under the three cylinders was a basket twelve feet long and sixteen inches wide. Nearby was a small ballast car that ran on tracks. When this car was moved forward the ship would dive, and rise when it was moved back.

Seamstresses of Perth Amboy sewed the cylinders from 1200 yards of Irish linen. John Wise, the noted balloonist, made the twenty-one inner cells from 1300 yards of cambric muslin.

Under Andrews' constant supervision the ship was finished by the end of May, 1863, at a total cost of 10,000 dollars. On June 1 the twenty-one cells were filled with hydrogen, and the strange airship was pulled out of the large balloon building. Andrews and his helpers dragged the three cylinders to the open Commons behind the barracks. There the basket was attached to the hundreds of ropes that encircled the cylinders: the balloon-house ceiling was so low that final assemblage could not be completed indoors.

The wind gently tugged at the airship as Andrews, tense with excitement, stepped into the basket. He nodded to architect Ellis C. Waite, who was holding onto the basket, and then shouted, "Cut loose!"

Hamilton Fonda, foreman of the U. S. Mail Lock Factory, cut the ballast ropes, and the *Aereon* shot forward rapidly. After forty years of dreaming the doctor was airborne for the first time.

Fonda was stunned. Although he had helped build the ship, he'd had no faith in the machine. The other watchers were amazed.

S. V. R. Paterson, cashier of the Perth Amboy City Bank, was standing, feet apart and mouth wide open.

One skeptic remarked that the *Aereon* was just floating with the
wind. So it seemed, for the thirty-foot-long streamer attached to the
rudder was standing out straight behind the airship.

But suddenly the odd-looking dirigible wheeled gracefully and
headed back toward them, rising to a height of 200 feet. Everyone
cheered. The amazing Dr. Andrews was actually flying against the
wind!

A moment later Andrews coasted into a gentle landing, his face
ruddy with elation and the wind. Paterson, Waite, and Fonda,
babbling incomprehensibly, pumped the inventor's hand. The
Aereon had briefly fulfilled the promise in her name.

A second series of flights took place in July. Since all but one of
Wise's inner balloons had collapsed half an hour after the first inflation in June, they had been taken out and the cylinders inflated
directly. This lightened the ship by 180 pounds, and longer trips
were hazarded by the flying doctor. By this time Andrews had become an excellent pilot. He had learned that the *Aereon's* seven-
teen-foot-square rudder was extremely sensitive—so sensitive that,
unless great care was taken, a simple turn would become a complete
circle. He had also learned that the ballast car wasn't necessary: he
could change the angle of the ship by merely shifting his weight in
the basket.

A month later the ship was brought out to the Commons for further trials. Two prominent citizens who had publicly expressed
their doubt about the *Aereon* were invited by Andrews to be on
hand. These men—John Manning, a prosperous merchant and ex-
Postmaster of Perth Amboy, and Judge Isaac D. Ward, the town's
Justice of the Peace—were established on a fence near the Commons when Andrews stepped into his car for the third trial. This
time the *Aereon* climbed high into the sky and zoomed over the
Sound. A moment later it returned "faster than a cannon-ball."

Manning jumped to his feet. "Three cheers for the success of Dr.
Andrews!" he shouted. The small crowd cheered. The judge took
off his hat in solemn salute.

After the successful August flights Andrews had supreme confi-
dence in his flying machine. As a last proof to the doubting War
Department he planned a spectacular flight from Perth Amboy to
New York and return.

But a close friend, a lawyer, warned him that the airship, even
though it had been turned down, was "contraband of war." Since a
public flight might reveal the *Aereon's* secret method of propulsion
to the Confederates, Andrews canceled the New York junket.

On August 26, 1863, he wrote a letter to President Lincoln. He told of the successful experiments, adding that he was going to make one final test. He would free the *Aereon* of all ballast and see how fast she could fly. Then he would destroy the ship so the Confederates couldn't copy her.

"Now all that I desire," he concluded, "is that your Excellency will select some suitable person, the more scientific and practical the better, and send him here that he may examine the machine and witness the trial."

No reply came from Washington, so the inventor decided to conduct his last "grand experiment" without War Department witnesses. On September 4, *Aereon* Number 1 was once more dragged from her balloon house and rigged up. The crowd for the final trial was large. Rumors of the fantastic airship had reached New York, and reporters from several of the big newspapers were present.

At five that afternoon the sky was clear with scattered clouds. A wind of about ten miles an hour was blowing from the west. Andrews cast off, skillfully drove the ship up to 1000 feet. To the utter amazement of newcomers the flying doctor headed directly into the wind.

James Allen, keeper of the City Hotel, who had come to scoff, stayed to admire. When he saw Andrews steer the airship easily into the wind, he cried out, "It's as easy as a steamboat could be turned!" At first N. H. Tyrrell, Collector of Taxes and Constable of Perth Amboy, couldn't believe what he was seeing; but in time he convinced himself. Through it all the young reporter from the New York *Herald* excitedly scribbled notes.

After several flights had proved to everyone the maneuverability of the *Aereon*, Andrews ordered the basket cut loose from the airship. A rudder cord was lashed to one side. There was a pause. Then the *Aereon* was released. The pilotless airship swiftly soared into the sky, making ascending spirals about three-quarters of a mile in diameter. It shot past clouds going in the opposite direction at a dizzying pace.

Foreman Fonda had never seen anything but a skyrocket or cannon ball go at such tremendous speed.

"I never saw any vessel, railroad car, or other thing of magnitude go so fast," declared Architect Waite.

The *Herald* reporter estimated that the speed of the airship was at least 120 miles an hour.

It was apparent to everyone that the ship was moving with the wind and then against it. About two miles above the earth, the ship went through the first stratum of clouds, seeming to scatter them in

all directions. After twenty great circles the *Aereon* disappeared in
the upper layer of thick clouds. It was never seen again.

The next day all Perth Amboy buzzed about the incredible last
flight. Dr. Andrews, who had always been considered the town's
most talented man, was cheered as a genius. A few days later, on
September 8, the New York *Herald* called the *Aereon* "the most
extraordinary invention of the age, if not the most so of any the
world ever saw——"

The fame of the ship and its eccentric inventor traveled far. The
Webster, Massachusetts, *Times* declared that "with such a machine
in the hands of Jefferson Davis, the armies around Washington would
be powerless to defend the capitol."

Inspired by the success of *Aereon* Number 1, Andrews hounded
the War Department until he was finally granted a personal interview with Abraham Lincoln.

Andrews told the President about his airship and the last conclu-
sive test.

"Were there any witnesses?" asked Lincoln.

Andrews nodded.

"Go home, Mr. Andrews, and request four or five respectable per-
sons to write to me what they saw. Then," promised Lincoln, "I will
take action on it."

Within a few days ex-Postmaster Manning, architect Waite, Constable Tyrrell, cashier Paterson, and Judge Ward had written enthusiastic letters to the President expressing their unqualified enthusiasm for Dr. Andrews' airship.

Months passed and nothing happened. In disgust Andrews returned to Washington, only to discover that Lincoln had never seen
the testimonial letters. Four times the President's secretary promised
to place these letters on Lincoln's desk. The promises were never
kept.

In January, 1864, Andrews sent a petition to the Senate and House
of Representatives, asking that action be taken. He threatened that
if nothing were done he'd fly over Washington in a new airship.

After weeks of interviews Andrews was allowed to give a demon-
stration of models of his dirigible to both military committees of
Congress. Andrews rushed an order to Paris for India-rubber models
of the *Aereon*. They arrived just before his scheduled demonstra-
tion in the basement of the Capitol building. Andrews filled the
four-foot miniatures with hydrogen. All previous models had failed
to sustain their own weight, and he was praying that the new
ones would work. He released the first little airship. It popped
out of his hand at a 40-degree angle and sped across the room
to the delight of the assembled witnesses. Andrews set the

rudder of the next ship; it described a perfect turn. Andrews lectured as he demonstrated, and his performance was so convincing that Senator Wilson requested that the Secretary of War appoint a scientific commission to examine the invention and make a report.

Andrews was elated. After many heartbreaking months of delays he felt he had won the battle of red tape.

A few weeks later, on March 18, 1864, the first meeting of the new commission was held in a library room of the Smithsonian Institution. Andrews' little models again performed flawlessly. Two other meetings were held, and the investigation was closed on March 27. Andrews returned to Perth Amboy satisfied that the commission had been greatly impressed.

The inventor was right. On July 22 the three esteemed members of the commission, Major J. C. Woodruff, A. D. Bache, Superintendent of the U. S. Coast Survey, and Joseph Henry, Secretary of the Smithsonian Institution, turned in a glowing report that recommended an immediate appropriation for the new airship.

A copy of the report was sent to Andrews. He was jubilant. But summer faded into fall and still there was no word from Washington.

Upon investigation Andrews discovered that the report had never reached Secretary Stanton. It had been somehow mislaid. And Andrews was asked to forward his own copy to the Chairman of the House Military Affairs Committee. He complied.

Another month passed. Then Andrews found out that a new problem had arisen: no action could be taken on a copy—the original was required.

Andrews returned to Washington to track down the missing document. He was shunted from one office to the next for weeks. Finally he was told the original report had been located and was at last on its way.

More time passed. Then on March 22, 1865, Andrews got a letter from Robert Schenck. No one else on the Military Committee, wrote Schenck, had the least interest in the airship. By now the war was almost over and such a machine was felt to be unnecessary. He advised Andrews to drop the matter, for it was a "hopeless effort against doubt and prejudice."

Dr. Andrews chose this time to fall from a carriage and break his arm. But for a man who thrived on adversity the enforced vacation was a splendid opportunity to write a book. In *The Art of Flying* he at last revealed the secret of his bizarre method of propulsion. The difference of specific gravity between the balloon and the atmosphere in which it floated, he declared, could be applied as a power to propel the airship in any direction. The New York *Herald* a few months later printed an authorized clarification of Andrews' theory. "If two cylindroids are placed horizontally side by side," explained the *Herald*, "there is formed between them a longitudinal cavity above and below. This concave surface offers more resistance to motion in air than a convex or plane surface, consequently rapid perpendicular ascent or descent is prevented and the power of rising or sinking perpendicularly converted into a force to move the balloon obliquely upward or downward in the direction in which it will move the most easily——"

To those who wished a simpler explanation Andrews merely replied that he sailed his ship as if it were a sailboat.

His book also proclaimed his personal philosophy of life. "The real and true inventor is never foiled except by sickness or death. His ingenuity and perseverance are equal to all emergencies. His greatest pleasure is in overcoming difficulties."

Immediately he put his philosophy into further practice by organizing the Aerial Navigation Company. Now that the war was practically over he was no longer restrained by patriotic scruples. He decided to build commercial airships and establish a regular line between New York and Philadelphia.

Eighteen thousand dollars, two-thirds from Andrews' own pocket, was raised for the new company. By the end of 1865 work had started on *Aereon* Number 2 in a shed on the corner of Greene and Houston streets in New York. Unlike the 1863 model, the new *Aereon* had only one cylinder—a huge lemon-shaped gas bag with sharply pointed ends. To ascend in the first ship Andrews threw out ballast, and to descend he let hydrogen escape through valves. For *Aereon* Number 2 he devised a new, complicated system of controlling altitude by manipulating cords and pulleys to expand and contract the volume of gas.

Two army-surplus balloons, the *Union* and the *Intrepid*, were cut up to make the envelope. The car from the 1863 ship had been saved and was slightly remodeled.

At nine o'clock on the morning of May 25, 1865, Andrews began inflating the newly completed airship with hydrogen. If the weather remained good, the first flight of *Aereon* Number 2 would take place that afternoon.

It was a busy day for Andrews and his three partners, George Trow, C. M. Plumb, and G. Waldo Hill. Few knew of the trip, and there was only a handful of spectators when the inflation was completed at three in the afternoon.

At last everything was ready. Andrews stepped into the car. He was followed by his nervous partners.

A light wind was blowing from the southwest. Andrews cried, "Cut loose!"

The great lemon rose quickly, easily clearing the tall buildings and chimneys that surrounded the "Balloon Works." But when Andrews pulled sharply on the rudder cords the airship refused to respond. The ropes had become tangled with the rigging. The *Aereon* soon reached 2000 feet and then drifted northward until it was directly over 14th Street and Fifth Avenue.

While Andrews struggled with the controls, the three passengers fearfully hung onto the edges of the pitching basket. It seemed certain that in a few seconds the entire Aerial Navigation Company would be dumped out of the airship. But as the basket tilted dangerously, Andrews at last freed the rudder ropes and turned the airship southwest, directly against the wind. Five minutes later he headed north again.

Below there was consternation on Fifth Avenue. Men shouted and children screamed. People streamed out of the fashionable houses to stare at this most remarkable phenomenon. At 21st Street even the staid members of the staid Union Club joined the street crowds. Little squares of pasteboard were now fluttering down from the airship. "*Souvenir* of her trial trip from the car of Andrews' *Flying Ship*," read the first sky advertisement in history. "*Tempus Fugit Tempore Fugit Homo,*" prophesied Andrews.

At 26th Street members of the Eclectic Club were in the street looking up in wonder. At 657 Fifth Avenue, near 52nd Street, the notorious Madam Restell, "the wickedest woman in all America," was enjoying the sight from the top floor of her large brownstone house. The famous abortionist, who did a yearly business of 30,000 dollars, waved a bejeweled arm at the intrepid Dr. Andrews and his three companions.

The airship now turned and headed across the East River for Brooklyn. At the Capitoline Grounds the large crowd watching the ninth inning of the baseball game between the New York Knickerbockers and the Excelsiors (won eventually by the Excelsiors, 56-42) looked up in disbelief as the floating lemon passed overhead and headed toward Astoria.

A few minutes later the first airship ever to fly over New York landed safely in Ravenswood's Wood.

Although Andrews was somewhat disappointed with the flight because of the balky rudder, those who saw the *Aereon* from below were greatly excited. The newspaper reports ran to extravagances of prose and praise. "Lovers can henceforth soar almost as near heaven as their aspirations can carry them already," exulted the New York

World in the next day's edition, "while above the terrestrial grandeur and fashion of Central Park pleasure, parties can partake of rarified sweets in rarified atmosphere."

The *Herald* man was just as rhapsodic. "After being *supra nimbos* for about twenty-five minutes," he wrote, "the docile and beautiful steam-winged bird was successfully persuaded to pay a terrestrial visit to Astoria where both her highness and her privileged masculine convoy were received with surprise and welcome acclimations by the astonished denizens."

Two days later the *World* had recovered enough to make a less poetic but just as enthusiastic judgment of the flight: "Navigation of the air is a fixed act. The problem of the centuries has been solved."

The applause was stimulating, but it did not relieve Dr. Andrews' insolvency. Before the famous New York flight the Aerial Navigation Company had a total indebtedness of $3119.74; and on May 18 a special assessment of 50 per cent had been levied against all the stockholders. Even after the successful May 25 flight the stockholders were not eager to invest more money in the airship. It wasn't until the morning of June 5 that enough had been scraped together for another expensive inflation of hydrogen.

Although the second flight was to be secret, rumors spread. By 5:30 P.M. on June 5 thousands of spectators were crowded on neighboring rooftops and outside the high fences surrounding the airship at the corner of Greene and Houston streets. Inside the enclosure there were about 100 friends, relatives, and reporters. On this trip Andrews had decided to take 400 pounds of ballast, Mr. Plumb, and the enthusiastic young reporter from the *World*. But just as the air travelers were about to cast off, Dr. Andrews, who was smoking a strange-looking pipe of his own invention (guaranteed to filter harmful nicotine), was forced to ask the reporter to dismount. The new rudder and larger basket were too heavy.

Andrews stowed away his pipe and ordered the lines cut.

The airship rose slowly, then started drifting horizontally. It looked as though it would smash into a six-story building across the street.

Plumb quickly threw out twenty-five pounds of sand. The *Aereon* shot up rapidly, just missing the building. Andrews tugged at the rudder, but the ropes were tangled. The ship drifted in circles, out of control, toward Canal Street.

Once again Andrews showed he was equal to emergency. Though the basket threatened to overturn, he worked the ropes calmly and finally freed the snarled controls. Then he brought his ship into the

THE AMAZING DR. SOLOMON ANDREWS

wind, and he and Plumb moved into the back of the car. The *Aereon* was now speeding along 1200 feet directly above Broadway.

Below, New York was in turmoil—a day-long turmoil set off by news that a Fenian Army of 1200, led by General Sweeney, had left St. Albans, Vermont, for an attack on the British in Canada. That day Colonel James Kerrigan, the former Congressman, had enrolled 1500 Irish volunteers at Tammany Hall, which was decked with dozens of green flags. Mobs of Fenians roamed the streets looking for—and finding—gangs of Non-Fenians. But the battles of brickbats and shillelaghs suddenly stopped when the strange airship of Dr. Andrews appeared in the sky.

Few downtown New Yorkers had witnessed the first flight of the *Aereon*. Most of those who hadn't actually seen the flight believed it to be a fake. Many still remembered the extras put out by the *Sun* on April 13, 1844, proclaiming the crossing of the Atlantic by Monck Mason's flying machine. It had turned out to be an elaborate hoax perpetrated by Edgar Allan Poe, who needed fifteen dollars to pay his rent.

But now thousands along Broadway could see the giant lemon-shaped airship right over their heads. There was near-panic in the streets. Women squealed and pointed their sunshades upward. Men found themselves tangled in the women's hoop skirts as they struggled to follow the airship's progress against the wind.

Traffic in the busy, eighty-foot-wide street was hopelessly tied up. Most of the 700 stages that daily traveled up and down Broadway had stopped. The passengers leaned out windows, shouting incredulously. Horses neighed in terror.

Patrons rushed into the streets from elegant restaurants like Taylor's and Delmonico's, and from "nickel" eating houses near the waterfront. Guests ran from cheap east-side lodging houses and from the lobby of the famous Astor House (one dollar a day on the European plan) at 221 Broadway.

Audiences deserted Barnum's American Museum (currently featuring the Tallest Giantess in the world, the three-horned bull, and Master Allie Turner, the Infant Drummer) for Dr. Andrews' wonderful airship.

There were a number of casualties.

High above, Andrews and Plumb were throwing out thousands of souvenir cards and waving to the throngs on rooftops.

Having demonstrated the *Aereon*'s ability to fly against the wind, Andrews turned the ship north again. Just over Blackwells Island (now known as Welfare Island) the gas expanded, and Andrews let the ship rise to 6000 feet. Dramatically it disappeared in the clouds.

After about twenty minutes Andrews valved gas, dropped to 2000 feet. The *Aereon* was over Long Island Sound. Although he had intended trying to make a sensational landing at the 100-foot-square enclosure at Houston Street, the doctor noticed heavy storm clouds gathering in the east; and since the rudder was still hard to handle he decided to land at once. A few minutes later he came down at the village of Oyster Bay.

Everyone in town rushed to the landing field to cheer the unexpected visitors from the sky. Andrews and Plumb were invited to a good dinner at the home of a man named Vernon. Later that night they were transported triumphantly back to New York in a wagon.

Once again the newspapers praised Andrews and the *Aereon*. Even more spectacular flights were predicted in the near future. But in spite of the public approval Dr. Andrews and the *Aereon* were never to fly again. In the postwar panic hundreds of banks failed, and the Aerial Navigation Company was wiped out with thousands of other businesses.

The doctor returned regretfully to his practice in Perth Amboy, taking up once again his duties as Port Officer and president of the Board of Health. His dream of flying was partially fulfilled, and he thought he'd left the secret of "gravitational" propulsion to posterity in his book. But since his second memorable day over the city of New York, no other man has been able to fly an airship without a motor.

THE MAN IN
THE WICKER BASKET

A strange procession was coming across a broad field in the beautiful Jardin d'Acclimatation (the new Zoological Garden of Paris) on a September day in 1898. Excited young Parisian dandies, some in caps and gaily checked knickerbockers, others in top hats and frock coats, were guiding their automobiles at a crawl; and as they drove they kept craning their necks to follow a curious yellow vehicle floating in the air. It looked like a badly shaped cigar.

Following the belching cars was a large, not-so-fashionable, but just as excited group of students and office workers, with girl friends in billowing skirts that swept the ground. They were jabbering and pointing at the eighty-two-and-a-half-foot airship, which several men were drawing on a long rope toward the leeward side of the field.

The crowd's excitement was understandable. There was a chance —only a slight one, but still a chance—that today, September 20, would be the day man would first navigate the air. It was a moment that would compete with the historic launching of Fulton's *Claremont* or the firing of Stephenson's first crude locomotive. That is, if the clumsy-looking airship actually flew.

A dapper young man about the size of a jockey stood nonchalantly in a deep wicker basket suspended by ropes from the gas bag. He was the inventor and navigator of the airship, the wealthy young Brazilian, Alberto Santos-Dumont. He was immaculate in a pin-striped suit, high collar, derby, and kid gloves.

When the floating dirigible approached the tall trees bordering the side of the field, Santos called out an order in a high-pitched, almost effeminate voice. The men on the ropes obediently stopped and pulled the airship down until the basket touched the turf. The Brazilian leaped nimbly to the ground. His peg-topped trousers were worn a fashionable two inches above his ankles, and the heels on his glossy shoes were more than an inch high.

He wrapped a strap around the wheel of the two-cylinder gasoline motor that was fixed behind the basket. Then he pulled sharply.

The motor started with a series of crashing explosions, and the gathering crowd jumped back in fear. At once several members of the exclusive Aero Club pushed forward and tried again to persuade their colleague to postpone his trip until a safe electric motor could be installed.

One young man anxiously pointed with his cane to the flame shooting several feet behind the exhaust. "It's going to explode the hydrogen in the balloon!" he shouted above the coughing of the tiny gas engine.

Santos amiably shook his head. It was his theory, and his alone, that the recently invented gasoline motor was the only answer to the seemingly impossible task of conquering the air. Solomon Andrews' motorless *Aereon* had proved to be too limited in cruising range. And neither Giffard's steam-driven dirigible nor Renard's electric ship had been able to go fast enough to maneuver successfully in the air.

An explosion was the least of Santos' worries, for the flames licking out of the exhaust were a good thirty feet below the hydrogen-filled bag. He felt that the extra horsepower was well worth the risk.

A half-dozen professional balloonists now strolled up to Santos and advised him, in a patronizing way, to start from the other end of the field where he could rise and float with the wind. When he refused to take their advice, they shrugged their shoulders and backed away to a safe distance, waiting for the crash they knew was sure to come.

Santos took a final look at the brilliant blue afternoon sky. Then, satisfied, he climbed into the willow car. The guide rope was slackened, and the elongated balloon began to leave the ground.

Now that the final moment had come, the crowd fell into a frightened silence. Everyone recalled vividly his favorite airship accident: Wolfert had been burned to death in the wreckage of his benzene-powered dirigible; just recently Schwartz's rigid monster had blown to bits in St. Petersburg; and there were many more—enough, indeed, to dampen the ardor of anyone but an airshipman.

Santos stroked his small but quite bushy mustache and calmly gave the signal to release the rope. To the crowd he looked bored. The ship rose rapidly, and Santos headed obliquely into the wind. There was a shocked gasp from the balloonists, who were positive that the ship would be tossed into the nearby trees. Miraculously, the dirigible did just what Santos had predicted: it bucked the wind. The wind acted as a lever, and in a few seconds the *Santos-Dumont* Number 1 was safely above the trees.

The crowd shouted with relief, then almost instantly became quiet again. The ship had wheeled as if blown around and was now skimming along with the wind. A dozen airships had done as much. The big test was to make steady headway in the teeth of the wind. It appeared that the *Santos-Dumont* Number 1 was going to flounder like all the others.

As if in answer to the doubters below, the big yellow dirigible made a sharp turn over the Jardin d'Acclimation and headed straight into the wind, moving briskly and easily.

The crowd cheered wildly. Women fluttered handkerchiefs, mechanics threw grimy caps into the air, and the young dandies from the Aero and Automobile clubs jumped up and down and waved their derbies and high hats. For the first time in history a powered airship had obeyed her rudder!

The ship was now twisting and turning with utter grace. It sailed in every direction of the compass. Then abruptly it made a steep dive. Women screamed in terror. But then the ship swooped up into a climb. The dive had been no accident—just a bit of cavorting by the spirited Santos.

High in the sky, in the willow car that looked like a laundry basket, Santos was tasting a new delight. Many hours of ballooning had prepared him for the sensation of height, even for the sensation of movement; but he had never before felt the wind blow in his face. A balloon always rode *with* the wind.

His flaming red necktie flapping behind him, Santos exultantly executed a neat figure-eight. Then he put two ballast bags in front of him, and the ship dipped. He shifted the bags behind him and the ship rose. He was intoxicated with the power of controlled flight. He was traveling in a new dimension. He was a bird.

Overwhelmed by the splendor of it all, he flew over Paris proper. But when he looked down and saw the lofty rooftops bristling with spikelike chimney pots, it instantly occurred to him that he was frightened. Quickly he headed for the Bois de Boulogne. In a few minutes the fields were an ocean of greenery below, and he felt safe once more. He climbed to what seemed a dizzy height, 1300 feet, then made a circle and started a steep glide toward the earth.

Something popped over his head. He looked up and saw to his horror that the big cigar-shaped balloon had doubled up like a jackknife. The hydrogen in the bag had contracted as the ship fell; the air pump, which was supposed to compensate for the contracting gas, evidently wasn't working; and the bag became limp.

The ship plunged helplessly toward the fields of Bagatelle. Santos didn't know what to do. If he threw out the ballast he would rise, and the hydrogen would again expand and straighten out the bag; but when he descended again the balloon would again collapse. He decided he might as well get it over with.

He let the ship plummet down. Now, as he abandoned hope of coming out of the crash alive, his fears evaporated. Instead he was thinking that in a few minutes he would be seeing his father, who had died several years before.

Three hundred feet from the ground he saw he was falling near a gang of boys. They were flying kites, he observed—and then the idea hit him. As his 200-foot-long guide rope struck the ground he called in his high-pitched voice, "Take the rope! Run into the wind!"

The boys were bright. They grabbed the trailing rope and ran into the wind. Just as the basket was about to crash, the falling balloon soared up like a kite. Santos landed a few seconds later with only a slight bump. He was ruffled but completely unharmed. Presence of mind had saved his life for the first time. It wasn't to be the last.

Even before the first flight of the *Santos-Dumont* Number 1, the Brazilian with the long patent-leather hair had captured the imagination of many Parisians with his daring stunts.

When he was eighteen, his father, the richest planter in Brazil, had given him his emancipation papers, a fat checkbook, and some unusual paternal advice: "Go to Paris, the most dangerous of cities for a young fellow. Let us see if you can make a man of yourself."

Santos sailed immediately for France and, to the wonder of his friends, took up divertissements less traditional than wine and women. He bought one of the newfangled automobiles, climbed Mont Blanc, and became an ardent balloonist.

He added a new fillip to ballooning. On his first trip in the air he took along a luncheon of roast beef, chicken, ice cream, cakes, champagne, hot coffee, and chartreuse. That night he delighted Parisians with his descriptions of his meal in the sky. "No dining room is so marvelous in its decoration," he told the titled and sophisticated members of the Jockey Club.

Santos was so enthralled by this first aerial trip that he designed his own balloon. Soon his balloon—so small that he carried it around in a valise—was a familiar sight over Paris. But even this dangerous sport became too tame for the high-spirited young man. His interest turned to dirigibles, although everyone told him it was impossible to make one that would actually fly. And when his friends of the Aero Club found out that he was going to power his airship with the gasoline motor of his tricycle, they told him flatly that the vibration would shake the airship to pieces.

But Santos was a devotee of Jules Verne and H. G. Wells, and a believer in the impossible. One day as dawn was breaking, he and a friend drove in his tricycle to a secluded part of the Bois de Boulogne. They picked out two trees with low-lying limbs and suspended the motor bike by three ropes.

Santos' friend then boosted him into the saddle of the tricycle. If the mechanics were right, the motor bike—like a bucking bronco—would soon throw Santos to the ground.

The young Brazilian took a deep breath and started the motor. To his delight there was less vibration than on the ground. It was his first triumph in the air! What was more, it taught him to trust his own instinct. Against all prophecies of doom he built his first *Santos-Dumont* and made his historic first flight.

Inspired by this success, the young inventor spent the next few years building and testing three more ships, each an improvement on its predecessor. By this time he had become the rage, not only of the young bloods (who imitated his clothes, his mustache, and his speech) but of all the citizens of Paris. He was a strangely contradictory figure. Although he was a man of the world, he was simple and direct, with the tenacity of a peasant. He was the companion of dukes and princes, chauffeurs and air-minded bank clerks. He would often work all morning in his shirt sleeves with his mechanics, and then turn up at the Cascade, the most fashionable café in the Bois de Boulogne, for lunch with Prince Roland Bonaparte, the Marquis de Dion, or King Leopold.

It was about this time that Henry Deutsch, a balding, bearded, and highly enthusiastic member of the Aero Club, offered a prize of 20,000 dollars to the first man who could fly from the grounds at St.-Cloud to the Eiffel Tower and back—a distance of about seven miles—in thirty minutes.

When Deutsch first announced his prize, he was criticized for having set a goal that couldn't be attained. Santos said little, but he became obsessed with the desire to win the Deutsch Prize, and quietly began building the *Santos-Dumont* Number 5, which featured several startling innovations. He built a triangular wooden keel with his own hands. It was fifty-nine and a half feet long and weighed only ninety pounds. The joints were made of aluminum and reinforced with piano wire instead of rope. To the horror of his mechanics he also changed all the suspension ropes to wire, cutting the dirigible's air resistance almost in half.

The four-cylinder, twelve-horsepower motor was located in the middle of the keel. Santos' basket was far front. A guide rope hung suspended still farther aft. To it Santos fastened the end of a lighter cord. Now, instead of having to shift sandbags to make the ship climb, he merely had to pull on the string, which in turn pulled back the heavy guide rope, shifting the center of gravity.

In the summer of 1901 the new ship was finished. Santos made a secret trial at four-thirty on the morning of July 12. Although his rudder cord broke and he had to land in the middle of the Trocadero Gardens, he was so pleased with the ship's speed and control that he at last had the courage to try for the Deutsch Prize.

He telephoned all the official judges and told them he'd make a run the next morning. The stage was now set for the first attempt in history to fly an airship over a closed course within a specific time limit.

That night Santos slept a few fitful hours near his big balloon house. Not long after midnight he got dressed and began to patrol the field like an expectant father, watching the threatening clouds overhead. By 4:00 A.M. the clouds had broken up somewhat, but there was a gusty wind from the west.

His friends advised him to postpone the flight; but since he had notified the judges the day before, as the rules specified, he felt obliged to go through with it. At five o'clock the spectators began arriving, and Santos gave orders to fill the gas bag.

At six-twenty the great sliding doors of the hangar opened and the airship was pulled onto the field, its pointed nose foremost. Santos was sitting in the basket in his shirt sleeves, a straw hat tilted jauntily on his head. This morning, contrary to his usual reticence, Santos was chattering and laughing like a schoolboy. The Scientific Commission, appointed by the Aero Club to judge the event, walked solemnly up to the basket. Led by the chairman, Prince Roland Bonaparte, each member shook Santos' hand and wished him good luck. Count Henri de la Vaux, vice-president of the Aero Club, who was planning soon to cross the Mediterranean in a balloon, said he hoped Santos would win. And Henry Deutsch, donor of the prize, wrung the Brazilian's hand and begged him warmly to take no chances.

Now the wind was blowing about six meters a second. One end of the balloon was waving in a sad and flabby manner: the sudden change from the warm hangar to the coolness of the morning had reduced the volume of gas. Although air was pumped into a ballonet inside the main balloon, the ship was still not quite rigid.

A mechanic told Santos the dirigible should be returned to the hangar for more hydrogen. But the Brazilian didn't want to keep the huge crowd waiting. He hopped to the ground and yanked the strap, starting the motor. It coughed and sputtered uncertainly. The head mechanic told Santos the motor needed overhauling.

But Santos would have none of it, even though he knew that if the motor stopped in the air it couldn't be started again until the ship landed. Yet he was no longer the gay and carefree adventurer: with his somber face spotted with oil and his striped shirt sleeves rolled up, he looked like a workman at his bench. He climbed into the basket, counted the ballast bags on the floor, checked the two canvas pockets that held loose sand, and saw that the guide rope wasn't fouled. Everything was ready for the flight.

Deutsch and several over friends shook his hand again. The official timer, Count de la Vaux, squinted at his watch. The nervous chatter of the crowd stopped. Santos raised his arm and shouted, "Everybody, let go!"

The guide rope was released and the ship rose.

"Six-forty-one!" called the Count.

To win the prize Santos had to cross the finish line by 7:11 A.M.

The ship rose slowly, drifting toward Versailles, and Santos threw overboard sack after sack of ballast. Those on the ground could see him pulling the rudder lines tight as the ship floated over the Seine. Now it pivoted gracefully and headed for the Eiffel Tower. The big canvas-covered propeller spun so fast that it was a blur, and the ship quickly picked up speed.

In a minute the putt-putt of the motor could no longer be heard at St.-Cloud. The ship got smaller and smaller until it was only a speck in the mist that hung over Paris. As the speck reached the tower it vanished, but a moment later it could be seen emerging out of the mist. A man with opera glasses said he was sure Santos hadn't gone around the tower. Another said he had. The argument was joined, and waxed heavy. It was still going on when a car bounced onto the field and stopped with a screech. The driver jumped out and ran toward the judges waving a piece of paper. It was a message from the official timer at the Eiffel Tower. Santos had successfully rounded the tower, almost scraping its sides, at 6:54 A.M.

The news spread rapidly, and soon everyone on the field was certain Santos would win. But as the minutes ticked by, the yellow dirigible seemed to be making little headway. At last it chugged over the Seine, fighting a stiff breeze. Now there were only three minutes left. The crowd shouted in unison, desperately exhorting Santos to hurry. But the motor was popping asthmatically; the ship was barely gaining.

It wasn't until 7:22 A.M., eleven minutes late, that Santos finally flew over the judges. Before a landing could be attempted, the ship was driven back toward the Seine, and across it. Twice Santos returned, but each time, like a swimmer struggling against a riptide, he was pushed back. Finally the motor stopped, and the ship was swept over the Bois de Boulogne, completely out of control.

"Something's happened!" cried a woman.

Then the balloon doubled up.

"He's falling!"

The horrified spectators watched as the *Santos-Dumont* Number 5 plunged out of sight. A dozen of Santos' closest friends leaped into their automobiles and raced toward the wreck. They expected to find him dead.

Half an hour later their roaring, sputtering cars rolled into the large estate of the Baron de Rothschild. They could see the yellow balloon tangled in the top of a huge chestnut tree. To their amazement Santos was standing in his wicker basket, high in the tree. He was nonchalantly eating a basket lunch sent up to him by his countrywoman, the Princess Isabel, Comtesse d'Eu, Rothschild's next-door neighbor.

"Are you all right, Alberto?" called a friend.

The little man pushed back his straw hat and said, "I should like to have a glass of beer."

The ship had been but slightly damaged by its fall into Rothschild's park, and three weeks later Santos was ready for a second trial. This time the weather was perfect. The ship rose quickly, headed for the tower with no swerving. Though it was six-thirty in the morning, the streets of Paris were jammed with spectators: the first trip, in spite of the accident, had brought Santos and his "miracle-airship" to the attention of the world.

In nine minutes Santos had turned the Tower. Most of the many thousands watching were positive the prize would be won, and won easily.

Only Santos realized he was in trouble. He'd noticed a loss of hydrogen halfway to the tower, but since he was making such good time he decided to take a chance and keep going.

Just after rounding the Tower he could see the balloon sagging. As he reached the fortifications of Paris one of the suspension wires that held the keel drooped so low it caught in the whirling propeller. Santos stopped the motor before the ship could chew itself to pieces.

Promptly Santos was hit by a strong, head-on gust of wind. Driven back toward the tower, the dirigible began to fall because of the continuing loss of gas. Santos was about to throw out ballast when he saw he'd be blown right into the Eiffel Tower. He let the ship fall.

From the hangar at St.-Cloud it appeared that the ship was dropping like a rock. Everyone realized even Santos had little chance of living through a fall onto the dreaded roofs of Paris. A moment later the ship disappeared below the jagged skyline. Another moment and there came a loud, hollow roar. The *Santos-Dumont* Number 5 had exploded.

The crowd screamed. Henry Deutsch, whose prize had caused the flight, burst into bitter tears.

Firemen at the Passy station, who had been curiously watching the flight, jumped into their engines as soon as they heard the explosion. Within seconds their horses were galloping toward the Trocadero section. Other alarms were rung, for it was generally feared Santos had set fire to one of the busiest parts of the city.

In a few minutes the steel-helmeted *pompiers* rounded the corner of the Rue Henri Martin. A big crowd was looking up at the top of a six-story building. The keel of the *Santos-Dumont* was braced at a steep angle against the side of a Trocadero hotel. The bottom of the keel was resting on the roof of a lower building. Fragments of the bursted balloon draped down forlornly.

A fireman asked where the body of Santos had been flung. A shop-girl excitedly pointed 100 feet in the air. There, perched precariously on the edge of a tiny barred window, was the indestructible Brazilian. When the balloon had struck and exploded on the top of the building, the keel had dropped, straddling the two buildings. Santos had jumped nimbly from the fragile keel, which was crumbling under him, to the tiny window. Someone inside the hotel had stuck a long pole through the bars, and Santos was hanging on for his life.

The firemen lowered a line from the top of the building and pulled Santos to safety. Half an hour later, after the motor of the airship had been rescued, he came into the streets. There he was mobbed by hysterical women who clung to him and smothered him with kisses.

Reporters asked how he had escaped almost certain death. The little man held up his right wrist. On a chain was a medal of St. Benedict. It had been given to him by the Comtesse d'Eu after his fall into Rothschild's chestnut tree.

"This saved me," he said, and reverently kissed the medal.

The crowd pressed around him, shouting, "*Vive notre Petit Santos!*" He couldn't escape. Young women snatched at his clothing, trying to get souvenirs. Finally his friends from St.-Cloud managed to push their way through to him. Deutsch embraced Santos. He offered to give him the prize then and there if he'd promise not to undertake another flight.

But Santos shook his head in refusal.

"What are you going to do now, Alberto?" asked another friend.

"Why, begin again, of course," said Santos in surprise. "One has to have patience."

That night he began building the *Santos-Dumont* Number 6.

Before his crash into the chimney pots of Paris, Santos had been one of the city's favorites. Overnight he became the idol of the youth of Europe. His two flights around the Eiffel Tower had made him an international celebrity. That September, news of the rapid progress of the *Santos-Dumont* Number 6 was topped only by the assassination of President McKinley.

By now Santos was recognized as the world's leading airshipman. Count Zeppelin's highly touted giant dirigible, four times larger than the *Santos-Dumont* Number 5, had proved to be such a dismal failure that it was dismantled. The New York *Tribune* categorically stated that Zeppelin "has now definitely retired from the field."

Santos was to make his third try on October 19, 1901. But the weather was so bad at 2:00 P.M., the announced time of the trial, that only five of the judges had bothered to be on hand. A treacherous southeast wind of six meters was blowing at the Eiffel Tower, and those acquainted with aeronautics thought Santos was insane to take off.

As usual the Brazilian refused to listen to advice. He seemed phlegmatic, almost bored, as he posed for pictures in front of his vermilion electric automobile. He was dressed in checked knickerbockers, coat, and panama hat; and a big flower was stuck in his buttonhole. His brilliant socks were not quite covered by extremely high spats.

The new ship was identical to Number 5 except for a more efficient ballonet which was constantly fed air by the water-cooled motor.

At 2:42 P.M. Santos got off to a fast start and headed straight for the Tower. The huge crowd at St.-Cloud was agog over the ship's phenomenal speed. Shortly the dirigible became a white spot. Then it tilted and sheered off to the left. After a few seconds the white spot veered sharply to the right.

Only eight minutes had passed. A moment later the cheering became delirious as the ship was cut in two by the outline of the Tower.

"He's coming back!" shouted thousands of voices.

The city itself was in a state of uproar. The spiral staircase of the Eiffel Tower was crowded with spectators who called out advice and encouragement as Santos cautiously circled them at a distance of fifty meters. Men put up their derbies on the ends of their canes, and women fluttered scarves and handkerchiefs. The streets surrounding the Tower were packed with screaming enthusiasts.

Suddenly the motor coughed—the cheering stopped. A little figure could be seen stepping out of the willow basket and walking calmly back to the motor.

Seeing the rudder flop uselessly, a man on the platform of the Tower shouted, "He's done for!"

Santos, seemingly oblivious to the danger, adjusted the carburetor and spark. In a few seconds the motor coughed and began picking up. The little Brazilian again crossed the frail keel like a tightrope walker and hoisted himself back into the basket. The crowd below cheered with relief.

Several minutes had been lost, and by the time Santos reached the Bois de Boulogne he was fighting for time. Now the cool air from the trees made the balloon heavier. Simultaneously the capricious motor began spluttering again, and the dirigible slowed down.

Just as the ship passed over the filled stands at the Auteuil race course, Santos pulled back his guide rope and shifted weights to the rear. The ship started to climb slowly.

The race-track devotees had forgotten their horses and were looking up. They applauded the airborne hero. Suddenly the motor picked up speed, shooting the ship up at a dangerous angle. The crowd cried out in alarm.

Santos shifted the guide rope and weights forward, and the ship leveled off. In a minute he had passed over Longchamps and crossed the Seine. He knew time was running out, so instead of landing he flew over the finish line at full speed. It was exactly 3:11:30.

He had covered the course in twenty-nine and a half minutes.

Santos turned the ship and landed.

"Have I won?" he cried.

"Yes!" shouted the crowd.

But even as his head mechanic was shaking his hand, the Comte de Dion came up to Santos. The nobleman's face was solemn. "My friend," he said, "you have lost the prize by forty seconds."

Angrily the crowd argued with the judges, who insisted the race wasn't over until the ship touched ground.

Santos, though bitterly disappointed, shrugged his shoulders. "Anyway," he said, "I do not care personally for the hundred thousand francs."

But the crowd refused to accept the judges' decision. As far as they were concerned Santos had won. They hauled him out of his basket like a conquering hero and carried him on their shoulders to the hangar. Many ladies threw flowers at him; others tossed him

fans, necklaces, and bracelets; and one handed him a little white
rabbit. A few lucky ones managed to pull him to their level and kiss
him.

At that moment Deutsch, who had just driven in from Biarritz,
reached the field. He ran up to Santos and embraced him. "For my
part," he shouted for the benefit of the reporters, "I consider that you
have won the prize." However Deutsch was merely the donor of
the prize.

At once Santos wrote an indignant letter resigning from the Aero
Club. But that night he tore it up. To his friends at the Jockey Club
he remarked with great sadness and patience, "It's more difficult, it
seems, to have the prize awarded me than it was to win it."

The dispute set Paris aflame. The press was vociferous. Angry
crowds roamed the streets shouting that their "Petit Santos" had
been robbed. The judges discreetly remained indoors.

After a few days of public-protest demonstrations the Scientific
Commission gathered to take a final vote on the matter. The Count
de Dion was still bitterly against giving Santos the prize, but Prince
Bonaparte insisted that landing had not been included in Deutsch's
original requirements. The vote was taken. The result: twelve to nine
—in favor of Santos.

The dapper twenty-eight-year-old Brazilian had won through to
new acclaim. His popularity rose even higher when he gave the
20,000 dollar Deutsch Prize to his mechanics and the poor of
Paris.

In the next few years Santos and his fleet of airships—he built
fourteen in all—became the outstanding ornaments of the Parisian
scene. To popularize flying he spent 1,000,000 dollars performing
innumerable stunts and demonstrations. He would delight boule-
vardiers by dropping down from the sky to have a drink at his
favorite bistro on the Champs Élysées. It was not uncommon to see
his airship sail down the Rue Washington and hover over his ornate
apartments until a butler, standing on the steps, would haul him in
for lunch. By this time his many tumbles from the sky had won him
the nickname "Santos-Dismount," but it was all in fun and affection.

Everyone was Santos-Dumont-conscious. Drinks and babies were
named after him. His picture graced thousands of French post-
cards. If a hostess could inveigle him for a week end, her entire
season was a success. And the Empress Eugénie came out of her
thirty years' retirement to see him and his famous airship in the
sheds built for him on the beach of La Condamine by the Prince of
Monaco.

To amplify his experiments Santos wrote books and articles predicting that there would soon be luxurious dirigibles ("floating houses" he called them), flights over the North Pole, huge heavier-than-air craft that would carry hundreds of passengers and tons of cargo. He even went so far as to disagree with his favorite author, H. G. Wells, who was predicting that the world of aviation was just around the corner.

"What do you mean, around the corner?" protested Santos. "The age of air is today!"

He proved it by new exploits. He flew over the Bastille Day Review in 1903; and to the astonishment of the marching troops and the President of France, he fired a grand salute of twenty-one blanks.

When a Cuban society girl implored him to let her pilot the *Santos-Dumont* Number 9, he gave her a few lessons and then said, "Head for the polo field. I'll bicycle over to meet you."

A few minutes later the crowd watching the Anglo-American polo match was pleasantly surprised to see an airship heading for the field.

"It's Petit Santos!" they all shouted.

Then they saw that the pilot wore a huge hat tied on with a veil. It was the lovely Aïda de Acosta, the first and last woman to solo in a dirigible.

When Santos was criticized for letting the young lady fly, he answered simply, "But it is not dangerous. Flying is so simple a schoolgirl could do it." He fervently believed in the safety of flying. When none of the professional chauffeurs dared to pilot Deutsch's airship, the *Ville de Paris*, Santos threw up his hands in dismay. "To think," he cried, "that they are willing to risk their necks daily on the highways and yet they are afraid to go a few hundred feet into the air!"

One summer day in 1903 he landed his airship among the boys and girls at the Children's Fete at Bagatelle.

"Does any little boy want to go up?" he called, remembering his own youthful desires to fly.

All of the boys, French and American alike, clamored to be taken for a ride. Santos chose the nearest, an American boy named Clarkson Potter.

"Are you not afraid?" asked Santos as the airship rose.

"Afraid?" the boy said disdainfully. "Not a bit!"

The age of air had begun in earnest.

3

PHOENIX AT
ECHTERDINGEN

Late on a warm afternoon in July, 1900, thousands of peasants, tourists, townspeople, and visiting scientists and journalists crowded the shores of Lake Constance near Friedrichshafen. The peasants had come almost reverently, for they believed they were about to see a miracle. The others had come to laugh at what promised to be the most colossal joke of the new century. For this was the day the "Crazy Count," the sixty-two-year-old Ferdinand von Zeppelin, was going to try to fly his ridiculous, sausage-shaped machine around in the sky.

Since noontime sight-seers on the shore and in hundreds of gaily decorated little pleasure boats had been watching a huge wooden building that floated on the calm waters. Although the nose of the Count's mysterious machine stuck out the open end of the great hangar, only a privileged few had actually seen the new invention. And there was much speculation as to the airship's actual size.

A few minutes before 6:00 P.M. there was a stop to the activity going on around the bobbing hangar. Laughter and idle conversation were replaced by a hush of anticipation along the banks of the lake and in the boats.

An old man walked thoughtfully from inside the hangar. He stepped onto a small floating platform and took off his white yachting cap. He was a stocky little man with a halo of white hair and a drooping mustache. No one had to be told it was Count Zeppelin himself. Although he seemed a ridiculous figure to the sophisticated visitors from Berlin and Frankfort, there was respectful silence as the old man bent his head in prayer.

Zeppelin, his prayer finished, put on his hat and walked back into the hangar. There were several moments of suspense. Then the float, on which the flying machine rested, crawled out of the hangar slowly, dramatically, like a huge slug.

The multitude burst into cheers and a rising gasp of wonderment as the dirigible grew longer and longer. Even those who had come to jeer were amazed at its length—425 feet! Nothing like it had ever been seen before.

A little steamer, the *Buchhorn*, began towing the machine against the wind. A large screen covered the steamer's smokestack to keep live sparks from falling onto the sausage bag, which contained thousands of cubic feet of flammable hydrogen.

Two little gondolas were suspended under the bulging gas bag. Five men rode in these cars: Eugen Wolf, the famous African explorer; the adventurous Baron Bassus; an engineer, Burr; Gross, a local mechanic; and the Count himself.

The gondolas were connected by a catwalk, from which hung a wire cable holding a 550-pound weight. To make the airship rise the cable was supposed to be shoved to the rear; to descend, the cable was to be set forward. Little rudders on each side of the bow and stern would, it was hoped, steer the clumsy-looking craft.

The *Buchhorn* gathered speed, and the huge sausage rose jerkily into the air like a kite. The flying machine's two four-cylinder Daimler marine motors, which had the horsepower of a modern motorcycle, began to pop like firecrackers; the big propellers turned slowly. Then the tow rope was dropped and the airship was free. It rose leisurely to 1312 feet and, as the little motors popped and barked more furiously, began to move slowly, majestically, over the lake.

There was a sustained roar and gasp from the crowd. The peasants were now sure they *had* seen a miracle: the monster was actually flying in the air!

For seventeen minutes the sausage flew above the shores of Lake Constance. Then, three and a half miles from the hangar, the sliding-weight lever broke. The airship's hull crumpled, and the rudder ropes became tangled. The ship nosed down. A moment later it settled gently on top of a sharp stake that anchored a buoy. Gas hissed out of the punctured hydrogen cell.

It was an embarrassing way to end the flight. But those aboard were moderately enthusiastic. The first voyage of the *LZ-1* (*Luftschiff Zeppelin* Number 1) could have been much worse.

That night Zeppelin gave a banquet for his employees. He thanked them for their loyal work, and they congratulated him on the success of his great invention. But the enthusiasm at Friedrichshafen was dampened a few days later when newspapers from Berlin and other large cities arrived. The visiting scientists and journalists had not been impressed. They had seen what the peasants had not—the ship's steering apparatus was poor, and the airship had been unable to fight the slightest wind.

"Yesterday we experienced a disappointment," said the *Frankfurter Zeitung* of July 4, 1900. "The entire countryside was invited to attend a performance, to which, as soon became apparent, not even the overture could be played successfully." The paper's correspondent concluded it was "much ado about little."

Far from being discouraged by criticism, the Count spent the next few months struggling to perfect his airship. On October 17 he made a second flight. After eighty minutes both motors sputtered and stopped. An overanxious mechanic had mistakenly put distilled water in the gas tanks. The ship fell 1000 feet to the lake. Luckily the motor boat *Württemberg*, piloted by the Count's faithful helper, Ludwig Marx, was on hand to pull the airship back to its hangar.

Again the dirigible was belittled by the journalists. One of the most sarcastic critics was a young economist and amateur yachtsman, Dr. Hugo Eckener. "We cannot be sure," he commented in the *Frankfurter Zeitung*, "that the slow forward motion of the airship may not principally have been due to slight currents of air."

Three days later Zeppelin made a third test. For twenty-three minutes the airship flew at ten yards a second, but it could make little headway against the wind. Army observers were disappointed: the ship was far too slow for military purposes. Zeppelin's few civilian backers were dubious of the dirigible's commercial possibilities. They withdrew their support.

The Company for the Promotion of Aeronautics, which had financed the building of the ship, was now penniless. On November 15, 1900, the organization was formally dissolved. It appeared that the Crazy Count's invention was a complete failure.

But, like Solomon Andrews, Ferdinand von Zeppelin had always thrived on difficulties. Born on an island in Lake Constance of wealthy Junkers parents, he made the army his career. At the outbreak of the American Civil War he left his Württembergian regiment to volunteer his services to the Union Army. Carl Schurz, a compatriot, brought the twenty-five-year-old Count to Washington to meet Abraham Lincoln.

The Count was introduced to the President, whom he later described as "a tall, gaunt figure with a large head and long, unkempt hair and beard."

"We Zeppelins have been counts for centuries," he assured Lincoln.

"That will not be in your way," answered Lincoln, "if you behave yourself as a soldier."

After the interview Zeppelin asked Schurz, "What in the world did the President mean by so strange a remark?"

The Count first joined General Hooker's Army of the Potomac

and later took part in the action at Fredericksburg and Ashby Gap. He fought with abandon. But it was the love of battle that had drawn him to America—not the issues involved. In his pocket he carried a personal letter of introduction to General Lee.

Bored with the New World type of warfare, Zeppelin abruptly left the Union Army in 1863 and joined an expedition to investigate the sources of the Mississippi River. It was a strange party, consisting of two not-very-bright Indians, two inexperienced Russians, and himself. The expedition ended at the point of starvation in St. Paul, Minnesota.

It was in St. Paul later the same year that Zeppelin made his first balloon ascension. While floating over the city, it occurred to him that a balloon that could be steered and propelled would be one of man's greatest inventions.

But the practical work of invention was much too sedentary for an adventurous young spirit like Zeppelin. Returning to Württemberg, he fought on the Austrian side against Prussia in 1866 and a few years later joined the Prussian army to attack France. In this campaign he led the first cavalry foray of the war—a harebrained adventure ending in death for all the Uhlan raiders except Zeppelin. Such madcap stunts won him a dozen medals and the nickname "The Crazy Count."

During the siege of Paris his interest in lighter-than-air craft was again aroused by the hundreds of successful balloon flights from the city. He drew up plans for a dirigible, but his army career kept him from further experiments. Then in 1887, while he was Württembergian ambassador to Prussia, the Count spoke too boldly too often, and incurred the hatred of Kaiser Wilhelm—a hatred that caused his premature retirement, as brigadier general, at the age of fifty-two.

Although this seemed to be a tragedy, it was actually the start of his true career. For now at last he had time to build the dirigible he had first dreamed about over St. Paul, Minnesota.

The failure of the *LZ-1* discouraged everyone but Zeppelin. The Count got permission from his staunch friend, the King of Württemberg, to run a lottery. This brought in 30,000 Marks for a second airship. With a few other contributions and 100,000 Marks from his own private fortune, Zeppelin built the *LZ-2*. The new ship had many improvements. The latticed girders of the *LZ-1's* frame were replaced with triangular girders; there was a horizontal rudder to make the airship ascend and descend; and the engine had been increased to 170 horsepower.

The *LZ-2* was badly damaged while being towed out of its floating hangar late in 1905, and the first flight actually did not take place until January 17, 1906. When Zeppelin cast off, the ship was so buoyant that it shot to 1500 feet before he could control its wild careening. Then the rudder controls jammed, and the LZ-2 drifted with the wind. Once more the ship began pitching up and down. Before long the two Mercedes motors were flooded, the ventilator belt ripped, and the bulky ship was a derelict.

Zeppelin, as unperturbed as ever, slid a message along a wire from the control car to the engine gondola. "Lower the drag anchor," it read.

While gas was valved, the anchor was thrown overboard. It dug into frozen ground and the chain snapped. More gas was valved as the ship drifted helplessly only a few hundred feet from the ground between two farmhouses. A girl, hanging up clothes in the front yard of one of these houses, looked up in surprise at the approaching dirigible. "Let me hang up my wash!" she shouted angrily.

A moment later the LZ-2 dropped gently and safely into a swampy pasture. Zeppelin was elated. The first landing on ground had been made—and without the slightest damage. The ship was lashed to trees and fences, but that night violent wind ripped the outer envelope and smashed the inner framework. The next morning the battered dirigible was chopped to pieces by overenthusiastic workmen before Zeppelin could salvage the undamaged parts. In one stroke the Count was back where he'd started from, considerably the worse for wear. "An airshipman without an airship," he said, staring at the wreckage, "is like a cavalry officer without a horse." Then he added with a wry smile, "And I am both."

A few months later he was promoting the LZ-3. He sold his horses and carriages, dismissed most of his servants, and talked the King of Württemberg into letting him run a new lottery. By the autumn of 1906 the third airship was completed. There were now two wing-shaped stabilizer fins and steering fins both at the stern and the bow. That October the trial flight was made. The ship steered perfectly and easily bucked winds of twenty-five miles an hour. The second trial was even more successful. Overnight everyone, including Kaiser Wilhelm, wanted to be associated with the venture.

The Count was decorated and honored by many societies. The Reichstag granted him financial aid for a fourth ship. "Zeppelin" cigarettes appeared on the market. The newspapers were filled with advertisements for "Zeppelin coats to be worn in the air." Pastry cooks made thousands of small "Zeppelins" out of sugar and marzipan; flowers were named after the inventor; and medallions containing his picture were sold by the thousands. And finally the government promised that if the new ship, the LZ-4, could make a successful twenty-four-hour-nonstop flight, a permanent yearly grant would be given the Count. His most farfetched dreams seemed about to be realized.

In its day the *LZ-4* was the largest ship built to fly in the air. It was 446 feet long and forty-two feet in diameter, and its gas cells held 519,000 cubic feet of hydrogen. Among its improvements and refinements, a small vertical shaft ran from the control car to the top of the gas bag where a small platform had been built for a machine gun. After several trial flights the ship embarked, on the morning of July 1, 1908, on its first great test—a twelve-hour flight. Eight men rode in the front gondola. Three engineers manned the two 104-horsepower Daimler motors in the aft car. A writer, E. Sandt, sat in the small saloon cabin, placed between the two larger gondolas.

As the *LZ-4* headed along the Rhine and Aar Valley toward Switzerland there was a great furor below: the outside world was getting a first look at the Count's airship. Church bells pealed and people ran into the streets. Zeppelin steered the ship at forty miles per hour over Lucerne and Zurich. In the evening the *LZ-4* returned, flying over Lindau and Friedrichshafen and landing at the floating hangar near Manzell.

The *Schweizerfahrt*, as the flight was called, set off a wave of national pride and enthusiasm. In Berlin a square was renamed *Zeppelin Platz*, and Frankfort on the Main boasted a *Zeppelin* park. A week after the twelve-hour flight Zeppelin retired to Girsberg to celebrate his seventieth birthday. The town was overrun by delegations from universities who came to honor the inventor. Large choral groups sang outside his home while fireworks were shot off. That night Zeppelin felt a surge of warmth for his fellow Germans. Now he needed only one thing to make his life complete—a successful twenty-four-hour flight of the *LZ-4*.

There wasn't a breath of wind as the sun rose the morning of August 4. Already it was sultry and close. At 7:00 A.M. the long *LZ-4* rose from Lake Constance. Durr was at the elevators and Lau and Captain Hacker at the rudders. Zeppelin, his face a mask, stood in front of the control gondola, giving orders calmly. Watching the old Count were members of the Imperial Commission who had come along to make a report on the ship's performance. In the aft gondola were Baron von Bassus, engineer Stahl, and four mechanics.

The airship flew serenely down the Rhine, passing Basle at nine-thirty. At every town factories were shut down as people crowded into the streets turning their faces to the sky. By noon the

LZ-4 was over Strasbourg. News of the historic flight was being telegraphed all over the world. If successful, the flight would prove to everyone the practicability of the rigid dirigible. If it failed, Zeppelin knew he wouldn't have the energy to build another ship.

Back in Friedrichshafen, Zeppelin's little office in the *Deutsches Haus* was crowded with excited workers from the airship factory. Also present were Herr Uhland, the Count's elderly secretary, and Dr. Hugo Eckener, who had changed from a critic of the Count's airships to an ardent admirer. They were following the ship's triumphal progress by calling the police stations of the cities on the *LZ-4's* route.

The reception in Worms, they learned, had been wild. Then Mainz was called. Eckener became anxious when he was told the airship, already overdue, hadn't arrived.

The atmosphere in the office changed instantly from light-heartedness to anxiety. The telephone rang. Fearfully Eckener picked it up. Then his huge body relaxed. It was the Count.

"We had to come down near Oppenheim," Zeppelin calmly told him, "and we're stuck here."

As the ship had passed over Darmstadt at four-thirty, the front engine overheated. Zeppelin, who never took a chance, quickly made an emergency landing on the Rhine River.

Not long after the Count's report to Friedrichshafen, the mechanics finished repairing the forward motor. With the help of a Rhine steamer the airship again took to the air.

The triumphal tour continued, reaching Mainz at midnight. Everybody aboard was jubilant. The emergency landing, instead of prejudicing the Commissioners, had impressed them. The airship was now floating above sleeping Germany, the first powered aircraft ever to make a night flight. Near Mannheim the front motor again sputtered and finally went dead. But the ship continued flying with one engine until the sun rose.

Zeppelin decided to try a second forced landing so that repairs could be made. Near the village of Echterdingen the ship slowly, gracefully nosed toward an open field. The gondola touched the ground lightly. Villagers ran onto the field and eagerly seized the dirigible's nose cable.

Zeppelin, his ears deafened by the constant roar of the engines, leaped to the ground like a youngster. His heart was full. Except for the delay on the Rhine the ship had flown nonstop for twenty-four hours. And even the two emergency landings had proven the safety and usefulness of his dirigible. He ordered a farmer's wagon buried in the ground to hold the ship's nose cable and then with a light heart set off for the local inn, the *Hirsch*.

News of the unexpected landing soon spread. By noontime 50,000 spectators had traveled to the little village by train, carriages, automobiles, bicycles, and on foot. A large detachment of soldiers had already arrived from nearby Cannstadt to act as a ground crew. Ropes were strung up to hold back the growing crowd. By two fifty that afternoon mechanics from the Daimler Factory in Stuttgart had overhauled the engines.

During the repairs only two regular crew members were on board the anchored ship. Chief mechanic Karl Schwarz was on watch in the aft gondola. Mechanic Laburda was far forward filling up the water ballast bags with the help of a soldier. The rest of the crew was finishing lunch in the village. Zeppelin was still resting at the *Hirsch*.

A wind suddenly sprang up from the west, hitting the ship broadside. The ground crew of sixty-five soldiers hung tighter to the gondolas and the trail ropes. Within a minute the wind had grown into a violent squall. The tail of the airship rose abruptly, lifting the men hanging onto the rear gondola into the air. The soldiers holding the trail ropes and the front car let go, and the ship shot up quickly. The crowd on the field screamed as the men on the rear gondola, looking like dolls, dropped limply to the ground.

Aboard the *LZ-4*, Chief Mechanic Schwarz ran along the catwalk to the forward car. With both hands he yanked at gas valves in a desperate effort to bring the ship down. The dirigible dropped, floating half a mile to the south. There the nose crashed into a clump of trees.

The huge crowd watched in amazement as a great ball of fire blossomed from the ship. After a second's pause there was a deep rumble, and the field shook.

Zeppelin heard the explosion as he was coming out of his room at the *Hirsch*. He then heard a mass scream of horror. He ran to the door of the inn. Across the wide field he saw the flaming *LZ-4* about to crash into the ground.

Schwarz was dazed. He heard the cry of "Fire" before he saw the flames. The bow of the ship had dropped sharply, and he was hanging onto the gondola to keep from being pitched to the ground. Leaning over the rail, he saw a strange bright light within the ship.

He let go the gas valves and got ready to jump. Overhead, ballonets were exploding, and the metal framework of the airship glowed a cherry red. Burning fragments of the envelope dropped into the gondola. He could see the fire blazing dangerously near the gasoline tanks. In a few seconds they would explode, and he was sure he'd be killed.

There was a dull crash. Schwarz didn't realize that the ship had struck the ground. He was catapulted out of the gondola, face down. He staggered to his feet and found himself surrounded by a red-hot network of wreckage. The burning mass collapsed on top of him. Without realizing what he was doing, he fought his way through the molten trap. "Now run like hell," he said aloud. He stumbled forward, choking from smoke. Finally he managed to put a hundred feet between himself and the wreck.

Then he turned and looked back. A soldier, his uniform smoking, ran drunkenly from the center of the wreckage. He stared stupidly at Schwarz.

"Where did you come from?" asked the mechanic.

"I was in the ship," the soldier gasped. "There's someone else back there."

Schwarz turned. A man was curled up, motionless, near a smoldering pile of girders. Schwarz and the soldier staggered back into the intense heat. Together they dragged the inert form to safety. It was Laburda. Blood was running down his face, but he was still alive.

The crowd was now silent, stunned. Slowly a little man wearing a white yachting cap came forward. He walked as close as he could to the smoldering ruins. Everyone knew it was Graf Zeppelin.

The Count looked at the charred gondolas and the mounds of metal. In the silence he could hear the moans of the burned and wounded. It was the first time anyone had been injured by his invention. The cries of pain were too much for him. His hands shook. He turned and walked away.

The crowd parted for him. Suddenly Zeppelin looked his age. Suddenly he was an old, old man, and for him this was the end. The men took off their hats as he passed.

At this same moment a victory celebration was being prepared in Friedrichshafen. Zeppelin's daughter, Hella, had just finished decorating the motor boat *Württemberg* with the Count's own colors, blue and white. Helmsman Ludwig Marx, one of the Count's most faithful workers, was helping her. A gay crowd had already gathered outside the *Deutsches Haus*. They had been singing national songs since noon.

A man in shirt sleeves ran from the office of the local newspaper with a telegram in his hand. He pushed his way through the crowd in front of the *Deutsches Haus* and tacked the telegram on a little blackboard at the entrance of the building.

The crowd pushed forward, thinking news had arrived of the *LZ-4's* departure from Echterdingen.

"The balloon has burned!" a man cried out.

The people didn't believe. They refused to believe it.

Then Dr. Eckener slowly walked out of the *Deutsches Haus.*
Tears were in his eyes. Then everyone knew that the telegram had
been right.

There was a hush as Eckener lumbered unsteadily through the
garden toward the boathouse to tell Marx what had happened.

Later that night Hella Zeppelin met her father at the train
station. All the flags in Friedrichshafen were either at half-mast
or had been taken down. Hella took her father's hand, and they
walked toward the *Deutsches Haus.*

The next morning Helmsman Marx started dejectedly down the
path behind the hotel toward his motor boat. Hearing a cheerful
voice, he looked up and saw the Count standing on the balcony
outside of his room.

"Good morning, Marx. How are you?" Zeppelin was immacu-
lately dressed and seemed in high spirits. Marx stared up at him.
"Why, Marx," chided the Count, "you still seem to be hard hit by
yesterday's accident. Come on up here a moment."

Wondering whether the old man had lost his mind, Marx climbed
up to the Graf's room. Zeppelin was beaming. He pointed to a
great pile of letters on his writing desk. "Well, Marx," he exclaimed, "what do you think of *this* accident?" He led the helmsman to the desk. Now Marx saw that every letter contained money.
"It was sent to me by the German people, and there's more coming!" cried the Count. His eyes were bright. "With God's help
we start again!"

Before the end of the day money for a new dirigible was
pouring in by mail and special messengers from all parts of
Germany: 150 Marks came from a Baden Bowling Club, and
20,000 Marks from the Aldermen of Stuttgart. The Mining Association at Essen gave 100,000 Marks. Zeppelin was especially
moved by an offering of seven pfennigs from a little girl who
wanted him to use it to "build another airship." Another youngster,
who had no money, contributed a book. "I am sending you my
Struwelpeter book to comfort you," she wrote, "because your airship burned up."

In a spontaneous outburst of national feeling Germany contributed 6,096,555 Marks toward an old man's dream.

On the day after the fire the Count was overwhelmed with
visitors. Even the King of Württemberg came. And everyone
brought the same message of faith.

That night, overcome with gratitude and affection, the Count

sat down and scratched out a letter to be published in all the
German newspapers. "I consider this magnificent national dem-
onstration," he wrote, "as a command from my countrymen to go on
with my work."

Out of the flame at Echterdingen had come the old man's
greatest triumph. The next day he and his men started drawing
plans for the *LZ-5.*

SHIPS OF WAR

Within a month of the fire at Echterdingen, Zeppelin had organized the Zeppelin Stiftung (the Zeppelin Foundation). Its capital was the millions of Marks contributed by the German people; its purpose, to study and promote air flight.

In the fall of 1908 the Count made a number of flights with the repaired *LZ-3*. They were so successful that even Prince Henry of Prussia and the German Crown Prince begged to be taken up as passengers. The Kaiser himself, observing how all Germany idolized Zeppelin, conveniently forgot his old enmity. That November he personally awarded the Count Prussia's most honored decoration, the Order of the Black Eagle. Then he kissed Zeppelin on both cheeks and called him the "greatest German of the twentieth century."

The next year Zeppelin and his new associate, Dr. Hugo Eckener, formed the world's first passenger air-transport line, the Deutsche Luftschiffahrts Aktien Gesellschaft. DELAG, as it was soon called, built air harbors all over Germany—Frankfort, Berlin, Hamburg, Dresden—and with the airships *Deutschland, Schwaben, Viktoria-Luise, Hansa,* and *Sachsen* began establishing records of safety and performance that many people outside of Germany found hard to believe.

In the United States there were special reasons for doubting the stories coming out of Germany. Walter Wellman, the noted journalist and adventurer, had already tried two flights to the North Pole in a 165-foot semirigid dirigible called the *America*. Both attempts had ended ignominiously a few miles from the base of operations in Spitsbergen.

Wellman, goaded by his critics, made an ever more dramatic bid for fame the next year. On October 15, 1910, without bothering to run a single test flight, he set out from Atlantic City in a 228-foot cigar-shaped airship, also christened the *America*. With a crew of five and a Maltese cat Wellman would span the Atlantic

Ocean—and make a proper prophecy of Poe's famous hoax of 1844.

The cast-off came early in the morning. By nightfall the *America* was reported just eighty miles from Atlantic City. One of its two motors—together they developed fifty horsepower—had given out. In the darkness the crippled ship almost rammed into the steamer *Bullard*. By morning bitter quarrels had broken out between Wellman and Melvin Vaniman, the ship's designer and chief engineer. Vaniman wanted to land in the ocean and row back to America in the lifeboat slung under the keel. But Wellman, preferring death to ridicule, insisted on going on. The damaged motor was smashed to pieces by Vaniman and dumped overboard when the ship began to lose buoyancy.

Two days and many arguments later they had drifted far south of their course. The ship was about to sink into the ocean when by a lucky chance it was sighted by the Bermuda steamer *Trent*. The adventurers were saved; the *America,* freed of its passengers, rose high in the air and drifted out of sight. It was never seen again.

Wellman and his men were given a ticker-tape welcome in New York. The journalist claimed two world's records: the airship had stayed in the air seventy-one hours and had covered a distance of 1008 miles. But most people realized the flight had been little more than a lucky piece of free-ballooning.

Two years later Vaniman, convinced that Wellman had been the cause of all his misfortunes, made a second attempt to fly the Atlantic. Backed by Frank Seiberling of the Goodyear Tire Company, he built the *Akron*, a 258-foot semirigid airship with a capacity of 400,000 cubic feet of hydrogen.

For months Vaniman was harassed by trouble. On the first trial flight in October, 1911, the gas leaked so badly the ship had to be landed almost at once.

Vaniman repaired the *Akron* all that winter. The second test flight on June 1, 1912, nearly ended in tragedy. One of the ship's eleven-foot propellers caught in a rope and the dirigible went into a steep climb. Calvin Vaniman, the inventor's younger brother, crawled out on a slender strut and whittled away the edges of the broken blade. A moment later the ship was righted.

The third test came on the morning of July 2.

"This is the day I've been waiting for," Vaniman told his wife as policemen and firemen dragged the long ship out of its Atlantic City hangar. "She'll make good today."

Vaniman climbed into the keel. He was followed by his brother and three other men, all of them confident that with its improvements the big ship would perform perfectly.

Vaniman waved cheerfully to the hundred men holding the ropes. "Let her go!" he shouted. Then he saluted his wife. His crew of four made a show of confidence for their wives.

The *Akron* rose slowly, under good control. As it sailed over the boardwalk at 500 feet, a great roar arose from the beaches black with people. The *Akron* sailed over the sea above Absecon Inlet and headed for Brigantine Beach.

A half-mile from the shore the dirigible suddenly rose. A tiny flash of light blazed on top of the gas bag, sputtering like an electric spark. A few seconds later there was a burst of flame. The gas bag split in two: dark billows of smoke hid the airship from the horrified thousands.

Then a deep rumble came across the water. The bow of the Akron began tilting. Women fainted. The ship nosed over and started its dying fall into the sea. Several hundred feet above the water a body, looking limp and unreal, fell from the wreckage. It was Calvin Vaniman.

The others crashed with the ship. All five died as their wives watched.

After the *Akron* disaster few dirigibles—and none of importance —were built except in Germany. Zeppelin's only real rival, Santos-Dumont, had long since turned his talents to heavier-than-air craft. On October 23, 1906, he made what at the time was popularly considered the first airplane flight.

By 1913 Zeppelin and his airships had gone on to greater triumphs. Although the first two airships built for the German Navy, the *L-1* and *L-2* had been destroyed with heavy loss of life, DELAG had made 1600 flights of 100,000 miles without the slightest injury to a passenger. And the next year, when the World War broke out, Zeppelin was the man of the hour in his homeland. The average German was confident that the Graf and his airships would frighten the Allies into an early surrender.

When Germany invaded Belgium she owned three commercial airships and six primitive military dirigibles. By the end of the war she had built eighty-eight Zeppelins, each larger and more efficient than the last. As the Allies kept improving their antiaircraft weapons and airplanes, the Germans were forced to make bigger and faster airships. Their last one 750 feet long, with a capacity of almost 70,000 cubic meters, was capable of flying as high as five miles.

One of the first innovations in this competitive development was the "spy car." Ernst Lehmann, former commander of the DELAG airship, the *Sachsen*, and Lieutenant Colonel Baron Max von Gemmingen, nephew of Count Zeppelin, first experimented with an old butter tub. The tub was hooked onto a steel cable 1000 feet long and lowered by a hand windlass from the bombing compartment. Before long, Zeppelins could fly high above dense clouds and yet bomb with deadly aim: a little observation basket, connected to the control car by telephone, would be swinging in clear skies a mile below the airship.

Early in 1916 the *LZ-77* inexplicably burst into flames above Revigny. A few days later the Germans discovered that the airship had been destroyed by a new incendiary rocket that could shoot higher than two miles. Suddenly it looked as though the rigid dirigible was a useless weapon of war. The German Army almost completely suspended its Zeppelin activities. But the Navy still had faith.

On May 31, 1916, the German North Sea Fleet, under Admiral Scheer, steamed toward the Skagerrak—the arm of the North Sea just below Norway—to lure the British Fleet into battle. Ten Zeppelins hovered over the German warships, acting as "eyes" for the Navy. The opposing fleets met near Jutland. The airships continually wirelessed Scheer important information—the most vital of which came on the morning of June 1. At five ten the *L-11*, captained by Commander Viktor Schütze, spotted a new flotilla of British battleships, and many destroyers, speeding northwest. Realizing that Scheer's fleet was about to be outflanked, Schütze wirelessed a warning. The English, now that their trap had been discovered, backed off. Scheer's fleet escaped.

A secret British report of the momentous battle gave the Zeppelins the full credit for saving the German fleet from complete destruction, And, said the report, "If the situation at the Skagerrak had been reversed, if airships had enabled *us* to discover the whereabouts of the German North Sea Fleet and destroy it—who can deny the far-reaching effect this would have had upon the outcome of the war?"

Zeppelin lived long enough to celebrate this great airship achievement. But the old Count, who had hounded the Ministry of War for months, trying in vain to get back into his old regiment, caught a cold the next year and died March 8, 1917. Thus he was spared the day, a few months later, that broke the hearts of all German airshipmen.

In spite of the incendiary rocket and the fast-improving fighter plane, Zeppelin attacks had been striking terror into the English people. Air raids, in those days, were such a shock that the entire populations of towns in Norfolk and Suffolk fled to find refuge in London, which was comparatively well protected.

One of the greatest of the hundreds of air raids on England was scheduled for October 19, 1917. At noon eleven naval airships left their docks to converge over England. At 6:30 P.M., the first Zeppelin sighted the English coast from a height of 13,500 feet. Antiaircraft guns began firing. As darkness fell, the fleet of gray bombers rose to 16,500 feet and spread out over Hull, Grimsby, and Sheffield.

There was no moon, and dark clouds completely hid the airships from searchlight beams groping below. In the next few hours the raiders, guided by lights and smoking chimneys, dumped their bombs. The damage was great and widespread. And because of the poor visibility not a dirigible was shot down by planes or rockets. The most devastating raid of the war had been accomplished without loss to enemy action.

But at midnight a storm blew in from the northwest. The eleven Zeppelins were driven across the Channel by a sixty-mile-an-hour wind. As they fought the wind, the airship could see in the distance to the east the brilliant flashes of an artillery duel in Flanders. At about 3:00 A.M. destroyers and land batteries spotted the airships and began firing rockets. The Zeppelins quickly rose to 20,000 feet, their motors coughing and sputtering as the air thinned out. The men suffered in the biting cold, and although they wore primitive oxygen masks, breathing was difficult. Strong varying winds scattered the air fleet, drove the ships far apart.

Six of the Zeppelins escaped to Germany. But when dawn broke, five were still drifting helpless over France. Then an Allied plane spied the L-55 and chased it up to 25,300 feet. The altitude made blood spurt from the ears, noses and mouths of the crew. The dirigible's water ballast soon froze, and the water for cooling the engines, too, despite the alcohol in it. In desperation the captain, Lieutenant Commander Hans Flemming, jettisoned all his ballast and fuel and came down near Tufenort. Now only four of the drifting raiders were left.

A few minutes later the L-44 was shot down by planes while trying to cross the lines near Lunéville.

The three survivors, the L-45, L-49, and L-50 were still flying at 20,000 feet over France. With only an hour's gasoline left, Commander Koelle ordered the L-45 to land in the Durance Valley. The airship sank lightly onto a sandbank in the middle of a small river.

The gas cells were punctured and the engines smashed. Koelle told the helmsman to fire a rocket-pistol at a cell containing hydrogen. The ship burst into flames.

At about the same time the *L-49* was coming to earth at Bourbonne-les-Bains. But when they landed the men were so groggy that French soldiers captured them before they could scuttle the undamaged ship. (Dimensions of the ship were carefully copied. Years later the *L-49* was to become the exact model of America's first homemade rigid dirigible, the *Shenandoah*.)

Now only the *L-50* remained aloft. Captain Schwonder turned east off his course toward Paris, hoping to cross the French Alps and reach neutral Switzerland. By the time the ship approached the mountains most of the mechanics had passed out. In the control car oxygen had been budgeted, but the men were weak, almost helpless.

The untended motors carried the *L-50* full speed ahead toward the peaks near Dommartin, but the helmsman was so exhausted that he couldn't turn the rudder wheel. The captain, feeling unconsciousness creeping over him, desperately rang up a "stop engines" signal. But there was no reply on the engine telegraph. All the mechanics were slumped over in their gondolas, unconscious.

The ship smashed into a peak, knocking off the control car and the aft gondola. A moment later the men in these cars, saved by the freak accident, crawled slowly out of the wreckage. Looking up, they saw their ship sailing over the Alps. Dazedly they watched the *L-50* hit another mountain, bounce high in the air, and then fade into the mist. No trace of the ship or the men aboard was ever found.

The greatest Zeppelin feat of the war was performed a month after the disastrous raid of October 19. The Fatherland's last colonial garrison in German East Africa, commanded by General von Lettow-Vorbeck, was badly in need of medical supplies and ammunition. The High Command decided that there was only one way relief could be sent—by airship. When news of the great adventure leaked out, every airshipman in the service volunteered.

The ship chosen for the mission was the one hundred and fourth Zeppelin designed, the *L-59*. Seven hundred and fifty feet long with a diameter of eighty feet, it had a capacity of 68,500 cubic meters. The airship was to be cannibalized when it reached East Africa. The envelope would be made into tents and uniforms, the framework would construct a barracks, and the five Maybach motors would run the garrison's dynamos.

Ernst Lehmann was put in charge of preparations. He collected fifty tons of equipment including 311,900 boxes of ammunition, 230 machine-gun belts, thirty machine guns, sixty-one bags of medical supplies, two sewing machines, and a case of cognac.

In November, 1917, the ship was flown from dock yards near Berlin to the airship base at Yamboli, Bulgaria. Dr. Eckener, now an instructor in the Naval Airship Division, was brought along as technical adviser for the trip into the desert.

At last on November 21 the ship, captained by Lieutenant Commander Ludwig Bockholt, was ready for departure. The stars were out as the men silently climbed aboard. The motors were tested and shut off as the ground crew detached sand bags and weighed off the dirigible.

"Ship ready for take-off!" cried Bockholt. A whistle blew. The ground-crew men grabbed the hand rails of the gondolas.

"Airship march!" commanded the ground chief. The ship turned slowly into the wind. Water shot out of the ballast bags, putting the L-59 in perfect trim.

Bockholt shook hands with Lehmann and Eckener and jumped into the control car. The trail ropes were pulled in.

"Up!" called Bockholt.

The nose of the L-59 went up.

"Stern engines full speed ahead!" The telegraphs rang; the ship slowly headed east. "All engines ahead!" ordered Bockholt.

The ship quickly disappeared into the early-morning darkness.

A few hours later the dirigible was flying over friendly Turkey. It hovered over Smyrna while planes scouted for enemy ships. When none was reported, the L-59 headed out to sea, over Crete, and into the Mediterranean.

At sunrise the rugged coast of Africa hove into sight, and the temperature shot up to 68 degrees. As the gas expanded, excess hydrogen hissed out of the emergency valves. A ton of water was dumped to compensate for the loss.

Hour after hour the airship flew over the dunes of the Libyan desert—over tiny lakes and oases. Once a camel caravan scattered in terror at the sight of the strange object in the sky.

Darkness fell. Soon afterward the L-59 crossed the Nile at the second cataract. Bockholt ordered his chief helmsman, Sergeant Major Grussendorf, a former DELAG pilot, to circle around Khartoum, which was held by the British. Sweat was pouring down the men's bodies: the sun had been down several hours but it was still 95 degrees.

The ship had traveled 2800 miles when the radio operator handed Bockholt a message:

ABANDON UNDERTAKING AND RETURN STOP ENEMY HAS OCCUPIED
GREAT PART OF MAKONDE HIGHLAND AND IS ALREADY AT KITAUGARI STOP

Although his goal lay only 400 miles away Bockholt, in bitter
disappointment, ordered Grussendorf to head back for Yamboli.

For hours the ship fought head winds. Suddenly a strong down
draft drove the *L-59* so low that the lead antenna weight dragged
along the sand. Bockholt quickly dumped 11,000 pounds of
ballast and cargo, including the crate of cognac. Munitions exploded as they hit the ground, rocking the ship dangerously. The
dirigible climbed painfully over the mountains along the northern
coast and soon was gliding over the cool Mediterranean. Below,
searchlights of British battleships, alerted by reports of the
flight, were raking the skies for them, but the dirigible slipped
through the blockade without being seen.

In two hours the temperature had fallen over 60 degrees to 23
degrees; the men suffered from the rapid change, but the ship
regained its buoyancy. By sunrise they were over Crete. At 10:00
P.M. the ancient city of Constantinople lay below. Five hours later
Bockholt and his crew of twenty-two were once more over their
home base, Yamboli. A violent crosswind was blowing, so the captain was forced to keep the ship aloft until 8:15 P.M.

Although the mission had been defaulted, the adventurers
were cheered as they stepped off the dirigible. The *L-59* had
flown for ninety-five continuous hours, at an average speed of forty-
five miles an hour; 4225 miles had been covered without a stop, and
there was fuel enough in the gasoline tanks for an additional
3750 miles.

The Allies readily admitted that the flight of the *L-59* was one
of the greatest aerial achievements of the war. Then they revealed that it could also have been a military triumph. The message to Bockholt ordering him to return had been based on a fake
British report from Malta.

As the *L-59* was turning around, General von Lettow-Vorbeck
was not losing the battle. He was actually winning it.

5

THE FLYING "LEMON"

In the late spring of 1919 the world—recently released from war—had succumbed to a new, more pleasant madness: flying. Airshipmen and aviators of a half a dozen countries were preparing for the conquest of the Atlantic Ocean.

Before the war airships and airplanes had been little more than curiosities at country fairs. Now they had proved themselves in battle. There was talk of regular airmail service and of passenger airships that would make long trips in something less than half the time of railroads. Of course sensible people took such nonsense lightly, but the air-minded breed thrilled to the sight of a patched-up blimp or a "Jennie" held together by bailing wire.

That spring the legion of aviators, mass-produced for war but now without an outlet for their new skill, caught transatlantic fever. Lord Northcliffe's London *Daily Mail* had offered a prize of 10,000 pounds for the first nonstop flight across the Atlantic. Eight English planes, based near St. John's, Newfoundland, were competing for the money and honor. Independent of the *Daily Mail* contest, three United States Navy flying boats, the *NC-1, 3,* and *4,* and the relatively untested English dirigible, the *R-34,* were prepared to attempt the first Atlantic crossing.

But the most serious contender was the *L-72.* Captain Ernst Lehmann was readying this German Navy Zeppelin, originally designed to bomb New York City, for a flight to the United States and return without stopping or refueling.

Suddenly there was a new and dramatic entry in the oceanic race. The *C-5,* latest of the United States Navy's nonrigid airships, took off from its station at Montauk with the bland announcement that it was going to fly the 1400 miles to St. John's and then shove off for Ireland.

Few outside of those in the Navy thought the blimp, with a capacity of only 170,000 cubic feet of hydrogen, had a ghost of a chance of even reaching Newfoundland. A few minutes past 8:00 A.M. on May 14 the ship, commanded by Lieutenant Commander E. W. Coil left Long Island and headed northeast. At ten forty-five the next morning it chugged over St. John's, and the aviation world was forced to take the impertinent little ship seriously. For the long and difficult hop had been made with no trouble and at the very respectable average speed of fifty miles an hour.

But news of the *C-5* was somewhat overshadowed by the scheduled take-off that very day of the United States Navy planes from nearby Trepassey Bay for the Azores.

Commander Coil felt he still had a good chance of reaching the mainland first because the flying boats, providing they reached their first goal, would still be held up a week or two before the final hop to Europe.

Harry Hawker, the world's most publicized flier, and his navigator, Commander Kenneth Mackenzie-Grieve, were also making frantic last-minute preparations on their single-engine Sopwith. A few miles away two other Englishmen, F. D. Raynham and C. W. F. Morgan gassed up their big Rolls-Martinsyde and waited for the green light from the weather bureau.

When the *C-5* finally landed in St. John's at 11 A.M. it was clear and fairly calm. The pilots, Coil and Lt. Jack Lawrence, went aboard the nearby USS *Chicago*, sent ahead of the blimp to provide a landing party, to get a few hours' sleep before the final jump to Ireland. The rest of the *C-5*'s crew refueled the rugged ship and put aboard provisions.

Soon the weather turned around. Treacherous gusts began to sweep down on the rocky point where the ship was anchored, pulling the ground crew along the uneven terrain like stubborn terriers. More sailors grabbed the straining lines, and word was flashed to the *Chicago* to rout Coil and Lawrence out of their bunks. The ground crew officers, Lieutenants Charles Little and R. A. D. Preston, figured that the storm might be a blessing in disguise. If their men could hang on to the blimp until the pilots got aboard, the gale-force wind would give the *C-5* a fast getaway in the Atlantic race.

But even as Coil and Lawrence hurried ashore, the wind grew stronger, reaching gusts over sixty knots. The ship was picked up like a child's toy and smashed down, breaking a propeller and damaging the control car. Little and Preston jumped aboard. If they could pull the rip panel and let out the gas they knew the ship would be saved and the trip resumed after a few days of repairs.

But the cord leading to the rip panel snapped. Although the ship was straining to get away, the two officers climbed up the bulging sides of the big gas bag, knives in hand. They would rip it by hand.

At that moment a strong gust hit the ship, shooting it into the air. Preston, afraid the crew would be carried away, shouted to let go. The ground crew obeyed just as the two officers jumped. Little broke his ankle.

The crewless *C-5* leaped high in the air and started across the Atlantic. Like the *Flying Dutchman,* the German *L-50,* it was never seen again. If the ship had been manned, it very likely would have been the first aircraft ever to cross an ocean.

The U.S. Navy seaplanes, delayed by rough water, didn't take off until the next afternoon at 6:06 P.M. Fifteen hours later the *NC-4,* captained by Lieutenant Commander A. C. Read, reached the Azores safely, but there was no word of either the *NC-1* or the *NC-3.* They were feared lost at sea.

The following day, May 18, Hawker and Grieve took off, quixotically dropped their landing gear, and began their daring but poorly prepared flight. Raynham and Morgan tried their luck the same day, but a gust of wind tipped over their Rolls-Martinsyde as it taxied for a take-off.

News of the missing American Navy fliers came over the wires. The steamship *Ionia* had picked up all the survivors of the *NC-1,* which had crashed in the sea a few hundred miles from the Azores. Then followed a flash that the flagplane, the *NC-3,* had also made a forced landing on the sea.

Finally, after fifty-two hours of sailing and spasmodic taxiing, the resourceful leader of the entire flight, Commander John H. Towers, had brought his flying boat safely across 200 miles of open sea into Ponta Delgada.

But there was no news of Hawker and Grieve. And when a week passed without a word, they were given up for lost. Then, on May 26, came word that Hawker and Grieve had been picked up at sea by the Danish steamer, *Mary.* The remaining airshipmen and aviators in St. John's staged a celebration that is still remembered in that Newfoundland city.

Hawker, called "the man who won't be killed" because of a dozen miraculous escapes from air and auto crashes, had done it again. His plane, the *Atlantic,* had developed motor trouble 1050 miles out of Newfoundland: a water filter in the feed-pipe became blocked with refuse. As their motor coughed, Hawker and Grieve quickly circled and located the steamer *Mary.* They landed near the steamer, but the seas were so heavy that they weren't picked up for two hours. The *Mary* had no wireless to broadcast news of the rescue.

The world was jubilant at the rescue of Hawker and his mate. They were received as heroes, rode on horseback through the clamoring crowds in London. To their amazement they were given a consolation prize of 5000 pounds.

A few days later the *NC-4*, the last of the three Navy flying boats still in the running, reached Europe. It had completed the first crossing of the Atlantic. But while Read's achievement was a landmark in aviation history, he had not flown the ocean in one hop. It was now a race among the British dirigible, the *R-34*, which was almost ready to take off from Scotland, and the remaining planes in the *Daily Mail* contest. On the eve of departure Captain Lehmann's *L-72* had been scratched from the competition by jittery German officials who felt America might not be so happy to see a wartime Zeppelin hovering over New York City.

On June 14, Captain John Alcock and his American navigator, Lieutenant Arthur Whitten Brown of the Royal Air Force, took off in a near-gale from their bumpy airfield at Mundy's Pond near St. John's in a cumbersome World War Vickers-Vimy bomber.

Sixteen hours and twenty-eight minutes later they landed, nose down, in an Irish bog. It had been a harrowing flight through almost constant fog, with wireless dead. Several times they had narrowly missed crashing, once inadvertently looping-the-loop and then flying upside down a few feet above the fog-bound waves. The first non-Atlantic crossing had been made in a plane that no one in his right mind would now fly from Newark Airport to La Guardia Field.

But the most remarkable of that year's aerial exploits was still to take place. The 643-foot *R-34*, commanded by Major G. H. Scott and carrying as observer the notable eccentric, General E. M. Maitland, left East Fortune, Scotland, on July 2. News of the big ship's progress was eagerly awaited.

Just after midnight on July 6 radio signals from the *R-34* calmly informed Roosevelt Field, the destination point, that it was running out of petrol fast, somewhere off Massachusetts. The ship would be lucky, it reported, to reach the tip of Long Island—Montauk Point.

Navy Chief Frank Peckham, one of the few Americans who had served on a British airship during the war, was ordered to gather an emergency ground crew and speed to Montauk. Peckham and his men made a wild dash in a Navy truck, almost ending several times in ditches, and finally reached their goal at dawn. Just as the landing crew climbed the barren rocks of Montauk Point the British airship hove into sight. The American sailors cheered and waited for the dirigible to valve and nose down for a landing.

But serenely the *R-34* passed them by. Peckham and his men jumped back into their truck and raced for Roosevelt Field. Coming into Mineola, they saw a parachute blossom beneath the hovering ship. Peckham was sure it was General Maitland, whose passion for parachutes was such that on air inspection tours he would dump his luggage attached to a parachute, then follow it down himself. The head of the British Balloon Forces seldom deigned to land the easy way.

A few minutes later Peckham discovered that the parachutist was not the redoubtable general, but Flight Lieutenant J. E. M. Pritchard. He had been dropped at Maitland's suggestion to organize a landing party. Of course the General would have much preferred to make the drop himself, but he feared the Americans might have thought it a "cheeky stunt" for the ranking air officer of Great Britain.

By the time Chief Peckham reached Roosevelt Field the ship was being hauled in, its gas tanks almost bone dry. The R-34 had made the first air east-west crossing of the Atlantic in 108 hours, 12 minutes, a new world's endurance record. It had another "first" to its credit: it carried the world's first transoceanic air stowaway, a British Tommy who had had an irresistible impulse and a fine disregard for the consequences. It surprised no one who had served with Maitland, that he used his influence to get the adventurous young man off with little punishment.

Three days later the famous airship won new laurels. It made the return trip to Pulham, 3200 miles, in seventy-four hours and fifty-six minutes, breaking several records and firmly putting England at the head of postwar development of the rigid dirigible. It was no wonder, then, that Britain was selected to build for the United States Navy a big rigid dirigible costing 2,000,000 dollars.

Early in 1920 a group of the U. S. Navy's most experienced airship officers and men were sent overseas to Howden Air Base. Practice cruises were made on the R-32, R-33, R-34, and R-80, so the Americans could get used to the English type of dirigible.

Months of annoying delays held up the completion of the new ship, which had actually been started in the last days of the war. The Americans were bored and impatient by the time work was finally completed late in June, 1921. Designated the R-38 by the British, the ship was a copy of a World War Zeppelin with an extra bay inserted in the middle to give it a ceiling of 25,000 feet. It was a monstrous affair, the biggest airship built up to that time. Its fourteen gas cells, looking from the inside like big slices of sausage, held 2,700,000 cubic feet of hydrogen. It was eighty-five and one half feet in diameter and stretched out for over two city blocks—699 feet (ninety-seven feet shorter than the Woolworth Building).

Six 350-horsepower Sunbeam-Cossack motors, each suspended in a tiny gondola, gave the ship a cruising radius of 9000 miles at sixty miles an hour.

On paper the ship looked better than anything the Germans had designed; and when it was brought out of its construction hangar at Cardington for its first trial flight on June 23, everyone from General Maitland to the most dubious reporter agreed that the R-38 was indeed a beautiful ship to behold.

But after the first test flight several veteran enlisted American airshipmen, who had gone along for the ride, were not so enthusiastic. They wrote friends at the new Naval Air Station at Lakehurst New Jersey, that the controls were "screwy," and the bay the English had inserted made the ship "hump."

"The damn gas bag," concluded the letter of one critical chief, "is a lousy lemon."

The third test flight was made on July 17. Just before midnight James "Red" Collier, one of the few American petty officers who had seen war airship service, relieved his shipmate, Charlie Aller, at the big elevator wheel.

The elevator man—the most experienced crew man was always put on the elevators—stood sideways in the control car so that he could feel the pitch of the ship and correct any rise or fall. The rudder man, who like the pilot of any ship, stood looking straight ahead, steered the ship right or left; his mistake could be more easily corrected.

Collier heard Flight Lieutenant A. H. Wann, captain of the R-38, talking with Commander A. H. Maxfield, who was to assume command when the ship was turned over to the United States Navy. It was decided to give the R-38 a modified speed test. Orders for full speed ahead were transmitted to four of the six engine rooms by the telegraphic annunciators. In a moment the big ship surged ahead powerfully.

Suddenly the elevator wheel felt peculiar to Collier. The ship nosed over and started to plunge down into the darkness. Flight Lieutenant Pritchard, the British officer who had parachuted out of the R-34 at Mineola, thought Collier had lost control. He grabbed for the elevator wheel.

Pritchard was a British officer, and the R-38 was still a British ship; Collier relinquished the controls even though he knew he had done nothing wrong.

Pritchard spun the wheel hard up. The ship shot up in the air at a dangerous angle. The telephone in the control car jangled. It was Charlie Aller calling from amidships. "Girders buckling at

Frame Nine, sir," he reported in what he hoped was a calm voice. Actually he was "scared as hell."

Lieutenant Wann quickly rang up the engine rooms, ordering all the motors slowed down to half-speed. The ship shivered and slowed. At last the elevator controls took hold again, and the ship leveled off. Pritchard looked apologetically at Collier; both of them knew now that the elevator controls were overly counterbalanced and had flopped over as soon as speed was poured on.

No one spoke in the control car for several moments. The danger was over, but it was obvious to all of them that if Charlie Aller hadn't been walking back to his bunk in the crew space at the right moment, no one would have seen the girders buckling—and the ship would have broken up in an attempt to fight the balky elevator controls.

But the accident failed to dampen the enthusiasm of the Americans. In two weeks the damaged girders were repaired. They were now even stronger than the other girders. This extra strength was to prove disastrous. The Germans could have told them that a ship must never be stronger at any one point than another.

All the Americans, even those who thought the R-38 was just a rebuilt "flivver," were anxious to take over "their" ship and start the trip across the Atlantic. Commander Maxfield, in particular, kept begging the British to hand it over.

But General Maitland, commandant of Howden, refused to be rushed. "I will not release the ship," he told Maxfield, "until I put it through all the tests I deem necessary."

August 23 was the date set for the final tests. The ship, now known by its American designation, the ZR (Zeppelin Rigid)-2, would fly to Pulham, tie up at the mast, and a few days later set off for America.

The transatlantic trip was causing a furor in the United States. At Lakehurst the ZR-2's new home was at last completed. Built at a cost of 3,000,000 dollars, the hangar was the biggest in the world and would house not only the ZR-2 but the ZR-1 (several years later to be christened the *Shenandoah*), which was then being built in Philadelphia. By the morning of the final tests five warships were already taking their assigned stations in the Atlantic as watchdogs. Each ship had aboard a meteorological officer who would keep the ZR-2 informed of surrounding weather conditions by radio.

Just after dawn on Tuesday, August 23, America's first rigid dirigible was readied for her last test flight. In anticipation of the turnover the American colors had already been painted on the

rudders and elevators. Sixteen American officers and men filed into
the hangar. They considered themselves fortunate to have been
selected to make the flight. Young Norman Walker, a wiry, boyish-
looking Texan, felt particularly lucky. Chief Sylvester Shields,
originally scheduled to make the trip, had become sick at the last
minute, and Walker had been given his place.

The Americans waved to their shipmates on the ground, who
were to bring the flyers' gear, already packed for the transatlantic
trip, to Pulham.

"See you at Pulham!" shouted Mechanic's Mate Steele.

"Say good-by to that barmaid!" called a rigger.

General Maitland walked under the big ship. He watched as
ballast was discharged to make the ship weightless. At last it was
"airtight."

"Now she's as light as a feather," Maitland told one of the ground
crew men. He looked up at the ship proudly. "She's a beauty!"

As the ship was dragged out to the field, a taxi was hurrying toward the airbase. In it was Lieutenant Richard E. Byrd, recently
chosen as navigator for the ocean trip. He was supposed to be
aboard the ZR-2 on this final test flight but had missed his train in
London. He urged the driver to hurry.

Now the six deep-throated motors were being tested. Lieutenant
Wann tried out all the ship's signal bells, and all men were ordered
to their landing stations. Everyone had an assigned spot on the
ship so it would be properly balanced.

Maitland waved good-by cheerfully to a group of officers. "I will
see you in Pulham," he shouted above the roar of the motors. Then
he climbed into the battleship-gray dirigible.

Commander Maxfield, the seventeenth American, said good-by
to his wife and his married daughter and was boosted into the
control car alongside Lieutenant Wann, C. I. R. Campbell, chief designer of the ship, who was also flying to Lakehurst with the
Americans, and three other civilians from the National Physical
Laboratory.

The commander of the ground party put a megaphone to his
mouth. "Cast off!" he cried.

At this moment Byrd ran onto the field. He looked up in
helpless exasperation as the ship slowly rose. Lieutenant Commander Coil's wife, an English girl, waved to her husband in the
control car. It was now seven-ten and morning fog rose from the
field as if from a thousand campfires. Villagers in nearby Howden
watched the ship disappear in the mist regretfully. For they
knew it was never coming back and during its stay in Howden it
had brought many shillings into the little town.

right: Dr. Solomon Andrews, who on May 25 and June 5, 1865, made motorless flights over Manhattan in his airship, the *Aereon* Number 2.

below: The British Army Barracks in Perth Amboy, N.J., bought by Andrews in 1849 and converted into "The Inventors' Institute." Andrews' airships were constructed in these buildings.

bottom: The motorless *Aereon* Number 1, the first airship to fly against the wind.

(Photos by Louis P. Booz)

left top: Albert Santos-Dumont in the *Santos-Dumont* Number 5 at St.-Cloud. Below is the first hangar ever built.

left bottom: Santos-Dumont in the wicker car of the *Santos-Dumont* Number 5.

above: The *C-5* arrives unexpectedly at St. John's, Newfoundland, on May 15, 1919. Below lie three rivals: the Navy seaplanes *NC-1*, *NC-3*, and *NC-4*.

below: Rescuers search the Humber River for survivors of the *R-38* (*ZR-2*), which broke in two over Hull, England, on its last test flight, August 24, 1921.

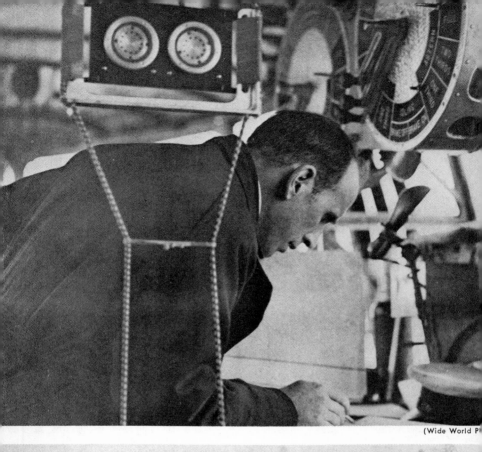

left top: Lieutenant Commander Zachary Lansdowne in the control car of the *Shenandoah*. Over his head is the annunciator, the telegraph system for relaying orders to the five engine cars.

left bottom: Tail section of the *Shenandoah*, which was torn in three parts by a storm, near Ava, Ohio, on the morning of September 3, 1925.

below: The wreck of the *Shenandoah:* (1) the control car; (2) engine numbers 4 and 5; (3) the crew space (note fragment of the tail in the trees); (4) the tail section. The nose, about one third of the airship, landed 10 miles away.

right:

(A) The *Italia* being whipped by a fierce wind at its mast in King's Bay, Spitsbergen, May 6, 1928. (B & C) During a lull in the storm the *Italia* is pulled off the mast by alpine skiers and volunteers from the mines at Ny Aalesund. (D) The *Italia* being walked into her domeless hangar.

General Umberto Nobile and his dog, Titina, in the doorway of the *Italia* at Stolp, Germany, on April 16, 1928, en route to Spitsbergen.

Mussolini presenting the Italian airship *N-1*—later the *Norge*—to Roald Amundsen at Ciampino on March 29, 1926. At the extreme right is Lincoln Ellsworth.

(Wide World P

A

B

C

D

Both photos by Wide World Ph

above: French gendarmes and soldiers inspect the skeleton of the *R-101*, which crashed near Bongenoult on October 5, 1930.

below: The *Los Angeles* and *Akron* (foreground) over New York City.

The *Los Angeles* standing on end on her Lakehurst mooring mast. (This picture, never before published, was believed by authorities to have been destroyed.)

above: The *Akron* being commissioned by Mrs. Herbert Hoover at Akron, Ohio, on August 8, 1931, before 250,000 spectators.

left: Robert "Bud" Cowart during his 90-minute ordeal on a mooring line trailing from the *Akron.*

right top: Crowd sings *"Deutschland"* as a glider is attached to the *Graf Zeppelin's* belly at the Berlin Airport.

right bottom: The *Hindenburg* and *Graf Zeppelin* over the Potsdam Railway station in Berlin in the spring of 1936. Loudspeakers aboard the airships broadcast appeals for the re-election of Reichschancellor Hitler.

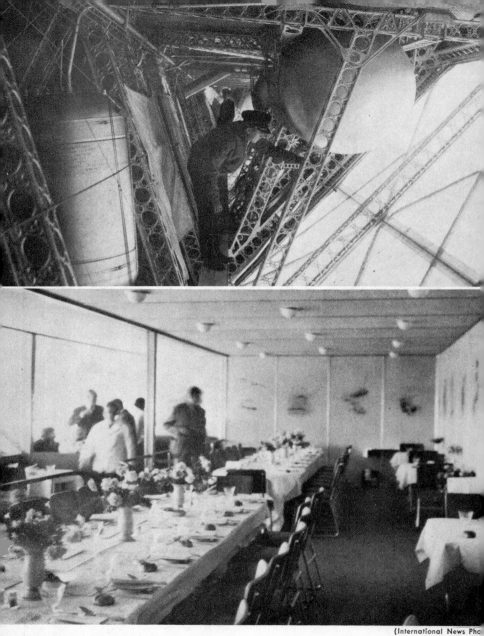

(International News Pho

above: The starboard keel of the *Macon,* showing gas and ballast tanks.

below: The dining room of the *Hindenburg.* (This picture was snapped in flight by the famed explorer Sir Hubert Wilkins.)

The last flight of the *Hindenburg:* over New York City at 3:12 P.M. on May 6, 1937.

The last flight of the *Hindenburg.* 7:22 P.M.: The nose mooring lines have been dropped and the ground crew at Lakehurst is picking them up.

The last flight of the *Hindenburg*. 7:25 P.M.: A split second after the first explosion.

The last flight of the *Hindenburg*. 7:25: 10 P.M.: The tail starts plunge toward earth.

The last flight of the *Hindenburg.* 7:25: 22 P.M.: The tail crashes.

The last flight of the *Hindenburg*. 7:25: 34 P.M.: The bow crashes.

The last flight of the *Hindenburg*. May 11, 1937: Nazi rites for the 28 European victims, on the pier at the foot of 46th Street, New York City.

On the ZR-2 everyone was in high spirits, confident that the ship's structural defects had been ironed out. But there was one man on the ground who watched his mates leave with an uneasy feeling. Red Collier had been the last man to take purity readings of the ZR-2's gas cells. His meter revealed that two of the cells aft of midships were "ripe"—that is, air had seeped into the hydrogen. Pure hydrogen, he knew, was safe. But air and hydrogen was an explosive mixture more dangerous than dynamite. He had made his report through routine channels, but nothing had been done about the two cells. They were still ripe—ripe for explosion.

The ZR-2 flew over the North Sea all that day and then started down the coast toward Pulham. But the fog was so dense that a landing was impossible. At 8:00 P.M. the ship radioed its headquarters, "Will remain out tonight to complete necessary trials. Several have been already successfully accomplished. Will land tomorrow."

That midnight the fog was so thick that Lieutenant Wann decided to make for Flamborough where there was a direction-finding station. The ship got its bearings and headed once more out to sea.

The next morning, August 24, the New York papers featured the test flight of the ZR-2. The ship would land soon, they informed their readers, refuel, and set off for America. President Harding and Secretary of the Navy Denby prepared speeches of welcome for the ship's arrival at Lakehurst.

The ZR-2 continued its trials all that morning. By 1:15 P.M. the fog had become so thick that Lieutenant Wann radioed, "Will not land at Pulham until cloud height increases. Trials proceeding satisfactory."

An hour and a quarter later the ship returned to its old base, Howden, and Lieutenant Wann told the radioman to request that a kite balloon be sent up 3000 feet so the probable wind could be determined.

An enlisted man overheard Wann's order. The ship's grapevine worked so effectively that within a few minutes all forty-nine men aboard knew that the final tests, the speed tests, were about to be made.

Everyone had been living on sandwiches, coffee from thermos bottles, and practically no sleep, and there was now an increased air of expectation on board the ZR-2. The English, who had been good companions for many months, had caught the excitement of the Americans, and there was much good-natured banter about the coming ocean trip.

In the control car, Lieutenant Marcus Esterly, the American radio officer, was being jollied about his elaborate precautions against a mid-ocean mishap. He had rigged up an emergency radio that would be carried 250 feet in the air by a tiny balloon if anything happened to the ZR-2.

In the crew space, amidships, half a dozen American sailors were loafing on their bunks. They were impatiently waiting for the last hour of the long flight to end. An old-timer, Chief Rigger A. D. Pettit, was telling the younger sailors a story about their skipper.

When Commander Maxfield first came to Wingfoot Lake, the American airship training base during the war, the enlisted men were suspicious of him. He wore a wrist watch and he smoked cigarettes—this in the days when real men smoked cigars and pipes and only women sported wrist watches. Their suspicions seemed well taken when, on his first Sunday morning, the Commander calmly walked out of his quarters in a bathrobe and headed for the dock. The new skipper had gone crazy; it was the middle of winter. When Maxfield got to the end of the dock he took off his bathrobe and dived into the icy water. He swam around leisurely for a few minutes, then climbed back to the dock and gave himself a rubdown in the near-freezing temperature. From that day on Maxfield had the respect of the toughest mechanics and riggers—in spite of his wrist watch.

Just as Pettit's story ended, the tempo of the motors changed and the ship lunged forward. The conversation stopped for a few minutes as everyone listened tensely to the roaring Sunbeam-Cossack motors. The ship vibrated slightly at top speed but remained stable. Fifteen minutes later the motors resumed the steady drone of cruising speed.

The men relaxed on their bunks.

"I bet we did over sixty knots," said Steele. He was right. Top speed had been sixty-two knots.

At long last the "big lemon" had passed her final test.

At the extreme end of the tail, in the tiny machine-gun cockpit, Harry Bateman, a civilian from the National Physical Laboratory, was closely observing the reaction of the fins. He was greatly relieved that at high speed the elevators hadn't flopped over as on the third flight.

A few minutes after the speed test, at 5:27 P.M., General Maitland and designer Campbell visited the tail. Bateman came out to talk to them, for the cockpit was too small for all three men.

Bateman told them how well the fins had responded to the speed test. Maitland was pleased. "I'm delighted with the ship," he said.

Campbell nodded in agreement.

In the control car Wann and Maxfield were pleased too. The ship was now ready for the long-postponed turnover. Howden had already been informed by radio that the ship had finished all its tests satisfactorily and would land at six-thirty. Everyone was relieved that the grind was about over.

At five-thirty-four the ZR-2's radioman, Flying Officer Wicks, acknowledged receipt of a routine signal. General Maitland was now in the keel gossiping with a rigger. The general was the hero of all the enlisted men, American as well as British: he was fearless, good-natured, and contemptuous of protocol and the privileges of rank.

Back in the crew space the off-duty American sailors, lying in their bunks, were making big plans. Young Coons was showing around the diamond engagement ring he'd just bought. He was going to marry an English girl as soon as he landed. Already ten in their detachment had repaid English hospitality by marrying local girls.

"I think we're over Hull," said Steele, one of the bridegrooms, as he looked out the window. The fog had been eaten up by the brilliant late afternoon sun. Two other men left their bunks to look down at the big port city. It was the first time they'd seen land clearly since the take-off.

Tired as they were after thirty-four and a half hours of rugged flying, the men became excited as the ship headed for the Humber River and Howden. They talked of what they were going to do when they got back to America. One was interested in seeing Babe Ruth in the World's Series. Another had saved all his money so he could go to New York and see Marilyn Miller in *Sunny* and Ann Pennington in the *Scandals*. Chief Rigger Pettit wanted only to see his family. His wife had gone ahead to Lakehurst with their two-year-old son Robert to get their new home ready. He became so bored with the talk he turned over on his bunk, Number 9, and went to sleep.

At this same time, not many miles away at a country estate in Weybridge, a man who had never been up in an airship was strangely worried about the ZR-2. This was American Ambassador George Harvey. He was telling his friends, Major Solbert, military attaché of the embassy and Captain Hyatt, the assistant military attaché, that the whole airship deal bothered him. He decided to send a cable to Washington advising the government not to buy the airship. But Solbert and Hyatt laughed at his fears and finally persuaded him to come out on the lawn and play croquet.

Just then the ship came from behind white clouds right over the center of Hull. The sun shone on the airship's silvery sides. Below, the streets were lined with thousands watching the graceful dirigi-

ble glide toward the Humber River. Its six motors were droning
steadily, reliably. It was now 5:37 P.M.

"It almost makes one wish to cheer," said one Hull greengrocer
to a customer as he pointed up at the ship.

At that moment the nose of the ship fell. Clouds of vapor seemed
to come from her sides.

"She's coming down to give us a better look," said the grocer's
customer.

But Chief Mechanist's Mate Charles Broom, standing nearby, was
sure something was wrong. He knew the ZR-2 as well as anyone, for
he was one of the American crew. He hadn't been assigned to fly
the last trials, so he was in Hull on leave seeing his English wife and
their two-weeks-old baby. He had been watching the ZR-2 for
several minutes. She had been moving peculiarly, her nose showing
a tendency to dip. He hoped the repaired center girders weren't going to buckle again.

Near the banks of the Humber River stood David Phipson, camera in hand. "What a beautiful object!" he told a bystander, trying
to focus his camera for a shot. Then he noticed a wrinkle in the middle of the ZR-2, "like a frown in a man's forehead." To his horror
the wrinkle deepened. In a few seconds the ship lurched and sagged
in the middle. The nose and stern went up simultaneously, and a
huge split appeared in the bottom of the ship. It reminded Phipson
of a huge, elongated egg being cracked.

"Good God," he said, "it's gone!"

The District Naval Intelligence Officer of Hull saw several men
jump from the great crack in the ship. He heard piercing screams,
but he couldn't tell whether they came from the ZR-2 or the
crowd. While the ship faltered over Hull, it appeared to him that
she was being deliberately steered toward the river to avoid falling
in the city.

Pilot William Henry Smith saw the accident from his tug in the
river. To him it looked as though the fore end broke away first
and then, after about twenty seconds, the stern end dipped down.
The ship was at an altitude of 2500 feet, and he could plainly see
beds, blankets, and men dropping into the calm river.

A parachute cracked open and a man, swaying lifelessly, drifted
toward the river. Then another chute opened. Two men could be
seen clinging together. They plunged down, soon passing the first
parachute.

A pier master named Martin was almost under the ship. He saw
her turn in from the northwest and head southwest. Then the
envelope crumpled in the center. He saw no flames at first but the
ship was surrounded by a slight fog. The crumpling got worse and

the ship broke in two. All at once the forward part caught fire at
the break. A few seconds later there was a terrifying explosion just
aft of amidships.

Fifteen miles away, at Grimsby, the explosion was heard. And
fifty miles away tremors, believed caused by an earthquake, were
felt. The concussion of this first explosion shook the entire city of
Hull.

From below it looked certain that the flaming ship was going to
drop right in the center of the crowded business section. Scores
were knocked to the street by the concussion. Many women,
shocked, burst into tears. Thousands of windows in a two-mile radius were shattered by the blast. Those in the streets rushed madly
for cover. A moment later others came running out of offices and
shops dazed by the explosion and the tinkling of broken glass. They
saw the ship dive toward the river and realized that by the grace
of less than a minute Hull had been saved from a major catastrophe.
Even so one Hull woman, Mariana Brown, died from shock, and hundreds were treated for cuts from flying glass. It reminded the citizens of a scene following one of the dreaded Zeppelin raids of a few
years before.

A second explosion soon followed the first. A large plate-glass
window behind photographer Phipson broke, showering him with
fragments. Although the people nearby were running around,
frantic with fear, he couldn't keep his eyes off the ZR-2. She had
split in the middle and the two halves hung with their open ends
down momentarily. He could see the black, gaping interiors of the
two sections. Gas tanks fell through the fabric of the ship and
crashed to the river. They burst as they hit, covering the water
with flammable fuel and filling the air with fumes.

Both ends of the ship floated in the air, drifting slowly for a few
seconds. But flames soon ate up the envelope of the nose, and it
plunged heavily toward the river. When it hit the gas-covered
water there was a concussion and a great burst of fire. The tail then
caught fire. It fell, but not as fast as the nose, with a long trail of
smoke and flames stretching behind it. It drifted east of the blazing
ring of oil that circled the fore section and, about 500 yards from
Victoria Pier, hit a spit in the river known as "the little sandbank."

Dazedly but automatically, Phipson snapped three pictures of
the wreck.

Inside the ship, the accident had happened with shocking suddenness. Lieutenant Wann was in the control car, in command. For the
past twenty-six minutes, following the speed trial, Wann had been
giving the dirigible rudder tests that became more and more severe. He had just ordered the rudderman to move the wheel from

hard over to hard over as they passed over the city at 2500 feet. Then he heard a violent crack like a burst of machine-gun fire. He guessed several girders had snapped as in the third trial. (The repaired girders at frames nine and ten actually were not the ones that crumpled. Those just aft had given way under the strain.)

The ship pitched forward, nose down. Wann saw men jumping or falling from the center section. He quickly emptied water ballast to level off the dirigible. As he did so there was a terrific explosion. The concussion knocked him to the floor of the control car. Debris piled on top of him, pinning him down helplessly. The ZR-2 seemed to halt; then it dropped like a rock. The next thing Wann knew, the ship had hit the river and water was pouring into the control car.

At bunk nine in the crew space, Chief Pettit, exhausted by the long trip, was in a deep sleep at 5:37 P.M. Perhaps he never woke up.

Aircraftsman Ernest Davies, off duty, was in the aft cabin at that same moment, snapping photographs of Hull. He was congratulating himself on the good pictures he was getting when he heard several sharp reports. The ship dipped, and then Davies heard two loud explosions. He felt the ship shudder violently and realized the tail section, where he was standing, had torn away from the bow and was falling. He saw men jumping into the river but decided to take his chance with the dirigible. Although clouds of black smoke were choking him, he clung to a girder. Several minutes later the tail struck the water and he fell, encompassed as by a huge tent, into a mass of wires. Water closed around the stern, and he knew he was going to die, trapped in the midst of twisted wreckage.

By coincidence another man was taking pictures at exactly five thirty-seven. A few minutes before, Lieutenant Pritchard had telephoned Harry Bateman, of the National Physical Laboratory, that the controls were to be moved with some rapidity. This would be the final severe test. Bateman believed pictures showing the pressure on the fins would prove a useful guide to future airship designers. He leaned out the window in the machine-gun cockpit and aimed his movie camera at the elevators.

Without any warning the ship was shaken three or four times in a lateral direction and then several times longitudinally, like a rat in a dog's mouth. There was a series of explosions, and the tail dropped abruptly. Bateman was knocked to the floor of the cockpit. He knew the ship was lost. Since he was wearing his rope harness, he quickly snapped on the ends of the only parachute in the cockpit. He tried to remember how the thing worked. Why hadn't he paid better attention when he was instructed? He remembered only that the chute was attached to the ship, and that when he jumped out his weight should pull it free and open it.

Bateman climbed into the cockpit window and jumped. He was jerked to a startling halt after falling only ten feet, and found himself hanging helplessly below the gunmounts. He wondered what he had done wrong.

Corporal Walter Potter of the RAF was climbing the ladder into the machine-gun cockpit when the ship lurched. The first big explosion knocked him off the ladder. Dazed, he got to his feet and stumbled up the ladder, thinking only of the parachute in the cockpit. He clambered into the cockpit just as Bateman leaped. Potter shouted, but it was too late. The bloody fool hadn't tossed out the ball of the chute! Potter leaned out the window and saw Bateman looking up at him sheepishly.

"Cut me loose and jump with me!" shouted the civilian.

"Too much strain!" replied Potter. "I'm getting my own."

He turned and started down the ladder, heading for the crew space where most of the parachutes were located.

At five thirty-four, three minutes before the first explosion, twenty-year-old rigger Norman Walker—the Texan who'd considered himself so lucky because he'd been a last-minute replacement for Chief Shields—got off Number 7 bunk in the crew space. He was tired of hearing what his shipmates were going to do when they got to America. Lloyd Crowel asked him where he was going.

"Back to the machine-gun cockpit," he said. He spent much of his spare time in the little tail nest, which reminded him of a hornet's stinger. He liked to sit back there, all alone, and watch the scenery. Most of the others were bored with scenery but it never ceased to fascinate Norman. He walked down the ZR-2's single keel or corridor, and then climbed into the lower fin.

Suddenly all hell broke loose. Screeching as if in pain, control wires and cables near his head grew taut and snapped. One wire knocked his hat off. He fell to the floor. It felt as if the ship had completey stopped, and he thought they'd run into the side of a hill. There were a half-dozen explosions, like gas tanks blowing up. If the hydrogen in the rear cells was touched off, he knew they'd all be blown to pieces. He got to his feet and scrambled to the keel. There were plenty of parachutes in the crew space forward. And that was obviously the only way to get out alive. He ran a few steps and saw daylight ahead. He couldn't believe it, but the ship had actually been torn in two. The forward part of his section started to burn. Big clouds of black smoke seemed to rise out of nowhere. He turned back once more toward the cockpit, remembering one parachute was there.

Just as he started up the ladder to the machine-gun nest, Corporal Potter came down.

"Go on back!" shouted Walker above the explosions and crackle of flames. "There's nothing forward!"

Potter climbed back into the cockpit. Walker followed. "The fellow from the Laboratory went over the side with the parachute," said Potter.

The American sailor and British airman grabbed hold of the ends of Bateman's parachute. They pulled him to the window. There wasn't enough room in the cockpit for all three, so Walker lowered the parachute container that was secured to the ship. Bateman stood on the container, holding onto the window ledge, while the others hung doggedly onto the parachute ropes. Nobody spoke. There was nothing to say.

Walker's main fear as the ship plunged down was a hydrogen explosion. Outside of that he wasn't much worried. Things could be a lot worse. He was just as glad he hadn't found a parachute. He had been the one assigned to make all the rope harnesses on the ZR-2. The chute snapped on in front and he always had thought it was a better than even chance a man's back would be broken.

When they were 100 feet from the water, Walker called to Bateman, "Hang on!"

The Texan crawled out of the cockpit window and climbed up on the fabric forward of the tail as Potter hoisted himself to the edge of the cockpit window next to Bateman's hands. Just as the tail was about to hit the water Walker jumped. To his amazement his feet touched bottom almost at once. He was on a sand bar in four feet of water.

The fins took up the shock of landing, and neither Bateman nor Potter was hurt; but the civilian was so dazed he told reporters a few minutes later that the ZR-2 hadn't broken in two. He swore he had seen the whole length of the airship lying on the surface of the water.

But the three were not yet out of danger. Flames were spreading rapidly toward them over the oil-coated water, and the rear cells of the airship were still filled with enough hydrogen to blow up everything within 100 feet.

As soon as the bow section of the ZR-2 hit the water, tugs and small boats sped to the wreck. Pilot Osborne of the Humber Conservancy Board was the first to go into action. His launch, the *Pilot,* reached the stern section first. He and several seamen cut open the envelope of the dirigible with jackknives. But they could see no one alive inside the cavernous shell. The bodies of two

American sailors floated by. The rescuers tried to reach the sailors with boat hooks, but the swelling tide swept the bodies away.

Thousands from the city now rushed to the banks of the Humber to watch the rescue work. A great wall of fire that almost surrounded the bow section momentarily held up the rescuers. Tugs then approached the rear section, which had fallen in the shallows, but were grounded by the low tide. Smaller boats had to be launched.

As the flames around the front section of the ZR-2 died down, one boat daringly went through a hole in the fire barrier and headed for the upturned control car. Two men were dragged from the wreckage just before the car sank out of sight. One was Lieutenant Little, who had broken his ankle jumping off the runaway blimp, the C-5. The other was the captain of the airship, Lieutenant Wann. Little died before the rescue boat reached the pier. Wann, though conscious, was too stunned to talk. He was cut around the face and bleeding badly, and his skull was fractured.

Other boats, meanwhile, reached the tail section. There they picked up Walker, Bateman, and Potter. Not one of the three had so much as a scratch. Potter, who had never left the windowsill, didn't even get his feet wet.

At the same time other river pilots were cutting open the envelope forward of the tail. At first they could see nothing in the dim interior. Then they heard a faint shout. It was Aircraftsman Davies, tangled in wire, his head almost submerged. The rescuers pulled him free and lifted him into their boat.

A few minutes later the boat carrying Little and Wann landed at Victoria Pier. The two—one dead, one alive—were carried through the solemn, shocked crowd that lined the waterfront. Then Davies was brought ashore. Almost collapsing, he staggered up the sloping landing stage of the pier.

Seeing that at least one man had come out of the holocaust alive, the crowd cheered. A reporter rushed up to Davies, asking him questions.

"I'm too ill to talk," he said in a strained voice. "But I will say we've had a terrible time. It was all over in a moment."

As soon as he saw the dirigible break up, Chief Charles Broom, the ZR-2 mechanic on leave in Hull, ran to the riverside. His one thought was to help his shipmates. He got to the pier just as a tug was starting for the wreck. He jumped aboard. When the tug was stopped by low water, he put out in a small boat. The after bag of the airship was still inflated with hydrogen and stood thirty feet above the water. He took off his coat and swam to the cockpit, not knowing that three of his mates had been rescued from there a few moments before. Broom crawled into the machine-gun cockpit. He climbed down the ladder into the rudder, which was now filling with water, and swam along the submerged keel looking for survivors. He saw an officer floating near the keel and dragged him back to the cockpit. It was Lieutenant R. S. Montague. But Broom was too late. The British officer was dead.

Broom passed out the body to other rescuers. He dove again inside the sinking wreck. A moment later he came up with Harry Bateman's logbook.

The entire rear section was now beginning to tip dangerously. Rescuers forward of Broom had cut a hole through the envelope. They saw an American sailor hanging by his coat to a girder. They crept cautiously over the tangled mass, trying to reach the American. Just then the whole section groaned and began to turn slowly over. The rescuers scrambled back and jumped into their boat as the wreck rolled over and began to sink from sight. The rescuers hoped the entombed sailor had already been dead.

At this moment Ambassador Harvey was playing croquet on his front lawn in Weybridge. His game was so bad his friends wanted to know what was the matter with him.

"I cannot rid myself of the fear," he said, "that something has happened to the ZR-2."

Several minutes later a servant came out of the house and told the Ambassador he was urgently wanted on the telephone. It was the news from Hull.

Lieutenant Commander Richard Byrd was in London when he heard about his shipmates. He remembered how disgusted he'd been the day before when he'd just missed boarding the ZR-2 by a minute.

At Howden Air Base the ground crew was being assembled for the ZR-2 landing. Red Collier was talking with a British photographer who early that afternoon had missed his connections for Pulham. Someone ran out onto the field, and soon everyone knew that the ZR-2 had crashed into the Humber. Collier and the photographer ran to a taxi that was waiting for a fare near the hangar.

The other Americans attached to the ZR-2 ran for private cars and trucks. Within a few minutes they were all racing for Hull.

When Secretary of the Navy Denby was told of the accident by Washington newsmen he shook his head, refusing at first to believe that the great ship had been demolished.

Those at Pulham had been disappointed when word reached them earlier in the afternoon that the ZR-2 wouldn't land at their mast because of fog. The airbase had been crowded with photographers and reporters who were to record the historic turnover of the airship. It was like a gala party at which the guest of honor failed to appear. But their disappointment turned to shock when it was learned the ZR-2 had crashed with only a handful of survivors. Major Scott, commander of the R-34 on her round-trip ocean crossing, was so stunned that at first he couldn't talk to newsmen. But the photographers and reporters wasted little time at Pulham now. Those still left at the field hurried for Hull—in the hopes of getting in on the tag end of the big story.

In Hull, Walker, drenched but uninjured, refused to go to the hospital. He was taken instead to the local jail. While he was waiting for his clothes to dry, a Navy chief came into his cell. It was Shields, the man whose place Walker had taken on the ship. The chief was so jittery his voice shook. "What do you want to do, Walker?" he asked.

The young Texan by now had recovered from the shock of the accident. "Go back to the base," he said.

Half an hour later the two men were in a taxicab headed for Howden. Shields had been very quiet, sitting on the edge of the seat. "You saved two lives, Walker," he finally said. "Yours and mine."

Walker was the only American to get out of the ZR-2 alive.

That evening the eccentric Hull tide was up forty feet, and the wreck of the ZR-2 was completely out of sight. Few bodies had been found. Most of the men had been trapped inside the ship.

Only then was it revealed that the British Admiralty had never authorized the American airmen to fly on the ZR-2. General Maitland, an expert cutter of red tape, had taken sole responsibility upon himself.

The disaster by this time headlined the front pages of all American papers. As usual in such stories, there were many inaccuracies. First reports declared that all the Americans had been killed— Walker had died in a hospital. There was also a lurid story of three men jumping out of the burning ship in one parachute. All three, according to this account, were saved. Finally, Lieutenant Wann was proclaimed a hero. When the ship started to break up, according to reporters, he gallantly headed the ZR-2 for the Humber River so thousands in Hull wouldn't die. Wann later denied the report, saying that the ship had gone too fast to do much of anything.

Soon messages of condolence were being exchanged by President Harding, King George, and Prime Minister Lloyd George. All the world was stunned. Of the forty-nine men aboard the ship, forty-four had been killed. It was the worst aviation disaster in history.

But Admiral Moffett, U.S. Navy's energetic Chief of Aeronautics, refused to lose faith in the airship. "We will carry on and build and operate as many big rigid dirigibles as are necessary," he told reporters, "so these brave men shall not have given their lives in vain."

On the streets of Hull that night some men cleaned away truckloads of broken glass and boarded up gaping windows. Others did a brisk business selling pieces of the ZR-2 as curios. In Lakehurst, New Jersey, there was mourning. Captain Frank Evans, commander of the temporary naval station, drove to the quarters assigned Chief Rigger Pettit's family. Evans had the hardest job of his career to perform: nothing in the book explained how to inform a wife that her husband had been killed.

The new Lakehurst hangar, 1000 feet long and 263 feet wide, looked like a huge empty tomb that night. And it would remain empty for some time. Congress had failed to make an appropriation, so work on the ZR-1 in Philadelphia had already stopped.

But Admiral Moffett was as good as his word. Mainly through his tireless efforts the American airship program was to continue in spite of the ZR-2 catastrophe.

In twelve years his faith in dirigibles would finally kill him as it had killed Maitland.

6

"DAUGHTER OF
THE STARS"

The world had scarcely recovered from the shock of the *ZR-2* tragedy when another took place.

The *Roma* was a 410-foot semirigid dirigible built in Italy by Umberto Nobile and three other Italian designers. Unlike the rigid Zeppelins, this airship kept its shape only by air and gas pressure. After twenty-two successful test flights, during which she reached the considerable speed of 110 kilometers an hour, the *Roma* was sold to the United States Army, dismantled, and sent to America. Three uneventful test flights were made and Liberty motors were substituted for the original Italian units. Then forty-five officers, men, and civilian observers took off from Langley Field, Virginia, on the *Roma's* fourth American flight on the afternoon of February 21, 1922.

For forty-eight minutes the biggest semirigid ever built, containing 1,193,000 cubic feet of hydrogen, behaved perfectly. At the forty-ninth minute one of the rudder cables broke. The ship went into a steep dive. Sandbags were tossed overboard and the dive was somewhat slowed down.

Richard Deal, a young airshipman, saw the dive from the nearby Hampton Roads Naval Air Station. He knew that the ship was out of control. The men were in for a good shaking-up, he thought, but the dive wasn't fast enough to kill them. The ship dropped out of sight. Seconds later there was a brilliant flash, followed by billows of smoke. Then, belatedly, came a terrific roar. Deal knew then that the hydrogen in the *Roma* had exploded. But he couldn't understand why.

Stunned army officers at Langley Field saw what had happened. As was true in so many of the old-time airfields, high-tension wires ran along one side of the landing strip. The gas bag, headed apparently for an embarrassing but not fatal crack-up, hit the high-voltage wires and burst into flames. Eleven men saved themselves by jumping. Thirty-three didn't.

This accident cooled off American enthusiasm for airships, but it had one good result: after that day flammable hydrogen was never again used in an American dirigible. Navy engineers developed a process of separating helium, an inert gas that could not be set afire with a match, from a natural gas found only in the United States. Airshipmen's greatest fear, fire, would now be a thing of the past.

In spite of the *Roma* disaster, work continued on America's first homemade rigid dirigible, the *ZR-1*. Started in 1920, at the Naval Aircraft Factory in Philadelphia, its construction had been held up many months by the failure of Congress to pass appropriations.

The plans for the American-made *ZR-1* were almost identical with those of the captured wartime Navy Zeppelin, the *L-49*. An extra ten-meter section was put in the middle, since helium, with only 92.6 per cent of the lifting power of hydrogen, was to be used. In addition the bow was strengthened for mast landings, the fins and rudders redesigned, and a walkway fitted along the very top.

There was great excitement at Lakehurst Naval Air Station when the big ship was walked out of the hangar for the first time late on the afternoon of September 3, 1923. Fifteen thousand spectators had come to see the "Made in U.S.A." rigid. The maiden flight lasted for an hour. The ship handled well and Navy officials were triumphant. Rigger Norman Walker, the only American to get out of the *ZR-2* alive, liked his new ship. "It's a lot better than that *ZR-2*," he told reporters.

The next day all the papers were filled with the tragic news that 250,000 Japanese had been killed in the world's worst earthquake, but the story of the *ZR-1's* successful first flight made most front pages.

On October 1 the long, graceful airship was flown to Lambert Field, St. Louis, to attend the Pulitzer Air Races. Rear Admiral Moffett, proving his practical faith in the ship's safety, made the trip. And the dramatic *ZR-1* stole the show from the hundreds of noisy airplanes that buzzed around her like mosquitoes.

A few days later Mrs. Edwin Denby, wife of the Secretary of the Navy, christened the *ZR-1* the *Shenandoah*, an Indian name meaning "Daughter of the Stars." Overnight America caught dirigible fever: thousands of Chambers of Commerce begged the Navy Department to fly their new battleship-of-the-air over their cities; a dancer at the Old Howard in Boston reportedly did a strip tease with a model of the ship; babies were named after the popular dirigible. Soon there was born of this enthusiasm a great and adventurous plan—a flight over the North Pole.

Those who thought Calvin Coolidge an unimaginative President gasped when he approved the flight. Among the press, eagerness for the daring trip was almost unanimous. The New York *Times* was almost alone when, like a cautious mother, it announced that "We had better look before we leap."

Plans were made to build mooring masts across the country and in Alaska. Ships at sea were to be provided with masts so that the *Shenandoah* could have portable roosts.

The Germans ridiculed. Helium and mooring masts, they said, were unfeasible departures from German airship procedure. But on November 16 the *Shenandoah* was successfully moored to the new landing mast at Lakehurst. The North Pole scheme boomed. Famed explorers Vilhjalmur Stefansson and Captain Bob Bartlett heartily approved the project. The spring of 1924 was set as the tentative date for the flight.

Meanwhile dirigible fever had spread to France. Of the seven war-time Zeppelins turned over to the Allies as spoils of war, the French had picked the *L-72*. This ship, originally designed to bomb New York City, had an astounding cruising range. A few days after the *Shenandoah's* first flight, the *L-72*, renamed the *Dixmude,* set out to establish a few world's records. The dirigible made the first air circuit of North Africa, flying 4500 miles and staying aloft 118 hours, 41 minutes.

The German builders warned the French that "he"—to the Germans dirigibles have always been masculine—had been designed for extremely high-altitude flying in clear weather and should not be subjected to rough trips. The French, eager for more records, ignored the advice, interpreting it as a sign that the Germans were jealous. The ship took off on December 18, 1923, for another long, strenuous cruise with a crew of forty and ten observers.

For two days all went well. The government assured its enthusiastic people that by Christmas new records would be won by the *Dixmude.*

On the third day the ship was sighted over Tunis. Then a storm came up, and the dirigible disappeared as mysteriously as the *Marie Celeste.* The day before Christmas the government announced that a message had been received from the ship at 1:00 A.M. Only two motors were now working, but a lucky wind had driven the dirigible across the Mediterranean Sea to Africa. Commander du Plessis de Grenedah, France's foremost airship pilot, was looking for a landing place. Later the same day the *Dixmude* was again reported over Tunis, and still unable to land. She had been aloft six and a half days; by now there was probably little or no fuel, and she was at the mercy of the storm winds.

That night, Christmas Eve, the Eiffel Tower broadcast a good-luck message to the fifty men stranded on the ship. But Christmas Day brought no news. An escadrille of French seaplanes was sent to patrol the Sahara Desert. Six warships crisscrossed an intricate pattern in the Mediterranean. Nothing was found.

On December 27 it was revealed that the *Dixmude* actually hadn't been heard from since December 21 at 3:00 A.M., when she had acknowledged receipt of a message. It was also discovered that the last reliable report of her whereabouts had been on the evening of the 20th, southwest of Biskra. Officials were now positive that the ship was down in the desert. Cavalry patrols were increased. Even natives on camels joined in the search.

The next day hope was revived. The *Dixmude* had been positively sighted two days before in the heart of the Sahara near an oasis fortress, Insalah. Since there were parachutes aboard, it was thought that the men may have bailed out and were wandering on the desert without food and water. More planes were sent out. The government was now thoroughly confused, and insisted that the last message had been received at 8:00 P.M. on December 21, when the ship was ninety miles south of Biskra.

The following day, December 29, two fishermen dropped a net six miles from the Sicilian coast near Sciacca. Their catch was heavy and they had difficulty in dragging the net to the surface. In it was the body of the thirty-one-year-old commander of the *Dixmude*. His wrist watch had stopped at two thirty.

Then it was recalled that the station master at Sciacca had reported that he had seen a brilliant light out at sea at two thirty on the morning of December 23. The light had lasted a few seconds and then disappeared.

All hope for the *Dixmude* was given up. Everyone believed she had been struck by lightning. This theory was strengthened when, on December 31, certain charred remnants were found near Sicily.

To add to the mystery a mail bag was later found in North Africa. It had been dropped on December 19. Letters indicated that the crew had been in high spirits.

To this day some wishful romantics believe the control car and a small part of the structure dropped into the Mediterranean, but that the bulk of the *Dixmude* and her fifty passengers drifted into the heart of Africa. They argue that more wreckage would have been found if the whole ship had fallen into the sea; and they firmly believe that survivors of the *Dixmude*, or their descendants, will one day be found in the darkest part of the continent.

Only after the disappearance of the *Dixmude* was it generally learned that Commander du Plessis had objected strenuously to the rigorous flights he'd been ordered to make. After his record-breaking flight of 4500 miles he had written, ". . . even in design the *Dixmude* is defective. She ought to be the last dirigible constructed on those lines."

She was.

In spite of the *Dixmude* mystery, plans for the *Shenandoah's* North Pole flight neared completion. In the middle of January, 1924, she was dragged out of her Lakehurst hangar and moored to the 172-foot mast. This was to be the final ten-day test of the ship's ability to battle Arctic gales. For four days the *Shenandoah* hung onto the mast. Occasional gusts of wind up to sixty miles an hour tumbled the men inside the ship, but the sturdy "Daughter of the Stars" showed no signs of weakening or structural defect.

Then, on January 16, a winter storm of great intensity broke. The ship was being slapped around like a pennant. At a little after four that afternoon the watch was changed. Commander McCrary, the ship's captain, came off with Lieutenant Charles Rosendahl. Exhausted, they left the field to get their dinner. The wind had moderated a few minutes before, and they both believed the worst of the storm was over.

But at six the storm picked up again. Gusts of over seventy miles an hour rocked the ship and its skeleton crew of twenty-one. Captain Anton Heinen, a former wartime Zeppelin commander who had been hired by the Navy to teach its officers the art of flying dirigibles, was in the control car. He was a small, explosive man with reddish-gray hair, a mustache and goatee; and his orders were delivered in a crisp Prussian bark that discouraged the slightest disagreement. With Heinen were Lieutenant Commander Maurice Pierce, the senior officer aboard; Lieutenant Commander Deem; and Lieutenant Earle Kincaid, a young officer with a mind of his own.

Lieutenant Roland Mayer, the construction officer, was walking aft on the eight-inch catwalk of the keel—a triangular tunnel running along the bottom of the ship. He had just learned that fabric in the upper vertical fin had torn, and he was trying worriedly to figure a way to repair the damage.

Machinists were at their posts in the six engine gondolas. One motor was idling, the rest were silent. On the keel, riggers who had nothing to do were placed by Mayer at strategic points, to keep the ship in trim. So delicate was the *Shenandoah's* balance that when its motors weren't running, one man could tip the 682-foot ship by as much as three degrees.

At 6:44 P.M. two sailors, carrying containers filled with a mixture of alcohol and water, were crossing the gangplank that led from the dirigible's nose to the mooring mast. Suddenly there was a scream of twisted metal and a loud pop. Rigger Eldredge, in the middle of the gangplank, leaped back into the ship. He was so shocked by the noise that he wasn't sure at first whether he was on the dirigible or the mast. As he jumped back he bowled over Chief Machinist's Mate Pasquale Bettio. At first Bettio, an innocent bystander who had just come aboard with a load of sandwiches for the crew, couldn't guess what had happened. Then he looked up to see a great tear in the nose of the *Shenandoah*. Heavy mooring winches and reels shot past Bettio and Eldredge and belched out of the ship's bow. Men on watch at the base of the mast, hearing the noise above their heads, leaped back and narrowly avoided being crushed by the winches and cables.

In the control car Kincaid was marking down wind velocities. He tabulated one at sixty-four miles an hour and then one at sixty-seven. Casually he looked out the front window. To his amazement he saw that the lights on top of the mooring mast were fast disappearing upward.

"There she goes!" he shouted.

Commander Pierce, an experienced sea navigator who was learning the intricacies of airships, at first thought that the control car had been wrenched from the ship and was dropping to the ground. Then he saw that the whole ship had been torn from the mooring mast.

Captain Heinen felt a sudden cessation of the constant trembling and vibration of wires. Instantly he knew that the ship had broken loose. To him it was a brief moment of peace after the buffeting of the past few days.

The nose was almost touching the ground when the four men in the control car instinctively pulled the ballast pulleys. All along the length of the dirigible water dumped to the ground—4000 pounds of it. The ship rose. Tail first it carried toward the pine trees at the edge of the field.

Engineers and riggers in the keel dumped three full gasoline tanks through the covering of the ship. The 724-pound tanks exploded as they hit the ground, but the wind was howling so fiercely that the men aboard the *Shenandoah* could hear nothing. Suddenly the tail of the ship rose, just brushing the tops of the stunted pine trees.

Captain Heinen grabbed the rudder wheel and spun the nose away from the wind. Their only chance, he decided on the spot, was to run with the storm.

Pierce had already ordered the five dead motors started. They coughed and sputtered as the ship drifted helplessly northward. First the tail would shoot up, then the bow; the men were bouncing around helplessly.

Lieutenant Kincaid climbed the ladder into the keel. Pierce, watching the elevator "bubble," shouted out the angle of the ship. Kincaid relayed the call to Mayer, who moved his riggers around like chessmen in an effort to trim the ship. The *Shenandoah* for a few minutes was like a huge teeter-totter, with men running up and down the narrow catwalk, sometimes scrambling uphill, sometimes sliding down.

At six forty-four Commander Ralph Weyerbacher, the *Shenandoah's* builder, had been walking, head down against the heavy winds across the big field at Lakehurst. He was scheduled to spend the night on the dirigible. He heard a crash and looked up, startled. Thirty-four floodlights lit up the *Shenandoah*. Weyerbacher saw that the nose of the ship, torn loose from the mast, was dropping toward the ground; and he knew immediately that the drop had been caused by an explosion of gas cells in the bow. As the *Shenandoah* careened toward the woods, stern first, it seemed impossible to save her. Weyerbacher saw the water ballast jettisoned and the fuel tanks explode. Miraculously the ship skimmed, tail foremost, over the trees. Just as she disappeared to the north he heard the roar of motors. He knew Heinen was at the controls. If anybody could save the ship, the doughty Zeppelin captain could.

In Bachelor Officers' Quarters, a few blocks away, the usual bridge game was going on. The dummy strolled to the window and looked out. To his amazement he saw the dirigible wrenched by a gust of wind and torn from the mast like a banana from the stalk. "She's gone!" was all he could say.

Chief Frank Peckham, who had been on the fruitless trip to Montauk Point to moor the *R-34*, was a few miles away on Clements' Farm Road. He saw the moored ship bouncing in the wind. In a few hours he was due back on her. It would be a rough watch, and he wasn't looking forward to it. Suddenly the ship left the mast. Peckham wondered why they were taking her out in such a storm. But then the dirigible's tail shot up, the bow settled, and the ship ballooned crazily above the trees; and he knew there'd been an accident. He remembered that only a few weeks before the *Dixmude* had disappeared in the same kind of a storm.

Peckham wasn't the only one who was thinking of the French airship. Back at the naval station, officers were trying frantically to radio the stricken "Daughter of the Stars." There was no answer. The *Shenandoah* had disappeared as strangely as had the *Dixmude*.

But within a half-hour dozens of phone calls came into Lakehurst. A strange object, believed to be an airship, was seen flying low over several Jersey towns.

The first definite word came in at about eight o'clock. R. P. Winslow, a member of the City Council of Westfield, saw a huge dirigible fly over his house only 400 feet in the air. He was sure the ship would crash in town, so he called the fire department and the police station. A few minutes later it hovered over the Westfield National Bank. A searchlight atop the bank played on the sides of the ship, which was now down at the bow and seemed to be in distress. Crowds of townspeople stood in front of the bank in the rain and wind. They watched the *Shenandoah,* pinned against the bleak sky by the searchlight, move slowly, painfully northward.

As soon as the dirigible was trimmed, Lieutenant Mayer and Rigger Smoky Reid crawled forward with flashlights to see how much damage had been done to the bow. The two men hung tightly onto the guide ropes on either side of the catwalk, for one jerk of the ship would pitch them through the gaping hole in the nose. They discovered that the two forward cells, numbers 19 and 20, had been exploded. Fragments of the large cells hung loosely. Mayer and Reid did their best to seal up the open end so the wind wouldn't destroy the other cells one by one. On their way back to the control car they saw Eldredge open a hatch.

"What do you think you're doing?" Reid called to the young rigger.

"I'm getting out of here," said Eldredge.

Reid grabbed Eldredge just as he was about to jump. Mayer hurried to help. It took the two men several minutes to convince Eldredge that a jump of four or five hundred feet wasn't very smart.

"We'll get out of this all right," said Reid confidently.

Four inexperienced men from the Army, who had come aboard to get lighter-than-air training, also needed assurance. Corporal Edward Douglas was standing a few feet from the nose when the ship tore loose. He turned, ran along the keel, and scrambled down the ladder into the control car, almost knocking over Captain Heinen.

"Take it easy," said the German in a heavy accent. Sweat was running down his face from his exertions. "There's no call to be scared."

Aviation mechanic Pasquale Bettio, the station's comedian, was rather enjoying his first ride in a rigid ship after many flights in blimps. From the moment he stepped aboard the *Shenandoah* with a load of sandwiches for the crew, he added to his reputation as a humorist. After helping dump 813 pounds of spare parts into the uninhabited piny wastelands, he rushed down the catwalk to Keel Officer Mayer. "I've thrown out everything I can lay my hands on!" he shouted, gesturing broadly.

Everybody on the catwalk broke out laughing, even though the ship was still bouncing dangerously.

"Well," Mayer grinned, "hike back and lay them on some more."

Bettio threw his hands in the air. "Pasquale goes on the *C-3*, she crashes!" he said. "Pasquale goes on the *C-2*—zzoom! Now I just bring a couple sandwiches to the *Shenandoah*, look what happens! These things are getting to be a habit!"

Again everyone laughed, even the soldiers.

Toward nine o'clock Gunner J. L. Robertson was finishing a long and difficult job in his radio room, located in the rear of the control car. He had spent the whole afternoon trying to repair his balky radio. At the time of the accident a hundred parts were neatly spread in front of him. After the wild plunges of the first few minutes Robertson began putting the radio back together again. He knew there was little chance of the *Shenandoah* coming safely through the storm unless he could get weather reports and find out their position.

By a little after nine the set was reassembled, but Robertson doubted it would work. The going had been so bumpy in the radio room that his tool chest had flown out of the window. (Later he learned that it landed twenty feet from Leslie Lambert of Alton, New Jersey.)

Finally at nine ten he switched on the transmitter. It seemed to be working. Hopefully he sent out a message: "All O.K. Will ride out storm. We think we are over New Brunswick. Holding our own. Pierce."

Several minutes went by, and there was no answer. Just as he was about to repeat his message he heard a strange voice say, "You are over Newark. The lights below you are from the Prudential Building. What can we do to help you?"

To Robertson's amazement he found he was talking with radio station WOR in Newark. "All O.K.," he answered. "Thanks, old man."

WOR immediately canceled all commercial programs in order to keep in direct communication with the lost ship. Other metropolitan stations like WEAF went off the air so they wouldn't interfere with the messages.

Radio operators Poppele and Barnett of WOR then got in touch with Lakehurst, relaying the reassuring news from the *Shenandoah.*

At ten o'clock direct contact was established between Lakehurst and the ship. "Everything fine," said Robertson. "Keep us informed about weather conditions. Little rough up here."

"Wish we could help you," said Lakehurst.

"You are helping," Robertson said.

"Can you make it?"

"Holding our own with four engines running."

Thousands stayed at their radios all night, earphones clamped on their heads, listening to the code messages between the *Shenandoah* and the naval stations that were picking her up. Later these countless messages about weather and direction were decoded and broadcast so that families of the flyers wouldn't be worried.

After passing over Newark the ship drifted over the flats of Bayonne. Great crowds, excited by radio reports, rushed to the streets as the long black shape, still nosing down slightly, rode with the wind. Half an hour later searchlights from the Brooklyn Navy Yard and the Sperry Gyroscope Company tried to pick the dirigible out from the Manhattan skyline as she circled over Governor's Island, then swung toward Staten Island.

Rockets were sent up at Port Richmond, Staten Island, to guide Captain Heinen. At midnight the storm, which had already killed five and injured twenty-two in the New York area alone, subsided. Until this time Heinen, out of fear that a heavy gust through the torn nose might collapse other gas cells, had avoided heading directly into the wind.

The ship recrossed the Kill van Kull and headed for home, Lakehurst. Heinen set the course and went up in the keel for a few minutes' relaxation. An Army sergeant offered him a sandwich.

"No thanks," said the little German with the goatee. "If I eat now it'll spoil my appetite. I'll have breakfast at six. And I'll eat it at home, too."

When Heinen returned to the control car he found Lieutenant Kincaid, at the rudder wheel, pointing the nose at an angle carrying the ship slightly off course. The German quickly told the Navy lieutenant of his mistake.

Kincaid replied that it was no mistake. The rudder was badly damaged, he said, and too much strain might rip all the fabric from it. The two men argued.

In the first moments of the accident Heinen had automatically taken charge. Since he was the instructor it had been assumed by the Navy officers that he knew best. But Kincaid was beginning to resent Heinen's attitude.

Their voices rose, became so loud and excited that Smoky Reid in the keel above could hear them.

"Who you giving orders to?" asked Kincaid. "I'm Officer of the Deck!"

"Do what I say!"

"You're not giving me orders."

"Oh, yes, I am. And if you don't follow them I'll throw you right off the ship!"

At that moment the senior officer of the ship, Commander Pierce, returned to the control car. A tense peace was quickly established.

The ship was now struggling homeward at four miles an hour. A large crowd of night factory workers cheered as she limped over Perth Amboy. Keyport was passed at twelve forty-five, and Captain Heinen climbed up to the officers' quarters for another break. Kincaid was sent back to the radio room to give Robertson a message for Lakehurst.

"Over Keyport, making some headway to south, cruising speed all engines. Please tell families not to worry," dictated Kincaid. Then he added, "Control cabin is delightful for first time because of not being overcrowded. Kincaid."

An hour later the police at Freehold reported that the ship had flown over their station at 500 feet going at thirty-five miles an hour. At Lakehurst all leaves had been canceled and everyone put on the alert. The rain had ceased and the skies cleared. At two ten on the morning of January 17 a sailor on top of the mooring mast saw a dark shape coming from the direction of Lakewood. He shouted to a man stationed at a siren. A loud, screeching whistle soon woke everyone for miles around. Floodlights lit up the field. Four hundred sailors and marines tumbled out of their barracks, ran toward the mast, and took their places in the landing crew.

At two twenty the battered *Shenandoah*, its six motors roaring, swept across the field. The wind was allowed to move the ship backward. Then the bow was dipped. Slowly the ship edged toward the ground. In a few minutes eager hands grabbed the railing around the control car. Others in the landing crew eased down the tail. The wandering "Daughter of the Stars" had finally come home.

A few minutes after the *Shenandoah* returned from her wild night, a young Navy officer took a count of the survivors. Twenty-one had left; twenty had returned. On second count it was discovered that only three of the four soldiers were on hand. A Corporal Mockowitz was missing.

"Damn the soldiers!" growled the officer.

A state trooper, hearing of the single casualty, left to spread the bad news. Only then did one of the corporal's comrades think to suggest that Mockowitz might be in the nearby barracks.

A minute later a searching party trooped into the barracks housing the visiting soldiers. There in his bunk, sleeping peacefully, was the "casualty." He had jumped from the ship the moment it touched ground, and, being properly exhausted by the long ordeal, had fled to his barrack without waiting for formalities.

The next day most of the papers in the country praised the gallant ship and crew. Instead of putting a damper on the North Pole trip, the accident had dramatically proven the fitness of ship and crew to weather the worst of storms. Not one plane had dared fly in a gale the damaged "Daughter of the Stars" had cruised around in for eight hours.

Cables and telegrams poured into Lakehurst. Among the first messages of praise was a telegram from President Coolidge. "I congratulate you most heartily," he wired the acting captain of the ship, Lieutenant Commander Pierce, "upon the fine exhibition of skill displayed by you during the storm which caused the USS *Shenandoah* to be cast adrift from her mooring Wednesday night, and upon your successful return to your base."

Immediately after he had landed, Professor C. P. Burgess of the Bureau of Aeronautics, who had been on board measuring mast stresses, allowed he was extremely impressed by the dirigible he'd helped design. "Can you imagine," he exclaimed to reporters, "a liner with two compartments caved in, a hole in her bow, half the steering gear torn away, bucking a gale of seventy-five miles an hour and returning to port? To me it was a rough ride but a good one!"

The men were just as proud of their ship but said little. Bettio expressed everyone's thoughts in a few words. "Man!" he said as he jumped to the ground, "what a ship!"

And America's greatest champion of the airship, Admiral Moffett, was the most pleased of all. "The *Shenandoah*," he said, "has demonstrated that she is the best and strongest rigid in the world." The North Pole trip, he declared, would soon be under way.

Captain Heinen, credited by almost everyone with saving the ship, gave a speech at a Princeton Club smoker the next night. He told his admiring audience that the *Shenandoah* was the strongest ship he'd ever commanded, and "fit for any task." As for the North

Pole trip, he concluded, "It will be the best joy ride ever made in the history of aviation!"

But in a few days it became apparent that the *Shenandoah's* famous night over New York City hadn't been entirely harmonious. The battle between Lieutenant Kincaid and Heinen leaked out. It was also hinted that Heinen had had to be quite insistent about flying the low course he had finally flown: an unnamed Navy officer, it seemed, had wanted to fly above the storm. Rumors of personal conflict at Lakehurst, common gossip for months at the naval base, reached the papers and were even discussed at congressional hearings. A well-concealed feud between Commander Weyerbacher, builder of the ship, and Commander McCrary, its first skipper, came to light. The story was that McCrary, an extremely able man at sea but an airship novice, had insisted on being the official captain of the *Shenandoah* on her maiden flight even though Weyerbacher had been in actual command. The reason was simple: McCrary outranked Weyerbacher. It was also revealed by the New York *World* that young Kincaid hadn't been assigned to fly on that first trip but had been so eager he stowed away. The episode had angered Weyerbacher, nor was he less angry because the young lieutenant was a good friend of McCrary's. To add still another complication, Weyerbacher and civilian Heinen were close friends. Both were old airshipmen, respecting each other's abilities. And every trip of the *Shenandoah*, rumor had it, was marred by this complex of tensions.

A climax was reached when Secretary of the Navy Denby, whose Democratic enemies were trying to link him to the Teapot Dome scandal, attempted to still critics of his favorite North Pole project by stating that every enlisted man who went on the dangerous trip would be a volunteer.

A list requesting volunteers was actually passed among the crew —with extremely embarrassing results. Very few would sign up. These realistic men weren't afraid of the Arctic; they had faith in the *Shenandoah*, particularly after her exploit in the storm; but they didn't want McCrary as the commander.

"The old man is all right," one chief told a *World* reporter, "but you won't catch us signing up ahead unless we're satisfied the skipper knows his job." A rigger added, "He just hasn't had enough experience in the air."

Reporters then asked the men whom they'd choose as their captain. "I'd fly to hell with that Heinie, Heinen," said a mechanic. The other men agreed. They said they'd also be glad to go with Commander Weyerbacher.

But neither of these men was available as captain of the North Pole flight: Heinen was a civilian and Weyerbacher had other duties.

Just when it seemed that the whole plan would be bogged down by dissent, the Navy solved the problem. A new man, belonging to neither faction, was brought in.

On February 16 Lieutenant Commander Zachary Lansdowne reported to Lakehurst to take over command of the *Shenandoah*. He was a tall man, an inch over six feet, with the rangy rawboned build of a Scottish highlander. In fact, he was the direct descendant of the fanatic reformer, John Knox. Lansdowne was a stern, reserved man; and with his high cheekbones and piercing eyes he had, according to a close friend, "the look of eagles."

On the ship Lansdowne was an uncompromising man—a strict disciplinarian who tolerated no laxity from officers or men. But on the ground he was an entirely different person, understanding and affable, often lending a sympathetic ear to the home troubles of his crew. Before he took over the *Shenandoah*, Lansdowne was already an experienced lighter-than-air man. And after a few trips together his crew respected and trusted him. (He and Commander Alger Dresel of the *Macon* are still remembered as the enlisted men's favorite skippers.)

The new commander brought a fresh enthusiasm to the North Pole expedition and soon fired everyone at Lakehurst with his own confidence. Work was started on mooring masts in Fort Worth, San Diego, and Camp Lewis, Washington. It was planned that the ship would fly west and up the coast to Alaska, where tankers with mooring masts would be anchored. From there the final dash across the Pole would be made.

The damage to the dirigible was quickly repaired. Two new cells were made in Akron by Goodyear. Goldbeater's skin, a lightweight but incredibly tough section of the lining of a steer's intestines, was cemented to the fabric, making the cells almost completely gas-tight. Expenses came to approximately 80,000 dollars. The greatest part of this, 50,000 dollars, was spent to replace the lost helium.

In the next few months many successful flights were logged by Lansdowne and his crew. Late on the afternoon of August 8, just off Newport, Rhode Island, the "Daughter of the Stars" approached the mooring mast on the Navy tanker, *Patoka,* commanded by Captain George Meyers. The airship made several passes at the tanker. Finally it nosed down. A steel cable was dropped to the deck of the *Patoka*. Sailors grabbed the cable and coupled it to one that had been lowered from the top of the mooring mast. The *Shenandoah* slowly rose as an engine on the tanker wound in the cable. Soon the cable was taut. The great dirigible was now dragged

toward the top of the mast like a fish being reeled in. In a few minutes the swivel pear on the *Shenandoah's* nose was fitted snugly into
the cup on top of the tower. There was silence. Then the sailors on
the deck of the tanker and the men in the airship realized what
they'd done. They cheered. It was the first time a rigid airship had
ever been moored to a floating mast.

When news of the important event reached Washington, stock
in the North Pole venture boomed. Now only one final test
remained: the airship was to fly across country, testing each
mooring mast, and return to its home base for final preparations.

Lieutenant Charles Rosendahl, already recognized as one of the
most promising in the new crop of airshipmen, was sent west to
inspect each mast. Since only half the ship's complement flew at
one time, a crew for the historic trip to the West Coast was
chosen. By this time there wasn't a man who wouldn't have flown
anywhere with Lansdowne.

There was great excitement from coast to coast when the trip
was announced. Everyone wanted to see America's only battleship
of the sky; and the triangular 9000-mile trip around the country
would give millions a look at what their taxes were buying.
Junius B. Wood, well-known writer for the *National Geographic*,
was invited by the Navy to go along as an unofficial chronicler of
the trip. Inevitably Admiral Moffett, that indomitable airship enthu-
siast, would make the trip. It was also planned to pick up a
Hollywood cameraman at San Diego to take movies of the west
coast from the air.

Just as the sun came over the horizon at five thirty-five on the
morning of October 7, the "Daughter of the Stars" was pulled out
of her giant hangar. It was a misty morning. With almost all of the
400 sailors and marines stationed at Lakehurst hanging onto the
ropes, the long, graceful ship was led into the wind toward the
tower far out on the field. It wasn't until seven that the dirigible
was safely moored to the lofty mast. In several hours she would
take off for the first airship flight ever made across the United
States. A skeleton crew went aboard, and the rest of those making
the flight left for breakfast.

The date, the seventh, had been chosen by Commander Lansdowne mainly because of favorable weather forecasts. It also had a
personal significance: this day was the second birthday of his
daughter Peggy.

There was good reason to moor the ship so early: Lansdowne
wanted the sun to heat up the helium. This would give the ship
"superheat," and make it capable of lifting many more pounds

of cargo. Since heat expanded gas, each degree of increased temperature meant that an extra 300 pounds could be carried.

By 10:00 A.M. the ship was almost ready to cast off. Crew and passengers were aboard. From the front window of the control car Lansdowne waved to his pretty twenty-two-year-old wife, who was standing at the base of the mast holding Peggy. Next to her was Lansdowne's son by his first marriage, nine-year-old MacKinnon, who had already taken one trip in the airship. When Mrs. Lansdowne had first suggested the idea, Lansdowne had refused, arguing that if he took Mac on a flight, his crewmen would want to take their sons. But like many another man, Lansdowne was unable to resist the long, insistent campaign waged by his young wife and son.

Junius Wood and Moffett stayed in the rear of the control car so they wouldn't interfere with the delicate and critical maneuver of casting off. Flying an airship was a combination of aviation, ballooning, and sea navigation, and it required a skill that few men possessed. Writer Wood watched in fascination as the complicated procedure began.

"We must weigh off right away, before we start to lose our superheat," said Lansdowne.

The enlisted man at the elevator wheel reported that the ship was heavy aft. Lieutenant Houghton, Officer of the Deck, told his skipper that there were three emergency ballast bags of water aft and two forward. A family man with a wife and four children, Houghton was small and dark, quiet and conscientious. Lansdowne liked him because he was completely reliable in a crisis.

Lieutenant Roland Mayer, the keel officer, then said there were 400 pounds of extra water at frame 40, near the tail.

Lansdowne held up his megaphone and leaned out the window. "Clear away aft," he shouted to the landing crew at the tail.

A man on top of the mast informed the captain that fuel was still being put aboard. Lansdowne, a little disappointedly, ordered the engines idled.

Lieutenant Sheppard, the engineering officer, swung the five levers on the annunciators, which were much like those on seagoing ships. Orders were transmitted telegraphically through the annunciators to the five engine gondolas. The sixth engine, the one at the end of the control car, had been removed to lighten the ship. This extra space now housed a generator for the radio and a two-burner gas stove used by the cook as the ship's galley.

Bells rang, indicating that the men in the engine gondolas had received and complied with the captain's orders: all engines were idling.

At last the mast reported that all fuel had come aboard. Lansdowne ordered the fuel shut off and the waterline secured.

"Aye, aye," replied the men on the mast.

"Is the ship still heavy?" asked Lansdowne.

An officer on the mast shouted, "Down at the tail, sir."

Everyone waited. Wood was surprised at the patience, the lack of tenseness.

"Elevators neutral," announced the burly chief at the elevators. He was Fred Tobin, better known as "Bull" because of his booming voice and commanding manner.

The ship was now parallel to the ground, at perfect equilibrium. But at that moment Houghton informed the captain that a cloud was coming over the ship. This meant that the temperature would drop—and so would the *Shenandoah*.

"Everyone at their landing stations?" asked Lansdowne.

Lieutenant Commander Hancock, the poised, dignified executive officer, told the captain that every man was at his assigned spot on the ship, assuring perfect balance. The cloud passed and the dirigible began to rise slowly again.

"She's coming up now, Captain," reported the mast.

There was watchful relaxation in the control car.

"Equilibrium!" finally called out the mast.

Lansdowne gave orders to release the mooring clamps that grasped the cone of the ship like fingers. As he did, he said, "Five seconds on one hundred and ten."

For five seconds Houghton, the stocky little Officer of the Deck, pulled on the ballast toggle which released water from frame 110, amidships. Each second sixty pounds were dumped.

"Free, Captain!" shouted the officer on top of the mast.

The dirigible swayed, then began to settle as she fell away from the mast. Lansdowne quickly ordered water dumped forward. The ship's nose stopped dropping and then slowly started up. The skipper, seeing the tail drop, ordered, "Water aft!"

A few seconds later water gushed from the tail. The ship swung up and down slightly. Lansdowne called for more water aft and then, noticing that the ship was far enough from the mast, said, "Standard speed."

Sheppard, with several deft movements, relayed the order to the mechanics. In seconds there was a concerted roar from all five engine gondolas. The dirigible hesitated, its nose pointing down. More water was dropped. The nose pointed up.

"Two men aft," said Lansdowne. "All the way."

Mayer hurried up the ladder to the keel and shouted. Swiftly two men ran to the very tail of the ship. The nose pointed up even more.

"Up twelve degrees, sir," said elevatorman Tobin, eying the "bubble" in front of him.

Lansdowne cautioned the rudderman to steer clear of the mast. Then he ordered Lieutenant Bauch, the tall, heavy-set second keel officer, to stand by to cut fuel tanks. Bauch scrambled up the ladder like a bear, pliers in hand. In a moment he was standing by a 724-pound gas tank, ready to cut it free in an emergency.

Lansdowne ordered a fast climb.

"She's climbing, sir," answered Tobin.

Executive Officer Hancock looked at the altimeter. "Five hundred feet," he called out. Since Lakehurst was almost at sea level everyone relaxed.

The ship circled the field until the altimeter read 1300 feet, then turned and headed south.

The first watch was now set. Ordinarily half the crew worked while the other half slept, but no one could sleep at the start of such a voyage. Those off watch spent their time amidships in the crew space, a plywood deck twelve feet square fitted over the keel. The ship's cook, J. J. Hahn, the only flying cook in the Navy, used the crew space as his headquarters. However he warmed up soup and made coffee in the galley next to the radio shack.

Those off duty had the run of the ship; now that the motors were driving the ship forward, the shifting of weight could be easily corrected by the elevatorman.

The keel was the heart of the ship. This triangular tunnel from nose to tail grew smaller at each end. But at the middle it was twelve feet wide and nine feet high. The two sides of the triangle were bounded by the gas cells. These bags, pressing against wire and twine networks that held them in place, were usually filled to about 85 per cent capacity at the start of a long trip. As the ship rose, the gas expanded and the bags became swollen. When the bags were 100 per cent full, pressure height was usually about 4000 feet.

A huge rubber hose ran along the top of the triangular keel and was connected to each of the twenty cells. When one cell reached its capacity, the helium leaked into the long hose, which transferred it to other cells not yet filled. When all cells were full, excess gas would escape through automatic valves.

There was another way of disposing of helium. In the control car was a row of pulleys similar to those that released water ballast. These pulleys let out helium through maneuvering valves. But helium cost fifty-five dollars for each 1000 cubic feet, and the Navy frowned on the use of the escape valves except in emergencies. When the Germans landed their Zeppelins, hydrogen was simply valved; and the ship, losing some of its buoyancy, would drop. To valve helium in this manner would cost up to 10,000 dollars. American airships, therefore, were forced to land at night, when the dirigible was colder and heavier.

Because of the helium problem the Navy devised an ingenious water-recovery system consisting of batteries of pipes rigged near three of the five engines. Water condensed by the combustion of each motor more than compensated for the weight of the gasoline consumed, since a gallon of water weighed 25 per cent more than a gallon of gasoline. As a flight progressed, the recovered water made it unnecessary to valve precious helium to keep the ship below pressure height. Before another year passed, this rigid economy of helium, made necessary by a parsimonious, antiarmament Congress, was to touch off a great military scandal.

At two ten that afternoon the *Shenandoah* was flying between Washington Monument and the White House, escorted by tiny airplanes. The ship had now settled into its regular schedule. Those who had served the first four hours of the trip were just off duty. Weary helmsmen loafed on the crew space, flexing their arms after the long grind with the rudder and elevator wheels. Mechanics, faces streaked with oil, pulled cotton from their ears. Everything would be a great buzz to them for some minutes.

"The noise makes you immune to hear anything," mechanic Joe Shevlowitz explained.

The leading chief on the keel was laboriously figuring out how many pounds of water had been recovered from the motors. He would then turn in his report; and if too much had been collected, the excess would be jettisoned. By this time the men were dying for a smoke, but they had to wait: there was never a match struck on the *Shenandoah*. She was built for war duty, not luxury.

During the day visibility was fairly good along the keel. The bottom hatches were open, and the cloth covering at the bottom of the dirigible was unpainted, unlike the rest of the envelope, letting in daylight. But at night the keel was a dark tunnel, for the *Shenandoah* had electric lights only in the control car and the five underslung engine gondolas. After dark every man carried a flashlight, and then the keel was an eerie place, with little lights bobbing around as riggers inspected gas bags and checked fuel and water tanks, nimbly treading the eight-inch-wide catwalk that ran down the middle of the passageway.

The men became so used to running down the narrow walk that they rarely held onto the guide lines along either side. A foot below lay only a covering of fabric. This gave a false sense of secu-

rity, for one misstep would plunge a man through the thin
envelope. More amazing than the crew's nonchalance was the fact
that no one had fallen through.

On the keel there were two other decks similar to the crew
space. The one just aft of the control car was the officers' "ward
room." Forward was a deck that held mooring equipment.

Men and officers slept on both sides of the keel in bunks suspended by wires from the girders. Unlike those of other Navy ships,
the *Shenandoah's* quarters were the same for officers and enlisted
men. And Commander Lansdowne ate the same food as Mechanic
Spratley—sandwiches, soup, and coffee. Upon these commonplace
equalities there developed a camaraderie that molded airshipmen
into a force of remarkable unity and efficiency. It was common
knowledge that any chief at Lakehurst would gladly clean up a
speak-easy that had done wrong to the lowliest airship sailor. But in
spite of the fact that the men and officers lived together—or
perhaps because of it—discipline was perfect. Every man knew
that an order must be carried out immediately, without question,
or the ship might be wrecked.

The next night Fort Worth was reached. The first leg had been
covered with no difficulties.

The *Shenandoah* drifted lazily away from the mast at Fort Worth
at nine forty-six on the morning of October 9—destination, California. Every man in the crew knew that, with the Rockies to be
crossed, the most dangerous day in the life of the ship was beginning. It would have been a simple matter to fly high above the
peaks, but to do so, much helium would have to be valved. Instead, the long ship would fly through a dozen narrow, winding
mountain passes.

For hours the dirigible skimmed over the open spaces of western
Texas. The terrain seemed to be flat, but the altimeter kept
mounting dangerously close to pressure height.

The foothills of the Rockies were passed. The air became more
rarefied. The ship rose sharply but so did mountains. It was now
evening. The moonlight was so bright that the ground was plainly
visible. At a few minutes before ten o'clock Van Horn, Texas,
was passed. The altimeter read 6600 feet. Everyone was tense,
watchful. It was like the moment before battle. The entire crew
was on duty, for the first pass was only a few miles away.

In spite of the evening's cold, the twenty gas cells were
swollen, pushing at their protective nets. Helium was seeping
slowly out the automatic valves, up wicker chimneys, and out of
the ventilators on the top of the ship. The *Shenandoah* was much

lighter because of the gasoline consumed. Already water from the recovery system and the ballast bags had been dumped to keep the dirigible a safe distance above the heightening terrain. Riggers with pliers in their hands, dressed in fur flying suits, stood along the keel next to gasoline tanks. In case of an emergency, fuel would have to be dropped.

There were now two men in every engine gondola. If a single motor went dead the ship might smash into the sides of one of the narrow mountain passes ahead.

Half the officers were in the control car. The rest were on the keel supervising the careful inspection of the gas bags. Below could be seen the friendly glow of the firebox of a locomotive that also was heading west. The little lights that looked like fireflies were the headlights of cars on a highway running parallel to the railroad tracks.

Below the control car hung a 400-foot-long copper wire. This was the antenna for the *Shenandoah's* main transmitting set. To it was attached a fifteen-pound lead weight.

As the twin walls of Sierra Blanca Pass loomed up, chief radio operator Lieutenant Carlton Palmer was receiving a message from an enthusiastic "ham" in a nearby town. Suddenly the radio amateur's voice went dead. Palmer looked out the window. The copper wire was whipping out far behind the ship. The lead "fish" had struck a telegraph pole and ripped free.

Quickly the radio operator reported the casualty to the control car. The altimeter was almost at 7000 feet, but the dirigible was actually less than 400 feet above the rocky canyon below. Lansdowne cautiously brought the ship up a few hundred feet. Dark, ominous peaks were now close on both sides of the "Daughter of the Stars" as she twisted and turned along the hazardous passageway. The town of Sierra Blanca, its lights glowing brightly, was below at ten fifteen. The locomotive, used as a guide by the rudderman, abruptly dove out of sight. So did the whitish highway. Lansdowne ordered more altitude to climb over the mountain ahead.

In a few minutes the valley of the Rio Grande spread out in front of them. The first ridge of the Rockies had been conquered.

Just before midnight thousands of lights below signaled that El Paso had been reached. As the ship slipped over the city, whistles blasted, and flares and searchlights lit up the sky.

But soon the city lights had disappeared behind them, and filmy clouds began forming in front. In an hour they thickened, and by three in the morning the moon was completely blacked out. The most dangerous pass of all, Dos Cabezos, lay ahead. On

the south of the pass were the peaks of Dos Cabezos, 7300 feet
high. The north wall, Pinaleno Range, towered over 10,000 feet. A
treacherous cross-wind was whipping around the peaks, forming
eddying winds in the canyon. The sky was almost black, and
Lansdowne squinted to pick out the right course through the
deceptive shadows ahead.

The airship headed into the tortuous channel, its five motors
roaring full speed. With the tail wind the *Shenandoah* was now
making seventy-five miles an hour. At last they were in the
narrowest part of the pass. The mechanics in the gondolas felt
they could reach out and touch a mountain wall on either side.
The channel made a sharp turn to the left. Lansdowne called for
rudders left. The rudder man obeyed. His mouth fell open as the
ship perversely turned to the right.

The 682-foot craft headed directly for a black mountain wall.
The helmsman desperately held the rudders to hard left. A hundred
feet from the mountain the rudders suddenly took hold and the
ship turned languidly to the left, its tail almost brushing the
northern mountain. Slowly, majestically, the ship slipped through
the dark pass. Everyone seemed to take a deep breath at the same
time. The danger had passed—for the moment.

Late that afternoon the *Shenandoah* crossed into California. The
sunlight was dimmed by dust. Then, after Indio had been reached
at five ten, darkness fell with dramatic suddenness. The crew was
lighthearted in spite of exhaustion. Only one more pass, San
Gorgonio, had to be threaded, and then they could enjoy the
warmth of southern California.

Strong winds hit the ship's nose as they entered the pass. But
soon the welcome lights of San Bernardino shone ahead. They were
at last in the land of oranges and lemons.

Suddenly the temperature dropped to 35 degrees. The lights
ahead were abruptly blotted out by a driving wall of white. They
were engulfed in a snowstorm. Once more they were flying
blind. The sturdy ship rocked and swayed but kept on its course.
Then a quick gust of wind drove the airship down. The radio
operator ran to the front of the control car. He had lost another
"fish." This time they were less than 300 feet from the ground
and still couldn't see it.

Lansdowne instantly ordered more elevation. The ship shot up.
Several crew men with vivid imaginations swear to this day that
they felt the tail scrape trees at the bottom of the canyon.

The ship rode through the snow squall and at nine fifteen that
night reached the Pacific Ocean off Seal Beach. An hour and a half
later the *Shenandoah* swung over the new mast at San Diego. A

green mooring crew ran onto the field as the visitor from the east approached for a landing. Ropes and wires were dropped from the descending ship. Officers in the control car leaned out windows and shouted instructions. Gently the long craft was lowered to the ground. It was going to be a perfect landing, a fit end to a highly dramatic trip.

The landing crew at the tail of the ship, instructed to grab the rear engine car before it hit the ground, took one look at the monster that was relentlessly descending on them. They jumped back, and Number 1 engine gondola bumped into the sand. The struts holding the car to the ship were punched up through the keel above. The first crossing of the continent by an airship had ended—with a bang.

A few minutes later Lansdowne was lowered in a basket from the high mast. He went to a telegraph office and sent the first message of the trip to his wife.

It said, "We made it."

The slight accident to the keel above Number 1 engine forced the *Shenandoah* to lay over in San Diego for a week. Repairs were made while the ship rode on the high mast.

Three days after the dirigible had reached California, it was learned that the ZR-3 had left Germany for Lakehurst. The ZR-3, numbered the LZ-126 by the Germans, was a modern Zeppelin made for the United States Navy as a part of war reparations. Earlier France, Italy, and England had been given two wartime Zeppelins as spoils of war and Japan one. Of the seven remaining airships the United States was to get a large share. Then German airshipmen, inspired by comrades who had scuttled the German Navy, destroyed the seven dirigibles. After months of negotiations it was agreed that Germany should build the United States a new nonmilitary dirigible, which would be used to train fledgling airshipmen.

At 7:30 A.M. on October 12, the new ship, which was twenty-four feet shorter than the *Shenandoah* but thirteen feet fatter, took off from Friedrichshafen with the eminent Dr. Hugo Eckener in command. Three lays later the ZR-3 passed over New York City, which greeted her with an enthusiasm that surprised the German crew. A few hours later the ship landed at Lakehurst, and an excited crowd almost tore the clothes off Eckener and his men. It was evident that America had forgotten the enmities of the World War and was willing to accept Germany as an equal.

In a long wire of congratulations to Eckener, President Coolidge expressed what most Americans felt. "It gives me and the people

of the United States great pleasure," he said, "that the friendly
relations between Germany and America are reaffirmed, and that
this great airship has so happily introduced the first direct air-
connection between the two nations."

Germany was overjoyed. Cities and towns were decorated with
flags, and there were wild celebrations in the streets. German
newspapers of all parties joined in praising the flight. Hearst
newsman Karl von Wiegand reported that it was like seeing a
whole nation come alive again. "Germany," he wrote, "has re-
habilitated herself in the eyes of the world."

The day after the arrival of the ZR-3 at Lakehurst the *Shenandoah* left San Diego for Fort Lewis, Washington. She arrived
safely through a storm, and, after a day on the mast, the ship
started on her long return trip. At 11:55 P.M. on October 25 the
"Daughter of the Stars" touched down on her home field, Lakehurst.
The trip east had been full of adventures, too. The dirigible had
gone through storms that had wrecked many ships, pierced fog,
and recrossed the Rockies in bumpy skies. She had, in all, traveled
9000 miles over uncharted country, proving that mooring masts,
helium, and the new water-recovery system were practical. And
what was more important, the historic trip proved that America
could make a good airship and fly it successfully with an all-
American crew.

An hour after landing, the famous craft was led into the big
hangar. There she was berthed next to her fat new stablemate.
Lansdowne and his men then headed for their homes. They now
had only one big goal ahead of them—the North Pole.

Now the public eagerly awaited the *ZR-3's* first American flight.

The hydrogen that the ship had used on its Atlantic trip had
been completely valved before it was docked in the Lakehurst
hangar. To fly, it now had to be filled with helium. And since
the Navy didn't have enough money to buy new helium, the
Shenandoah was forced to lend its nonflammable gas to the newcomer.

In spite of her triumphs the heliumless *Shenandoah* was tempo-
rarily retired from service. For the rest of 1924 and the first half of
1925 the ZR-3, now christened the *Los Angeles*, made many successful flights. Twice she flew to Bermuda. Then a trip to Minneapolis was scheduled. The ship left Lakehurst but was forced to
return after battling head winds in Pennsylvania. It was discovered
she needed an overhauling. Her German-made cells were leaking
badly, and her keel had been corroded by drippings from an anti-
freeze mixture.

Late in June helium was bled from the *Los Angeles* back into the *Shenandoah*. The "Daughter of the Stars" was ready for new triumphs.

But by this time President Coolidge had reconsidered the North Pole flight: he refused to give it his final approval. Early that summer Roald Amundsen and Lincoln Ellsworth had been forced down on the ice in an attempted Polar airplane flight. No word was heard from their two planes for a week. Lansdowne begged the Navy Department to let him take out the *Shenandoah* on a rescue mission. He pulled wires, telephoning every influential person he knew. But Secretary of the Navy Denby turned down his request.

Instead he was ordered to make the trip the *Los Angeles* had failed to finish. The *Shenandoah*, he was told, would make a junket of the Midwest in late August. The *Shenandoah*, he was told, would visit several state fairs.

Lansdowne liked these new orders not at all. A native of Greenville, Ohio, he was familiar with the line squalls that swept over that part of the country in late August and September. "I'd rather take four trips to the North Pole," he told his young wife, "than attempt one to the Middle West at this season."

The commander officially requested that the trip be postponed. The Navy put back the date to the first week in September. The day the postponement was granted, Lansdowne told his wife with some relief, "We've got it put off for the time being. I only hope it'll never go through."

A few days later he requested another delay, but this time he was turned down. The Navy saw no good reason for another postponement. It would disappoint many thousands in the Midwest. After all, the "Daughter of the Stars" had flown fifty-seven flights totaling 25,000 miles, in all kinds of weather. The fifty-eighth flight, therefore, would take place as scheduled, the first week in September.

7

THE LINE SQUALL

The sky was unsettled on the afternoon of September 2. At times it was almost clear; then ominous clouds would scud across the field at Lakehurst and disappear as suddenly as they had come. The *Shenandoah,* nose to her high mast, was floating gracefully with the variable breezes. Her twenty gas bags were about ninety-one per cent full, her tanks loaded with 9075 pounds of water and 16,620 pounds of gasoline. Sailors in dungarees, carrying duffel bags, were riding in groups of two and three up the narrow, open elevator to the top of the tower. The "Daughter of the Stars" was almost ready for her fifty-eighth flight.

The first stop would be Scott Field, near St. Louis. Then would come a jump to the state fair at Minneapolis. The third leg would bring her to the new mooring mast at Dearborn, Michigan. This mast had been erected by Henry Ford at his own expense. Ford was as enthusiastic as a schoolboy about dirigibles. He had met Eckener and his assistant, Captain Lehmann, and had become so intrigued with the vast commercial possibilities of the airship that he put his best engineers to work building the best of all possible masts. What was more, although Ford had always given airplanes a wide berth, he planned to ride in the *Shenandoah* on the last leg of her trip, from Detroit to Lakehurst.

Almost all the crew of forty-one officers and men making the trip had gone aboard. Now the two guests climbed into the elevator. One was elderly Colonel C. G. Hall of the U. S. Army Air Service, the other, Reserve Navy Lieutenant Walter Richardson, a civilian in charge of the photographic section of the Bureau of Aeronautics. Richardson was to be official photographer of the trip. He was also detailed to make a photographic record of the new mast at Dearborn. He carried his case with exceptional care, for it contained a camera recently designed at Anacostia Naval Air Station.

At the enlisted men's two-story wooden barracks half a mile

away, young Julius Malak, mechanic's mate second class, was looking out the window at the ship. He had made twenty trips on her. He'd been aboard during the first mooring on the *Patoka;* he'd gone to the recent Governors' Convention at Bar Harbor. And, coming back over Boston, he'd seen the Fourth of July fireworks blossom from the sprawling city. He'd never forget those fireworks, nor the terrific electrical storm the *Shenandoah* had battled on her way down the New England coast a few hours later.

But Malak, who had spent several years digging coal in a Hooverville mine before enlisting in the Navy, wasn't scheduled to make the big Midwestern trip. The ship would probably fly over his home town and he wouldn't be on her. He flopped on his bunk, closed his eyes, and waited for the whistle that would call the casting-off detail to the field.

Then he felt his arm being shaken roughly. "On your feet, Shellac!"

It was one of the lucky crew men making the trip. "Brennan's got a cold," the man said. "He's confined to sick bay. You're taking his place."

Malak bounced happily to his feet. In a minute he had stowed a set of clean whites—jumper, ducks, and hat—into his duffel bag. He swept in his toilet articles and stuffed a blanket in on top. Others in the barracks laughed at his excitement, but they knew how he felt. A man from St. Louis shouted out a girl friend's address as Malak ran down the hall and out onto the field.

At about the same time Mrs. Zachary Lansdowne was driving toward the field. At first she had decided not to see her husband take off. Two-year-old Peggy was in bed with tonsilitis, and Mrs. Lansdowne didn't want to leave her alone with the nurse. Then, at the last minute, she decided to go. She ran outside to the Navy car that was waiting on the chance that she would change her mind. She peered at the sky. It looked threatening to her. She asked the sailor-driver what he thought. He agreed.

The ten-mile drive from Lakewood was covered quickly. As the car plowed across the sandy landing field that stretched in front of Hangar Number 1, Mrs. Lansdowne saw a small group of officers at the foot of the mast. She hoped Zach hadn't yet gone aboard. The car reached the mast, and she saw her tall, slender husband talking with Captain George Steele, commandant of the base.

Lansdowne and Steele were discussing the disappearance of Commander John Rodgers and four men in the Navy seaplane, the *PN-9*, Number 1. Rodgers had taken off from California on the first attempted flight across the Pacific to Pearl Harbor. But no news had been heard of the men for over twenty-four hours. The

loss of the five Navy fliers put a damper on the heady excitement
that marked an important flight.

Lansdowne saw his wife and walked quickly to her car.

"I don't like the look of your weather, Zach," she said. "What are
you getting into?"

Lansdowne turned his sharp, stern features toward the sky.
"Doesn't look bad, Betsy," he said reassuringly. "There are going to
be thunderstorms in northern Ohio, but I think we can get around
them." Then he asked how their baby was.

"Everybody's come aboard, sir," called an officer from the control
car high above them.

The skipper waved his arm. "Coming aboard."

He made his last good-byes and walked toward the mast. As he
was about to enter the elevator, he turned to Captain Steele and
saluted him. "Shove off with your permission, sir."

Steele nodded. A minute later the skipper was leaning out a
window in the control car. He held a small megaphone to his
mouth. "Cast off!" he shouted to the men on the mooring mast.

At two fifty-two the cone of the ship slid gently from the socket
of the mast. The dirigible lifted slowly. Water ballasted first from
amidships, then from the tail—2225 pounds of it in all. The
Shenandoah swung around the mast and a few minutes later
headed west into the uncertain sky.

Margaret Lansdowne turned her back as the dirigible headed
over the piny woods. So did the other wives who had come to the
field. It was considered bad luck to watch your husband's ship fade
out of sight.

In an hour and twenty-six minutes the "Daughter of the Stars"
was high above Philadelphia. The city welcomed her with factory
whistles and thousands of car horns. The door of the radio room
opened and a sailor leaned far out, balancing himself with a hand
clenched on a wire. The man opened his other hand and a tiny
white parachute fell in the wake of the ship. The man was Chief
George Schnitzer, who was sharing the radio duties with Warrant
Officer Raymond Cole. Schnitzer was on board only because of
a stroke of luck. He and Harry Manley, the other enlisted radio
man, had matched fifty-cent pieces to see who would go. Schnitzer
was glad he'd won, for he needed the extra 50 per cent flying pay.
Attached to his parachute was a message addressed to a friend in
Philadelphia, Herbert Foster. It asked Foster to telephone his wife,
Althea, and their two children at Tuckerton, New Jersey.

The man in the little radio shack with Schnitzer had also had a
good break. Mechanic Jimmy Moore, one of the two men assigned

to the generator that kept the radio going, had never been on an important trip before. He was such a careful and polite chauffeur that Commander Lansdowne had always kept him home as his wife's driver. Several days before, Moore had asked Mrs. Lansdowne to put in a good word for him. She had. Besides the excitement of the trip he, like Schnitzer, wanted the extra flying pay. His wife was going to have a baby in a few months.

Ralph Joffray, the enlisted man at the rudder, was on board only because of the generosity of Dick Deal, who'd drawn the original assignment. Joffray, who came from St. Louis, had begged Deal to let him make the trip so he could see his old home town.

Darkness came quickly that evening. Lights began to pop on below as the ship passed York. An hour and forty minutes later, at eight thirty-five, Chambersburg was a mass of yellow pinpoints off the starboard bow.

Soon the rolling, wooded Alleghenies were reached. The men off watch turned into their bunks along the keel. They slept aft of the crew space, and the officers bunked both fore and aft of the control car. Every five meters along the keel was a triangular frame of latticed girders, corresponding to the circular outer ribs. Each of these frames was marked with phosphorescent numbers so the men would know where they were. The numbering started at the base of the ship's rudders. The first girder—the important crucifix girder—was called frame 0. The frame above Number 1 engine car, the gondola farthest aft, bore the number 60. This meant it was sixty meters from frame 0. The crew space, amidships, ran from frames 100 to 105. The control car hung twenty feet below frame 160. At the tip of the nose the most forward frame was numbered 194.75—it was 194.75 meters from the rudders. The frames aft of frame 0 to the end of the tail, a distance of ten and a half meters, were unnumbered.

The sky was still partially overcast at midnight. But the air was not rough. It was warm in the keel even though the plywood hatches were open, and the men sleeping had no need for the blankets they'd brought along.

The tunnellike keel was dark except for the glowing numbers and letters on the girders and emergency gear. Rigger James "Red" Collier took a reading of gas cell Number 9 near frame 85. His light flashed on a perpendicular eight-inch strip that curved along the side of the ship. Numbers on the strip ran in fives from 0 at the top to 100 at the bottom. Collier squinted, lining up the bottom of the slightly pulsating gas bag with the canvas indicator. It came to 88, meaning that the cell was 88 per cent full of helium. When loaded to capacity the bag pushed down to the 100 marker.

Collier made a notation in a little black book. After he'd checked all the bags, he would report his findings to the Officer of the Deck in the control car.

As the dark, round tops of the Alleghenies slipped by below, Bill Russell, the mechanic in charge of engine Number 1, climbed sleepily down the long, unprotected ladder from the belly of the ship to the top of his gondola. He stood for a moment, holding onto a strut, looking back. The wind felt warm but refreshing on his face after the stuffiness of the keel. Then he opened the door to the gondola and stepped in.

"Anything new?" he asked his assistant, Walter Johnson.

Johnson shook his head and yawned. Then he climbed up the ladder to take a four-hour sleep. Russell looked at the annunciator dial. It was set at two-thirds speed. His motor, making 1000 revolutions per minute, sounded good. He checked everything, then climbed to the top of the gondola and sat down, leaning nonchalantly against a strut. The moon had come out and the fishlike shadow of the ship ran across the western foothills of the mountains. He could see by the shadow that they were making pretty fair speed. The men had a simple way of telling ground speed. They would fix an eye on a point ahead of the ship's shadow. When the front of the shadow hit the point they'd start counting the seconds. They stopped counting when the shadow passed.

Russell picked a point and soon began to count out loud. He got to nine. That meant the ship was moving along at about fifty-five miles an hour.

Up in the keel near frame 90, Chief Bart O'Sullivan was pulling Malak out of his bunk. "Time to get to work, Shellac."

The young man drowsily pulled on his rubber-soled shoes, which cut down the possibility of sparks. Jimmy Cullinan, a rigger who held the coveted enlisted rating of aviation pilot, came down the keel singing. He told them his little girl, Taffy, was going to be six years old in two days.

O'Sullivan laughed. "Wait'll you have four, like me, then you'll never keep track."

Cullinan said he remembered because the *Shenandoah's* maiden flight came the day before Taffy's fifth birthday. He looked at his watch. "Hey, it's after midnight," he said. "It's tomorrow. It's the ship's second birthday."

Forward in the control car, Lieutenant Commander Lewis Hancock had just climbed down the ladder from frame 160. Unlike the ladders into the five engine gondolas, this one was enclosed. Hancock went over and relieved Lieutenant Commander Charles

Rosendahl of his navigator's duties. They talked about the trip for
a few minutes. Then Rosendahl climbed up to the keel and turned
in at frame 150.

At the same time young Tom Hendley, a radio officer who
was learning engineering, took over from Chief Machinist Shine
S. Halliburton. Quickly Hendley inspected all the engines; they
were running smoothly. He hurried up the keel, went down into
the control car and back to the radio room. Gunner Raymond
Cole, the radio officer—earphones clamped on his head—nodded
and smiled. Silently he handed Hendley the midnight weather report from Lakehurst. Hendley walked a few feet forward and gave
the report to Lieutenant Joseph Anderson, the ship's studious
young aerologist. Anderson began to draw up his usual midnight
weather report from the new information.

Hendley watched with interest. "Thunderstorms over the Lakes,"
muttered Anderson. He shrugged his shoulders noncommittally.
"Don't think they'll come south enough to bother us."

It was now twelve fifteen. Malak was checking the gasoline tanks
that were hung up along the sides of the keel in nests of three.
With Sully sleeping, he was now "Oil King," the man in charge of
every drop of gasoline on the ship. He looked out a port hatch
near frame 90. He could see engine car Number 2 below. On the
starboard side was car Number 3, but it was out of his sight.

On the very top of the ship, Rigger Frank Peckham, who had
helped inspect the *Shenandoah's* gas cells in Akron, was sharing
the keel watch with Red Collier. He was walking forward on a
little catwalk on top of the ship. Once every watch somebody had
to go along the top to inspect the outer covering and the maneuvering valves. Peckham leaned into the wind, bent forward at a
steep angle. He remembered the first time he'd ever come across
the top. It was on an English blimp during the war. An old
hand was walking in front of him. Both the men leaned against the
force of the wind. Suddenly the man in front of Peckham stood
up straight, cutting off the onrushing wind. Peckham had flopped
to his face, too surprised to be scared.

Either a man could take it or he couldn't. Every newcomer got
the same initiation. He had to learn to respect height—but not fear
it. Peckham flashed his light at a maneuvering valve. It was O.K.
He wondered how the flashing light must look to the people far
below.

A few minutes later, deep inside the ship on the keel, Lieutenant
Roland Mayer, who'd already spent many rough hours on the
ship, relieved his junior, Lieutenant Charlie Bauch, as keel officer.

"We've passed the mountains," said Bauch, a brawny fellow

known as "Boom-Boom" to some of the men. "Didn't have to valve any gas or water." He told Mayer they were flying at 3000 feet.

By now Anderson, a young man of medium height with blond hair and blue eyes, had finished his weather map. He got up from his little desk and walked forward. Lansdowne was staring straight ahead. The weather officer handed the skipper the map. Lansdowne studied it a few minutes, then nodded. Things weren't as bad as they could be.

He started for the ladder. "Don't call me," he said wearily, "unless something unusual comes up."

Anderson opened his mouth as if to say something.

"Talk it over with the officers in the control cabin first," the captain added. He stifled a yawn. It had been a long, hard day. The first day, with the complications of take-off, was always the hardest. He climbed nimbly up the ladder and soon was in his bunk—the same kind of bunk his men slept in. It was hard getting to sleep after so many hours' tension. But he knew the ship was in good hands. All officers and men of the "Daughter of the Stars" had been carefully selected. His executive officer, Lewis Hancock, was an intelligent, dependable man who could never be panicked into a rash move. Hancock had recently married Joy Bright Little, widow of Lieutenant Little, killed in the crash of the ZR-2.

Like Hancock, Lieutenant Regg Houghton, the Officer of the Deck, was a reliable, steady officer. On the other hand Lieutenant Jack Lawrence, one of the watch officers, was a brilliant, imaginative officer, as well as an extrovert, a lover of crowds and parties and practical jokes. Lawrence had been one of the pilots of the luckless blimp, C-5, which might have been the first aircraft to cross the Atlantic if she hadn't broken loose from her moorings in Newfoundland. Lansdowne was fond of Lawrence and had complete trust in his judgment as an airshipman.

The engineering officer, Lieutenant (j.g.) E. W. Sheppard, was another brilliant officer. Almost painfully conscientious, he made life miserable for any mechanic who wouldn't keep up to his perfectionist standards. Sheppard, in addition to being a practical engineer, was responsible in large part for the success of the ingenious water-recovery system.

And the leading keel officer, Lieutenant Roland Mayer, rounded out a fine staff of officers. He was a quiet man with gifted hands who worked efficiently, unobtrusively, and without prodding.

As he had done so many nights, Lansdowne went over and over in his mind the problems that faced the ship in the next few days. There was the landing at Scott Field, the trip to Minneapolis, the tricky business of mooring at Ford's new mast, and finally the leg home. This was to be his last flight for a long time, perhaps in his career, for he was scheduled to report for sea duty in two weeks. He wanted the last trip to be a good one.

While the skipper was trying to get to sleep, Malak was checking the service gasoline tank above car Number 5 at frame 120 on the starboard side. It was O.K. He crossed to the port side of the ship on one of the four lateral runways that crossed the keel at right angles. He checked Number 4's tank. It was down to twenty gallons. He decided to go down to the control car and get permission to pump some fuel in. He started up the keel.

But he stopped momentarily at an automatic hatch, which was flapping up and down as the pressure inside the ship changed. He got a glimpse of flattening countryside and caught the twinkle of lights of a faraway town. Maybe it was Hooverville. He smiled. Smiling came easily to him—so easily that when he wasn't called "Shellac" he was called "Smiley."

Malak walked up the catwalk. Now he could hear snoring from the officers' bunks. He was careful not to let the glow of his flash hit those bunks as he passed by. A warm breeze floated through the flapping hatches. The concerted double roar of engine Numbers 4 and 5, just aft, was deep and reassuring. Malak couldn't help smiling again. It was something to be Oil King on the only flying battlewagon in the whole Navy.

At just three that morning Bill Russell, head mechanic of engine Number 1, saw lightning flash in the east. Being in the lowest and sternmost gondola, he had the best view in that direction. Thank God, he thought, we missed that storm. The old *Shenandoah* didn't seem to miss many.

The control car was ghostly. All lights were out except the small, dim ones over instrument boards. Radium dials gleamed eerily. At the elevator wheel, Chief Lou Allely felt a little heavier pull than usual. He hadn't studied aerology, but he guessed a storm was brewing somewhere not far away. He was standing sideways, facing the south. He turned, looking west. Intermittent lightning was flashing ahead. He was just about to report the lightning to Lieutenant Commander Hancock, who was in command of the ship while Lansdowne slept, when he saw Lieutenant Mayer lean forward and look to the northwest. Allely craned his neck and saw even more lightning farther north.

"Take a look over there," Mayer told Hancock.

The executive officer, who had been checking the fuel and water charts, walked forward. For a few minutes he and Mayer studied the northwest and the increasing flashes of lightning. Finally Hancock made a decision. "Wake up Andy and the captain," he ordered.

Mayer turned and climbed up the ladder.

At three ten Anderson was roused from sleep by a hand on his shoulder. "Hancock wants you," said a voice. It took the tired weather officer a moment to realize it was Lieutenant Mayer speaking. "Lot of lightning. May mean trouble."

Anderson dressed quickly and made his way to the control car. Commander Lansdowne, his eyes alert though he'd just been pulled out of bed, was already studying the electrical display in the northwest.

The skipper turned to Anderson. "We're bucking strong head winds, Andy." He pointed out the starboard window. "Look at those thunderstorms and tell me what you think."

Anderson pulled out the weather résumé from Lakehurst and again went over it carefully. The captain looked over his shoulder. Astern, the lightning in the east grew in intensity. Below, the lights of Cambridge, Ohio, seemed stationary, for the ship was making little if any progress against the increasing westerly winds.

Anderson then went forward and scanned the skies. In the northeast the lightning was vivid and frequent but far away. It was partly cloudy in the north and northwest. To the west was one large, heavy cloud—directly on their course. The skies in the south and southwest were now generally clear.

"Nothing to worry about in the storms to the east and north," Anderson said presently. "That cloud out west though——" He looked at it again. He was told that just before he came into the control car, they had changed their course slightly to the south to avoid it.

The young aerologist discerned, then, that the darkness of the cloud ahead was due to shadow and not rain. "That's nothing to worry about either, sir," he said with relief.

The captain nodded and spoke softly to the rudderman. The course was changed back to due west. To make headway Lansdowne now tried various altitudes and combinations of engine speeds. But nothing worked.

Back at frame 60, Arthur Carlson, an experienced rigger, who was patrolling the keel with his veteran watch mate, McCarthy (Peckham and Collier had just been relieved), looked through the hatch that led to engine car Number 1. The lights of Cambridge still lay below, but at that moment Carlson saw them go out. He climbed down the long, open ladder to the engine room and found Russell sitting in the seat near his engine.

"Did you see that, Bill?"

"See what?"

Suddenly the lights went on again. But before Russell could say anything they disappeared a second time.

"Somebody didn't pay their light bills," said Russell.

In the control car Anderson saw the lights of Cambridge go out the second time. Hit by lightning, he guessed. There was darkness for several minutes before the lights blinked on again. The ship was now passing under the northern edge of the big cloud that had at first worried him. He couldn't help feeling relieved when the ship broke through safely. He'd been right—it wasn't a storm cloud.

He saw that the altimeter read 2500 feet and that all engines were once more at cruising speed. But at that moment Lansdowne ordered engine Numbers 1, 2, and 3 stepped up again. Even so they could make but little headway.

"Why don't you bring her down to one thousand feet?" suggested Anderson.

"Too dangerous," said Lansdowne. But he did order Allely, at the elevator controls, to lower them to 2000 feet in an effort to find a hole in the wall of wind. It was useless.

The sky in the north and northwest suddenly began to cloud heavily. Fifty miles to the north lightning scrawled across the sky. Anderson got a hunch—every weatherman gets them occasionally. "The storm is backing up, sir," he told Lansdowne, "and I don't understand it." He decided to go out on a limb. "I think we should turn south, sir."

Lansdowne looked at the storm, which appeared to be moving from the north to the west in front of them. He shook his head. "That storm's still a long way off." But the skipper saw that the young aerologist was unhappy. "We've been ordered to fly over a certain course," he explained patiently, "and I want to keep that course as long as I can."

Anderson started to speak up, but changed his mind.

"We'll keep on our regular course, Andy, until some definite danger threatens us." Lansdowne knew that thousands of Midwesterners had been told the exact course the ship would take. If possible, they shouldn't be disappointed. He knew the value of public opinion—it resulted in big appropriations.

At three forty-five O'Sullivan woke up Malak again. The Oil King was still yawning when Lieutenant Tom Hendley passed him on the keel and said, "Malak, turn the clock in the crew space back an hour when it gets to be four."

Malak went forward. Coming into Central Time made him realize how many miles they were putting behind them.

At 4:00 EST, the clock in the control car was also turned back an hour. The dirigible, now flying at 2100 feet, was making better progress; but she was drifting to port and then, a few minutes later, to starboard. Lieutenant Regg Houghton, now Officer of the Deck, asked Keel Officer Mayer to check drifts. Mayer checked one at 40 degrees to port and another to starboard at 36 degrees. Even so, the air was still fairly smooth.

It was a strange situation.

At frame 60 Malak noticed the service tank that fed engine Number 1 was down to twenty-two gallons. He hustled to the control car, where Engineering Officer Sheppard was at the annunciators, ringing up for more speed from engine Numbers 1, 2, and 3.

"Number One is running low on gasoline, sir," reported the Oil King. "I'd like to transfer fuel."

Sheppard checked the master gasoline chart. "Transfer from reserve tank Number Fifteen."

"Aye, aye, sir." In a few minutes Malak was back at frame 60. He began to transfer gasoline with a wobble pump, which looked like an old-fashioned water pump. Soon sweat beaded his forehead. This was hard work, and it would take at least a quarter of an hour's steady pumping.

At about that time E. P. Allen relieved Allely at the elevator wheel. The ship was handling nicely now, and the two friends talked for fifteen minutes before Allely headed for his bunk.

It was the last time Allely would see Allen alive.

Lieutenant Tom Hendley had been visiting Schnitzer in the radio room. He followed Allely from the control car and went to the officers' bunks. They were all filled, so he continued aft to the enlisted men's sleeping section. At frame 70 he found an empty and flopped down. He hadn't had any sleep for twenty-four hours and he was exhausted. He fell asleep immediately, confident the ship would be hard by her destination, Scott Field, when he awoke.

Moments later Colonel C. G. Hall, the Army officer, awoke in his bunk far forward. Obeying an impulse he has since been unable to explain, he dressed and headed for the control car. When he got there, Anderson was pointing to clouds and lightning in the west and northwest. Neither the weather officer nor Lansdowne seemed particularly concerned, but the clouds looked menacing to Hall.

At 4:35 EST Lieutenant Commander Rosendahl climbed down

into the control car to relieve Hancock. But the senior navigator, thinking he might be needed, decided to stay in the car a bit longer.

In engine car Number 3, mechanic Ralph Jones, serving the four-to-eight watch, was informed by the annunciator that the captain wanted full speed; but when he stepped up his engine to the required 1400 revolutions per minute the little cab began to buck. It was like driving suddenly off a cement highway onto a dirt highway. His engine was preigniting. It exploded and sputtered.

There came a rapping on his ladder. He knew it was one of the engineering officers giving him the bump signal. He crawled from his cab to the top of the ladder and dimly saw Sheppard's face peering down from the dark background of the keel.

"Slow down your engine!" said Sheppard, speaking distinctly and slowly so the noise-deafened mechanic could hear him. "We'll have to dope your fuel. When we do, return to your original signal."

Jones nodded and crawled down the shaking ladder. In rough weather it was no picnic hanging onto that damn ladder. He looked down and saw dark ground several thousand feet below. Then he scrambled quickly into his cab and slowed down the motor to two-thirds speed, 1000 revolutions. He wondered why it was acting up.

Several miles away in Caldwell, Ohio, a man was wakened by a slamming noise on his front porch. He went downstairs and discovered it was only a wicker chair, overturned by a gust of wind. The air felt damp, as though a storm was coming or had passed. He saw in the distance a dark shape in the sky like a big panatela. It took him a minute to realize he wasn't seeing things. It must be the *Shenandoah*. He remembered reading that she was supposed to pass some time early that morning. Then he saw a cloud far above the airship. It was dark and seemed to be in great turmoil. It looked to him, he later told friends, "as though two storms had gone together."

A woman in Ava got an even better look at the same cloud. She was watching the *Shenandoah* pass out of view over a hilltop, half a mile away. A huge, dark cloud hovered directly over the ship. It was in such commotion she called her husband into the yard. "Come out and see the boiling cloud!" she cried.

But no one in the control car could see the boiling cloud above the ship. The men on the "Daughter of the Stars" were unaware that a line squall was being born directly over their heads.

At a few minutes after 5:00 EST, Lieutenant Sheppard crawled down the ladder into the control car. He was worried by the way the three motors, recently ordered stepped up to full speed, were acting.

"Captain," asked Sheppard, "can I dope the fuel tanks?"

Lansdowne, who was sitting on a seat on the port side of the cabin with Mayer, nodded. They had been discussing the new lightning that was flashing in the northwest.

Colonel Hall and Anderson were sitting alongside listening. It was now five eight.

Suddenly Allen, the elevator man, leaned over Mayer's shoulder. "Captain," he said with a slight tone of nervousness, "the ship has started to rise."

Lansdowne slowly got to his feet. "Check her."

Allen pulled the wheel clockwise to drive the ship down. It was obvious he was fighting the controls. Sweat covered his forehead. "She's rising two meters per second. I c-can't check her, sir."

Lansdowne glanced uneasily at Sheppard and ordered the remaining motors, Numbers 4 and 5, speeded up. But despite the increased power from the engines, the ship continued to rise. As Allen strained at the elevator wheel, Rosendahl flashed his light at the large inclinometer mounted on the chart board. The nose was pointing down 18 degrees.

"I can't hold her down," said Allen. There was a note of panic in his voice. This had never happened to him before. He started to pull the wheel even farther down.

But Lansdowne stopped him. "Don't exceed that angle," he said in a calm, confident voice that reassured everyone in the cabin. "We don't want to go into a stall." He ordered Rudder man Ralph Joffray to change his course to port, the south.

Joffray tugged at his wheel counterclockwise. He had to put his whole body into the effort. "Hard over, sir," he grunted, "and she won't take it."

"I've got the flippers down and she won't check," said Allen, his voice again rising nervously.

"Don't worry," said Lansdowne as if there were nothing to fear.

The ship still shot up, tail up about 15 degrees, heading relentlessly into the stormy west in spite of elevators, rudders, and motors. The ship was rolling now. Rosendahl thought it was rolling like a raft in the sea.

Civilian Richardson was wakened by the sudden rise. He got up from his bunk on the starboard side of the keel at frame 80. He had been sleeping fitfully for several hours. Riding a dirigible at night was like nothing he'd ever experienced before. He walked aft to the enlisted men's lavatory at frame 35. A moment later he started forward. He picked up his new camera at the foot of his bunk and continued on toward the control car. It might be light enough to get some good pictures.

At the crew space he stopped and got a drink of water. He looked at his watch. It was only a little after five—too early. He yawned, mumbled something to Cook J. J. Hahn who was getting breakfast ready for the crew, and went back to his bunk. He closed his eyes and tried to get back to sleep. Then he was wondering if the roughness was caused by the mountains east of Wheeling. Or maybe it was some kind of little local storm. He fell asleep before he could decide.

The men in engine car Numbers 4 and 5 guessed something was wrong when they got the order to push their engines to full speed. In the starboard car, Number 5, Mechanic Joe Shevlowitz was sure they were in big trouble.

"Take it easy," said the chief mechanic, Charlie Broom. He had been in a lot of hot water in his day, and it took something special to get his pressure up. He'd missed going down on the old ZR-2 only because he had a pass to see his English wife in Hull. That day he'd risked his life several times diving vainly for his comrades in the submerged wreck in the Humber River.

Lester Coleman, chief of engine Number 2, one of the two middle motors, was upset because his motor was beginning to miss. Like a mother taking the pulse of a sick child he felt the clutch to see if it was overheating. Suddenly a hot blast of air from the radiators hit his face. The water-temperature gauge shot up above the boiling point. He turned off the engine and hurried up the ladder into the ship, where he began to run off all the reserve water into the hot radiator. The trip back to the gondola was rough, for the ship was down sharply at the nose and seemed to be pitching. He started up the motors again.

By this time Lieutenant Sheppard had a free moment in the control car. He picked up the phone and called the station at frame 105. (There were also phones at 60, 180, and the nose.) He wanted to tell Malak to start putting fifteen cubic centimeters of ethyl-lead in each tank to enrich the gas. They'd really be needing it now. The ship had started its rise at 2200 feet and was climbing as if it would never stop.

Lou Allely, in his bunk at 95, was awakened that very moment by the rapid rise. The nose was down and he'd almost been rolled off the bed. He was worried, and he got up and walked barefoot toward the crew space nearby. He wanted to see how high they'd gone. The phone at 105 was blinking red. He picked up the receiver. It was Sheppard from the control car.

"Send Malak up here on the double." Shep sounded as if he meant business.

Allely hung up the phone. He saw Malak sitting on a tool chest a few yards away, resting. He didn't know the Oil King had just finished pumping fuel and deserved a breather.

"Hey, Shellac," he called. "Get off your butt. Sheppard wants you in the control car."

Malak got to his feet and started up the keel. He made fast time even though the nose was now pointing down almost 25 degrees. In the control car everyone at last knew that the situation was critical. A freak current had caught hold of them, and there was nothing they could do to stop the rise.

Lieutenant Mayer watched the altimeter anxiously for another minute. Then he turned and scrambled up the ladder. It was obvious they were going over pressure height. The bags were already about 95 per cent full, and he had to tell Carlson and McCarthy to take off the jam-pot covers that fitted over the automatic valves and kept them from operating. He knew he had to hurry. If the covers were still fastened on at pressure height, the extended gas bags would explode.

As he started aft, the ship began to roll and pitch heavily. He had to grab the hand lines to steady himself. At frame 150 he saw a flashlight coming forward. It was Malak, smiling as usual. The enlisted man politely leaned far to his right to let the officer pass.

As soon as Mayer left the control cabin, Regg Houghton, still Officer of the Deck, glanced at the altimeter. He called Anderson.

"Yes, Regg?" said the weather officer.

"Go up and tell Lieutenant Bauch to stand by the automatic valves."

Anderson started up the ladder.

"Tell him the condition of the ship and the rate of rise," added Houghton.

The young aerologist shot up into the keel, almost bowling over Malak who was about to come down. Then, in spite of the ship's antics, he hurried toward the officers' sleeping quarters. He finally found Bauch at frame 137.5. Anderson shook the big man by the shoulder.

Bauch blinked, his eyes heavy with sleep.

"The ship's rising. We're going to hit pressure height in a minute."

Bauch came awake with a violent start, jumped out of bed, put on his shoes, and hurried aft. He flashed his light at the nearest bag. It was already 97 per cent full. He ripped the panel on the jam pot that fitted over the automatic valve like a housewife's outsized refrigerator-jar cover. Only those covers at frames 80 and 160 had been removed when the ship had left Lakehurst.

Bauch met Rigger Carlson amidships. "Remove the jam-pot covers at forty!" he said. Carlson nodded and hurried aft.

When Malak got into the control car it was quiet—so quiet that he failed to realize that the ship was in serious trouble. Lansdowne was giving orders in an undertone. It had a soothing effect: even though the ship was still rising the men at the elevators and rudders were no longer panicky.

Grinning, the Oil King reported to Sheppard.

"Dope the fuel tanks at each power car," ordered the engineer.

"Aye, aye, sir." The young man climbed back up the ladder. He knew that the fuel wasn't doped unless there was trouble. He wondered what was going on.

Coleman in engine Number 2 was sweating over his balky motor. He shut it off and climbed into the keel. He saw Malak coming into the crew space. "Smiley!" he shouted, "I need some water for my radiator!"

The Oil King was puzzled. Now he had two orders and he didn't know which one he should carry out first. He ran aft to the bunk of the senior Oil King, O'Sullivan.

Malak almost pulled the older man out of bed. "Hey, Sully!" he called above the rush of wind. "I need some help."

O'Sullivan groaned but slowly rolled out of bed.

Malak told his chief of the emergency.

"I'll take care of Number Two," said O'Sullivan. "You dope the fuel."

In the meantime Sheppard had decided to make a tour of his engines. He climbed out of the control car and started down the keel. At frame 135 he saw his assistant, Halliburton, sleeping. He woke him up.

"Stand by for emergencies," said Sheppard. "We're running into bad weather."

Halliburton, an older man with sparse hair, had slept in his clothes. He laced on his rubber-soled shoes and started to follow Sheppard aft.

"Everything's O.K. in the engineering department—so far!" said the lieutenant. "Stand by at one thirty-five."

Halliburton stopped while Sheppard hurried aft, steadying himself on the guide lines. In a moment he came to a little group hovering above engine Number 2 like consulting physicians. "What's wrong?"

"Detonating at standard!" called Coleman from the top of his ladder.

"I'll give y'all a hand," said Halliburton in his Southern drawl.

Coleman went back to his car. He watched from the window as O'Sullivan and Lieutenant Sheppard doped his fuel. Then when he got the go-ahead signal he started up his engine. It detonated worse than ever.

Sheppard came down the ladder into the little engine car. "Shut her down, Coleman!" he shouted.

Coleman once more shut off the troublesome engine.

"Wait'll we get some more water for your cooling system," said Sheppard. "These steep angles are raising hell with the motors." He climbed back into the ship.

"What's the matter?" asked Lieutenant Mayer, who had been passing by.

The engineer told him, and said that Number 1 was sounding bad, too. Mayer nodded sympathetically but he couldn't stop to gossip. As head of the riggers he had his own problems with the cells. He worked his way to the crew space. The ship's nose was by now so far down that he sat on the catwalk and slid down.

When he got to the crew space the ship leveled off somewhat. He found J. J. Hahn swearing and picking up loose thermos bottles and canned goods. The cook asked angrily how the hell he could get breakfast ready for forty-three men if they couldn't even keep the damned ship level.

Allely was watching the altimeter in the crew space. Mayer looked over the off-duty elevator man's shoulder at the dial, which was eighteen inches in diameter. They were still climbing. Mayer put up his hand and felt the inflation manifold that ran along the top of the keel. Ordinarily the manifold was flabby; now it was swollen fatter than a two-foot water main. Even so the pressure wasn't dangerous. The helium was now being distributed evenly among the twenty bags, and the automatic valves were blowing satisfactorily. But if they went up much higher, even the automatics couldn't handle the pressure.

Mayer started forward. At frame 120 he found Jimmy Cullinan doping engine Number 4. The keel officer looked down at the gondola. Both the mechanics, Celestine Mazzuco and W. H. Spratley, were on the job. Their motor was running smoothly.

He turned back to Cullinan. "Jimmy," he warned, "we're going to start dropping pretty soon. When we do, stand by to slip fuel tanks."

Mayer went on to frame 130 while Cullinan balanced his way aft to the lavatory.

Ten meters forward, Lieutenant Jack Lawrence stirred in his bunk. He looked up at a bobbing flashlight that was coming toward him. "What's wrong?" he asked.

"Nothing particular," answered Rigger John McCarthy from behind the light. "Ship's rising, sir."

"I'd better get down to the control cabin." Jack Lawrence got to his feet just as Mayer reached frame 140.

"All O.K. forward, sir," reported McCarthy to his boss, Mayer. Lawrence, still buttoning his clothes, pushed between the two men and hurried forward. If there was trouble he knew the old man would want him in the control cabin.

Somewhere nearby two wires snapped in rapid succession. They sounded to Lieutenant Mayer like bullets ricocheting over the surface of the water. Apparently Lawrence didn't hear the noise, for he continued forward without stopping.

Mayer looked at his chief rigger. "Did you hear those wires go?" he asked, wondering if he was beginning to hear things.

"Yeah," said McCarthy without alarm.

Mark Donovan was trying to sleep near the crew space. Ordinarily nothing woke him up. But when the ship lurched so badly that he was almost thrown from his bunk, he decided he'd better get up and report to his landing station. He picked his way wearily to frame 60. There he saw big Charlie Bauch inspecting gas cells. The lieutenant was checking to see if the helium manifolds were untied.

"Donovan!" called Bauch. "Let me know if anything unusual happens back here." Bauch staggered forward as the ship lurched again.

Donovan began to patrol his area. He saw a light at the head in frame 35. It was Jimmy Cullinan. "I expect we'll lose some gas, Jimmy," Donovan said.

Cullinan, who rarely worried, was worried now. "I hope we don't ride at this angle much longer," he said. He frowned, shook his head, and started forward. "If we do, we'll have real trouble with the lousy motors." The two men passed each other on the narrow catwalk, arching away from each other at the same moment. It was an unconscious movement, graceful in spite of the rocking ship.

Lieutenant Bauch, in charge of the aft end of the keel, was now at the auxiliary control station. Rigger Carlson swung down from the rigging above the keel, dropping in front of Bauch like a monkey. He told his boss he'd been up looking at one of the gas cells.

Just below them in engine car Number 1, Second Mechanic Walter Johnson was in trouble. A few minutes before, he'd had a bell for full speed. But as soon as his motor had been opened up, the water-jacket petcock on Number 6 cylinder began to vibrate. It had finally jiggled open and water spurted out. While Johnson was stemming the flow, the water line to the carburetor radiator broke, and there was another gush of water. The mechanic angrily shut off the motor. He climbed up the ladder to frame 60 and turned on water from his emergency tank.

"Hey, Art!" called Johnson, catching sight of Rigger Carlson and Lieutenant Bauch. "Give me a hand."

Carlson came forward.

"Stand by the valve and shut it off when my radiator is full." He clambered down the ladder, disappearing in his gondola.

Carlson stood at the valve. He could hear Johnson starting up his motor. It pounded badly. As Carlson listened, the ship went into a sudden lurch.

A few frames forward at frame 95, Rigger Franklin Masters was rolled out of bed by the lurch. Sleepily he got to his feet. He wondered how close they were to Akron, his home town. His wife had just given birth to a son, and Lansdowne had given Frank permission to bail out in a parachute when they flew over Akron. He was too lazy to put on his rubber-soled shoes; instead he dug his feet into a pair of leather-soled house slippers. Then he heard engine Number 1 pounding like an old truck going uphill. He walked back to the engine hatch, wondering vaguely what was going on.

"What's the word?" he asked.

Carlson looked up from the water valve. "Hey, Frank," he said, "you better tell Russell his engine is knocking like hell."

Masters, still half asleep, nodded. Then he started forward. His leather slippers were like ice skates on the tipping keel. He almost fell off the catwalk several times before he reached Russell's bunk.

Russell, head engineer of Number 1, who reputedly could sleep through a cyclone, was running true to form: when Masters' flashlight beam hit him, his face was full of peace and satisfaction. It took a few good shakes to rouse him, but when he found out his beloved motor was coughing, he was immediately wide awake and climbing into his dungarees.

The atmosphere in the control car was quiet but tense. The altimeter had passed the 5000-foot mark. They had long since gone above pressure height, 3800 feet. In spite of every corrective measure the ship was still rising.

In his little shack in the rear of the control cabin, Radio man Schnitzer was unconcernedly receiving and sending messages. A message came in requesting their position. He got up from his transmitter and, earphones on his head, walked to the forward part of the gondola.

"What's our latest position, sir?" he asked Navigator Rosendahl, who was busy with other problems.

"Our position hasn't changed appreciably since the last report," said Rosendahl. "And besides, there's too much going on right now to figure it out for you."

"Aye, aye, sir," said the radio man. He turned and walked back to his compartment, carefully shutting the door behind him.

The *Shenandoah* struggled on. In the blenched predawn light a dozen men and women came out below to watch the strange antics of the big dirigible. It was hilly, rugged country, lined with deep valleys. Ridges ran between stumpy hills thick with scrub timber. The people knew nothing of dirigibles, but they realized this would be a bad place to make an emergency landing.

To R. K. Murphy of Caldwell, Ohio, it seemed the ship was swinging back and forth like a huge pendulum. D. A. Groves, a Pleasant City farmer who had always been an early riser, was in his yard sniffing the morning air. A storm seemed to be making up. He had just gone back to his house and closed the door against a sudden shower when he heard a loud buzzing. From behind a hill a huge airship came straight toward him. Suddenly, nose down, it started to shoot up in the air. He wondered why they were playing tricks practically over his house.

In the control car Allen called out, "Still rising two meters per second, sir!" They were up to 5500 feet.

Lansdowne glanced at the altimeter and held a quick conference with Hancock and Jack Lawrence, whose opinions he valued highly. Then he turned to Houghton. "All right, Regg," he said, "Open the maneuvering valves."

The lieutenant yanked at the yellow helium toggles. Rosendahl, looking at his watch, called out the time at fifteen-second intervals.

The sky was now solid overcast except far to the south and southwest. Anderson peered ahead, trying to figure out the best course. Directly north of the ship and above, at an angle of 45 degrees, he saw a huge, threatening cloud. It had developed out of nowhere. Then he saw that the cloud actually extended above them to the west. If their rise didn't stop soon they'd shoot straight into the eye of a squall.

"Rising one meter per second," called Allen hopefully.

The valving of thousands of cubic feet of helium was finally taking effect. Even so they were close to 6000 feet and still rising.

"Get up in the keel, Andy," said Lansdowne, realizing that at any moment the rise would stop and they would begin a fast plunge to earth. "Pass the word to stand by the slip tanks in case of an emergency."

Anderson dashed up the ladder. He heard Rosendahl intoning, "Three minutes," just as he left the control car. The young aerologist almost knocked over Lieutenant Mayer as he popped onto the catwalk.

"The captain says to stand by slip tanks!" gasped Anderson.

"They'd better start using the maneuvering valves," Mayer said fretfully.

"They've been valving for three minutes."

Mayer looked relieved. "O.K., tell the captain we're just waiting an order to slip the tanks."

Anderson turned back to the ladder.

At frame 95 Elevator man Bull Tobin suddenly awakened. He opened his eyes and saw Allely, a fellow elevator man, sitting near his feet. Rigger Masters was sitting on a bunk across the keel. Bull wondered what they were gabbing about so early. Before he could ask them, Allely disappeared up the keel forward and Masters went aft. Tobin was beginning to resent being awakened when he heard a hissing, like escaping steam, over his head. He looked up. It was the gas bag overhead, swollen like a child's balloon. He jumped up. "Hey, Henry!" he called.

Across the keel his buddy, Henry Boswell, who was usually rudder man while he was at the elevators, sat up in bed, his eyes blinking. "What's going on?" he asked.

At his bunk in frame 75 Charlie Solar, generator mechanic in the control car, came fully awake after sleeping fitfully for the last few hours. Something seemed to be wrong. Solar started to put on his shoes, figuring he'd better take a look around. Then he noticed that engine Number 1 was coughing and sputtering as if it was about to conk out.

In Number 1 car Walter Johnson was struggling to keep his engine going. Water was still streaming from the broken radiator, and the temperature was going up fast. For the third time he rang a high-temperature signal, but the control car didn't answer. Finally he realized they were in bad trouble and needed every possible revolution. He tried to nurse the engine along, but it made a final splutter and then stopped completely. Johnson flopped back in his chair in disgust.

Just then his chief, Bill Russell, his hair tousled, clanked down the ladder and into the car. "What the hell's the matter?"

"Engine's hot," growled Johnson.

"Well, let's crank the damned thing." Russell got down on his knees and started to crank. The ship was now at such a steep angle that he was lying on the radiator in front of the car. He tried several times. It was no use. Water began dripping from the gauge. Hearing the water, Russell got up and went to the after part of the car. The ship was tilted so severely that it seemed he had to climb almost straight up. Then he saw water coming from the jacket around Number 6 cylinder. As if one leak wasn't enough!

The violent rolling and pitching finally woke up Frank Peckham. At once he smelled the rich, bitter odor of ethyl-lead. He reached up and touched Number 9 gas bag over his head. It was fat, as if the ship were flying at pressure height. No intimation of danger registered on him, he dropped back on his bunk in a dreamy half-sleep. At the time seven others were still sleeping in the enlisted men's quarters, including Lieutenant Tom Hendley, who hadn't been able to find an empty officers' bunk.

In the control car, Rosendahl, the timer at the helium valves, called out, "A total of five minutes."

"Close the helium valves," ordered Lansdowne. "Now look out," he added tensely but quietly. "We'll begin to fall." He looked down at Houghton, who was standing short and stolid beside him. "Stand by the ballast controls, Regg."

Above them, Anderson was starting back down the ladder. Suddenly a blast of bitter cold air rushed down the keel through the ventilating hatches, hitting him in the face.

Photographer Richardson, who was still vainly trying to sleep, felt the cold blast too. The gust flapped the curtains violently around his bunk.

Mechanic Gus "Quinny" Quernheim, carrying water from frame 120 to Number 2 engine, had just reached frame 90 when the chilling wind hit him. His ears were singing from the dizzy rise.

And Lieutenant Mayer felt the terrific rush of cold air as he was passing the ventilating hatches forward of 170.

All of them felt the cold air, but none realized at the time that the ship had just risen into a line squall—a clash of opposing winds, one moist and warm, the other dry and cold. The ship was now in the grip of two opposing forces, each twisting the ship in a different direction.

The fantastic rise stopped sharply at 6300 feet. The "Daughter of the Stars" wavered for an instant and then began to plunge.

The first one to notice the fall was Elevator man Allen, who was facing the altimeter.

"The ship's falling!" he cried out. "She's falling fast, very fast!"

By this time no one had to be told. Eardrums pounded and blood shot to the head as the *Shenandoah* plummeted down twenty-five feet a second.

"Water ballast!" called out Commander Lansdowne.

Houghton pulled desperately on the water controls, holding as many of the plain toggles in each hand as he could. Lansdowne ordered the ship nosed up about 10 degrees. But, in spite of the tons of water being dumped and the inclined elevators, the sickening fall continued.

"She's still falling!" called out Allen.

"She's all right, Allen," said Lansdowne evenly. "We'll stop her." He looked at the altimeter. "Yes, she's falling fast. But we'll slow her up." The captain's self-possession once more had its calculated effect. In spite of the ship's frightening drop there was no panic.

Mayer had just stepped onto the officers' platform at frame 180. He saw the gas cells alternately cupping upward and flapping badly. He knew the rate of descent must be terrific. He scrambled to the emergency ballast bags near the platform. Just then they emptied. He knew the control car was on the job.

Coleman and O'Sullivan were still draining water for Number 2's boiling radiator. Coleman, a flashlight in one hand, had just got a funnel under the emergency tank when the bottom seemed to fall out of his world. He dropped the funnel. It fell to L girder and rolled forward. Heedless of the breath-taking heights, O'Sullivan went through the netting that protected the gas cell and crawled forward to get the pesky funnel. Coleman shouted directions, pointing the beam of his light at the errant funnel. Neither man worried about the ship's dive. Let them worry about that in the control car.

Bull Tobin, still groggy with sleep, got to his feet just as the plunge began. He struggled to pull on his clothes, but the ship kept teetering, throwing him off balance. Henry Boswell, trying to dress across the keel from him, was having the same trouble. Then a ray of light from a rigger's flash momentarily lit up the scene. Boswell, seeing his big friend wrestl'ng on his bunk with a pair of dungarees that didn't seem to have leg holes, began to laugh. Angrily Bull grabbed his clothes, crawled and sprawled up the ship toward the crew space. Boswell followed close behind.

Down in engine room Number 5, Broom and Shevlowitz were now, for the first time, having trouble with their engine. It had suddenly become crackling hot.

"Top her off!" shouted Broom above the whistling of the wind. Joe Shevlowitz climbed out of the gondola and started up the open ladder. The ship seemed to be spinning like a merry-go-round, but he'd never heard of a big dirigible doing any such thing. He could only advance a step at a time, for the wind was trying to blast him off. He finally reached the belly of the ship and staggered forward for some water. He had to get Number 5 started up again or Sheppard would really read him off.

Bill Russell was still trying to crank the frozen Number 1 engine. But when he saw the ship was dropping like a rock he figured they were going to crash. And Number 1, the lowest-hanging of the five engines, would probably hit the ground first.

"Get up in the keel!" he ordered his assistant, Johnson.

As Johnson struggled up against the force of the wind, Russell glanced forward. To his horror the hull of the ship was writhing, making big, twisting lurches toward its starboard side.

Rain now spattered sharply on the ship.

Up above in frame 80, Warrant Officer Cole finally awoke and started forward. He wanted to get to his landing station, the radio compartment. Maybe Schnitzer would need some help. The morning air was cool; it was a relief after the hot, stuffy night. He found the keel as slippery as a patch of ice.

Gus Quernheim was having an even harder time negotiating the keel. With one hand he held onto a guide line, and with the other he was trying to carry a collapsible bucket so the water wouldn't slosh out. Engine Number 2 needed every drop he could get. He wished he had two spare hands to put to his ears. His eardrums seemed about to burst.

From a top altitude of 6300 feet, the ship had now dropped to 3200 in less than two minutes. The men stationed at the slip tanks, pliers in hand, made ready to cut loose the heavy gasoline tanks as soon as the order came from the skipper. They knew he'd give the order at just the right moment, but they wished it would come fast.

Peckham, who had been awake only a few minutes, was estimating the rate of fall by the contracting gas cell nearest him. He judged they must have come down a good 3000 feet. He was thinking they had just crossed the last of the mountains and were coming down to a better altitude.

Red Collier felt something push down on his face. He woke up with a start. It was Number 9 gas cell, bloating and bulging over him. He figured they must have gone far above pressure height. Then he noticed that next to it cell Number 10 was gone! It hung down in flabby folds, like a burst toy balloon. The ship tipped down abruptly, as if it were out of control. He looked across the dim keel at the youngster sleeping near him. Ben Hereth was a good mechanic but he hadn't had much experience in the air. Collier felt responsible for him. He started across the keel to wake him up.

Oil King Malak was a man who always did one thing at a time, with a fine disregard for distractions. He had been told to dope the fuel, so was going to dope the fuel. He was conscious that the ship was giving him a rocky ride, but that was none of his business. A few minutes before, he'd opened his tool box in the crew space and taken out a pair of pliers. From the cargo net that swayed crazily several feet above the plywood flooring he took out a gallon can of ethyl-lead. Then he sat on the tool box and placed the container between his legs. The cap stuck but he finally got it off. He was so intent on his job he had no idea the dirigible had just fallen 3500 feet.

By this time the rain had suddenly stopped, and Gunner Cole had staggered to the crew space. He wondered how Smiley Malak could sit calmly on his tool box while the ship was bucking in this wild way. And the others in the crew space didn't seem especially concerned either. Cook Hahn was securing a pile of supplies that had once again spilled over the floor. Allely was engrossed in watching the antic altimeter. Cole looked over his shoulder at the big luminous dial. It read 2600 feet.

Allely laughed. His relief man at the elevators was getting a workout. "Allen is sure doing his stuff!" he said. He had no idea what was really happening.

At that moment Quinny Quernheim, half the water in his bucket spilled out, reached frame 90 and the water tank above his engine, Number 2. O'Sullivan had finally rescued the dropped funnel. He handed it up to Quinny while Coleman lit them both up with a flashlight.

The ship stopped with a jolt. It leveled off. Thank God, thought Quernheim, the damned thing had finally stopped dropping. There couldn't be too much room below. And now they could get Number 2 cooled off.

A wire snapped nearby.

Quernheim jumped in surprise. "What's that?" he asked Coleman. His chief shrugged his shoulders. As Quernheim handed the funnel to Coleman and started to go forward, O'Sullivan took the bucket away from him.

"I'll make this trip, Quinny," O'Sullivan said.

In the control car, Colonel Hall went to the after window to observe the ground. He noted a drift to port of about 45 degrees and called out this information to Anderson, who was looking out the front window. There were clouds in the north and northwest. To the south was a big opening.

Lansdowne gave an order so quietly to Joffray at the rudders that no one else heard. The ship headed south. Then the captain picked up the telephone.

Rigger Mark Donovan, at the auxiliary control station near frame 60, was the man farthest aft. He was watching the telephone at eye level on the starboard side of the keel, and he was wondering what he should do next.

The telephone glass flashed red.

Donovan grabbed the receiver and sang out, "Sixty. Donovan."

"How are all the cells aft?" asked Lansdowne quietly.

"O.K. aft of sixty, sir. Fully intact."

There was a slight pause. "Pass word forward," said the skipper, "all men on their toes." His voice was calm but insistent. "We are going through together."

Donovan hung up and started forward. As he did there was a weird whistle of wind and the ship surged upward, even faster than the first time.

In Lakewood, New Jersey, Commander Lansdowne's dog, Barney, began howling.

Betsy Lansdowne, who had been sleeping poorly, woke with a shiver. "Lie down and shut up!" she called sleepily.

But Barney kept up his keening howl. He had only done this once before—the night the *Shenandoah* had been so long overdue on its stormy return from New England.

Betsy called out again, but the dog wouldn't stop his frightening moans. Finally, afraid the noise would wake up the two children, she threw a telephone book at Barney. Then Mrs. Lansdowne looked at her watch. It was five thirty. She wondered where Zach was at that moment.

8

BREAKUP

Donovan hurried forward to carry out the captain's order. At 90 he ran into O'Sullivan carrying an empty bucket. He told him what Lansdowne had said.

"I'll pass the word forward," said O'Sullivan. "I have to go up to one twenty-five and get water anyhow." He turned and started up the keel. Donovan hesitated and then went back to his post. The change of direction probably saved his life.

The engine telegraph was ringing almost constantly in the control car. Engine Numbers 1 and 2 were out, and the mechanic at 3 had just reported it was heating up again.

Lansdowne ordered Allen to nose down the ship as far as he could without stalling her. They were shooting up incredibly fast. The rise had to be stopped. He turned and said, "Full speed!"

In preparation for the fall that was bound to come, Lansdowne now ordered Jack Lawrence to go into the ship and have the men stand by to slip the gas tanks.

The altimeter was back at 3500 feet. Joffray was pulling at the rudder wheel, straining away, throwing his whole body into the struggle. It was a sight Anderson was never to forget.

Aft in the enlisted men's sleeping section, Red Collier was about to wake up Ben Hereth. But a sudden lurch rolled Hereth out of his bunk. He looked up at Collier in wide-eyed surprise.

"Hereth," said Red tensely, "the ship's done for. Look out for yourself." Then Red started aft to investigate Number 1 gondola.

Hereth's mind was in a whirl. He shook his head to wake himself up completely. "Here we go, I guess," he mumbled. He had to do something—he didn't know what—and here he wasn't even dressed.

Charlie Solar, sitting not far away on his bunk at frame 75, was still struggling to put on his shoes. In the darkness he couldn't unknot the shoelaces.

"Hey!" called Yeoman Richardson Wilson, the assistant cook, from the bunk across the keel from Charlie. Wilson yawned hugely. "What's the matter around here?" he asked.

"I don't know," answered Solar, fighting the snarled laces. "But I'm putting my shoes on to stand by."

The ship suddenly careened up at the nose.

Masters, the rigger scheduled to make the parachute drop at Akron, had been wandering aimlessly up the keel in his leather house slippers. He was caught off balance by the violent elevation of the nose. His feet came out from under him, and he fell on his face. To him the ship felt to be starting a gigantic loop-the-loop.

Shevlowitz and McCarthy, standing together at 140 taking a moment's breather, had to grab on girders. They both thought the ship was standing straight up on end. Ahead of them, at frame 170, Keel Officer Roland Mayer was going aft to tell his riggers to stand by to slip fuel tanks. The steep rise reminded him of an airplane in a spin. He noticed that, in addition to the amazing inclination, the dirigible's nose was turning to port while the tail rolled to starboard. The torsion was terrific. The whole structure vibrated wildly, and he was afraid that something was going to give. He hung onto a girder lest he be thrown into the netting on the port side of the keel.

Far below, farmer J. P. Davis had just finished lighting the fire in his kitchen stove when he heard the noise of an airship. He rushed outside and saw the *Shenandoah* a few miles to the northwest. It was going sideways. Near it were two storms, one in the north and one in the southeast. They were almost together. As he later told friends, the ship "came a piece, stopped, turned and nosed down. And then it raised a piece." He saw strange flickering lights in the dirigible. These, though he didn't realize it, were the bobbing flashlights of riggers and mechanics dashing up and down the keel, trying desperately to save their ship.

W. H. Danford of Pleasant City had been awakened by a "right smart" wind that rattled doors and windows. Looking up, he saw the dirigible due north, its nose swinging back and forth between north and east. Then it went up, making an odd grating noise.

A mile southeast of Danford's place, another farmer, L. D. Archer, was out in his yard in the gray dawn, shoveling corn to the hogs. He was an old man and he thought he'd seen everything. Then "his woman" called to him from the door of their farm. "Look up yonder at that funny-looking cloud," she said.

He looked. "That's no cloud," he replied. "It's a big balloon or flying machine." Its nose was pointing down and turning around and around. Suddenly the ship shot up like a "skyrocket." There was a "tolerable strong wind looking for a storm" at the time. Archer figured this wind had blown the airship high in the sky.

In the *Shenandoah* Quinny Quernheim thought they were going into a loop. So did Peckham. For the first time Frank was alarmed.

He jumped out of his bunk, went down the walkway to Number 2 car, and climbed down the ladder. Coleman was at the door of his gondola.

"What's the matter?" asked Peckham.

Coleman didn't know. He thought the ship was going over on her back. But he returned to his gondola and waited for a signal from the control car.

Radio man Schnitzer kept on the job. The radio was giving him trouble, but he continued to send out messages. At 5:43 EST he started another, "Hope to ride out storm. Unable to get radio to function——"

A few feet forward of Schnitzer, Lansdowne was worrying about the problems yet to come. He knew their second rise would soon end. Then would come another rapid plunge, and he didn't know if the ship could live through it.

A drop of any sort was going to be harder to stop this time: five minutes of helium had been valved, and all the water ballast dumped. Now they had left only the slip tanks—the middle three of five tanks, with a capacity of 700 pounds each rigged on the keel for emergency purposes. He knew riggers were standing by, pliers in hand, waiting for his order to cut the wires that held the slip tanks.

Lansdowne eyed the altimeter, then told Rosendahl to carry an order up into the ship: the men were to stand by for the command that would soon be transmitted by mouth up from the control car.

Rosendahl dashed up the ladder.

Chief Machinist Halliburton was standing at frame 140 when Jack Lawrence passed him, going forward.

"Stand by to slip tanks," said Lawrence. Before Halliburton could answer Lawrence was off at a lope toward the control car. Lawrence wanted to get down where he was needed most.

About ten yards aft of him, near frame 130, Halliburton made out a small group of mechanics drawing water from special tanks for their overheated engines. They were O'Sullivan, Cullinan, and Shevlowitz. Lieutenant Sheppard was talking to them.

"Looks serious, doesn't it!" shouted Halliburton to his boss, Sheppard. Then he drew pliers from his pocket and took up his position near the slip tank at 140.

It was exactly 5:45 EST. Malak, sitting on his tool box, had taken off the cap on the container of ethyl-lead. He was about to reach for a glass centimeter measure lying in the cargo net.

The ship gave a lurch. Malak almost slid off the box.

Then there was a loud, roaring crash. It came from forward near frame 130. He turned to see what had happened.

Halliburton heard the crash, but it was behind him. He swung around, pliers in hand. The keel had snapped like a twig at frame 130. It was impossible. Halliburton couldn't believe it, but there was a yawning hole in the bottom of the ship! And the four men he'd seen only a moment before—Sheppard, O'Sullivan, Cullinan, and Shevlowitz—had disappeared.

Shevlowitz was stunned. There had been a roar, and the keel broke almost at his feet. He fell but grabbed a girder. As if in a nightmare he saw Sheppard, a few feet aft of him, drop as through a trap door.

At first Shevlowitz thought the engineering officer had fallen out through the big hole in the keel. Then he heard someone climbing back into the ship. He couldn't see, but he realized that Sheppard had grabbed onto a tangle of wires at the very break in the keel. Cautiously the enlisted man crawled aft to give the lieutenant a hand. The torn wreckage underneath Shevlowitz began creaking ominously.

"Never mind me!" cried Sheppard from below. "Look out for yourself!"

But Shevlowitz inched down. Just as he reached out his hand, the wires in front of him were ripped out. He waited a moment hopefully. There wasn't a sound. He knew Sheppard was gone.

Colonel Hall had been looking out the starboard window of the control car. The ship was turning rapidly in a circle; obviously she was caught in a terrific blast of wind. The tail was suddenly thrown up and wrenched to the right. The ship had been caught by opposing winds. The "Daughter of the Stars" was being wrung out as if by two giant hands.

There was a shrill screech—the tearing and twisting of girders.

"There she goes," said Hancock, without raising his voice.

When Anderson heard the tear of girders he guessed the ship was breaking up amidships. Then the control car began to jar and shake.

Every man in the car knew what was happening. The struts that held the big gondola to the ship were being wrenched by wind and torsion. It was only a question of minutes, perhaps seconds, before the car would be torn loose from the dirigible.

Lansdowne didn't move. His face and eyes showed no emotion. "Anybody who wants to," he said, "can leave the car."

"Everybody out!" shouted Colonel Hall. He scrambled up the ladder.

"Quickly, Colonel!" cried Anderson, who was right behind him.

The others did not move. Moore, on his first big trip, stood fast. Schnitzer continued trying to get out a message. Houghton held his station at the ballast controls. Lewis Hancock acted as if he hadn't heard the skipper. Allen clung tightly to the elevator wheel. Joffray gripped the rudders. Jack Lawrence stood fast at his post next to Lansdowne.

Hall pulled himself up to the top of the ladder. He stepped onto the catwalk and started to run aft.

When the keel snapped, the ship had opened at frame 130 like an egg being cracked from the bottom. But the two sections were held together by the many control wires that came up from the control cabin and ran along the bottom of the keel to the huge fins.

Cullinan and O'Sullivan were hanging desperately onto the torn end of the stern section of the ship. Broom, a few yards away in engine car Number 5, and Spratley and Mazzuco in engine car Number 4, saw them dangling. But there was nothing the three mechanics could do to help.

On the port side of the crew space, Malak and Cole stared in horror as daylight appeared forward. Allely and Cook J. J. Hahn had been watching the altimeter on the starboard. They both saw it reach 6200 feet. Then there was a great roar forward, and they forgot about everything but saving themselves. Hahn saw gas tanks twisting in the keel nearby. He was showered with something wet, but he didn't realize for a long time that he was covered with gasoline.

Malak dropped the glass centimeter measure and jumped up, spilling the gallon can of ethyl-lead.

"Climb!" shouted Allely, realizing that the keel was the worst place to be in case of a crash. Malak grabbed the girder above his head and crawled on top of it. Cole was right behind him. Hahn hesitated for a moment. Then he, too, started for a girder.

Tobin and Boswell, who had almost reached the crew space, heard the crash of girders forward. They turned and started aft.

There were six men at frame 90 when the ship began to break up. On the port side, Coleman and Quernheim were still in their car, Number 2. They looked forward and saw objects dropping from the crack in the ship. Frank Peckham was on engine Number 2's ladder, trying to see what was wrong with the ship. He heard girders break and carry away above him. He figured she'd broken her back near amidships. He hurried back into the dirigible.

In the starboard engine car, Number 3, Jones was sitting as calmly and pleasantly, as if he were at a picnic. His motor, now that it was doped, was running like a charm, and he didn't have a worry in the world. Then he heard a crash of metal. A second later the lights in his car blacked out. He looked out of the forward end of the car and knew the *Shenandoah* was lost. Her nose was floating at a crazy angle above the rest of the ship. The front section looked as if it were trying to free itself.

The other two men at frame 90 were on the keel. Ben Hereth was still sitting on his bunk. Red Collier thought he heard someone screaming up forward. It was the strange, womanlike screech of metal breaking. He saw that Number 9 cell was deflating fast, but Number 8 was up to pressure.

At frame 80 Mr. Richardson, the ship's only civilian, was finally completely awake. He sat upright in his bunk. When he heard the noise he thought that the tail had hit a mountain and was being torn off. Just aft of him Charlie Solar was still having trouble with his shoelaces. Yeoman Wilson, in the next bunk, sat up. He didn't know what else to do so he just stayed put. Masters was standing up between the two men, his legs spraddled so he wouldn't fall. He was on his way back to his own bunk but the terrible noise made him stop dead in his tracks.

At frame 70 Lieutenant Tom Hendley, who had slept through everything, was awakened by the screaming of metal. When he opened his eyes he found himself plunging, bunk and all, through the port side of the dirigible. Two of the wires that supported his bunk had snapped off. He grabbed at several dangling wires, stopping the bunk as it jammed a hole through the outer envelope. He cautiously climbed back onto the keel. Then he started for a cluster of gas tanks, figuring he should stand by to slip them in case of emergency.

Russell was in engine car Number 1 when the ship first broke. He quickly started up the ladder. His assistant, Walter Johnson, who had been told a moment before to get into the keel, was standing in the middle of the ladder looking forward. Johnson saw car Numbers 4 and 5 sagging a few feet below their normal height, their motors still going full blast. He hoped nobody was in them. It was obvious they'd tear loose any second.

Above these two mechanics was Rigger Arthur Carlson, standing stolidly at the auxiliary control station, waiting for orders.

Ten meters behind Carlson, at frame 50, was Lieutenant Bauch. He heard a breaking of girders somewhere forward but he could not see that the ship had been fatally damaged: the keel in that section was as dark as a cave.

The man farthest aft was Donovan. From his position at frame 30 he, too, was in the dark. The crash of breaking girders hadn't been alarmingly loud, but he was alarmed by the feeling that the starboard bow of the ship had run into a stone wall. Then the *Shenandoah* began to quiver, and Donovan smelled burning cloth. Nauseated, he hurried forward to frame 40 and opened a hatch, leaned far out and took deep, gasping breaths. Below him the ground was dim and spinning rapidly. He could see a field covered with clay, or something whitish. The landscape twirled sickeningly around him.

Just then something snapped in the tail. A trail of sparks shot up under the keel. Red Collier, at frame 90, was the first to realize what had happened. The main cable controls had broken loose from the elevators and rudders and were running wildly up the ship. Collier wondered what was happening to the control car.

Rosendahl had been working his way up the keel, intending to go to the slip tanks amidships. Suddenly he heard a terrible clashing. He turned and saw the bottom panel of the ship's outer covering, and several of the transverse structural members of the keel, cut loose along one side. He saw the severed control wires being pulled out like the guts of a fish by the falling control car.

Mayer, a few yards forward of the control car ladder, saw a man scramble up the ladder from the control car and start aft. It was Anderson. There was a great roaring like the protracted rumble of thunder, and a large hole opened in front of the keel officer. The control car had torn loose and was dragging hundreds of feet of control cables with it. The shock of the rupture threw Mayer to one knee between two ballast bags at frame 170. Anderson threw up his hands and disappeared.

Hall saw the whole thing from frame 170. After he'd come out of the control car and stepped on the catwalk he was only able to take two steps. Then the catwalk was pulled from under him. He reached out, catching a girder, and dragged himself to the top of the apex girder of the keel.

McCarthy was at almost the same spot. He felt the keel dropping away from him and grabbed a box girder. Then he started cutting a path through the cord netting that had once held a gas cell in place.

But the man who had the last look at the control car was Anderson. He'd had no trouble getting to the top of the ladder just a few feet behind Colonel Hall. But as he was stepping onto the catwalk there was a splintering of the control car struts. The gondola was wrenching itself loose from the ship. He looked over his left shoulder and saw the control car hanging down, no longer in a vertical plane but listing to starboard. Suddenly the ladder he was still holding was yanked away, and the control car took its plunge to earth.

Stunned, Anderson felt the catwalk and the girders on both sides of it collapsing like a match house. He was pulled off the catwalk. But just as he was about to drop through the great hole torn open by the control car, he managed to get hold of something—a wire or part of a girder. The next thing he knew he was sitting on a fragment of the catwalk that was suspended directly over the center of the wide hole. A few wires were all that held Anderson, and the fragment he was perched on, to the rest of the ship. He didn't make a move for fear he might topple off. And the slightest movement might pull out one of the wires, and he'd go hurtling after his shipmates in the control car.

J. P. Davis, a mile away, saw the ship break near the middle, its ends down. One part went down out of his sight, behind a hill. The other part ballooned into the air, first bearing southwest, then southeast toward Caldwell.

W. H. Danford was only a quarter of a mile away. He saw the ship break "by heaving up in the middle." He heard part of the dirigible crash on the nearby farm of T. R. Davis. Danford ran for the barn, got out a horse, and rode bareback toward the crash.

A mile from the Davis Farm, D. A. Groves saw the ship break upward in the middle. Then he saw things fall out. He, too, ran to help.

Another Pleasant City man, C. M. Larrick, was a mile away. He saw the dirigible tip up almost perpendicularly, drop back, and break completely in two.

At the crew space, Malak was hugging a triangular girder tightly. Looking forward he saw nothing but daylight; the bow section had broken off and ballooned high above the stern. Then there was a groan aft of the crew space, followed by a second shotgun-like report. Malak turned. To his amazement and terror he saw daylight in the stern too. The ship had broken again, this time just forward of engine Numbers 2 and 3, at frame 100. To this day he remembers the tail section fading away lazily, like something in a slow-motion dream, with strips of torn fabric waving like ragged pennants.

The crew space, holding four men, was now being dragged downward at terrific speed by engine gondolas 4 and 5. Allely, like Malak clinging to a girder, saw the crew space torn away at frame 100. He noticed that gas cells 10 and 11 had been exploded by the first break of the ship. Their section now had little to keep it buoyant. Gunner Cole knew nothing of all this, for early in the drop he had been knocked off his girder. He had fallen to the floor of the crew space, rolled off to the bottom of the ship, and was balanced precariously across a network of wires—unconscious.

The crew space section, frames 100 to 130, suddenly made a lurch. There was another shrill shriek of metal and fabric. A moment later the crew space itself, as if relieved of a great weight, was floating gently, easily, with sky at both ends of it.

Two men in the tail fragment of the *Shenandoah* saw what had happened. Johnson and Russell, clinging to the ladder of Number 1 engine, saw gondolas 4 and 5 abruptly wrench themselves from the plunging middle section. The two motors tore out great hunks of the structure of frames 120 to 130. Cullinan, clinging to the ragged ends of frame 130, must have been flung off almost immediately (his body was found, hours later, in a gully a quarter of a mile from the engines). But O'Sullivan rode the wreckage down. With him went Mazzuco and Spratley in engine car Number 4, and little Broom in Number 5.

Below, on the T. R. Davis farm, tenant Andy Gamary, his wife, and five children were just getting up. It was a few minutes before 6:00 EST. Andy had always been afraid of storms, so he was at the window watching the clouds apprehensively. Then he heard a different sound, a roaring that grew louder. It was a twister, he guessed. He shouted to his wife to take the children to the "storm house."

But before they could move there was a deafening crash outside their door. Then they heard something go over the house. There was another crash. They ran to the window and saw what they thought was a big white cloud floating down the hill toward the valley.

Each of the three drifting sections of the ship was following a different course. The bow, relieved of the weight of the control car, had soared to 5000 feet and was traveling in a huge circle. The rear section was gliding toward the rolling hills, tail first, at high speed—dragged down by the weight of engine gondolas 1, 2, and 3.

The smallest section, the crew space, had at first dropped much faster than the tail. But when engine Numbers 4 and 5 were yanked out by the force of gravity, its plummetlike descent stopped suddenly. It floated gracefully past the Gamarys' home.

Inside, Cook Hahn was hanging onto P girder. Looking overhead, he saw no gas cell. Then he looked down. Through a hole in the port side of the hull he saw the ground coming up at him. Allely had been hanging onto a nearby girder, but the sudden jerk with which the engines ripped out had knocked him to the plywood flooring. Cole was still lying unconscious on tangled wires a few inches from the outer envelope. Malak was hugging his girder grimly. The gas cell above him pushed down on him. He could hear the wind whistling. He thought, "Boy, this is it!" For two and one-half years he'd risked his neck mining coal without a scratch. Now he was going to get his—on an airship.

The little section, jagged wreckage dangling at both ends, skimmed down Gamary's hill, losing altitude rapidly now but miraculously remaining on the level. A little hump of earth stuck up. The crew space smashed into it and then skidded down the slope.

Hahn suddenly "went stunned." The next he knew he was lying on the ground.

Malak was catapulted through the side of the ship, through a

network of wires. As he hit the ground he felt himself being pulled
by his left ankle. Wires had trapped him. The crew space, sliding
downhill toward a clump of trees, dragged him for fifty feet. The
wreckage skidded into the trees and stopped.

In the dim light of early morning Malak untangled the wires from
his ankle. He noticed it was much darker on the ground than it had
been in the air. For a moment he thought he was alone. Then he saw
Cook Hahn standing a few feet away, dazed. They looked at each
other but didn't speak. They thought they were the only survivors
of the *Shenandoah*.

Malak heard a faint groan from somewhere inside the wreckage.
"I hear somebody," he said.

"Let's check," said the cook.

The two went inside the tangled mess. Allely was sitting silently,
looking unconcerned, on the crew space platform. The groans resumed. They were coming from under the plywood flooring of the
crew space. Malak lifted up one corner of the platform. There was
Gunner Cole.

The three rescuers pulled the radio officer out of the wreck and
stretched him on the ground. He said his leg and back hurt. His face
was bruised and slashed from his rough ride along the ground with
only the ship's outer covering to protect him. The first thing the
injured man did was to look at his watch. It was 6:06 A.M.

Malak sat down on the ground, his face twisted in pain.

"What's wrong with you, Smiley?" asked Allely.

Malak struggled to his feet. "Lou, there's something wrong with
my right leg," he moaned.

"Your leg isn't broken," Allely said. He pulled back his foot and
kicked the Oil King sharply in his right shin. "See?"

There were eighteen men in the tail section. Rigger Mark Donovan, far aft at frame 40, had leaned out an open hatch, watching
the strange behavior of the crew space and trying to dispel the nau-
sea caused by a burning smell. He saw the little detached section
fall rapidly for several hundred feet. Then, when engine car Numbers 4 and 5 snapped off, it stopped as if it had hit something solid.
Immediately the crew space righted itself and floated out of sight.

Donovan got up out of the hatch and felt his way farther aft. The
tail assembly was higher than the jagged end.

At frame 50 Lieutenant Bauch knew they were falling at great
speed. At first the tail itself was up about 30 degrees, but as the
section neared the ground it straightened to a 5-degree angle. Bauch
had no idea how far away the ground was; he could see nothing
inside the dark keel.

Many of the men in the tail section stayed where they were when the ship first broke up. Mechanics Johnson and Russell didn't. They had been hanging onto the ladder of engine car Number 1. Both men crawled into the ship after watching gondolas 4 and 5 rip from the crew space. They figured their car was about to do the same thing. Johnson ran back to frame 50. Russell hung on to a girder at frame 90.

Lieutenant Tom Hendley, recently shaken out of sleep, tried to act constructively. At the breakup he wanted to dump gas tanks, but he had no flashlight and he couldn't find any wire cutters. He did stumble over a nest of tanks. He tugged and strained in the dark at one tank. It wouldn't budge.

Near him Charlie Solar was hanging to a girder. Assistant Cook Wilson was sitting, as if hypnotized, in his bunk. A moment later civilian Richardson scrambled past, heading aft. He slipped on the steep keel and caught at a gas tank for support. The top fastenings broke loose, and the tank tilted and teetered. It seemed about to topple over and crush him. Richardson fell. As he was about to tumble off the catwalk and over the side, he grabbed a guide line. He steadied himself and continued on his way, too surprised to realize what a narrow escape he'd just had.

Then Red Collier raced by. More familiar than Richardson with the narrow catwalk, Red had no trouble reaching frame 60. He lowered himself down a hatch and climbed down the ladder to engine gondola Number 1, which had recently been vacated by Russell and Johnson. He stood on top of the gondola, hanging onto a strut. If something was going to happen he wanted to see it.

Frank Peckham, Richardson's watch mate on the keel, went the other way. Frank had been on engine Number 2's ladder talking to Lester Coleman. When the ship broke up he figured the safest place would be inside, as high up as possible. He climbed back into the dirigible and, just as girders crashed behind him, moved down the port side to frame 85. He didn't know Coleman and Quernheim, whom he'd been talking to a moment before, had just been cut off from the keel. When his fragment of the *Shenandoah* began to go up higher at the tail he tightroped across a diagonal wire, balancing himself with another wire. Eventually, precariously, he reached the keel. Then he climbed to the top of the triangular tunnel. As he reached the apex he was amazed to see a face pop up from the other side of the keel. It was Hereth. The two stared at each other as if each were looking into a mirror.

Mechanic Ralph Jones left his engine car, Number 3. He climbed to its roof mainly out of curiosity. It took him a minute to accept the fact that *his* ship was going to pieces. Then he realized his motor was still running at 1400 revolutions. He wondered if he should climb down and turn off the ignition: they always turned off the ignition in stories about air crashes. But the ground was getting closer; trees began to form out of a dark blur. He decided he'd better stay on top of the gondola, holding onto a toe cable. As the trees grew larger he figured it was just about time to jump——

Les Coleman and Quinny Quernheim were in their engine car, Number 2, to the port of Ralph Jones. After the first crash inside the ship Coleman said, "Let's go up in the ship and drop gas tanks." They started up the ladder into the dirigible. But when they got to the top there was another crash. The crew space broke away from them only a few yards forward. They saw the walkway was blocked off by nearly fractured girders. There was nothing to do but hang on to the top of the ladder.

Their chunk of the *Shenandoah* was heading for the ground, tail first, like an arrow in reverse. Both men saw a field suddenly jump up at them. Then the bottom of their engine gondola hit a hill. They saw a kaleidoscope of trees rush at them. They jumped. At that same instant Ralph Jones leaped off the top of engine Number 3.

Just slightly forward of these three men were Bull Tobin and Henry Boswell, only a few feet from the jagged break where the crew space had torn loose. They were clinging to girders. It had been a queer ride since the first break, thought Tobin. There was a second crash, and the crew space pulled loose only a few feet in front of them, almost jolting them out the jagged end of the tail section. But after that—not a sound. They had drifted down in what seemed like a deep, deathly silence—this although Jones' motor was roaring full speed only a few yards away from Bull. Tobin had tried to go aft after the second and final break. But the open end of the great fracture, trailing down about twenty feet, jumped up dangerously under his feet, cutting off his retreat. He crawled as high as he could and hung on. He concentrated so desperately and exclusively on hanging on that he didn't notice when the two engines below him were knocked off.

Charlie Solar knew what had happened to engine Numbers 2 and 3. He heard a crash. Then the cloth covering below him ripped off with a screech. The dark keel was suddenly light. They'd hit trees, and two of the tail section's three engines were scraped off. Freed of the weight, the tail shot up, dragging across the tops of a big clump of trees.

Stern first, the tail sailed into a small valley.

When he felt the ship taking off again, Rigger Art Carlson ran back to frame 40, to an emergency valve control wire. To bring the ship down he let out helium as fast as he could.

The ship floated gracefully, if backward, across the tiny valley. Abruptly the port side snagged against something. Bill Russell saw a hole in the covering and jumped. To his astonishment he found himself in a tree. He dropped to the ground. He was on a steep hill. He ran after the ship which was slowly, silently, drifting away. "Jump! Jump!" he shouted. "Jump through the keel!"

The quiet, peaceful Ohio countryside echoed to Russell's shouts. Inside the ship Carlson heard him. He let go the valve line and ran forward to a hole in the keel. The ground was only ten feet below. He hung onto a girder and dropped through the covering to the ground.

Mark Donovan heard Russell too. He jumped through the hole Carlson had enlarged. He thought he landed on his hands and feet, but Carlson, only a short distance away, saw him dive out and flop on his right side.

Lieutenant Bauch heard Russell. He walked forward but he didn't jump. Solar, Wilson, and Masters jumped without hearing Russell. A moment later Hereth and Boswell followed.

All this time Red Collier was standing unconcernedly on top of Number 1 gondola. Finally the bottom of the little car hit the side of the steep hill. To this day Collier insists he never made an easier exit from an airship. He must have jumped the very moment the gondola, striking the ground, was severed from the ship.

Standing right over the hatch, Richardson saw engine car Number 1 torn loose. He thought of jumping, but it was quite dark and the ground might be much farther away than it looked. He slid down the ladder that had led to car Number 1. But the wrench that pulled the gondola free had bent back the broken end of the ladder. The photographer's hands somehow got wedged in the bend of the ladder. After an agonizing few seconds he tore them loose and dropped to the ground. But his troubles weren't over. A wire hung down from the ship like a fisherman's troll line. The end snatched Richardson by his right ankle and dragged him down the hill after the careening tail section.

Mechanic Walter Johnson saw Richardson disappear down the ladder. It looked like a good idea, so he followed. He was luckier. He landed safely just as the uplifted tail of the descending ship was about to hit the side of the hill.

Only three men were now left aboard the tail section, the two officers, Bauch and Hendley, and Chief Bull Tobin. When the tail itself finally crashed into the hill, Bauch was thrown through the side of the ship. The husky officer hit the ground, rolled over and got up, good as new. As the ship struck, Tom Hendley was hit on the head. He landed on the ground slightly stunned but uninjured.

The last man out was Bull Tobin. A moment after the tail struck the hill, his footing crumpled. There was a crashing and snapping of girders, then Bull tore out the open end of the section like a fullback. He looked back and saw where he'd been standing a few seconds before. It was as flat as if a giant had stepped on it.

As the tail fragment hit, it began to pivot in a huge arc, threatening to crush the men who had jumped on the downhill side of the slope. Johnson escaped by running uphill. Peckham went the other way. Richardson, after being dragged like a roped steer for fifty yards, got the wire loose from his right ankle and scrambled back up the hill. He ducked just in time to avoid the downward sweep of the 350-foot segment.

Donovan had been momentarily dazed by his headlong dive from the dirigible. Somebody grabbed him by the hand and pulled him to his feet. It was his buddy, Bill Russell. The two men ran down the hill hand in hand.

Donovan didn't know what it was all about. Suddenly Russell let go and Donovan sat down with a thump.

"Look, Donovan!" shouted Russell. "The ship's rolling!"

From his sitting position Donovan saw the long, dark shape bouncing towards him. He got to his feet and started to run. He looked over his shoulder. The ship was coming faster than he could run. He stopped and watched, fascinated. As the big form loomed up frighteningly, he flopped down on his stomach, hoping the ship would bounce over him. He closed his eyes and held his breath wondering if the luck of the Irish was with him. Nothing happened so he opened his eyes. The tail section had bounced over him, continued on a complete circle, and ended up with its stern again pointing forward.

Slowly, dazedly, the men began to collect. There were fifteen of them.

"Look," said Photographer Richardson. He pointed to the northeast sky. There, riding at an even keel at about 7000 feet, was the bow section of the "Daughter of the Stars." It headed up into a storm cloud and vanished from sight. A moment later it came back, only to disappear again behind trees on top of a hill.

Anderson, sitting on his fragile suspension bridge of two wires, was still afraid to stir. The bow was spinning on a horizontal plane. He felt seasick. There was no sound but for the high wind and the creaking of the wreckage. He was alone on a derelict ship, rising higher and higher. Soon the gas cells, expanding with every foot of rise, would explode.

In frame 175, not far forward of Anderson, Lieutenant Roland Mayer also thought he was alone. When the senior keel officer saw the tail section break away and fall, the horror of it all sent him into a state of shock. Now he was out of sight of the ground, spinning giddily. Mayer had to hang onto a girder to keep from being flung out of the ship. At 9000 feet a torrential rain began. For some reason the rain stopped the merry-go-round spinning, and at last Mayer could act. He crept forward, opened a maneuvering valve. He let helium escape until, at 10,000 feet, the wild ascent was halted. Then he rested and began to collect his thoughts. All during the long battle with the storm and the subsequent wild moments of breakup, he had been too busy to be afraid. Now, in the deadly quiet, he was afraid. He was afraid, mostly, of being alone.

Then he heard a frightened shout from aft. There was an answering shout. Mayer shouted, too.

The first shout had come from Navigator Charles Rosendahl, who was near the officers' quarters at 150. His shouts had roused two men farther aft—Chief Machinist Halliburton and one of his mechanics, Joe Shevlowitz.

Mayer tried to join the group of three but found the hole made by the control car was a dividing chasm.

"Hey!" called another voice. It came from the depths. Mayer recognized Weather Officer Anderson's voice.

"Are you all right?" called Mayer. There was no answer. As he scrambled down to help his friend, another figure emerged from the gloomy interior of the bow. It was Rigger McCarthy. The two men crawled as close as they could to the suspended Anderson. From a height of about seven feet they lowered a line, but Anderson didn't reach for it. Then they saw that if Anderson let go the wires he was sitting on, he would fall. Mayer made a lariat. After several heartbreaking misses, he finally looped the rope around Anderson. Cautiously the aerologist withdrew one hand from the wires and worked his arm under the bowline. Mayer and McCarthy then drew the line tight.

At that moment another survivor appeared—Colonel Hall.

"What can I do?" he asked Mayer.

Hall was told to go forward and valve helium at frame 180; Mayer would call out instructions. The colonel crawled over twisted girders toward the nose.

At the same moment McCarthy and Mayer were pulling Anderson up from the great hole in the bottom of the bow. Only when

Anderson reached temporary safety above did he realize that he was drenched with gasoline. A tank had burst apart overhead.

Now that Anderson was secured, Mayer held a long-distance conference with Rosendahl across the jagged gap. Mayer shouted that he had found a helium valve, and one bag containing 1600 pounds of water ballast. It was hard to tell in the dimness inside the bow, but he felt sure the mooring wires in the nose were O.K.

Rosendahl shouted back that there were some fuel tanks that he, Halliburton, and Shevlowitz could drain from the bottom as ballast. At the right moment they could climb up the rigging and slash gas cells with their knives. It was decided to descend and try for a landing.

With the plan of action settled, the free-ballooning of the runaway nose began. It was going in a large circle with a radius of about ten miles. Now, as they sank, they could see the ground through the huge hole in the bottom. For a brief moment they glimpsed the wrecked tail section. From above it looked in good shape. The men in the air hoped that those on the ground were safe.

As Colonel Hall valved helium, the 300-foot bow section dropped toward the earth. Hall was taking orders from Mayer, who was taking his from Rosendahl across the gap.

Now the wind was blowing them at a speed of about twenty-five miles an hour. The truncated ship fell faster. McCarthy, thinking they were going to land at any moment, walked out on a flying strut to go aft. Then something hit the envelope that covered him like a tent. The thing, whatever it was, seemed to grab him and pull him right out of the ship.

The low-flying derelict had hit a tree, then shot up in the air again. McCarthy was left dangling, unconscious, in the branches of a large walnut tree.

At the fairgrounds in Sharon, a mile away, Charles Ferguson was watching the drifting wreck through field glasses. He saw a man plucked out of the *Shenandoah* by the branches of a big tree. It looked as if he were hanging from the tree by a rope. Ferguson and George Love jumped into their car and raced to the scene. A few minutes later they found McCarthy lying at the bottom of a tall walnut tree, seriously injured. Gas tanks and pieces of wreckage were littered under the tree.

At that moment a telephone was ringing in the house of Ernest Nichols, a nearby farmer. Nichols wondered who would be calling so early. He picked up the receiver. It was a neighbor telling him a crazy story about some runaway airship that was heading straight for his house.

Nichols hung up and went into the yard. A big object, like a low cloud, was coming over his orchard. It headed for the house. Out of the corner of one eye he saw his oldest boy sticking his head out of the upstairs window.

"Look out!" cried Nichols in fright.

Then, from above, he heard men shouting, "Grab hold! Grab hold! Turn her south!"

Wires were hanging from the nose of the derelict airship. Nichols grabbed a dangling cable and quickly wrapped it around a fence post. The post snapped off like a twig. He ran after the ship, grabbed the cable again, and threw it around the stump of an old maple tree. The cable pulled loose. By now Nichols was backed up against a fence. He turned and jumped over it.

The ship turned slightly from its course, knocked off the top of a shed, flattened a wheel on a well, and then bowled over a grape arbor. It skimmed over the ground and settled down gently, open end first. Mayer and Anderson jumped out of the tip of the nose and made the lines fast to posts and trees. The after end still stuck up twenty feet above the ground.

Mounted atop the after end, knives in hand, were Halliburton and Rosendahl. At the last moment they had climbed high in the rigging and punctured the helium cells. A line was thrown to them. They clambered down, hand over hand, and landed safely. Rosendahl looked at his watch. It was six forty-five.

The last section of the "Daughter of the Stars" had reached the ground. The wreck moved uneasily in the wind, tugging at its restraining lines. To his surprise the men borrowed a shotgun from Farmer Nichols. Nichols was even more surprised when, a moment later, Halliburton blasted holes in the gas cells.

Its helium gone, the wreck finally settled down.

Malak rubbed the ankle that Allely had kicked. Looking up, he spied a farmhouse on a hill. He pointed it out to Hahn.

"I'm going to notify the authorities," said the cook, starting up the hill.

"Hey, wait for me." Malak ran after him. He didn't want to be left near the wreckage all alone. The Oil King was out of breath when he got to a clump of trees in front of the farm. Then he saw a pile of wreckage near a little cornfield. Engine car Numbers 4 and 5 lay in the midst of a great snarl of wires and twisted girders. And there lay Broom, Spratley, and O'Sullivan.

Malak heard groaning from car Number 4. He opened the door and pulled out Celestine Mazzuco. Mazzuco suddenly held out his arms. Then he died. Malak laid him on the stubbly ground.

Soon Malak's gaze lit on a tangled mess at the other end of the cornfield. He walked fifty yards and found a hole gouged in the corner of the field by the control car. Seven men were scattered in grotesque positions outside the smashed car. They seemed to be sleeping. Jack Lawrence's battered wrist watch read five forty-seven.

An eighth man, Jimmy Moore—the mechanic who had begged Mrs. Lansdowne to get him a berth on the ship—was in the compartment containing the radio motor generator.

Now people were coming from all directions through the morning mist. They asked Malak questions. Stumblingly he tried to answer them. He looked again at the control car. Elevator and rudder cables ran from the car in a long, jagged line down the hill he had just climbed.

He noticed it was a warm morning. His right ankle began to throb.

At 7:30 EST that morning, Betsy Lansdowne's telephone rang. She was nervous as she answered it; Barney's strange behavior two hours before was still preying on her mind.

It was a marine in the Communications Office at Lakehurst. He asked for Mrs. Lansdowne.

"This is she."

The voice on the other end of the wire stammered, "Mrs. Lansdowne, there's been an accident.

"There's been an accident," he repeated.

She questioned him for a few minutes but could get no sense from him. He seemed to be crying. She asked for the officer on duty. After a tense pause she got him.

"One of the press services," he told her, "said there'd been an accident to the ship in Ohio."

She asked for details. The officer said there were none. The Station hadn't heard anything official.

She hung up the phone.

At nine thirty it rang again.

"We've had wire from Hahn," said a marine excitedly. "Two men in the after car were killed, but all the officers in the forward section are free-ballooning, looking for a place to land!"

Now she knew Zach was safe. Zach and Jack Lawrence knew more about free-ballooning than anyone in the Navy.

A few minutes later a call came from Washington. It was her aunt. She was coming immediately to Lakewood. Betsy tried to find out if there'd been any later information. Her aunt said there was nothing definite, but her nervous voice made Betsy suspicious.

Ten minutes later the wife of a Lakehurst officer drove up in front of the Lansdowne home. Betsy saw her coming slowly, reluctantly up the walk. She knew now, without being told, that Zach was dead.

First came the rescuers. They did everything they could to make it easier for the stunned survivors. Then the officers, leaving the enlisted men to guard the wreckage, hurried to Belle Valley and Caldwell to set up emergency headquarters.

Soon came the looters. They came in buggies, buckboards, and broken-down Model-T Fords. Within hours curious thousands had crossed the rutted back roads to the Davis farm. Other thousands had collected on the Nichols farm. Many were full of pity; many treated the disaster like a picnic.

By lunchtime souvenir hunters had torn almost all the covering off both large sections of the ship. Women, carrying yards and yards of fabric from the envelope, left the wrecked fragments of the *Shenandoah*, staggering under their loads. The looters were armed with knives, hatchets, pliers, and even wrenches. They went away with logbooks, girders eight feet long, blankets, and valuable instruments.

Nothing was too small or too large. One man was seen leaving with a huge piece of twisted piping and an armful of girders. A single house slipper was sticking out of his pocket.

At the crew space a man found an aluminum locker. It was locked, but a hammer soon opened it. Half a dozen enterprising men and women quickly cleaned out canned soup, condensed milk, and other supplies.

They worked while the surviving enlisted men tried to keep guard. Still dazed, the men didn't know how to stop the pillage. Soon the two main sections of the ship—miles apart—looked like skeletons picked to the bones.

Presently Major Frank Kennedy, an Army airship expert stationed at nearby McCook Field, arrived on orders to offer his services. He found Frank Masters, who had been scheduled to parachute over Akron at about that moment, trying desperately to guard the control car. The young rigger was nervous and confused. He didn't know how to stop these crazy people from taking things. As he rushed from one point to protect another, a group of looters would dart in behind his back. He had had nothing to eat for many hours. Sympathetic farmers offered to take him to breakfast, but he refused to leave his post.

Later in the day Major Kennedy went to Belle Valley. There the fourteen bodies were being placed in plain black coffins, and the local American Legion post was scouring the neighborhood for four-

teen American flags. Kennedy wanted to discover what had caused
the catastrophe. He could find only one living Navy man in town.
It was Red Collier. Red, like Masters, was disturbed, nervous.

"Chief," said Kennedy, "for God's sake, what happened?"

"Major," Red replied, "the cells ruptured. I saw them!"

At nightfall, in spite of National Guardsmen who threatened to
open fire, the looting continued. By morning the control car had
been picked clean. Every instrument had been stripped from it, all
the toggles ripped out, everything movable torn free. Just the naked
hull was left, and even that had been moved twenty yards from the
place where it had come to rest.

The Annapolis class ring was missing from Zachary Lansdowne's
finger.

It had taken the "Daughter of the Stars" three hours to die piece-
meal and all day to be picked bare. The resulting military scandal,
incited by Billy Mitchell, would last many months.

9

FLIGHT OF THE
"NORGE"

As Zachary Lansdowne was preparing the *Shenandoah,* in the late summer of 1925, for what was to be her last flight, plans were being completed in Europe for the first serious assault on the North Pole by air.

Earlier that spring, Roald Amundsen, discoverer of the South Pole, had attempted a flight across the Polar Sea with Lincoln Ellsworth, Leif Dietrichson, and Hjalmar Riiser-Larsen in two Dornier seaplanes. The planes had been forced to land on the ice pack and for twenty-five days were given up for lost. Airmen of many countries were in the midst of rescue expeditions when one of the Dorniers was repaired and made a remarkable take-off with all four men. As soon as the Amundsen party returned safely to Spitsbergen, the grizzled fifty-three-year-old leader, who had aged at least ten years in the first five terrible days on the ice pack, could talk of little but a second flight. This time Amundsen, having no stomach for another forced landing in a plane, insisted on an airship. Riiser-Larsen, who had taken an airship pilot's course in England, suggested that the *N-1,* an Italian semirigid dirigible built by Colonel Umberto Nobile, would be the safest and most practical type of ship for the expedition. A tentative proposal was made to Nobile. The Italian airshipman was enthusiastic. He had long been mulling over just such a trip himself. He agreed to come immediately to Norway and talk things over.

Ellsworth, a wealthy American, put up 85,000 dollars for the expedition, and the Norwegian Aero Club agreed to be sponsor. Late in June, Nobile arrived at the Amundsen home in Bundefjord, near Oslo. A small, energetic man of forty-one with deep, brooding eyes, he told Amundsen, Ellsworth, and Riiser-Larsen that Italy's dynamic Premier Benito Mussolini, was greatly interested in the trip and would donate the army airship, *N-1,* if the Italian flag were flown.

Amundsen, a strange, tormented, hypersensitive man, refused bluntly: as far as he was concerned, the expedition was strictly a

Norwegian and American venture. Nobile quickly made a new proposal. He said Mussolini would be willing to sell the ship for
75,000 dollars. The others eagerly snapped up the offer. In August
they went to Rome to sign the contract.

At this second meeting Nobile promised to pilot the ship if experienced Italian mechanics and riggers were signed on. The proposal was agreeable to Amundsen, provided his old comrade, Oskar
Wisting, one of the four men to accompany him on his successful
race to the South Pole, would man the elevators, Emil Horgen the
rudder, and Riiser-Larsen take charge of navigation.

Nobile made no objections. But when Amundsen kept insisting
that he and Ellsworth would be in absolute charge of the expedition
and make all the major decisions, the colonel became quite evidently
worried. The only non-Italian who had ever been inside an airship
and understood its peculiar limitations was Riiser-Larsen; and Nobile wanted it understood that if, in his opinion, conditions were too
bad, the ship would return from the Pole to Spitsbergen instead of
flying, as planned, on to Alaska.

"No," Amundsen snapped. "You're only a hired pilot."

Nobile decided that the flight meant more than his pride. "At any
rate," he said, "if an important decision comes up, you'll ask my advice?"

Amundsen, stony-faced, nodded.

In spite of the brief clash, the meeting between these oddly
matched partners closed on a note of friendliness and enthusiasm.
Amundsen was delighted to have not only the N-1 but also its famous designer and builder as commander. And Nobile was delighted to have as leader of the entire expedition a man considered
to be the greatest of all living explorers. The ravages of success and
time were to work strangely on this mutual admiration.

For years man had been trying to fly over the North Pole. In
1897 the Swedish engineer, Salomon Andrée, conceived the fantastic idea of free-ballooning over the Pole. With three companions he
left Smeerenberg, in north Spitsbergen, in a great balloon. Like flying saucers of a later day the balloon was "sighted" for many
months afterward all over the world—from Kansas to Russia. But no
concrete trace of the expedition was to be found until 1939.

An even more fantastic try was made ten years later by Walter
Wellman in the dirigible, *America*. Wellman, like his flamboyant
fellow journalist, Richard Harding Davis, believed in making his
own news. In a hastily constructed, 165-foot semirigid dirigible,
Wellman and his party took off from Andrée's jumping-off place,
Smeerenberg, on September 2, 1907. The trip ended dismally after

thirty-five miles. Two years later Wellman made a second attempt. Sixty miles from Spitsbergen the airship's "equilibrator," a leather monstrosity that dragged along the ice and water as a sort of guide rope, broke off. Since it contained all the emergency rations, the *America* was forced to limp back to Spitsbergen.

Even Count Zeppelin was fascinated by the North Pole. But, unlike his predecessors', his plans were thorough and sound. He formed the German Arctic Zeppelin Expedition in 1910 to investigate the possibilities of a Polar flight. Zeppelin sailed to Virgo Bay in the arctic steamer, the *Fonix*. There he ascended in balloons, made many observations, and rode for miles in a sled. After extensive research he concluded that a trip over the Pole could be made in a dirigible. But before he could put his careful plans into operation, World War I broke out.

Preparations for the Polar flight of the *N-1* were proceeding according to schedule. The Norwegian Aero Club supervised the construction of an ingenious topless hangar at King's Bay, Spitsbergen, in the constant darkness of the winter of 1925. Meanwhile Amundsen and Ellsworth organized emergency rescue plans in case the airship had to land on the pack. The Norwegian members of the crew were then sent to Rome to train with Nobile in the reconstructed *N-1*.

Compared to the *Shenandoah*, the *N-1* was a midget. It was only 348 long, with a capacity of a little less than 550,000 cubic feet. Its gas bag was divided into a number of compartments by means of transverse diaphragms. Unlike the rigid ships, this great gas bag was not enclosed in a metal frame but was covered simply by rubberized three-ply fabric. A V-shaped keel that ran along the bottom of the ship gave the *N-1* semirigidity. An ingenious system of air ballonets (similar to Santos-Dumont's) compensated for any loss of hydrogen and kept the ship from losing its shape.

Three 250-horsepower motors drove the dirigible at a top speed of 71.4 miles an hour. But for long flights only two motors were used, giving the *N-1* a cruising speed of fifty miles an hour. The motor in the rear gondola, just aft of amidships, was always in use. The other two motors, located just forward of amidships, were run alternately. The idle motor was kept warm through pipes connected with its active partner.

The control cabin, fastened directly under the forward part of the keel, was divided into several sections. Forward were the controls. As in American airships, the rudder wheel was centrally located near the front window, but the elevator wheel was on the starboard side. Over the helmsman's head were toggles for the hydrogen valves and controls that regulated the air pressure in the air ballonets.

In the rear section of the gondola was a compartment for the navigator, containing the only two chairs on the ship. In the stern on the starboard was a tiny radio room and, on the port, a lavatory. In front of the radio room, a vertical ladder led up to the open keel.

The top of the aft section of the control car was covered with a cloth roof, but the forward part was open. Without leaving his post directly under the engine telegraph system, Nobile could look up and shout orders directly to riggers on the keel.

All in all, the N-1 was a tight, carefully conceived, and exceedingly practical little ship.

But even as plans for the Amundsen-Ellsworth Expedition were going smoothly, trouble was brewing behind the scenes. It came to a head in January, 1926, when the Norwegian Aero Club sent a wire to Ellsworth in New York City asking that Nobile be given permission to write about the aeronautical aspects of the trip. Characteristically, Ellsworth wired his immediate consent. A few days later the Norwegian Minister to the United States advised him to refuse the request. A second wire was sent by Ellsworth. But the Aero Club answered:

SORRY BUT CONTRACT NOBILE SIGNED AFTER RECEIVING YOUR CABLE 16TH

Amundsen was angered when he learned of the Aero Club's action. Although Nobile had designed and built the airship, he would be its "hired" captain, and the Norwegian resented sharing any of the glory with a member of a southern nation. Italians, he declared (forgetting, presumably, the successful explorations of the Duke of the Abruzzi), weren't at all suited for polar regions.

Nobile became "so fed up with the whole mess" that it took all the persuasion of Dr. Rolf Thommessen, head of the Aero Club, to keep him from dropping out of the expedition.

On February 26 the maiden flight of the remodeled N-1 took place at Ciampino near Rome. It was the first airship ride for all the Norwegians except Riiser-Larsen, and their enthusiasm knew no bounds.

Concurrently the Cygnus left Italy with twenty-nine tons of motors and equipment and 140 tons of hydrogen cylinders. The ship reached King's Bay on March 9. As they watched the equipment unpacked, the Norwegians were amused to find that motor generators and floodlights for illumination of the hangar had been included. The Italians had forgotten that May and June would be favored by the midnight sun.

On March 26 Amundsen and Ellsworth arrived in Rome for the
ceremonies in which the *N-1* would be transferred to the Norwegians and rechristened the *Norge*. Nobile was a hospitable host, doing his best to wipe out past unpleasantness. But now Amundsen
was beset by a new aggravation: the Aero Club, in recognition of
the wholehearted cooperation of the Italians, had officially renamed
the venture the Amundsen-Ellsworth-Nobile Polar Expedition.

In an impressive affair of state on March 29 Mussolini turned over
the airship to Amundsen. None of the Norwegians could understand
what the Premier was saying, but all were impressed by his magnificent gestures and booming voice.

The formalities over, Ellsworth and Amundsen set sail for King's
Bay to make final preparations for the airship's reception. Work was
hurried on the mooring masts at Oslo and Vadso, which were to be
way stations on the rigorous trip north.

On the morning of April 7 a great crowd assembled at Ciampino
for the take-off of the *Norge*. Although an attempt on his life had
been made the day before, Mussolini was present—with a large
piece of adhesive tape on his nose. But the weather was bad and the
departure was delayed until the morning of April 10.

At five fifty on the afternoon of April 11, after a rough, exciting
trip, Nobile brought the ship down at Pulham, England. The *Norge*
was pulled into a hangar and berthed next to the *R-33*, which was
more than four times larger.

Two nights later, on April 13, the *Norge* slowly rose from the
Pulham field to the friendly farewells of British airshipmen.

"Good-by, all of you, and a good trip," shouted a veteran English
coxswain. "If any harm comes to you up there, we'll take our old
omnibus out and fetch you."

The trip over the North Sea was uneventful. As the *Norge* flew
over Norway, every town put out flags in its honor. A huge crowd
greeted the fliers at Oslo on the noon of April 14. When the *Norge*
left the next morning at one eight there was an even bigger crowd
on hand. The people sang the national anthem, "*Ja, vi elsker*," as
the airship parted from the mast.

That evening the Norwegian navigator lost his bearings, and Nobile had to swoop low over a small railroad station to read a sign. To
his surprise they were in South Finland. At 6:16 P.M. the ship
reached its destination, Gatschina, near Leningrad. It was a strange
scene coming so soon after warm Italy. The snow was deep. The
soldiers, lined up in a large V to moor them, wore high boots, coats
that nearly touched the snow, and odd helmet caps decorated with
red stars. The reception was friendly, if unusual. The airshipmen
reclined in long sledges covered with straw and were driven to a

bizarre palace, almost barren of furniture, where they were given tea and sandwiches.

For two weeks the *Norge* was tied up in Gatschina while Nobile impatiently waited for the masts at Vadso and King's Bay to be finished.

Although the relationship between the Norwegians and Italians was always friendly, the temperamental differences between the two nationalities were sometimes a strain. The Italians awoke singing joyfully and shouting to one another. The Norwegians refused to utter a word until they'd had their morning coffee. Throughout the long, idle days, the northerners were baffled by the incessant bursts of southern laughter. For their part, the Italians couldn't understand the northern jokes, even when they were translated. The Norwegians constantly poked fun at the one Swede in the crew, aerologist Finn Malmgren.

"You know the Swedes are awfully fond of anything to do with royalty," a Norwegian would say. "Do you know what a good north wind is called in Swedish then? The Royal North Blast!"

The Norwegians, and even Malmgren, would laugh until their faces grew red, while the Italians shook their heads in wonder. Then there were the Norwegians' comic nicknames for Malmgren: the Swedish Imp and Uncle Poodle. The Italians tried hard but could never appreciate the humor of these names.

At last on April 29 word came from Spitsbergen that the dirigible could leave in a few days. It was also learned that Commander Richard Byrd's expedition had arrived in King's Bay the same day. Byrd planned to fly over the Pole in his blue Fokker, the *Josephine Ford* (named after Edsel Ford's young daughter). News of another rival came from Point Barrow, Alaska: an Australian, Captain George H. Wilkins, of the Detroit Arctic Expedition, was almost ready to take off on an attempted flight over the Pole. The competition added new tension to the suppressed antagonism between the *Norge's* leaders and the natural hazards of the expedition.

At last Nobile received the go-ahead from Amundsen. On May 5 the *Norge* left Gatschina, flew over Leningrad in salute to the Russians, and, at six thirty the next morning, landed at Vadso, in northern Norway. The whole town was on hand to fete the explorers. But the elaborate celebrations had to be postponed: Nobile decided to leave for Spitsbergen the same afternoon at three o'clock.

That night the Italians got their first real taste of excitement. They saw South Cape and its snow-covered mountains; and at midnight the sun, to the Italians' delight, gave off a bright yellow light. It seemed unreal.

Although one of the three motors was disabled, the ship drew near to King's Bay the next morning. First the enormous black hangar loomed up. Then Byrd's supply ship, the *Chantier*, became visible in the bay. The Norwegians gave a shout when they recognized their own supply ship, the *Heimdal*. Finally, near the shore, the crew of the *Norge* saw their rival, the *Josephine Ford*. They didn't know it, but there was gloom in the American camp; Byrd had broken a ski on the first attempt to get off the snow a few days before. It was a clear, still morning. Smoke from the chimneys of the airship base climbed almost straight up.

On the field Major Vallini shouted orders in Italian to the motley landing crew. Next Lieutenant Hoven shouted the same orders in Norwegian. Then both men shouted at once. The crew, confused, did nothing.

The stubby ship flew in circles around the field while the crew was being organized. Finally a mooring line was dropped from the nose. The ship was hauled to the ground at 6:40 A.M. while the band from the *Heimdal* played the Norwegian, American, and Italian national anthems. Then, in honor of Uncle Poodle, there was a chorus of the Swedish anthem.

Apothecary Fritz Zapffe recognized his old friend, Emil Horgen, in the descending control car. "Morgen, Horgen!" he shouted.

"Good day, Zapffe," Horgen called. "Shall we soon skaffe [eat]?"

The Norwegians laughed loudly, but this exchange of puns puzzled the Italians. A moment later the Norwegians were puzzled as the Italians greeted their compatriots on the ground with great shouts, hugs, and kisses.

Nobile told Amundsen that a new motor had to be installed, and it would take about three days to ready the *Norge* for the flight over the Pole. The Italian mechanics toiled far into the night, and American mechanics at an adjoining field continued their work to repair the *Josephine Ford*.

Early on the morning of May 8 the cold, silent air was suddenly blasted by the roar of motors. The Italians and Norwegians jumped out of bed and ran to their windows. Most of them caught a glimpse of the *Josephine Ford* as slowly, heavily, she lifted off the snow and headed north, straight into the midnight sun.

Now that Byrd had beaten them to the start, Amundsen and Nobile were as anxious as the Americans for the *Josephine Ford* to reach the Pole and return safely. There was a natural solidarity among Polar explorers that transcended their bitter rivalries; and if Byrd were to have an accident, the *Norge* would instantly and automatically go to the rescue—even though this would probably mean cancellation of their own flight to Alaska.

There was nervousness at King's Bay all that day. Americans clustered around the radio on the *Chantier*. Ashore, Italians and Norwegians worked on the *Norge*, stopping every few minutes to listen for a faraway drone.

At five in the afternoon Amundsen, Ellsworth, and Nobile were sitting down to dinner when an Italian burst into their hut.

"I can hear a motor!" he shouted.

Everyone ran outdoors, many without hats or coats. Far to the north a speck became larger. Amundsen plunged across the wide stretch of deep snow that separated the two airfields. The others followed him. The American base was a wild scene as the blue plane skimmed in for a landing. Mechanics and reporters swarmed onto the field, and Byrd's pilot, Floyd Bennett, had to circle the field until it was partially cleared. Soon the skis of the *Josephine Ford* lightly touched down at almost the same spot they had left nineteen hours before. Ellsworth and Amundsen pulled the Americans from their plane, and the *Heimdal's* band played "The Star-Spangled Banner."

Then, to the surprise of those who considered Amundsen a cold, reserved man, the Norwegian explorer embraced Byrd and kissed him on both cheeks.

Two days later final repairs on the *Norge* were finished. Now all that was needed was calm, moderately clear weather. Late in the afternoon it was learned that a great high-pressure area was building up over the Pole. This promised cold weather, clear skies, and slight winds. Even though Point Barrow on the northern coast of Alaska reported fog, Malmgren recommended leaving. The three leaders agreed that they should start with the hope that the fog would clear before the *Norge* reached Alaska. The take-off time was set for ten that night.

But when local winds sprang up, most of the men were sent to bed. Nobile and Malmgren started the long night watch. Twice the wind slackened, and messengers were sent to rouse the sleepers. But each time the wind increased in fury. At last at 6:00 A.M. the wind quieted. Everyone was awakened. With the exception of Ellsworth and Nobile, who wore reindeer and bearskin suits that gave more freedom, everyone climbed into specially designed fur-lined clothing. Rations of pemmican, chocolate, and biscuits for fifty days were stowed in the keel. In addition every man carried a little basket of hard-boiled eggs and sandwiches. Hot coffee was poured into forty thermos bottles. One huge thermos container held many quarts of bouillon and meat balls.

At a little after eight the wind sprang up again. Nobile was uneasy about bringing the airship out of the hangar, for there was only about a yard's leeway on each side of the ship. But Amundsen insisted on an immediate start; and at eight thirty on May 11, during a lull, the ship slowly glided out of its unique roofless hangar and was led safely onto the field.

King's Bay was beautiful in the yellow light of the seasonal sun. Snow-covered mountains surrounded the long arm of sea, enclosing it in a kind of amphitheater of snow and ice. So brilliant was the sun that the hydrogen inside the ship expanded, and some had to be valved. This meant that only sixteen men could make the trip. Three would have to stay behind.

Gustav Amundsen, the leader's nephew, was one of the three. He went up to say good-by to Nobile.

Knowing how disappointed the young man was, the Italian did not shake hands. "Wait a little," he said hopefully. "Perhaps—perhaps."

Young Amundsen, his hopes revived, ran back to the hangar to get his knapsack. A few minutes later, skis over his shoulders, he saw the *Norge* slowly rise. He felt lonely and forsaken.

Those on the ground were worried as the airship gracefully headed north. But those on board felt only joy and relief. At last, after months of preparation, they were off.

Suddenly there was a roar and the *Josephine Ford* whizzed past the *Norge*. Byrd waved in greeting. For an hour the blue Fokker hovered around the plodding airship. Then came a final wave from Byrd and the *Josephine Ford* turned back toward King's Bay. The *Norge* held on its northern course.

The sky was pure turquoise. The shadow of the ship ran over the broken ice below, startling three white whales, which darted under the shelf of a floe. Polar bears, frightened by the strange monster in the air, dove from ice cakes, sending up columns of spray. At ten thirty the ice edge was passed. A thousand feet below lay the snow-covered ice field of the Polar Sea. Glittering in the sunlight, it was inspiring yet terrifying in its immensity.

Stolid Emil Horgen, sitting on the large container of bouillon and meat balls, was at the rudder wheel. To his right, at the elevators, stood Oskar Wisting, leather-faced, imperturbable. Nobile looked over Horgen's shoulder. Unlike the other Italians, Nobile said little and rarely smiled, but he was always on the alert, giving the Norwegians a sense of security. Curled at his feet was his constant companion, the little terrier Titina.

Now that the voyage was under way, the months of bickering and petty jealousies were over. The crowded cabin was a scene of peace and competence. Even the walls of the gondola reflected the general equanimity: side by side hung pictures of the King and Queen of Norway, Mussolini, a snapshot of Nobile's young daughter Maria, an image of the Madonna, and a four-leaf clover donated by the English airshipman, Major Scott.

Meanwhile the newsmen at King's Bay, bored by the serenity of the take-off, were concocting stories of bitter fights in the control car.

Now Renato Alessandrini, the head rigger, was clambering all over the ship looking for trouble spots. He examined the keel. He climbed the narrow passageway up to the very top of the airship so that he could inspect the gas valves. When he took a full step aft, his foot sank into the yielding gas bag. Instantly the rubberized material began to ripple and roll. Alessandrini quickly took two short steps. The rolling motion broke down as nonchalantly the rigger walked over the top of the *Norge* like a circus performer on a trampoline.

Oskar Omdal, who had helped Amundsen find the North East Passage, was in the starboard gondola with Ettore Arduino, a fair-haired, blue-eyed man who looked more Nordic than some of the Norwegians. The ship's greatest comic, Attilio Caratti, held down the port gondola. And in the stern engine room was Vincenzo Pomella, fair-haired, quiet, and gentle. The chief mechanic, Natale Cecioni, went from gondola to gondola. A huge, heavy-set man of thirty-nine with gray hair, he seemed like a father to the others. And his advice had a paternal effect—calming when it did not command.

In all there were sixteen men and one dog aboard. Riiser-Larsen was almost constantly at his navigation desk, assisted by Ellsworth, who was glad to do the most menial jobs aboard. In the radio room were Birger Gottwaldt and Storm-Johnsen. In the navigation chair the Norwegian journalist Ramm was scribbling dispatches for the operators to relay to King's Bay. Weatherman Malmgren stood at Ramm's side, studying the fog that was beginning to close in threateningly.

The sixteenth man was Amundsen. He sat alone on an aluminum water tank, his sunken eyes fixed on the ice pack as it slowly disappeared in a swirl of fog. He was thinking, "I wonder what I shall see next."

At ten thirty the little *Norge* was enveloped in dense fog. Ice began to form on all the metal parts of the ship. The celluloid windows of the control car were encrusted in rime ice like thick wool. Nobile ordered Wisting to bring the ship up to 2130 feet. There was no improvement. Nobile called for more altitude. At 3160 feet the ship stuck its nose out of the fog bank. The temperature had now sunk to 12 degrees below zero.

Suddenly a shout came from the radio room. Storm-Johnsen and

Gottwaldt came forward. Beaming happily Gottwaldt held a radiogram in his hand. The King of Norway had just decorated him with
a Gold Service Medal. Everyone shouted congratulations.

Soon latitude 87 degrees, 43 minutes, was reached. Amundsen
peered down at the ice hummocks. A year ago he had spent twenty-
five days at this spot. He grimaced. "Not this time, dear friend, not
this time," he said to himself. Ellsworth caught his eye and the two
men smiled. They were both happy to be in a safe dirigible this
trip.

At 6:00 P.M. the port motor coughed and stopped. Caratti heaped
insults on his engine. He discovered that water had got into one of
the pipes and had frozen, stopping the gas supply. The starboard
engine, idle till now, burst into action and the ship went on without
losing its momentum. At 7:55 P.M., after almost two hours of explosive tirades, Caratti again had his motor in operation. Omdal then
shut down his.

Soon it began clouding. By eleven twenty-five the fog was a thick
wall ahead. Since the ship was only 100 miles from the Pole, the
two regular compasses were behaving erratically. The *Norge* was
sent up to 3000 feet so that Horgen could steer by sun compass, a
device that caught the midnight sun in a periscope and cast its reflection on a glass plate marked with a calibrated wire cross.

It was Riiser-Larsen's job to see that the axis of the periscope was
always parallel with the axis of the earth. Once, while engrossed in
other duties, he forgot the sun compass, and Horgen unwittingly
steered the *Norge* in a complete circle.

At midnight there was a second celebration. It was Ellsworth's
forty-sixth birthday. Except for the mechanics on duty, everyone
crowded into the control car. Nobile brought out a flask of eggnog.
Every man took a swig and shook hands with Ellsworth.

"It isn't often," said Amundsen, his arm over the younger man's
shoulder, "that you can fly over the North Pole on your birthday."

As the ship neared the Pole, the excitement mounted. At 1:00
A.M. the sky, to everyone's relief, began to clear. It would have been
a bitter disappointment to fly over the roof of the world without
seeing it.

At 1:15 A.M. Riiser-Larsen, bulky as a bear in his suit, knelt on the
floor near a starboard window. He was squinting at his sextant, which
had been set at the height and declination the sun should have at
the Pole at the date. The reflection of the sun and the bubble of the
artificial horizon drew closer and closer.

"Ready with the flags!" he called.

Amundsen opened a window and stuck out the Norwegian flag.
Its staff was weighted and pointed at the end so that it would stick

in the ice. Ellsworth was ready with the American flag sent him by President Coolidge. Nobile called up to Alessandrini on the keel to get the Italian flag.

"Hurry up, Alessandrini!" he shouted. When the rigger finally arrived with the flag, it was hastily fastened to a spear.

Riiser-Larsen grew tense. "Now we are there!" he cried suddenly. It was exactly one thirty on the morning of May 12, 1926. Amundsen flung out his flag. The men watched it spin down to the sunbathed Polar basin. Now, through the hazy atmosphere, they could see that the ice below was broken up in a mass of small floes. The end of the flagpole stuck in the ice. Amundsen, his throat choked with emotion, turned. He clasped Wisting's calloused hand. Neither spoke. Both were thinking that not quite fifteen years before they had planted a similar flag at the South Pole.

Nobile ordered the motors slowed down. Horgen steered the ship in a circle. Next, the American flag went over the side. A moment later Nobile excitedly tossed the Italian flag overboard. It glided, caught in the drift gauges, and finally fell.

The men all shook hands. It was a moment of unqualified triumph for everyone.

Now began the hardest and most important part of the expedition —to navigate the unexplored territory that lay between the Pole and Point Barrow, Alaska. Peary had thought he had seen mountains beyond the Pole. It was Amundsen's dream to find out if there actually was land in that bleak area.

"You're forty-five again," someone told Ellsworth jokingly. Since the time at Point Barrow was about eleven hours later than King's Bay time, as soon as the Pole was crossed the morning of May 12 had become the afternoon of May 11. And every direction was south.

"Your birthday lasted only an hour and a half," said Amundsen sympathetically.

"Yes," Ellsworth said. "But I'll have another one in a few hours."

The men in the control car crouched down for the only hot meal of the trip. Horgen was ousted from his thermos jug seat; mugs were filled with meat balls and hot grease. The sandwiches, by now, were stiff and the tea and coffee ice cold.

For hours they floated over the monotonous glittering ice, rifted by wind and tide into cracks and occasional leads of open water. Then the ice became a solid, formidable mass.

"We are at the Ice Pole," announced Riiser-Larsen. Again everyone shook hands. The center of the Polar ice mass was the least accessible spot in the world.

Fog drifted in from the east. Riiser-Larson was the only one who welcomed it, for it gave him a chance to sit down for the first time since leaving King's Bay. He napped for half an hour while the ship plowed ahead. Now the sluggish English aperiodic compass, which reacted so slowly it seemed stuck, was being used alternately with the quixotic German Ludolph compass, which oscillated wildly at the slightest provocation.

At five nineteen that evening an excited cry rang out. In the west a mountain ridge reared up out of the fog. Amundsen, his heart beating wildly, rushed to a window. Peary was right! There *was* land in the "empty" Polar Sea! Nobile ordered the ship steered toward the mountain. The suspense was greater now than during their approach to the Pole.

Then Amundsen began to laugh, almost to himself. "It's just a Cape Fly-away!" he said. Even as he spoke the mirage mountain dissolved into nothingness. The men were familiar with the phenomenon, but they felt the disappointment keenly.

At five thirty they were back on course, skimming over billows of fog. Then the fog rose. So did the ship. But then the cloud roof above them began to drop. Soon the two banks met, surrounding the ship completely. Since they were already at 3500 feet, Nobile couldn't go higher without valving precious hydrogen. After a conference with Riiser-Larsen, Nobile decided to go down to see if the fog reached the ice. The dirigible sank slowly, so that the air ballonets could be filled to compensate for the contracting gas bag.

Ice began to form on the ship. Malmgren was called into the conference. It was decided to go up again. The situation was becoming grave. The sun compass, which was mounted on an outrigger, was frozen to a solid block of ice. The guy wires were covered with an inch of ice. As these wires quivered, ice broke off, and some of it was falling into the propellers. Then, like small projectiles, the ice would be driven through the canvas into the keel, often making holes in the ballonets. Each time an ice "bullet" pierced the canvas it sounded like a gunshot. Then Cecioni would propel his bulk into action, quickly mending the holes with rubber patches.

For hours the fog had prevented speed or drift measurements. Soon after the ship had passed the Ice Pole, the ship's aerial was encased in thick ice and the radio had gone dead. Riiser-Larsen was navigating on instinct alone.

Now icicles hung from all the projections of the gondolas and along the radiators and gangways. Even the propellers were ice-coated. Everyone remembered the prophecies of experts that the *Norge* would eventually be forced down by the weight of ice and snow.

The tension grew as ice continued to fly into the keel, narrowly missing the gas bag itself. Occasionally a patch of the ice-pack appeared underneath but never long enough for Riiser-Larsen to take an observation. No sign of life was seen—no birds, not a seal or walrus or polar bear.

Early in the morning of May 13, the fog began breaking up. At three twenty the sun shone through long enough for a reading. It was found that Riiser-Larsen was almost on course. He calculated that land should be sighted between six and eight.

At six thirty the navigator noticed some dark spots off the port bow. He blinked his eyes, afraid he was seeing another "Cape Flyaway." To avoid setting the men up for another bitter disappointment, he said nothing. In fifteen minutes Riiser-Larsen had no doubts.

"Land ahead on the port bow!" he cried.

The men—in the air for almost two days—forgot their exhaustion and the numbing cold. The good word ran from gondola to gondola. Soon little gravel pits appeared ahead. At 7:25 A.M., forty-six hours and twenty minutes after leaving King's Bay, the *Norge* crossed land a few miles from Point Barrow. Beyond the gravel pits lay snow-covered flatland, stretching out as far as they could see.

Once again Nobile passed around the flask of eggnog. To Riiser-Larsen it felt like fire going through his body. Then Nobile, overwhelmed with joy, leaned far out of a cabin window. His face tingled in the cold wind.

The helmsman followed the Alaskan coast for an hour. Suddenly Amundsen cried out, "Look!"

Below an Eskimo was dancing on the ice, waving his arms. His dogs were howling in terror.

A few minutes later a group of shacks appeared, then a reindeer training field and a small house with a red roof.

"It's Wainwright!" shouted Amundsen, leaning forward. He pointed at a house that grew larger. It was Maudheim, built by Amundsen and his home for two years. People stood on the roof of Maudheim and waved at the explorers.

Instead of landing, the *Norge* continued its voyage. In spite of fatigue, every crew member wanted to push on to Nome, the announced goal. Several hours later they began to regret their enthusiasm. A violent gale came up from the north and blew the ship sideways in and out of massive clouds of fog. The ship, its flexible keel bending in the wind, was driven almost to the Siberian coast. Then, falteringly, the *Norge* fought its way back across the rough, foaming waters of the Bering Strait.

Fog closed in.

At last, an hour later, a slight opening appeared below. The ship sank tentatively. The rugged, mountainous coast of Alaska jutted up at them. Nobile ordered Horgen to follow a narrow mountain ravine southward. Jagged hills, reaching above the fog, were on both sides of them. A gale-force wind began to blow across the ravine, rolling the little ship sickeningly. The windows fogged up. Titina, Nobile's terrier, began to move restlessly in the cabin. Nobile, taking the elevator wheel from Wisting, told Riiser-Larsen to lean out the window and shout if they came to a rise. The ship moved slowly through the blinding white billows. Everyone in the control cabin peered ahead, straining his eyes to see the danger before it was too late.

Riiser-Larsen suddenly shouted back a warning. Nobile jerked the wheel to the right and the nose of the *Norge* shot into the air. The black wall that had leaped in front of them dropped away.

"Did it knock off the rear gondola?" asked Nobile, his face pale. A moment later the message came forward that Pomella was safe. His gondola had dropped so low he felt he could have touched the hilltop.

Now, high in the fog again, they were lost again. Nobile lowered the ship carefully until the ravine could be seen, then resumed the perilous job of threading a trail through the hills. Riiser-Larsen again leaned out the window. A second time his alert warning saved the ship. By four in the afternoon they all agreed it was suicide to continue at that altitude.

Nobile decided to climb above the fog so Riiser-Larsen could take a reading of the sun. The engines were slowed down and the ship rose quietly. At last, above the 3000-foot mark, the ship came into sunlight. But the sun was so high that no observation could be taken from the control cabin: from every angle the gondola was in the shade. A reading would have to be taken from the top of the ship. The navigator climbed up the steep bow ladder onto the top of the pitching dirigible.

At last Riiser-Larsen finished the reading and started down the ladder. But the gas bag, exposed to the sun's rays for a long time, began to swell dangerously. The hydrogen had expanded so rapidly that Nobile couldn't control it by opening the gas valves. Titina, silent until this moment, skittered back and forth in the gondola, howling and whining.

Since the ship was cruising at low speed, it was impossible to drive her down. Nobile, watching the hydrogen gauges shoot up, knew he had to act quickly.

"Run fast to the bow!" he shouted in English to the Norwegians in the control car. They looked at him quizzically. "Run to the bow!" he cried, gesturing. Three Norwegians finally understood and scrambled up to the keel. They ran to the bow, tipping the nose down.

By this time all three motors were at full speed, and the ship nosed even further down. Nobile watched the hydrogen gauge waver at the danger point and then drop. In a minute pressure was back to normal. For the time being, the danger was over.

Hours passed. There was no coffee or tea. The sandwiches were frozen to the consistency of wood. The meat balls were frozen into ice crystals. Amundsen, no stranger to tedium, told humorous stories to shorten the hours. He gave everyone the feeling that if the worst happened and they were forced to the ice, he would take over and lead them to safety.

At one thirty in the morning radio signals from Nome could be heard distinctly. Gottwaldt tried to reach the station but got no response.

A few minutes later a winding river could be seen through the fog.

"It's the Serpentine!" cried Amundsen.

Now there was no further need for navigation: it was necessary only to fly low and follow the coast. Riiser-Larsen took over the watch from Nobile, who hadn't been relieved for sixteen hours. The exhausted commander slumped into their only armchair to get a few minutes sleep before tackling the tricky landing maneuvers.

As they drew near mountains to the leeward, the balky port motor sputtered. The ship began to drift toward a crag. Riiser-Larsen ordered the idle starboard motor started up, so the *Norge* wouldn't have to risk rising into the fog. But there was no response on the annunciators. Riiser-Larsen quickly signaled the aft gondola for full speed. His order was executed, and the ship moved safely ahead.

There had been nothing wrong with the starboard engine. Cecioni heard the bell and saw the indicator on the big disc move. But he was so weary that he couldn't grasp the meaning of the signal. The efficiency of the whole crew was impaired by dulled reflexes and diminished powers of concentration.

At 4:30 A.M. a tiny dot was spotted. Amundsen thought it was Sledge Island. Nobile was awakened.

"We're near," Riiser-Larsen told him. "In half an hour we should be over Nome!"

Nobile leaned out a window to refresh himself. The sea was somber, rough, foamy. The skies were an ashy gray, striped with black clouds. Every few minutes a snow squall would cloud the windows. The ship was constantly buffeted by furious gusts of wind.

"Prepare landing ropes!" called Nobile to Alessandrini on the keel above.

Riiser-Larsen began writing out directions for the landing party, and the men off duty went to work folding up the sleeping bags on the keel. Wisting, his eyes red from fatigue, was at the rudder wheel. Amundsen, his old comrade, stood next to him. Together they tried to pick out familiar landmarks. A cluster of shacks appeared on the snow. Then they spied an abandoned three-masted steamer lying on her side in the middle of the ice.

Now the wind began blowing so hard that the *Norge* was brought to a standstill. Nobile ordered all three motors speeded to 1200 revolutions. Still the ship made little progress against the gale. It was obvious that an even greater storm was building up. The sky had become black, and the *Norge*, tilted at an angle of 30 degrees, was pitching heavily.

Amundsen and Wisting shook their heads. They didn't recognize the little community, and no one knew where Nome lay from the village. The three leaders had a quick discussion.

Everyone agreed that the men had reached the end of their endurance, that it would be insane to fly on with a great storm threatening to strike, that an immediate landing should be attempted even though the ship was bouncing crazily in the wind.

Riiser-Larsen feared that they were in for a crash landing. He suggested that the panels of the control cabin be kicked out. It was a trick of the British, he explained.

Nobile objected heatedly. Amundsen sided with Riiser-Larsen. But Nobile refused to be panicked. He headed the ship down.

"Look!" cried Riiser-Larsen to Amundsen as the ground loomed into detail. "There's plenty of help! I see a lot of cavalry down on the shore."

Smiling, Amundsen shook his head. The "cavalry" was merely irregular brown stripes in the coastal sand.

A mooring line was dropped. Eskimos and traders rushed from the village to grab it. One Eskimo boy thought the ship was a giant flying seal. He called to his father, told him to take his gun and shoot the animal.

Riiser-Larsen leaned out a window and shouted directions in Norwegian.

"You must speak English here," said Amundsen in amusement. The navigator had not oriented to their arrival on the other side of the world.

Abruptly the gusts of wind stopped. During this momentary lull the *Norge* approached the ice with cautious haste. The big air fender under the main gondola touched ground, and the ship bounced a yard in the air. Then, at exactly seven thirty on the morning of May 14, she settled serenely. It was a perfect landing.

The men staggered out onto the ice. Their legs were wobbly, their eyes glazed. Amundsen went up to Nobile, who was ordering the crew to deflate the gas bag quickly, before the strong wind started up again. The great Norwegian explorer thanked Nobile warmly for bringing them safely through the long storm.

Ellsworth wrung the Italian's hand gratefully. "My house in New York is yours!" he cried. "My villa at Florence is yours!"

At that moment no one thought of personal glory or national pride; to a man they were simply relieved—relieved that the intolerable tension was at last over. The Norwegians went into the village, led by the impassive natives.

Now the *Norge* was shrinking fast. The control car was dragged under the retreating folds. Then the engine gondolas disappeared under the empty rubber envelope.

Now only Alessandrini and Nobile stood watching their beloved airship. The two men looked at each other. At this moment of great triumph, they both had a strange feeling of sadness.

10

THE "ITALIA"

Word was flashed to a world that believed them lost that all sixteen on the *Norge* had reached Teller, Alaska—a tiny Eskimo village of fifty-five. There was international rejoicing.

The flight across the top of the world was immediately recognized as one of the most daring and important adventures in history. Many thousands of square miles of iceland had been explored for the first time. And it was finally learned that no great land mass lay between the Pole and Alaska. Peary had seen another "Cape Fly-away."

Soon after landing at Teller, Amundsen and Ellsworth left by dog sled for the fifty-five-mile trip to Nome. Nobile and most of the crew remained to dismantle the *Norge*.

Already the dormant bitterness between Nobile and Amundsen— forgotten during the long, dangerous flight—had come to the surface again. It was intensified when only half a dozen people turned out to welcome the Amundsen party to Nome. And the streets were all but deserted as the Norwegian, who had expected a wild welcome, passed through. A friend told him that everyone had been very disappointed because the airship hadn't landed at Nome.

The quarrel broke out in earnest when dispatches from Nobile began to come out of Teller. Mussolini didn't ease the situation. Il Duce's Fascist press made the trip appear to be almost entirely an Italian triumph.

Amundsen angrily asked the Norwegian Aero Club to restrain Nobile from further writing about the flight. Dr. Thommessen tried to explain the situation in a radiogram to Ellsworth.

CONTRACT WITH NOBILE, SIGNED IN PRESENCE OF RIISER-LARSEN AS REPRESENTATIVE YOU AND AMUNDSEN HAS FOLLOWING ARTICLE QUOTE—IT IS UNDERSTOOD THAT NOBILE WILL COMPILE THE TECHNICAL AND AERONAUTICAL PART OF THE WORK UNQUOTE

At that moment Amundsen's hatred became large enough to divide between the Aero Club leaders and Nobile.

When the Italian party finally arrived in Nome the entire population showed up and staged just the exuberant celebration Amundsen had expected for himself. The local Catholic priest was held responsible by Amundsen for the well-planned affair. For the first time, but by no means the last, the ugly issue of religion was produced and put into circulation.

On June 27 the steamship *Victoria* landed at Seattle with the sixteen explorers. To Amundsen's indignation and disgust, Nobile and one of his officers appeared on deck in uniforms, complete with decorations. It was Nobile who had constantly harped on the value of weight, and Amundsen was incensed that extra uniforms had been carried on the *Norge*. And as the three leaders of the expedition stepped onto the dock, a little girl ran forward with a bouquet of flowers and gave them—not to the grim-faced Amundsen but to the man in the uniform, Nobile.

Dozens of other petty differences cropped up in the next few days. These were climaxed when Nobile, accompanied by Titina, started a lecture tour of the United States. Amundsen was furious because he felt that the Italian was taking the edge off the tour he himself had planned. Ellsworth, who said ill of no one, tried in vain to act as peacemaker. He was a tortured man for, although he admired Nobile, he had a deeper affection for the sensitive Norwegian explorer.

Newspapers and magazines reported each passage-at-arms, blowing them far out of proportion. Amundsen made many insinuating remarks to reporters, but Nobile tried to ignore the attacks. The first authorized story of the expedition, written mainly by Amundsen and Ellsworth, appeared in the New York *Times* and later in the book, *The First Flight Across the Polar Sea*. Although Nobile's part in the voyage was greatly minimized, the authors did declare that for commander of the airship, "a better selection could scarcely have been made."

Nobile also wrote a long account of the trip in the *National Geographic*. In it Amundsen's contributions to the expedition were politely minimized. This article was evidently too much for Amundsen's Nordic pride. Soon two long, violent articles by the Norwegian appeared in *World's Work*, accusing Nobile of everything from incompetency to cowardice. Amundsen declared that Nobile had only been a paid chauffeur—and a poor one at that. Twice Riiser-Larsen had saved the ship from crashing in the fog by grabbing the elevator wheel from the "stupefied" Nobile. And once the navigator had had to shout a "rough command of warning to Nobile to change our elevation."

When the ship rose unexpectedly and the gas bag threatened to explode, continued Amundsen, "Nobile made a frantic effort to get the nose of the *Norge* pointed downward. The ship did not respond to the rudder. Then Nobile lost his head completely, with tears streaming down his face and wringing his hands, he stood screaming, 'Run fast to the bow! Run fast to the bow!' Three of our Norwegians dashed forward on the runway under the bag and by their weight forced the *Norge's* nose downward."

Nobile was too hurt and angry to make a judicious answer to these highly colored charges. He replied in a succeeding issue of *World's Work* that Amundsen had just come along for the ride; that he had merely sat in an armchair and enjoyed the scenery. It was, said Nobile, "A pleasure trip, more or less, for Amundsen."

The Italian, now a general, did not bother to explain that his "resplendent uniform" at Seattle was the same one he wore under his reindeer flying suit; or that Riiser-Larsen's "rough command" to change elevation had come when the navigator, his head out the window, was acting expressly as guide. He merely wrote, "This story is cause for laughter to those who know that no Norwegian on board was skilled in handling dirigibles."

When Nobile announced that he was going on a second Polar trip, Amundsen and many Norwegians, who felt the northland was the exclusive purlieu of the Nordics, sarcastically predicted that the affair would be a great fiasco ending in disaster.

The idea for the expedition had come to Nobile while in Teller. As soon as a safe landing was made, every crew member had enthusiastically offered to go on another trip with Amundsen. But the Norwegian, worn out by his many rigorous expeditions, shook his head. "Another generation," he said with a heavy sigh, "can now take a hand."

But Nobile was still obsessed by the north. He asked Riiser-Larsen if he would come on a Polar flight in a new airship, already being built in Italy, which was much larger than the *Norge* and could fly from Spitsbergen to Tokyo. They would call it the Nobile-Riiser-Larsen Expedition. But the feud between the two leaders had already come into the open; and Riiser-Larsen, faithful to his hero, coolly declined to join forces with the Italian.

A little later in Nome, Nobile asked Oskar Wisting if he'd join the new expedition. The old Norwegian consented readily, and Finn Malmgren was also eager for a second Polar flight. But Mussolini had other ideas. He ordered Nobile, instead, to start building an airship three times as big as the *Norge* for a nonstop flight to Buenos Aires.

A few months later high Fascist officials in the Air Ministry, jealous of the adulation Nobile was receiving from the people, per-

suaded Il Duce to abandon the ambitious South American project.
Then work was ordered stopped on the big airship Nobile had
planned to take to the Pole. The general's enemies were now confident he had been forced into oblivion.

But Nobile was not to be discouraged this easily. Rather than give
up the second Polar trip, he began work on a small dirigible similar to the *Norge*. Plans were considerably progressed when Dr.
Thommessen, president of the Norwegian Aero Club, came to Italy
in August, 1926. In spite of the tempestuous battle still going on
between Amundsen and Nobile, the Norwegian official maintained
that Nobile was being maligned. He agreed to let the Italian use the
Aero Club's roofless hangar at King's Bay.

Nobile laid out an ambitious scientific and geographic research
program for the new expedition. He wanted to explore the mysterious Nicholas II Land and the coasts of Greenland and Canada, and
make an actual descent at the North Pole for oceanographic observations. Now all he needed was approval of the project from
Mussolini.

In May of 1927 aviation was given fresh impetus by a dramatic
solo flight from New York to Paris. As young Charles Lindbergh was
winging over the Atlantic, a huge, rowdy fight crowd at Yankee
Stadium stood for a moment in silent prayer. The world was soon
enchanted by the young man's simple charm. Once again everyone
became air-conscious. Preparations for a dozen exciting plane and
dirigible flights were set in motion. It was obvious that the spring
of 1928 would be the most thrilling and productive in the history of aviation.

Several months after Lindbergh's flight Mussolini, eager for more
Italian air exploits, finally gave his consent to the new Polar trip.
The dictator promised to provide a ship and crew if the Italian
Royal Geographic Society would sponsor the event and the city
of Milan pay the expenses. Since Nobile was one of Italy's greatest
popular heroes, these arrangements were soon made.

The new ship proved, with its modifications, to be superior to the
Norge. The control car was larger and more comfortable. The envelope was made of lighter material and reinforced with heavy
rubberized fabric at the bottom as protection from splinters of
ice. The keel was reinforced with two extra layers of cloth to protect the ballonets and gas bag from the ice "bullets." Observation
cupolas were fixed to the windows; thus the navigator could take
readings and adjust the sun compass without letting in gusts of icy
air. The radio antenna was redesigned to be pulled more easily into
the car when it became covered with ice.

Nobile worked out an ingenious device for descent on the Arctic

Ocean. A chain of bronze balls, threaded on a steel cable, could be dropped onto ice or water, acting as a brake. Then two men were to be lowered in a pneumatic basket. The ship's instruments were also improved. Now four compasses, more suitable for Polar use, were installed.

Since the altimeter had been very erratic on the previous trip, with barometric pressure readings usually unavailable, Nobile devised a simple but effective altimeter. Glass balls were made and filled with a red liquid. When they hit the snow the balls would break, making a red mark. The time of fall indicated the altitude. Three seconds, for example, meant the ship was 187 feet above the ground.

With all of these improvements, the ship was 2866 pounds lighter than the *Norge*, which gave it a greater cruising range.

Nobile took many months to pick his crew. To avoid offending Amundsen, Wisting had withdrawn. But Malmgren volunteered eagerly, and with him five other veterans of the *Norge*: engineers Cecioni and Arduino, mechanics Caratti and Pomella, and Rigger Alessandrini.

Calisto Ciocca, a veteran workman who had helped prepare the *Norge* at King's Bay, was chosen as the third mechanic. Felice Trojani, the general's work assistant for twelve years, was signed on to help Cecioni at the elevators.

From a large group of volunteers two young radio operators were chosen: Ettore Pedretti, blond, blue-eyed, and slender; and Giuseppe Biagi, short, dark, and rugged. Biagi was to become the most famous radio operator of the day.

Three naval officers, highly recommended by the Air Ministry, were assigned to Nobile as navigators and aerologists. Nobile instantly took a liking to Lieutenant Commander Alfredo Viglieri, a tall man of dignified composure. The other two, Commanders Adalberto Mariano and Filippo Zappi, had excellent records as airshipmen; and since they were far superior to the other applicants, Nobile chose them. He was to regret it bitterly.

In addition to Malmgren, two other well-known scientists were selected: Dr. Aldo Pontremoli, of the University of Milan, and Dr. Francis Behounek of the Wireless Institute of Prague, who had been at King's Bay when the *Norge* took off. Behounek was a big, stout young man with the rosy face of a schoolboy.

Two newspapermen rounded out the ship's complement: Francesco Tomaselli of Venice and Ugo Lago of Syracuse.

The expedition was planned in meticulous detail, with great foresight and patience. Nobile conferred with Nansen and Otto Sverdrup for survival items. The keel of the new ship would be loaded with two sledges, snowshoes, skis, a Vickers rifle, two Norwegian seal-hunters' rifles, three Colt revolvers, and even mosquito netting in case they were forced down in the Mackenzie section.

For food a special pemmican mixture that appealed to the Italian palate was prepared under Norwegian supervision. It consisted of pulverized meat and fat, peas, oatmeal, potatoes, onions, and celery. Chocolate, malted milk, and biscuits were also on the menu.

The same care went into the clothing. As an undergarment the men were to wear a three-piece outfit of tunic, trousers, and hood. The outside garment was a buttonless lambs' wool suit that weighed less than eight pounds. Its fur was turned inside and the skin covered with a thick wind-and-rainproof material. In addition to reindeer skin shoes and *finsko* (Russian felt boots), every man was provided with reindeer leather shoes, heavy hiking boots, and several pairs of catskin socks.

On March 19, 1928, the *City of Milan*, under Captain Romagna, left Spezia for King's Bay with extra engines and supplies. On the same day the airship, now named the *Italia*, was transferred from Rome to its sponsor city, Milan. A week later the sturdy Norwegian whaler, *Hobby*, left Tromso for Spitsbergen, bringing canvas for the hangar and 300 tons of matériel for refueling and repairing the *Italia* should the *City of Milan* arrive too late. On board were Amadeo Nobile, the leader's young brother, who was to be in charge of the weather station, other Italian experts, and ten Norwegians. Special ground crews soon arrived at the way stations on the *Italia's* long northern trip—Stolp, Germany, and Vadso, Norway.

The whole operation was working smoothly, in spite of veiled ridicule from newsmen who disliked anything connected with fascism on general principles. On March 31 the crew of the *Italia* was received by Pope Pius XI, an ardent mountaineer, who understood the danger of ice and snow. He had followed with keen interest all details of the expedition's preparations.

The Pope himself had prepared a six-foot oak cross, and he presented it to Nobile to be dropped on the North Pole. "Like all crosses," he said with a smile, "this one will be heavy to carry."

A few days later Nobile had a farewell audience with the King, who had twice visited the Arctic with the Queen on hunting trips. On April 11 the general was received by Il Duce. Nobile explained the ambitious plans and told of the careful preparations.

"Good!" said Mussolini, jutting out his lower lip. "You have foreseen everything. That's the best way to succeed. To provide for everything—one hundred per cent. That's my system too!"

The two men parted with the warmest words of good will.

At 1:55 A.M. on April 15, despite discouraging weather conditions, the *Italia* left Milan with twenty aboard. "We'll have some excitement," promised Malmgren, "but we can't hope for anything better during the next few days."

There was more excitement than Malmgren had bargained for. For thirty and a half hours the sturdy ship plowed through rain, fog, hail, lightning, ice, and snow. The left horizontal fin was damaged in a squall over Trieste, but the flight continued. While flying over the rugged Sudetes, the ship was attacked by a violent electrical storm. Then, amid deafening peals of thunder, hailstones pelted the ship. Nobile brought the *Italia* down to 500 feet to escape the lightning and bear toward the light part of the sky. He piloted a wild course, rising into dense fog to avoid mountain peaks, then sinking again to thread a way through the passes.

At last the ship broke onto the plains, and at seven fifty on the morning of April 16 Nobile set down at Stolp, Germany. Not a single pound of ballast was left; the upper fin was now broken, too; and the propellers were pitted by hailstones. No further proof was needed that Nobile had lost none of his skill as a pilot and that the ship was rugged enough for the severest Arctic storms.

On April 26, after ten days of repairs, the *Italia* was ready to proceed. The same day Amadeo Nobile telephoned his brother that the King's Bay hangar and mast were ready.

But disconcerting news came from Tromso. The *City of Milan* had been held up by Captain Romagna. His excuse was that he'd heard King's Bay was frozen over. Nobile impatiently sent a telegram to Romagna, telling him to start at once and, if necessary, to carry the cargo across the frozen bay as the *Hobby* crew had done. It was the first indication that Romagna was not as enthusiastic about the expedition as he might have been. His reluctance puzzled Nobile but didn't worry him. He assumed that Romagna was merely cautious of strange waters.

The airship left Stolp early May 3, battling a steady north wind of twenty-five miles. At 11:00 A.M., the explorers flew over Stockholm, circled Malmgren's house, and dropped a letter of greeting to his mother. As they crossed Finland that night, a report told of a depression forming over the Barents Sea, moving eastward. Nobile, in an effort to beat the storm, speeded up all three engines. At 8:55 A.M. the mast at Vadso appeared out of the fog. The ship was hurriedly refueled, but the storm from Spitsbergen, according to reports, had grown so savage that it would be foolhardy to leave. Nobile crawled into a collapsible boat and fell asleep. But soon he was awakened. The winds began mounting to gale force and swinging the *Italia* around and around. Remembering how the American dirigible, the *Shenandoah,* had been torn from its mast, Nobile ordered two of the engines to be kept running at low speed. Snow fell so thickly Nobile became worried about the added weight. Alessandrini, who had grown fat since the flight of the *Norge,* hoisted himself to the top to make an inspection. He reported the wind was sweeping off the snow.

The danger was such that by this time only a skeleton crew remained aboard. One of the journalists, young Ugo Lago, refused to leave. If there was going to be a disaster he did not want to miss a firsthand view of it.

A tube in the framework broke, but Alessandrini quickly repaired it. Snow then turned into rain, which soaked through the ship, into the control cabin. By noon meteorological conditions over the Barents Sea had improved slightly, and Malmgren advised a quick start.

Nobile needed no urging. By now he felt the ship would be safer anywhere else—even in a storm at sea. At eight thirty that evening the ship swept off the mast. At Malmgren's suggestion the dirigible went slightly off course to pass over the Bear Island meteorological station. As the ship flew over the island, the crew waved a salute to the two lonely weather men whose reports had been so helpful. Then at 5:30 A.M. Nobile turned the ship's nose north.

Now the weather worsened. They found themselves in the head of a cyclone coming from Iceland. Violent winds up to forty-five miles swept from the southeast. Along the west coast of Spitsbergen the ship was smothered in a snowstorm. Great masses of clouds scudded from the northwest.

"A magnificent sight," said Nobile drily to Malmgren.

The aerologist nodded. "We were lucky the last time we flew this way," he said. Then he added in his impersonal manner, "The situation is rather dangerous. The atmosphere is full of energy."

The ship was now being driven almost sideways by the heavy wind. Since they were making excellent time and had three days' gas left, Nobile was tempted to go all the way to the Arctic Ocean. But one of the engines went out of commission, and Nobile headed straight for King's Bay.

Just before noon the *City of Milan* lay below them in the bay, its rigging gay with flags, its deck spotted with tiny, black, fast-moving figures. Next to it was anchored the little *Hobby.*

At 12:45 P.M. Nobile gave orders to drop the mooring cable. A group of alpine skiers, brought along as a rescue party, grabbed it. Sailors from the *City of Milan* joined them, and the airship was steadied. In apprehension of the strong wind, the *Italia* was moored to the mast. The crew, except for Nobile and three others, was lowered to the ground.

Soon the wind began to rise. Nobile ordered fifty men put on the ropes to keep the ship from whipping around. But Captain Romagna refused to let Nobile use his sailors. The general was nonplused and quickly he sent an emergency call for volunteers to the nearby mining town of Ny Aalesund. For an hour Nobile and the alpinists fought against the gale, with everyone certain the ship would be torn from the mast and destroyed.

At last reinforcements, organized by the mining directors, arrived. During a brief lull in the storm the ship was brought off the mast and led into the hangar. It was then that Nobile realized he had been too busy building and flying airships to play politics or to look to his own best interests. For the first time he realized he had enemies.

In four days the *Italia* was completely overhauled. The Tromso weather station wired that conditions were favorable for a flight to Nicholas II Land; and at 7:55 A.M., on May 11, the ship took off. Because of the rise in temperature, gas had to be valved; and only eleven crewmen and two scientists, Malmgren and Pontremoli, were taken along. Shortly after the ship had started on its northward course, Alessandrini spotted a wire rudder cable which was badly frayed. It was repaired at once, but Nobile was very upset. He had specifically ordered the ground crew to inspect every control wire. Such carelessness was unforgivable in the Arctic—if indeed it was carelessness.

Pressure began to fall. Within a few hours the ship was in the middle of a gale. Ice began forming all over the dirigible, and snow piled up on its back. Then a strong northwest wind sprang up. Malmgren and Nobile decided that since the scientists were accomplishing little in the dense fog, it was futile to continue. At 4:10 P.M. the ship arrived safely at the base.

The foreign journalists assigned to cover the expedition reported happily that the entire flight had been a dud. Little mention was made of the faultless airmanship by which commander and crew had brought the *Italia* through the storm.

For the next few days it snowed steadily. Since there was no roof on the hangar, and the weight of the snow could break the back of the ship, this period was a nightmare to Nobile. Each hour a ton of snow collected on top of the *Italia*. And sweeping off the fragile envelope was a difficult, painstaking job. The control car and rear gondola began to drag on the floor of the hangar. The stern was so heavily weighted that metal plating underneath started to buckle.

Nobile slept little, spent every waking minute at the hangar supervising the sweeping.

Finally the temperature rose and the snow melted. Water dripped down the sides and spouted from all parts of the ship. Nobile now feared a freeze would set in and seriously damage the envelope. Fortunately the snow stopped, the sun shone, and the ship dried out.

While repairs were made to the outer covering, several foreign journalists ridiculed the hangar with no top. The hangar, originally built by the Norwegians, was the same one that had been praised so highly two years before.

Nobile made plans for another trip to Nicholas II Land. This time several tons of scientific equipment, including the device for landing on the ice pack, were put aboard. In all the little ship lifted a load of 26,000 pounds.

The *Italia* took off early on the afternoon of May 15 with thirteen crewmen, two scientists, and one journalist. Tomaselli and Lago flipped a coin to see which of the newsmen would go. Lago won, but Nobile decided the older man had priority.

In four hours the ship passed over Cape North. The sea was frozen over. Snow began to fall, but the scientists could see clearly for six miles. Clouds had covered the pearl-gray sky by the time they passed over Franz Josef Archipelago. Below, patches of freshly frozen ice showed white and were bordered with thicker, bluish ice.

By early evening the *Italia* was penetrating deeper and deeper into unexplored territory. Only a few black birds were seen. Near Alexandra Land a polar bear looked up at the airship and scuttled away. For hours Nobile flew at 500 feet under a fog bank. Then the sky began to clear and visibility extended over thirty-five miles.

At 11:15 P.M. a vague outline appeared on the horizon. As they drew closer, a fantastic city of white and blue crystals rose from the ice. The illusion lasted for several minutes and then disappeared.

The ship pushed on and on to the north for a day and a half. Still no land was in sight. Gillis Land did not exist—at least in its position on the maps. After flying over 31,000 square miles of unknown territory Nobile turned the ship around. The *Italia* landed at its Spitsbergen base on the morning of May 18, after a rigorous and successful flight of sixty-nine hours. Though the newsmen at King's Bay seemed to think little had been accomplished, Malmgren had collected important data on meteorological conditions and the state of the ice, and Pontremoli had made readings and surveys, which until then had been unavailable to scientists.

Nobile began preparing the ship for a flight to the Pole that same afternoon. By May 22 the *Italia* was ready and the apparatus for landing on the ice had been personally tested by Nobile. That night, on the strength of favorable weather reports, Malmgren recommended an early start.

At two thirty in the morning Nobile ordered the ship filled with hydrogen. He walked under the ship, carefully inspecting the envelope for undiscovered damages inflicted by the snowstorm. Near the stern he heard a little hissing noise. In a moment he found a small slit in the envelope. It looked more like a gash than a tear. The damage was repaired and a thorough examination of the ship made for other flaws.

At 4:00 A.M. the *Italia* was dragged from the hangar and weighed. Its extra buoyancy permitted Behounek to come aboard with the other two scientists.

In sharp contrast to the departure of the *Norge*, this leave-taking was charged with emotion and camaraderie. After a champagne toast (which was enlarged to a drunken brawl by several correspondents) the crew members embraced their fellows who were to stay behind. Every man went to his landing station.

Then Father Gianfranceschi, chaplain of the expedition, recited a short prayer.

"Let go!" shouted Nobile from the control cabin.

At 4:28 A.M., May 23, the ship rose from the snow. The crowd of 250 below cheered. The *Italia* circled the field and then headed north. It had started on its last voyage.

There were sixteen on board, including Viglieri and the young newsman, Lago. Fourteen of the crew were Italian, one Swedish, and one Czechoslovakian. Of the Italians, seven were blond and blue-eyed; and Malmgren remarked jovially that their voyage to the cold northlands was simply an instinctive answer to the call of their Nordic origin.

The ice pack, shrouded in fog, was crossed at 6:50 A.M. In the middle of the afternoon the fog thinned, and they saw the coast of Greenland. At 6:00 P.M. they were a few miles from Cape Bridgeman. The sky was clear and amazingly blue, and a radiant sun glistened on the snow. There was an air of expectancy on board.

The three naval officers took turns at the rudder, while Trojani and Cecioni spelled each other at the elevators. Malmgren, wearing glasses, stood marking the weather chart, and Biagi brought in periodic radio reports.

Pontremoli and Behounek, intently working their complicated instruments, looked like scientists in a laboratory. In the stern engine was Pomella. Dapper Caratti held down the port gondola and

"Old Man" Ciocca, the starboard. Arduino, whose forehead was perpetually creased with worry, walked up and down the keel supervising his mechanics and checking the gas consumption. Fat Alessandrini began to patrol the ship as soon as he'd pulled up the maneuvering ropes. When he'd finished his inspection he came into the control car to take a turn at the elevators.

The *Italia's* route to the Pole lay between Peary's and that of the *Norge.* Once more they were flying over unknown land. The sky was so clear they could see sixty miles, but there was no land.

As they neared the Pole, a strong tail wind sprang up. Nobile asked Malmgren if it wouldn't be wiser to continue on to the mouth of the Mackenzie River after passing the Pole. But the Swede advised going back to King's Bay; then they could make one more flight. Nobile was worried because the strong wind at their back would have to be fought head on throughout the return trip.

But Malmgren shook his head. "No, this wind won't last," he said.

At 10:00 P.M. a high cloud barrier rose up ahead of them. "There's no getting through that," Nobile thought to himself; and he feared they would have to turn back before reaching the Pole. In half an hour they reached the clouds. The ship rose to clear sky at 2500 feet. Nobile relaxed.

Tension on board began rising an hour later; the *Italia* was now only fifty-five miles from its goal. At midnight Mariano, the first officer, set his sextant. He squinted through the sights. Twenty minutes later he called out excitedly, "We're there!"

The engines were slowed, and Nobile ordered the helmsman to steer in a circle. The wind made a landing on the pack impossible, so the giant cross and flags were brought out and prepared for dropping. Twenty minutes later they were again in sight of the pack. The ship circled under the fog bank, and a large tricolor cloth was fastened to the cross to guide its fall.

At one twenty in the morning Nobile leaned out a window and dropped the Italian flag. The gonfalon of the city of Milan followed, and then the little medal of the Virgin of the Fire, which the people of Forli had begged Nobile to take to the Pole. At one thirty, from an altitude of 500 feet, Nobile dropped the cross.

The Italians were overcome with emotion. The motors were almost silent, and now everyone could hear a little Gramophone playing the wistful folk song, "The Bells of St. Giusto."

Zappi cried, "Viva Nobile!" Others took up the cheer.

Malmgren held out his hand to the Italian commander. "Few men in the world can say, as we can," he said, "that they've been twice to the North Pole." Seven had done it—one Swede and six Italians.

Their faces flushed, Alessandrini and the four other veterans of the *Norge* crowded into the cabin. Nobile longed to embrace them but natural reserve held him back. Instead he brought out his flask of eggnog and passed it around.

Then telegrams were sent to the Pope, the King, and finally Mussolini. At this point Pontremoli, who had been taking readings, hurried up to Nobile. He was agog with excitement. He had measured the horizontal component of the terrestrial magnetic field at the Pole.

At this moment Nobile's brother was anxiously pacing the deck of the *City of Milan* with Father Gianfranceschi. Newsmen clustered in front of the door of the radio room, waiting for news. Captain Romagna came out of the room.

"Your station," he angrily told one of the foreign newsmen, "is too active!" He did not tell the reporters that the *Italia* had already crossed the Pole: it seemed proper to him that the announcement come from Italy.

At length Rome proudly informed the world that Italians had once more conquered the Pole. As the dirigible passed over the top of the world, according to the first dispatch, the Fascist hymn was played on a Gramophone, and the crew members raised their right hands in the Fascist salute.

For twenty-four hours the *Italia* sailed back toward King's Bay under the fog at an altitude of about 500 feet. The pack, pallid and uniform, was covered with snowfields, hummocks, and crevasses. The cheerfulness of the outward journey was gone. As the strong head wind increased, the men lapsed into silence. Now and then their progress could have been matched by a man crawling over the ice. An occasional loud report like a rifle shot would tell them that a piece of ice had struck the ship and torn a hole. Then Cecioni and Alessandrini would search desperately until they had found the hole and mended it.

Before long, ice had formed all over the dirigible's outer shell—to a thickness none had seen before. Biagi pulled in his aerial and knocked off an icicle two inches thick. It was hung up in the control cabin as a trophy.

Little headway was being made against the strong wind. Malmgren became annoyed, anxious. "Let's get out of this zone quickly," he urged Nobile. "Afterward, things will be better."

Nobile ordered the third engine started. An air speed of sixty-two miles an hour was registered, but their ground speed did not increase appreciably. As time passed Nobile grew more and more fearful of the strain on the ship. Finally, at three o'clock in the morning of May 25, he ordered the speed reduced.

Now Malmgren's anxiety returned. "We're not going ahead," he complained. "It's dangerous to stop here. The weather might get worse."

Again Nobile accelerated all engines. The hurricane raged; the ship was continually being blown off course by snow flurries. Everyone was silent, exhausted, depressed by the thirty-hour struggle.

All that day the ship plowed through thick fog. At 500 feet nothing could be seen but the colorless, monotonous pack below. Malmgren took over the helm. Pontremoli and Lago were sleeping in their fur bags in the stern of the keel. Behounek, steady and impassive, was at his instruments.

Nobile directed a zigzag course, trying to find a hole in the wind. Their position was uncertain: the radio signals from the *City of Milan* were only given in approximate figures, and fog prevented solar observations. The general peered anxiously out the front window, searching for the northern coast of Spitsbergen. But all he could see was fog and floe. He glanced up at his daughter's picture on the wall. She seemed to be looking back at him sadly, her eyes misted with tears.

At 7:00 A.M. he decided to plot the *Italia's* position by steering west and then measuring off two points. But the wind was too strong. The course toward North-East Land, due south, was resumed. Nobile walked back to the radio compartment to find out if any report had come in.

It was 9:25 A.M.

Trojani at the elevators suddenly cried out, "The elevator wheel! It's jammed!"

Nobile ran from the radio room as Trojani tried to pull the ship's nose up. But the controls were jammed. The ship headed for the ice, only 800 feet below.

"Stop the engines!" ordered Nobile. Viglieri finally released the elevator controls with a sharp blow.

The general opened all the air valves so the gas pressure would be reduced. Then he looked back. The propellers had stopped. When he turned around he saw Viglieri tossing out four tins of gasoline that had been stowed in the control cabin. Nobile angrily reprimanded the naval officer for wasting precious gasoline.

Even as Nobile spoke the ship, now only eighty-five yards from the pack, began to rise gently. Cecioni, who'd been asleep on the keel, climbed down into the cabin and, at Nobile's orders, paid out the ballast chain lying on the floor. The ship slowly rose to 2800 feet—out of the fog into the brilliant sunlight. Cecioni took the casing of the elevator mechanism apart but found nothing wrong. They decided ice had formed inside. Now the controls worked perfectly. Once more Nobile descended toward the pack to check speed and drift. Viglieri had been able to take the height of the sun while Cecioni was examining the elevators, and thus their course for King's Bay was finally set. Nobile figured that they would reach their base at three or four that afternoon.

Cecioni was at the elevators. Beside him, between the pressure gauges and engine telegraph, stood Trojani, his brow furrowed as usual. Malmgren was steering and Zappi passing him instructions. In the rear of the cabin Nobile sat at the navigator's table with Mariano and Viglieri, who were taking speed measurements with the Goertz apparatus—an instrument clamped to the side of the table.

Pontremoli and Lago were still asleep on the keel. The mechanics —Pomella, Caratti, and Ciocca—were all at their positions. Arduino and Alessandrini were patrolling the keel. The ship, now flying at 300 feet, was so light Cecioni had to tilt the nose down to keep the proper height.

At exactly 10:30 A.M. Nobile walked to the front of the cabin to take an altitude measurement. He looked out the right-hand porthole between the two control wheels and then dropped a glass ball. He stood timing the ball's descent with a stop-watch.

"We're heavy," said Cecioni tersely.

Nobile, startled, pulled in his head and looked at the instruments. The ship's nose was up to 8 degrees, but the variometer showed the *Italia* was falling a half-yard per second.

Without raising his voice, Nobile ordered the third engine started and the other two speeded up. The pack drew nearer. He ordered Cecioni to lift the nose higher. Then he shouted up to Alessandrini on the keel, "Go on top and see if the stern valves are working!"

Pomella and Caratti brought their motors up to 1400 revolutions. Ciocca, with surprising speed, had already started his. The nose was now tilted up at about 18 degrees, and the ship moved faster.

Nobile's eyes were fixed on the variometer. The ship was dropping even faster. He knew a crash was coming.

"Stop all engines!" he cried. This would lessen the crash and keep the ship from catching afire. "Take the elevators," he told Zappi.

Then he ordered Cecioni to lower the ballast chain again. In spite of the steady drop no one became panicky. Cecioni tugged at the rope that tied the chain. He swore as he struggled with it.

"Hurry up! Hurry up!" cried Nobile, knowing the chain would help deaden the fall. Then he noticed that the left engine was still running. He leaned out of a porthole and shouted at Caratti, "Stop your engine!"

As he looked back he saw the stern car was sixty feet from the pack. He quickly drew in his head.

Zappi, sweat rolling down his thin face, hung tightly onto the elevator wheel.

Malmgren was squeezing the rudder wheel with his fingers. His eyes widened as he saw the jagged pack rise up in front of him.

Behounek grabbed onto something for support.

Biagi tore off his earphones and leaped up from his seat at the radio.

Viglieri and Mariano stood, feet apart, braced for the shock.

Just as Nobile reached the spot between the two controls, Malmgren flung up the wheel. He turned, his startled eyes meeting Nobile's. Instinctively the commander grabbed the free wheel, wondering vaguely if it was possible to bring the ship down with less shock.

There was a jar in the stern of the ship. A few seconds later uneven masses of ice rose up. The control car struck with a great crash.

Something hit Nobile on his head. Clearly, without pain, he felt an arm and a leg snap. Something fell, knocking him to the floor of the ship. He shut his eyes. With perfect lucidity he thought, "It's all over."

Malmgren felt himself thrown forward roughly. A sharp pain raced through his left shoulder.

Biagi struck his head on a table.

Zappi's right arm seemed to crumble.

Behounek found himself kneeling on the ice, surrounded by the wreckage of the control cabin. He looked up. The dirigible, nose in the air, was drifting away. In a daze Behounek wondered what had happened. Then he saw a hole in the bottom of the ship where the entire cabin had ripped out. From the hole trailed torn strips of fabric, ropes, pieces of metal. The left wall of the cabin was still attached to the airship. There were a few creases in the ship's envelope.

A man was standing on the gangway to the starboard engine, staring down. It was Arduino. His face wore a look of utter disbelief.

Figures began moving drunkenly on the ice pack. Trojani and Viglieri looked blankly at each other. Biagi rubbed his bloody face. The first to speak was First Officer Mariano. "All right, all right," he said quietly. "We're all here."

The men looked around, still stupefied. The pack was formless—a contorted jumble of pointed ice crags, stretching to the horizon. It was a terrifying wilderness of ice.

"Where's the general?" asked Mariano.

Viglieri pointed. Next to Malmgren, who was seated on the ice dazedly rubbing his arm, lay Nobile. His eyes were closed.

There was a sharp, excited bark. Then Titina dashed across the ice, happy to be free from the confining dirigible. The crash hadn't even frightened her. She sniffed the little hummocks of snow and ice.

Nobile opened his eyes. His right arm and leg were throbbing. His face and the top of his head ached. His chest seemed upside down. He was sure he was dying. He looked around at his men, who seemed to be in a state of shock. The wreckage was a dreary gray against the clean white snow. A stain of bright red, like blood, marked the spot where the gondola had crashed. It was not blood but a glass altitude ball that had burst.

Nobile, breathing with great difficulty, felt he had only a few hours to live. He was glad he wouldn't have to watch his comrades die of hunger one by one. For they were lost on the pack with no tent, no radio, no sledges, no food—no hope.

"Steady, boys," he said when he saw everyone looking at him with despair. "Keep your spirits up. Lift your thoughts to God." No other words came to him. Impetuously he cried out, *"Viva l'Italia!"*

Everyone but Malmgren cheered. Then Mariano ordered those who could walk to look for salvage.

Malmgren still sat beside Nobile as though he were alone. He hadn't stopped stroking his left arm. His face was ashen, his blue eyes stared fixedly at nothing. He seemed lost in despair.

"Nothing to be done, my dear Malmgren," said Nobile.

Malmgren looked down at the Italian with glazed eyes. "Nothing but to die," Malmgren said. "My arm is broken." Suddenly he got to his feet. He couldn't stand straight because of his injured shoulder. In English he said tonelessly, "General, I thank you for the trip. I go under the water!" He turned away.

"No, Malmgren," said Nobile gently. "You have no right to do this. We'll die when God has decided. We must wait. Please."

The Swede seemed surprised. He stood still, as if undecided. Then he sat down next to Nobile again.

"The field station is intact!" came a cry from behind a hummock. It was Biagi. He'd found the little emergency radio set. A moment later a box of rations was found. The men's spirits rose.

Nobile, believing there was no hope for an injured man on the ice pack, called First Officer Mariano. "I think I have only a few hours to live," he said quietly so the others couldn't hear. "I can't do anything for you. Do everything you can to save yourself and the men."

"There's still hope," said Mariano. "We've just picked up a case of provisions. We can hope."

Nobile put his hand on Mariano's cheek. "Men like you ought to be saved." He looked up pleadingly. "Do what you can for my little girl and my sister's children."

"Yes, General, don't worry. I've always been fond of you. In my own way, always."

At that moment Nobile spied, between two hummocks of ice, one of the two waterproof bags he and Pontremoli had prepared for the descent at the North Pole. It had been strapped to the ceiling of the radio room. His arm trembling, the general pointed the bag out to Mariano. "Get that sack opened!" He knew it contained provisions and a tent. "There's a sleeping bag in it, too," he added. "Please bring it here to me and get me into it, if you can. Then I'll be able to die in peace." Nobile, who preferred to be unrestricted in his movements, did not wear the standard lamb's-wool suit.

The sack was opened. The men clustered around, staring avidly as each treasure was pulled out. In addition to the tent and fur bag were pemmican, chocolate, a Colt revolver with 100 cartridges, a Very signaling pistol, and a case of matches.

Then the men slid Nobile slowly into the bag. His face was white. He clenched his teeth so he wouldn't cry out in pain. Once he was inside the warm sack he thought of Titina and called her name.

She scampered gaily past him, refusing to understand. She continued frisking about, wagging her tail and sniffing the cold, clean air.

"Take care of her," he told Mariano. Then the commander put his head inside the bag and lay motionless, waiting for death.

Cecioni thought he was dying, too. He lay a few yards away, his leg bent crazily under him. He struggled to get his leg straightened out, then tied on a clumsy bandage. He cursed angrily.

Biagi searched tirelessly for more salvage. He was convinced that Arduino, seeing them stranded on the ice, had tossed overboard emergency supplies.

Behind an ice crag he came upon a wrecked gondola. It was the

stern engine. And beside it he found Pomella, its mechanic. Pomella
had taken off one of his shoes and was sitting motionless on the ice.

Biagi was about to call. Then he saw the empty look on his
comrade's face. Pomella didn't seem to be injured, but he was dead.

Biagi sat beside the body. He took off his own *finsko* and tried
on the sturdy leather shoe that lay on the ice. It fit perfectly.
Biagi unlaced the dead man's other shoe. He put it on and then
went slowly back to the main wreckage.

Nobile's head was now out of the sleeping bag. His face had lost
its pallor.

Cecioni was still cursing his luck. "I've broken my leg, General!"
he called. "My leg. It's broken."

Malmgren was still sitting, staring and rubbing his arm. On his
left Zappi was stretched out. He complained of a pain in his chest
near one of his ribs.

"Do you think it's broken, General?" he asked.

"If it doesn't hurt you much when you breathe," said Nobile,
"that means it isn't broken." The general wondered if there was any
medical truth in his statement.

Viglieri, Trojani, and Mariano held a conference to pick out the
best place to pitch the tent. There was only a light breeze, but in
the intense cold it was unbearable. They knew they would soon
freeze if they didn't find shelter. Finally a surface of ice fifty feet
square was selected.

The three men set to work while Biagi, in a state of elation over
his new leather shoes, began to improvise a wireless mast. Behounek
leaned down to console Nobile. "We'll all be saved," he said.

The general smiled. "I hope so—for your sakes."

Soon the tent was pitched. It was nine feet square, supported in
the center by a wooden pole. Designed for four men, it was now the
home of two men with broken legs, Nobile and Cecioni, and seven
others.

Nobile was dragged across the ice in the sleeping bag. He almost
fainted from the pain. He was stretched out at the back of
the tent, facing the entrance. Cecioni, grunting with pain, was
then carried in and laid beside the general. The sleeping bag was
ripped up the middle so both men could have a common bed.

By this time Biagi had set up a transmitter near the aerial. He
began sending out an SOS to the *City of Milan*. Then he listened at
the receiver. There was no answer.

An inventory was taken of the provisions. There were fifteen and
one half pounds, enough for twenty-five days. The men jammed into
the tent while Mariano divided half a pound of pemmican. Trojani

ate his portion at once, his face puckering with distaste. Cecioni and Nobile put their pemmican aside. Neither had an appetite.

After the meal the general was told of Pomella's death. The mechanic was an old friend, but his loss left Nobile unmoved. He envied Pomella, for he had escaped the lingering death that awaited the rest of them.

The men began discussing the fate of their six mates in the damaged airship. Smoke had been seen half an hour after the crash on the ice. Some thought the *Italia* had fallen and burned; others thought it was just a signal.

Soon their talk died out. The nine huddled down for the first sleep most of them had had for several days. Outside, the arctic wind howled. The canvas of the tent flapped monotonously. Cecioni, half-conscious and racked with pain, rambled on until exhaustion overcame him.

When everyone was asleep Nobile looked around at the tangle of human limbs. He wondered which of them would die first. He hoped he would be the first. Then he, too, fell asleep.

11

WILDERNESS OF ICE

In Italy news of the flight over the Pole had caused great celebration. The dropping of the flag and cross at the Pole, according to the Rome correspondent of the New York *Times*, had "seized the popular imagination here as has nothing else recently."

But when the *Italia*'s radio stopped on May 25, people were instantly worried. Officials in Rome scoffed. Nothing, they declared, could possibly have happened to the great Fascist dirigible.

The men on the floe slept for only a few hours. Then, while Malmgren and Zappi stayed in the tent with the two invalids, Mariano, Viglieri, Behounek, and Trojani went outside to hunt for more salvage.

Biagi continued to send out an SOS on the fifty-fifth minute of every hour, as arranged with the *City of Milan*. After each signal he hurried back to the tent where the receiver was now located and put on his earphones. But there was never an answer.

Later in the day Zappi, realizing his rib was bruised, not broken, took over the medical duties. He made a splint with two wooden boards for Cecioni's broken leg. Nobile's leg was bandaged with strips cut from the control car's varnished covering. Then Zappi discovered that Malmgren's arm was badly mauled, but there was no break.

All day an icy wind blew. And every few minutes the salvagers were forced back to the tent to get out of the raw blasts.

That evening Biagi intercepted the news bulletin from the station at San Paolo in Rome. Now the government, too, was becoming alarmed at the *Italia*'s silence. After a meal of pemmican and chocolate the men, depressed by the failure of the transmitter, huddled up for another "night." Cecioni was almost out of his head with pain and worry. While the others slept he threw his great hairy arms around Nobile's neck, his eyes wide with terror. He asked the general if there was any hope.

"We must trust in God," whispered Nobile.

When everyone had fallen asleep, there suddenly came a long-drawn-out crash. The tent shook.

"Everybody out!" someone cried. Cecioni and Nobile were dragged onto the snow. Other floes, driven by the wind and current, were smashing into their floe from two sides. It felt like an earthquake. Then the crashing stopped as suddenly as it had started. Snow began to fall. The new quiet was terrifying. A strange thought occurred to Nobile: the moon must be like this.

The trip back to the tent was unbearably painful to Cecioni and Nobile.

When the men had settled into their beds again, Malmgren crept up to the general. "This is a bad site," he said quietly. "We ought to move as soon as possible." He explained that the jagged ice meant that they were exposed to the action of winds and currents. "We'd better find a smoother place pretty soon," he warned.

Soon only Biagi and Nobile were awake in the silent tent. About an hour later the radio operator crawled outside to transmit his call for help. Then he returned, clamped on his earphones, and listened intently. After a while he nestled into his place on the floor.

"Nothing, Biagi?" whispered Nobile.

"Nothing."

The night's sleep cheered everyone. Now, at the beginning of their third day on the ice, they were determined to hold out till the end. Biagi was sending signals at two-hour intervals. There was still no reply. Zappi claimed that the radio was too weak; but Nobile told them to be patient, it was the best radio of its type.

A daily routine was established, with special jobs assigned to each man. Nobile took charge of the food. He worked out a daily menu of an ounce of pemmican and a tiny piece of chocolate per man. Titina's ration came from the general's scanty portion. Before each meal he placed her share in an old shoe.

Malmgren, completely recovered from his depression, volunteered for the difficult water detail. Surrounded as they were by tons of ice, it was still an arduous job to get enough drinking water each day. Fresh-water ice had to be found and melted. The precious liquid was passed around at mealtimes in the lid of a thermos bottle, the lid becoming dirtier and dirtier as each man drank.

That evening an event of major importance took place. Malmgren made pemmican soup. It was their first hot meal in four days. When Malmgren, after two hours of preparation, brought the steaming tin into the tent, the men greeted him with shouts of joy. The odor was delicious.

Mariano knelt next to the tentpole—where the Colt and the

Queen of Italy hung—and ladled the soup into a large round nickel container. This soup dish, which had once been the top of a giant thermos, was passed from man to man. All nine of them confessed that it was the best meal they'd ever eaten. When they had finished, Trojani told them that as an experiment he'd prepared a similar soup from the yellowish stuff in Rome. But even his dog refused to eat it.

Everyone laughed. It was their first laugh on the ice.

An hour after the meal the men were still discussing the fine qualities of the soup. The taste of raw peas had been particularly pleasing. Then Mariano started to clean the community soup dish.

"No, no!" growled Trojani. "Let the grease accumulate. It would be a shame to waste good food!"

That day Biagi's signals still went unheard. But the receiver was working perfectly. "We imagine you are near the north coast of Svalbard [Spitsbergen], between the fifteenth and sixteenth meridians," wired the *City of Milan*. "Trust in us. We are organizing help."

The men growled sarcastically when Biagi relayed this message. Trust in them! They weren't even looking in the right area! And why hadn't the *City of Milan* heard their radio?

Biagi believed that the message had "skipped," but most of the men thought the *City of Milan* operators simply weren't listening closely enough.

The loss of the *Italia* had already precipitated elaborate search-and-rescue preparations in many parts of the world.

While Roald Amundsen was attending a banquet in Oslo in honor of the two arctic fliers, Wilkins and Eielson, a message from the Norwegian government was read aloud. It requested him to lead a rescue expedition. Amundsen, whose last two years had been darkened by his fierce feud with Nobile, rose to his feet. "Tell them," he said in his crisp manner, "that I am ready to start instantly."

Swedes, Finns, and Russians volunteered their services. United States Secretary of the Navy Wilbur told reporters that he was thinking of sending the *Los Angeles*.

At 9:00 P.M., the San Paolo bulletin told nothing of these international rescue plans but all about a florid round of ceremonies, fetes, and speeches. Biagi then heard the *City of Milan* reply with long newspaper reports full of wild theories. One journalist was pleased to suggest that the *Italia* had probably hit a mountain.

"They ought to let the newspapers go hang," said Viglieri angrily, "and listen for us steadily."

When the men woke up on the 28th, their fourth day in the

wilderness, they discovered that a strong north wind was blowing. Their floe was drifting southeast at about fifteen miles a day. Soon Charles XII Island appeared on the horizon.

"We're drifting toward Franz Josef Land," said Malmgren. This unwelcome observation was confirmed when *Arctic Pilot*, a navigation book in English, was found on a hummock. "The principal direction of the ice stream in North-East Land," it said, "is toward the east."

After dinner Mariano and Zappi began talking of a march to the coast. They had no faith in the radio, and they believed that the floe would drift far from any rescue expedition.

Malmgren nodded toward the two invalids. "With them?" he asked.

Mariano nodded.

"That's impossible without sledges," said Malmgren, the only man who knew the Arctic.

Malmgren's judgment forestalled the proposal briefly, but later in the evening Mariano and Zappi went up to Nobile. They suggested that the three naval officers and Malmgren go to the coast for help.

Nobile told them to call everyone in the tent for a discussion. Cecioni began to shout wildly. "They mustn't be allowed to go!" he cried. "They can't abandon two helpless men like that! We should all march together." His eyes wild, he turned to Nobile. "If I didn't have a broken leg I'd take the General on my back!" He was answered with silence and tried a new tack: "I'll make a sledge. My arms are strong and sound!"

Patiently Nobile tried to pacify the big man, to show him that they had neither the tools nor the materials to make a sledge, nor the manpower to propel one. "If things become desperate, the others will have to go," he said firmly. Cecioni looked terrified. "I'll take care of you," said Nobile.

Cecioni began to cry like a baby.

The projected march threatened the unity of the little camp. Bitter personal differences broke out, but Nobile suppressed them with an astute combination of benevolence, psychology, and rank.

After the broadcast that night, Mariano and Zappi insisted on still another discussion of the march.

Malmgren supported them. He, too, had lost faith in the radio. "We're drifting farther from North-East Land," he argued. "Our only salvation is a march toward Cape North."

"Who would go?" asked Nobile.

Mariano volunteered at once.

"And how many will you be?" asked Nobile, growing weary of the same argument.

"At least four," said Zappi quickly. His thin face was eager. "The three naval officers and Malmgren as a guide."

"That will leave Biagi, Trojani, and Behounek with you two invalids," said Malmgren. The Swede was a man of action, and the plan made him eager and optimistic again.

"We'll take Biagi too," snapped Zappi.

Malmgren shook his head. "No, no, their one hope is the radio."

"For my part," said Behounek angrily, "I'm remaining with the general." He glared with unconcealed animosity at Zappi. "But I insist that one of the naval officers stay. We've got to have someone who can take our bearings. Otherwise what's the use of the radio operator?"

Nobile nodded. Then he looked at the other men in the tent. Trojani, Biagi, and Viglieri were silent, expressionless.

But Cecioni sat up in alarm. "No!" he cried. "We can all march together." He again told them he could make two sledges. He looked pleadingly from man to man.

"That's a good idea," said Nobile, as though talking to a child. "You build a sledge." Then he turned to Malmgren. "Why don't you three wait a few days? Maybe the drift won't keep carrying us east."

The three who wanted to march glanced at each other. Zappi was about to protest, but a look on Malmgren's face warned him to keep quiet.

The next morning, May 29, Charles XII Island disappeared. Soon two small islands, close together, could be seen. These two islands, Broch and Foyn, were only ten miles away, which served to make the would-be marchers more impatient than ever.

Nobile stayed in the tent, but Cecioni, fired with energy and good purpose, had himself dragged onto the ice. He made Trojani and Behounek bring him steel tubing from the cabin wreckage. He hammered the tubing into a crude skeleton of a sledge. All day he worked feverishly, grumbled fiercely, and cursed Behounek and Trojani for their slowness and stupidity. The two shrugged their shoulders and continued to look for bits of wire, aluminum, and sticks.

Mariano and Malmgren disappeared on a reconnoiter. Zappi and Viglieri rearranged provisions. And every two hours Biagi sent out an SOS, running back to the tent to clamp on his earphones and listen for a reply. Then, good-naturedly, he would join Cecioni's labor battalion.

That evening, as they ate, they talked of several things. A wide channel had opened up about 100 yards away. They wondered if it extended all the way to the islands. They discussed their six comrades on the *Italia*. Some thought the ship had exploded, the others that it had landed not far away. Biagi suggested that two men hike toward the place where the smoke had been seen. Perhaps they could find their comrades and get the rifles stowed in the keel. But such an expedition over the pack seemed too vague and dangerous and was finally abandoned.

Biagi faithfully continued sending his SOS—with no results. Everyone but Nobile had discounted the radio entirely. The *City of Milan* was transmitting nothing but newspaper reports and hundreds of personal telegrams each day.

"They think we're dead," said Trojani bitterly. "They're not even trying to listen to us."

The truth was that Captain Romagna had convinced himself Biagi was dead. The last communication with the *Italia* had been at 10:30 A.M. on May 25, the moment before the crash. Then there had been silence, total silence.

"It's as plain as a pikestaff," Romagna explained to his subordinates. "Biagi leaned out the porthole. The radio propellers came loose and cut off his head."

But young Pedretti, the *Italia's* reserve operator who had been left behind, still believed his mates were alive. During the few moments of the day when the *City of Milan* wasn't transmitting to San Paolo, Pedretti would listen intently for his lost comrades.

On the evening of May 29 he was at the *City of Milan's* receiver. Suddenly he heard the word *Italia*. He stiffened. The message continued, "Reply via Ido 32 K."

Pedretti jumped to his feet, grabbed Chief Operator Baccarani by the arm. "The *Italia* is calling us!" he cried. "Ido" was the code word for the San Paolo station; "32" indicated the airship's wavelength. "K" meant, "Hurry up, answer us."

"You're crazy," said Baccarani. Captain Romagna's theory had been so firmly planted in his mind that he couldn't imagine Biagi was alive.

"But they said so," protested Pedretti.

"It can't be the *Italia*," insisted Baccarani. "It's probably Magadiscio." With a wave of the arm he dismissed his assistant's further protests. Baccarani was so sure that the men of the *Italia* were dead that he didn't bother to ask Magadiscio if it had been their message.

That same day a false rumor spread all over Rome: contact with the *Italia* had been made! There were celebrations in the streets.

In Washington, D.C., Representative Fiorello La Guardia of New

York blocked a bill conferring a gold medal on Lincoln Ellsworth for the polar flight of 1926. The "Little Flower" insisted with feeling that Amundsen and Nobile also be honored.

On the ice, talk centered on their Colt revolver. Malmgren insisted that it was a poor weapon in the Arctic. Nobile disagreed. "Our Queen," he said, "is a fine shot, and has hunted bears and seals in Spitsbergen. She told me a Colt was excellent for big game."

Malmgren politely refrained from expressing his opinion of the Queen as a hunter. "Tell me," he said to the general, "do you think that we wouldn't have had a crash if we'd gone straight on to the Mackenzie as you wanted?"

"That's hard to say," answered Nobile. "At least we wouldn't have had to fight wind for twenty-six hours." Then he saw the look of guilt in the Swede's face. "My dear Malmgren," he added with a smile, "you only gave me the advice. I didn't have to take it."

Malmgren walked out of the tent. He went up to Behounek, who was watching the ever-widening channel. "The general is a truly great man," he said, as if to himself. "Compared with him the rest of us seem very small."

Behounek nodded: the general was a great man, and the cold was unbearable.

After listening to the nine o'clock news bulletin, which next to the evening meal had become the most important event in their daily life, Zappi again brought up the subject of the march. The arguments were repeated with maddening monotony. Cecioni still opposed wildly. Nobile continued to delay the issue by talking optimistically of the radio.

"While we put it off," snapped Zappi, who was fast losing his respect for Nobile's braided general's cap, "the provisions are growing less."

Mariano, though still respectful of the general, agreed with Zappi.

For a moment Nobile was silent. He absently scratched Titina behind the ears. Then he said, "No, you'd better put it off a few days." He suggested they let Cecioni demonstrate his handmade sledge the next day. It would be most effective, he thought, for Cecioni himself to prove how difficult it was to drag a helpless man across the terrible ice pack.

"Carrying a load like Cecioni is absurd," said Zappi brutally. "We'd better stop wasting time and decide right away to start."

"All right," sighed Nobile. "Why not just two of you go? You could move faster."

"No," said Mariano quickly. "There has to be at least three. Then if one gets sick, the second could stay with him while the third goes on."

"Four!" Zappi snapped. "We need the three naval officers and Malmgren."

"We could make six miles a day," said Malmgren eagerly. "Nine, when we're nearer land."

The map was examined. From Foyn Island to Cape North was 100 miles. That meant the trip should take about fifteen days.

"All right," said Nobile with a sigh of resignation. "Now I'm going to ask each man whether he wants to go."

Malmgren, Zappi, and Mariano quickly nodded their heads.

Nobile looked at Viglieri. The tall, quiet man nodded.

"I'll go!" cried young Biagi.

Behounek stood up. "I'm staying with the general," he said stolidly.

Trojani glowered at Biagi. "Me, too," he said.

"I'll think things over," said Nobile. "Tomorrow we'll try to shift the camp five hundred yards. Afterward, we'll see."

"How can we move all the supplies and the injured in one trip?" Zappi objected.

"By making two trips," Nobile said simply.

Mariano spoke for Zappi's objection. In the fog, he declared, some would get lost. It was obvious to the general that neither man would stay on the floe much longer.

By way of concluding the argument Nobile lay back and shut his eyes. Malmgren, trying to find a comfortable place for his injured arm, lay down at the foot of the sleeping bag. In a few minutes Cecioni was mumbling in a half-sleep. Soon everyone but Nobile and Mariano was asleep. The general watched his first officer, who was staring out toward the ice pack. The last few days, thought Nobile, had changed Mariano a great deal. Now he was too eager to leave his friends.

Finally Mariano dropped off to sleep.

Nobile closed his eyes. A few minutes later Cecioni woke up with a painful start and convulsively grabbed the general's arm. The two talked in hushed tones. Nobile made Cecioni repeat a prayer. Then there was silence on the ice pack except for the rustling of the light wind, which was driving them always to the east.

All that night the sun was under dark clouds, creating a semblance of nightfall. Early in the morning of the sixth day on the floe, the sun came out. Nobile poked Cecioni, who woke up Zappi. The naval officer shook Mariano.

"Make an observation," whispered Nobile, "and check our position."

Zappi and Mariano both left the tent. A few minutes later Zappi's sharp face peered in the tent. "There's a bear!" he said in an undertone.

Everybody was immediately awake. Malmgren sat up, startled. "Give me the pistol!" he said. "I'm going to kill it!"

Nobile sat up and painfully stretched toward the tentpole. He handed the Swede the pistol and cartridges. There was no sound as Malmgren hurriedly loaded the gun.

"Keep quiet," warned Malmgren. Then he crept out onto the ice pack. Everyone followed. Cecioni and Nobile were helped onto the ice. In their excitement they felt no pain.

The sun was once more covered with clouds. It was bitter cold, but there was no wind. The clear, translucent air made the bluish ice crags stand out distinctly against the glaring white snow. Finally they saw the polar bear, twenty-five yards away toward the two islands.

"Shh! Don't move!" whispered Malmgren, turning back toward the tent. Then he stole forward slowly, the pistol clutched in his hand. Mariano and Zappi, armed with a knife and ax, followed warily at a distance.

The others stood stock-still and silent in front of the tent door. Each was armed with some crude weapon—a nail, a file, or a piece of tubing. They held their breaths as they eyed the animal. It was the first time any of them had been near a polar bear outside of a zoo. Nobile smothered Titina to his chest so she couldn't bark. She struggled, eager to join in the hunt.

This moment superseded the tensions of their six days on the floe. The bear could mean weeks of fresh meat—or an immediate death for all of them. In spite of the danger Nobile could hardly keep from laughing. It was a strange scene: nine ragged, dirty, bearded men stalking one huge white animal which was standing placidly as a cow staring at them, slowly wagging its head.

Malmgren crept to within fifteen yards of the bear. Then he raised the Colt slowly and fired.

"He's hit!" cried Biagi.

Malmgren ran toward the bear, followed by Mariano and Zappi. The Swede fired two more shots. The bear turned and ran clumsily across the floe. After a few steps it fell. It did not move.

There was great joy in the camp. Now they had 450 pounds of fresh meat and a bearskin! Malmgren was the hero. Everyone slapped his back, praised his outstanding skill with the pistol.

When the hunter came triumphantly back to the tent, Nobile extended a hand in congratulation. "You see," laughed Nobile, "the Queen was right!" The floe on which the action had taken place was henceforth and ceremoniously known as the "bear floe."

Malmgren supervised the skinning and cutting. "It has to be done while the animal is warm," he said.

Trojani and Zappi proved to be excellent skinners. Now Trojani broke his silence. He was so excited that he talked as much as Biagi. To their amazement they found nothing in the bear's stomach but some ragged pieces of paper printed in English. This mystery gave them much food for thought. Days later they realized that the bear had been so hungry that he chewed up a part of one of their navigation books.

They were too busy and too cheerful that day for arguments. After dinner they all dropped off to a euphoric sleep. With the extra 450 pounds of food they no longer need count off their lives on the little calendar that hung on the tentpole. And now, thought Nobile, the march could be delayed for at least a week.

Next morning, May 31, Zappi began talking of the march again. He had become obsessed by the floe's drift. Now Foyn Island was only seven miles away.

Mariano agreed with Zappi.

"We can all go together!" Cecioni said.

Zappi looked down at Cecioni coldly. "Last night," he said, "we tested your sledge by bringing one hundred pounds of meat from the bear floe. It's just forty yards but it took us over an hour."

Nobile stopped Cecioni's protests. He felt that he no longer had a right to hold up the marchers. "Get ready, Zappi, and go," he said. Then he asked for Malmgren.

A few minutes later the Swede crawled into the tent. "You're the only one who knows the Arctic," said Nobile. "Trojani and Biagi think you ought to stay on the floe."

"But the marchers need me," replied Malmgren. Then he thought a moment. "I'll do what you wish, General. Stay here or go with them."

"If you want to go," said Nobile, "I have no objections."

That day, the seventh on the floe, Malmgren prepared bear broth. The men eagerly awaited the moment when the broth was carried into the tent. But they were all bitterly disappointed. It had no taste, and they couldn't chew the tough lumps of half-raw meat. The pemmican was much better.

After the bear broth, Mariano turned to leave. "I want to speak with you alone," said Nobile.

Mariano ignored him and went onto the ice. Then he began speaking loudly to Zappi, knowing that Nobile could hear him. "No, we two should go! We're such good friends!"

Nobile realized that the statement had been for his benefit and he decided to make no more objections. He called everyone for a final conference.

"Three will leave," he said. He ordered the supplies and clothing divided. The pemmican and chocolate and malted milk were distributed equally. They all agreed that the bear meat should stay on the floe.

"We'll take the pistol," said Zappi.

"You will not!" shouted Cecioni.

"What should we do if more bears come along?" protested Viglieri. Trojani nodded in agreement.

"We'll keep the pistol," decided Nobile. "You take the knife and ax."

The marchers were given windproof suits, and all the extra woolen clothing. The charts and instruments were shared. Each of the three marchers took a watch and compass.

"When do you intend leaving?" asked Nobile.

"This evening," said Malmgren. Mariano and Zappi went outside to make preparations. Malmgren squatted down at the general's feet. They were silent for several minutes.

Finally Nobile said, "What do you think will happen?"

"They don't understand," said the Swede, nodding toward his two companions on the floe, "how difficult and dangerous à march on the pack is."

"And we?"

"You'll have the drift. It'll carry you to the east." He paused, then said in a lowered voice, "Both parties will die."

Half an hour later Biagi came into the tent with a heavy frown on his face. He sat down and stared accusingly at Nobile.

"What's wrong, Biagi?" asked Nobile with affection. Thinking back on what he knew of the young man, he admired most his tremendous energy and boundless optimism.

"I'm fit to march too," Biagi said sullenly.

"Why, of course, my dear Biagi," said Nobile. Then he added, "If you think it better to go, then you shall go. You've done your duty and you needn't have any scruples about leaving. Go and get ready."

Biagi's face brightened. He jumped to his feet and hurried out of the tent.

Viglieri, who had been sitting silently beside Nobile, said quietly, "If he's going, then I want to go too."

Nobile nodded. It was logical and just. He knew that Viglieri, who had been quiet for so many days, had always thought his only hope was to march.

Nobile called Malmgren, Mariano, and Zappi. "Biagi is coming with you," he said. "And all the others who can walk. I'll stay here with Cecioni."

The giant with the broken leg began to protest. Nobile quieted him.

"Two invalids can't stay alone," growled Zappi.

Mariano agreed.

"I'll look after Cecioni," insisted Nobile. He glanced around at the men. "I intend that whoever wishes to go shall go. Now I'm going to question you one by one . . . for the last time!"

He suddenly turned to Viglieri. It took the naval officer off his guard. Viglieri hesitated and then said, "We made up our minds before that just three should go. I don't see why we have to go back on our word."

Behounek hunched his massive shoulders. "I'm staying with the general."

"Me, too," Trojani said.

"All right," said Nobile, looking at Biagi. "Go and get ready, then."

Mariano, Zappi, and Biagi left. Malmgren stayed. He sat silent at the general's feet. "Well," he said after a minute, "if they leave, I stay."

"Why, Malmgren?" Nobile asked.

Malmgren's steady blue eyes seemed to go right through the Italian. "I could never go back to Sweden and say that I abandoned the leader of the expedition. That I left him and another sick man here without any help." He looked out the tent door. "It would be unworthy of a gentleman." He got to his feet. "No, if Biagi leaves, I stay. He's the only hope you have left."

Minutes passed. No one in the tent spoke. Then Biagi sidled in through the opening. He sat down cross-legged and looked fixedly at Nobile.

Then he began to grin.

"Forgive me, sir," he said impulsively. "It was a moment of weakness. I've decided not to go. You might need me for the wireless."

Biagi's smile was catching. First Nobile smiled, then Viglieri and Behounek and Cecioni. At last even Trojani broke into a semblance of a smile.

Food for three was put into two small bundles and the knapsack found near Pomella's body. The marchers also took the blanket, two bottles of gasoline, half the alcohol from the compasses, and rope. Nobile gave them the only pair of ice glasses, three pair of ski socks, catskin slippers, and Russian felt boots.

Now Malmgren, ready to go in Biagi's place, asked for the radio operator's shoes.

"No," replied Biagi without hesitation. He explained that he had to make countless trips from the tent to the transmitting set and back. Biagi kept his shoes.

The Swede, his pack prepared, sat down next to Nobile for a last talk. Now that he was about to go into action, all his depression had gone. But he regretted leaving Nobile.

"I'm sure we'll get through!" he said.

"And then?" asked Nobile.

"Then I'll come back to look for you myself with Swedish airplanes! Put four red flags at the corners of a square, two hundred twenty yards on each side, with the tent in the center. And be sure to eat the bear meat first and save the pemmican for a march when everyone is able-bodied. Another thing: don't let the bear meat touch the ice. Hang it up." He put his hand on Nobile's shoulder. "Keep quite still, General. Then your fractures will heal soon."

"We will be all right, Malmgren," said Nobile.

"Don't use the radio for twenty or twenty-five days," went on Malmgren quickly, almost guiltily. "Save the batteries until we've had time to get there and send a boat as near you as possible."

Nobile asked if they should change their campsite.

"Yes, find a safer spot. Keep your eye on that channel. If it comes within fifty yards, get out of here as fast as you can." The Swede warned about the movements of the ice and then asked what messages Nobile wanted sent to Italy.

"Tell them my comrades and I are staying here calmly," said Nobile. "Just see that they look after our families."

Malmgren held out his hand. "All right, General. And just remember that the greater number of lost expeditions have been saved at the last moment." He stood up. "If you have any letters for your families give them to us."

The men staying scurried for paper and pencils. Trojani shrugged his shoulders. "What's the use?" he said, giving Nobile his fountain pen.

The tent grew silent, the silence accentuated by the scratch of pen and pencils. Nobile wrote to his wife, Viglieri to his mother. Behounek began a letter to his fiancée. Tears rolled down his filthy cheeks. Only Nobile, who was struggling to suppress his emotion, and Trojani, who was impassively wrapping up money for his wife, remained dry-eyed and composed.

Cecioni wrote a few lines, then dropped his head down and sobbed. Nobile picked up the letter. It was full of his grief and despair.

"No, not like that, Cecioni," said Nobile. "It's not certain we're going to die here." He crumpled up the letter. "Here, let me write. You copy it." Putting his own letter aside, Nobile wrote Cecioni's wife a long letter full of hope and advice. When he finished, he wrote seven pages to his own wife, making many suggestions for Maria's education.

"Perhaps God wills that we shall embrace each other again one day," he concluded. "That will be like a miracle. If not, don't mourn my death but be proud of it."

He added a few lines to Maria. "You must keep Mummy from crying, if I don't come back again. Titina is perfectly happy here, but perhaps she'd still rather be with you."

The letters were handed over to Malmgren. Then Nobile distributed the last meal they all would share—three tablets of malted milk and a few lumps of sugar.

There was little talk during the meal. Afterward Mariano slid over and embraced the general. So did Zappi. The men were weeping. The bitter quarrels of the past days were forgotten.

Nobile embraced Malmgren.

Mariano, remembering that Cecioni's greatest fear was the widening channel, went up to the big man. "If it stretches up to the island," he promised, "we'll come back to get you. Don't worry. We'll march quickly and bring help."

The three marchers went outside and fastened the bundles on their backs. Nobile called from the tent, "Good luck! God go with you!"

Slowly the marchers moved away.

Viglieri, Trojani, Behounek, and Biagi stood for a long time in front of the tent, watching the three figures struggle across the ice pack toward the islands. At last they filed back into the tent.

In Italy special church services were now being held. The Pope had given orders that he be awakened, even in the middle of the night, if any word of the lost men was received. Rescue operations were stepped up. Swedish, Norwegian, Finnish, and Russian planes were being rushed to Spitsbergen. Only the Italians seemed strangely lethargic; they insisted that a wide air search should not be made yet. "Official circles in Norway," read a special cable to the New

York *Times* from Copenhagen, "are at a loss to understand Italy's attitude toward the rescue expedition."

But the world's attention had become distracted by a more newsworthy story. The seaplane *Southern Cross,* with Captain Charles Kingsford-Smith and three Australian companions, was halfway across the Pacific on its way to Hawaii.

The day after the Malmgren party left, Viglieri passed his time scanning the pack through glasses. The men had forgotten about him when he let out a shout. "I think they're turning around!" he called to those in the tent. "Maybe the channel runs all the way to the island!"

"They're coming back!" cried Cecioni joyfully.

"No, they're not!" said Nobile. "They're never coming back!"

The utter finality of the general's statement sobered the others. From that moment on they thought less and less of the marchers.

A new schedule was set up. Viglieri was put in charge of dispensing provisions and making solar observations. Trojani was made chef, with Behounek as his assistant. Cecioni, who had found a large needle in his pocket, was put to work making slippers. His first project was a pair, made out of two waterproof bags, for Viglieri's massive feet.

Within a day their industry had revived their spirits. They were now united, an abandoned family, with Nobile as father. Cheerfully the four able-bodied men instituted and divided a night watch. They kept a continual lookout for bears and dangerous rifts in the ever-moving ice.

Nobile followed Malmgren's advice except as it applied to the radio. He still felt their only hope lay in the radio. If, as he was convinced, the *City of Milan* wasn't listening faithfully, perhaps another operator would pick up their signals. He wrote out a message in Italian and French and gave it to Biagi.

"Starting tomorrow," he said, "transmit it every day for an entire hour."

Biagi, who obeyed an order without discussion, nodded.

Every day, as soon as the men awoke, someone would ask the man on guard, "Can you see Foyn Island? How far away is it?"

This island became the only real measure of their aspirations. Except for it, the world was silent, desolate, frozen. When they floated near the island, sea gulls came down to inspect them. The birds settled on the hummocks, making raucous cries. The birds and their sounds were a source of pleasure to the men. When the birds were there, the men weren't alone.

One day, while sending out a message, Biagi heard a sound behind him. Turning, he saw a great bear. The animal had knocked down one of his wires. Biagi ran to the tent. "There's a bear!" he cried. "Where's the pistol!"

Nobile, forgetting his broken leg, got to his feet. He reached for the Colt, which still hung on the center pole directly under the Madonna of Loreto. A stab of pain went through his leg. Biagi grabbed the gun and ran outside. He fired three times. The bear trundled off toward Foyn Island.

The next day, while eating, they heard Titina barking furiously on the floe. Behounek and Viglieri rushed out of the tent. They were right—it was the bear again. The tiny white terrier was chasing it across the ice. The bear didn't return for three weeks.

On their tenth day, June 3, an icy north wind began blowing again. The men huddled together against the increasing cold. The tent cover flapped continuously. Soon Broch Island disappeared and Foyn began fading rapidly. The men felt as if they were on a sailing ship.

Remembering Malmgren's prophecy, the men lapsed into a deep despondency. Nobile tried to cheer them up. "Think of the millions all over the world praying for us," he said. "A million prayers have to be answered."

Viglieri agreed. So did Cecioni and Behounek. But Trojani grunted his sarcastic grunt. Quickly the general made a joke. Biagi, always susceptible to humor, guffawed. The others watched Biagi laugh, tried to laugh with him. Trojani remained impassive, unsmiling.

As the days slipped by Nobile watched Trojani, who continued to do his work efficiently. But he was following every order through discipline—not because he thought that they had the slightest chance of being saved.

Even though Biagi no longer had faith in his radio, he was positive they'd be saved. One morning the men woke up to the sound of singing. It was Biagi. "Gina, My Lovely Gina!" he sang exuberantly. The others picked up the tune one by one. Finally Trojani joined in. To everyone's surprise he had a good voice.

To encourage singing, Nobile handed out sugar as a reward. But when the bitter northwest wind continued blowing through June 5 and 6, even Biagi became depressed. The singing stopped.

Nobile realized that something—anything—must be done to sustain morale. He decided that when the floe drifted within ten miles of Cape Leigh Smith he'd order the four able-bodied men to march for land. He told Cecioni of the plan.

The big man protested mildly, almost as a formality. He had

grown calmer with each passing day, till now he seemed reconciled to staying alone with his leader.

Nobile explained his plan carefully to Trojani and Behounek; Viglieri and Biagi, he knew, would obey him without protest.

Trojani shrugged his shoulders. "I'll do what you command," he said.

The general turned to Behounek.

"I don't know why you ask me this," said Behounek sharply. "I've come here with you and I'm not going away without you."

Nobile did not know whether to be pleased with the professor's loyalty or dismayed by his belligerence. Certainly the man was not easy to understand. Every morning, his face filthy, his hands black, the shoes almost falling from his feet, he would shuffle onto the pack and take his scientific observations. It was a religion to him. It sustained him.

After their meager dinner that evening, Biagi, as usual, intercepted the San Paolo broadcast. The others were watching him with halfhearted interest. Suddenly his face lit up.

"They've heard us!" he cried.

The men jumped up and crowded around him. Nobile dragged himself across the tent floor. Biagi was writing as fast as his trembling fingers permitted. Nobile leaned over his shoulder and read aloud, "The Soviet Embassy has informed the Italian government——"

The rest of the dispatch soon followed. A young Russian farmer from Archangel, Schmidt by name, had picked up fragments of their SOS on the evening of June 3.

Then the tent was a scene of wild joy. The men hugged each other. Those who could walk danced around. Trojani himself was jubilant. "But do you truly believe we shall return home?" he asked Nobile.

"So much depends," said the general. "We can hope." He ordered a celebration banquet of a ninth of an ounce of malted milk and half an ounce of sugar. Alcohol was carefully drained from the compasses. The men drank a toast to their unknown friend, Schmidt.

But the celebration on the floe was somewhat premature. Few outside of the Soviet Union believed that the Russian operator had actually heard them. Those at King's Bay, in particular, insisted it was all a hoax.

The next day, the fourteenth on the ice, Biagi transmitted with zest. That evening everyone except Trojani, who was sentry, listened intently to the evening bulletin.

Biagi copied out the bulletin as he spoke. An American radio amateur had intercepted a radiogram from the *Italia* survivors. "No shelter except remains *Italia* which crushed against mountain," said the false message. Then it gave their position—near the 85th parallel in the Arctic Ocean.

The men were frantic over the hoax. It was unintelligible, but it was scrambled artfully enough to be convincing. And it would make people even more skeptical of the true report from Schmidt. Nobile passed around an extra ration of sugar to ease the blow. At this moment Trojani, the hairs in his nose frozen stiff, stuck his head into the tent. When he learned what had happened he sighed. "These ups and downs of hope are enough to drive you crazy."

"Not quite crazy," replied Viglieri calmly.

A moment later Biagi, still at the receiver, held up his hands for silence. The men waited expectantly. It was a newspaper dispatch from the *City of Milan*. That morning, it said, the supply ship had heard fragments of what could have been a call from the *Italia*. The message had been, "SOS—Franceso."

Biagi's head bobbed wildly. "That was ours!" he cried. "They ran together the words 'Foyn' and 'circa'!" Then Biagi's face fell as he read aloud the rest of the dispatch: the Italian officials were sure the message was another fake.

"I'll make you a promise, Biagi," Nobile consoled. "When you really are heard by the *City of Milan*, you'll get an entire chocolate bar as a reward."

The following day Biagi transmitted a new message: "SOS *Italia*, Nobile, longitude twenty-eight degrees east, about twenty miles from the northeast coast of Spitsbergen."

After a dinner of bear stew, which Trojani by some magic had managed to make tasty, the men settled around the receiver for the evening bulletin.

Biagi grew impatient as he copied page after page of trivial news. Finally he took off his earphones and began gossiping with the others. A few minutes later he lazily put the earphones on again.

"*Italia! Italia!*" he heard. He gave a start. "They're calling us!" he shouted.

"It can't be," Nobile murmured.

But Biagi's face was radiant. " 'The *City of Milan* heard you well this morning,' " he repeated aloud.

The men hung on Biagi's words, holding their breaths for fear of disturbing the reception.

" ' . . . and has received your coordinates. Give Biagi's registration number.' "

The men laughed and shouted. They looked years younger in spite of their filthy, bearded faces. Nobile decreed a special feast of five lumps of sugar, ten malted milk tablets, and two ounces of chocolate. Never had there been such a feast.

Then Nobile remembered his promise to Biagi. He ordered Viglieri to hand over an entire half-pound chocolate bar.

The young operator, his lips moving in anticipation, took the candy. Slowly, ceremoniously, he tore off the wrapping. The men watched him with mixed pride and envy.

Biagi opened his mouth for a bite of his fantastic wealth. Then he glanced around, closed his mouth. Without a word he broke the bar in two, offering his comrades the bigger piece.

The next morning, their sixteenth day on the ice, Biagi heard a fragment of a message from the *City of Milan*. "Be ready to make a smoke signal. Airplanes will . . ." At that point the message broke off.

"We are on the pack drifting slightly with the wind," Biagi replied. "We will make smoke signals and fire Very lights as the airplanes approach. Remember that our batteries may run out in a few days but we shall still be able to receive." He also gave the local weather conditions and listed the provisions they needed. Then he told the *City of Milan* about the Malmgren party, giving its approximate position.

There was great hubbub in the little camp as preparations for the arrival of the planes were made. Using the liquid in the glass altitude balls, the men painted wide red stripes on the tent. The cartridges for signaling were a little too large, and Cecioni went to work filing down the chamber of the pistol. In the process the head of a cartridge flew off. There was a small explosion and the tent began to burn. Nobile smothered the blaze with his jacket, but the men were frightened. Now that rescue seemed near, their only home, and main hope for survival against the freezing winds, took on new importance.

The next few days were the happiest on the pack. Sentries pulled their shifts eagerly, vigilantly, not as a meaningless chore. Foyn Island was nearer than ever. In celebration Nobile decided to wash his hands. Cecioni had found a tiny piece of soap in his bag. Biagi brought in a wooden box full of snow. The general rubbed his hands briskly with soap and snow. A dense, black liquid ran off into a wash dish. Everyone gathered around and watched.

A sensuous look came over Nobile's face as his hands showed white again. But he soon learned that cleanliness was a dangerous luxury: the dirt and grease had been a protection against the bitter cold.

The greatest danger now lay in the widening channel. There was also a good chance that at any moment their floe would split in two and dump them in the icy water. Nobile radioed the *City of Milan* for medical equipment and a collapsible boat. He advised sending a hydroplane. "The pack here is extremely broken. Canals often open which are large enough for a hydroplane to moor."

But the *City of Milan* cut them off almost pettishly: "You had better economize your batteries. It is our business to speed up the rescue work. Three Swedish planes are on the way. Captain Riiser-Larsen is in the *Hobby* near Maffin Island but blocked in the ice. The Russians are preparing a large ice-breaker while we are trying to reach you with dog teams, and to meet your three comrades who are marching for Cape North."

The news on June 11, their eighteenth day, was so good that they forgot their hunger pangs. The Swedish expedition was en route to King's Bay. The *Hobby* was clear of ice and pushing ahead with Riiser-Larsen and two small planes aboard. Major Maddalena had left Italy in the hydroplane, S-55. Major Penzo was about to leave in another. A Russian ice-breaker was to sail that day from Archangel with two planes, and another would leave soon. Finland was sending a trimotor with skis, and Germany had offered men and machines.

But the men on the ice found their greatest hope in the announcement that Amundsen was almost ready to take off. They knew that if anyone could find them, it would be the old Norwegian.

After listening to all the details, Nobile remarked, "It's an interesting problem, our rescue."

"It's a hell of a problem," Trojani grumbled. "And if they don't hurry up, they won't solve it."

The two Russian ice-breakers, *Malygin* and *Krassin*, raised their hopes. The men on the floe knew that the Russians were just obstinate enough to push through until they found them. The idea of going back on a ship appealed to them. Reverently they put their dream into words: one day the stillness of the pack would be broken by the blast of a whistle; then they'd see smoke in the distance, and the ice-breaker would approach.

"We'll get on board," mused Cecioni, "and, without even stopping, go straight to Archangel and thank Schmidt!"

Everyone laughed. They made jokes about the red flags they'd hoisted beside the Alpini pennants flying over the tent.

"When the Russians arrive," said Biagi, "they'll be glad to find their flag flying beside our own."

Then the talk shifted to Malmgren, Mariano, and Zappi. The

chances of the three crossing the ice pack safely were gone over and over. Finally the discussion drifted off into a gloomy silence.

If only they had had faith in the radio, repeated Nobile to himself. He squinted across the floe into the distance. His eyes were smarting. It was snow blindness.

By now the heat of their bodies had melted the snow and ice under the tent. They leveled off a new position a few yards away, then repitched the tent. That night they slept in comfort on a soft, freshly made bed of snow.

On June 12 a turbulent west wind blew them away from their two islands. To make matters worse the radio was working badly, and Biagi heard nothing from the *City of Milan*. Hours later, when the storm was over, their two islands had disappeared and the sea gulls had flown away. They were back on the face of the moon.

Next day the strong wind returned, agitating the ice dangerously. A channel about seven yards wide suddenly opened near the tent. The sentries, their teeth chattering and their faces battered by the wind, watched the channel closely. By the next afternoon the cleft had widened. A few sheets of ice broke away from the floe. Then a large block near them slid into the channel. Trojani, the man on duty, gave the alarm. The men rushed out of the tent, Cecioni and Nobile bringing up the rear on their hands and knees.

An argument sprang up. Half of the group wanted to move, half didn't. Nobile pointed to the bear floe 40 yards away. "We'll move there," he said. "Right now."

The two invalids sat on the ice while the others took down the tent and shifted the stores. Their floe, after twenty days of habitation, was a dreary place. The ice was dirty, covered with puddles of slush. Everywhere were scraps of wreckage—twisted tubing, broken instruments, rags.

Out of a desperate pride, and to spare the men from carrying him, Nobile started to crawl to the new campsite. But after a few yards he came to a wide crevasse. Humiliated, he crawled back to the tent. Finally he was loaded into Cecioni's improvised sledge and carried, litter-style, from floe to floe by the four able-bodied men. It was a dangerous trip and painful to Nobile. Cecioni, who was almost twice as heavy, was then loaded into the sledge. The porters struggled on, and Cecioni moaned in pain for more than an hour. Finally they reached the new floe. The four men, exhausted and gasping for breath, collapsed on the ice. The sweat froze on their faces.

The spacious new location was surrounded with boulders of ice ten feet high. Beyond the hummocks lay little flat stretches that rested the eye and mind. Except for a few footprints the floe was spotlessly clean, with no wreckage to remind them of the disaster. The only landmark was the bear's skeleton, which jutted up short and thick between two hummocks. Next to it lay a great black mass, the animal's liver. It was a good place.

In three hours everything had been moved and the tent, now a faded pink, set up. At first the men were uncomfortable inside the tent. Any new home was a little difficult to get used to.

That day Biagi was informed that the *City of Milan* would only listen to him at 8:55 P.M. This was annoying: it meant they had to forego one of their greatest daily pleasures, the 9:00 P.M. bulletin from San Paolo. But Nobile decided not to protest. For the next few days reception was poor. The *City of Milan* picked up no more than fragments of Biagi's messages. But King's Bay didn't seem at all worried.

"We have nothing new to tell you," they said each night with monotonous regularity. "Good-by till the next hour." Then, instead of listening for Biagi's reply, they would switch off at once and send personal telegrams to San Paolo.

"When you call us you must listen in too," was Nobile's curt message the next day. "We might have urgent news to communicate."

But the next message from the *City of Milan* was the same: "Nothing to tell you. Good-by till the next hour."

On June 17, the twenty-fourth day, Nobile dictated an angry message: "For three days we have not managed to give you our coordinates because you persist in listening to us only at 8:55 P.M., when the reception is often very bad. Once more, then, we beg you to listen in to our station for ten minutes every time you call us." The message gave their new position—about five miles from Foyn Island. The weather was good, said Nobile, and visibility excellent. Romagna should take advantage of conditions to send at once the minimum supplies. "Our situation," he concluded, "is still dangerous."

Now that they were once more near Foyn Island they were again visited by birds and bears. During a meal the sentry, Trojani, stuck his head in the tent. "There is a bear," he said with quiet formality.

He reminded Nobile of a butler announcing an unwelcome guest.

Biagi seized the pistol and ran out to the ice. The bear was out of range, standing over Pomella's shallow grave. He had uncovered an arm. Biagi shouted and fired for effect. The bear lumbered off. When the radio operator told of the uncovered grave, Nobile sighed.

"Well," he said, "we'll have to bury poor Pomella in the sea."

Later in the afternoon a faint hum was heard. It grew louder. The men shouted and ran about helter-skelter as two planes approached from the south. Nobile ordered signal fires burned and the Very pistol shot. The two planes came within two miles and then turned back. Biagi immediately radioed that the planes had been sighted. The following morning the *City of Milan* told them the planes—piloted by Riiser-Larsen and Lützow Holm—would try again that day at the same hour.

The men kept constant watch all day, but the planes did not appear. That evening they learned through the bulletin that Maddalena had arrived in his hydroplane at King's Bay. Then came the glorious news that Amundsen had left Tromsö that day for Spitsbergen in the French plane, the *Latham*. Once Amundsen took charge of the rescue work, they were as good as home.

At 7:05 A.M. on the nineteenth of June, the men on the floe heard a plane. They knew it was Maddalena, who had taken off from King's Bay at four twenty-five. Trembling, prayerful, helpless, they watched him circle twice to the northwest, coming within a few miles. Then at seven thirty the big plane turned and disappeared.

Nobile quickly sent instructions. "At least two airplanes flying parallel should be used," he advised. "Fix up a wireless in Maddalena's hydroplane. Observe with sun at your back. Today we also saw Riiser-Larsen but he was too far east. Tell him all I have said."

Later another Norwegian plane came close. It traveled in zigzags from Foyn Island heading toward the floe. A few miles away it turned and flew away.

That night Nobile decided to make biscuits. A box containing a few pieces of bread had fallen into a crevasse; the bread was soaked in the salt water and inedible. Nobile washed his dirty handkerchief as best he could. Then he put the bread in the handkerchief and squeezed it until water oozed through the silk. With the paste he made eight little round rolls and set them out to dry in the midnight sun.

The next morning, their twenty-seventh day on the pack, while the others were enjoying the rolls, Biagi learned that Maddalena had left King's Bay at 6:00 A.M. He was carrying a radio.

Nobile ordered Viglieri and Trojani to prepare the smoke signals and Very lights. Biagi stood by the radio. Behounek was holding a tin to be used to flash signals. Viglieri stood on top of a hummock to shout directions to Biagi. Trojani was ready to light a fire primed with gas, oil, rags and paraffin.

Nobile and Cecioni sat on the sledge. The big man held a tinfoil "mirror." To protect his snow-blinded eyes, Nobile was wearing an eye shade made of the wrapping from Biagi's chocolate bar.

At seven thirty-five Biagi made contact with the plane. Half an hour later engines could be heard. Everyone waited tensely. As soon as the hydroplane appeared, Viglieri shouted directions. Biagi passed them on to Maddalena: "Turn five degrees to your right."

The plane did wheel to the right!

"Ten degrees to the left!" called Viglieri when the plane went too far to the right.

A moment later the hydroplane was heading straight for them. "The tent is on your course," radioed Biagi. "Three kilometers in front. Come ahead!"

The plane kept coming toward the floe. It swooped down to 100 yards.

Biagi gave the signal "VVV!"—"You're on top of us!"

The men were hysterical. They could see the Italian colors painted on the wings. As it passed overhead, two figures leaned out of the cabin and waved wildly in greeting.

Viglieri and Behounek were shrieking like madmen. Biagi, Cecioni, and Trojani were shrieking. Nobile tried to shout but his throat was stoppered tight. He took off his general's cap and waved it. The men began shouting unintelligibly to each other and sobbing and laughing, and Titina ran frenziedly over the ice barking shrilly.

The plane had passed far beyond. Now it wheeled and started back—but in the wrong direction. It changed its course several times, as if searching. It had lost sight of the floe.

Biagi ran to the transmitter. Frantically he signaled the plane. But it continued to wander aimlessly, out of touch.

"Oh, hell!" said Trojani. He had known all along they'd never be rescued.

Biagi kept scrambling from transmitter to receiver. After half an hour he made another contact with the plane. The men sighed with relief. Their faces were covered with nervous sweat. Once more the plane was guided back painfully to the floe. As it neared the tent Nobile shouted, "KKK!"—the code signal to drop the provisions.

Biagi was sending the message even as Nobile spoke. A figure leaned out of the back of the plane's cockpit. Packages fell. All the men, including the general, began to shout. The plane circled back; more packages were thrown out. Then the hydroplane wheeled and headed south.

Viglieri, Trojani, and Biagi scattered over the ice searching for the far-flung packages. Soon they began bringing them back. There were six pairs of shoes, two collapsible boats (which were greeted with the loudest shouts of glee), smoke signals, two sleeping bags, two rifles with broken stocks, a few shattered batteries, and a bag of provisions. The men quickly put on the leather shoes and danced

around the ice. Viglieri watched. There were no shoes large enough
for his large feet.

But when they took an inventory of the provisions the men were
cruelly disappointed. Instead of pemmican and chocolate they
found oranges, lemons, a pot of marmalade, a package of cocoa, fifty
bananas, and thirty fresh eggs—most of them broken.

That night, June 20, Nobile radioed the *City of Milan:* "Thank
you for the thrill you gave us this morning when we saw our country's colors overhead." He asked for more batteries (better
packed, this time!), pemmican, a Primus stove, medicine, snow
glasses, wooden stocks for the smashed rifles, and "a pair of *very*
large shoes for Viglieri."

He asked for news of Malmgren, Mariano, and Zappi and concluded by advising, "I think you should put yourself entirely in
Amundsen's hands, as he is the only expert collaborator with you."
He knew that only a man like Amundsen, who had himself been lost
on the desolate ice pack, would realize how vital speed was.

But Amundsen and his mates in the *Latham*, already long overdue,
were never to reach King's Bay. The great Norseman had already
disappeared somewhere in the mysterious Barents Sea. He would
never be found—dead or alive.

Two days later Maddalena returned to the floe, accompanied by
Major Penzo's hydroplane. Many packages were dropped, some in
chutes. One heavy box fell a few feet from Cecioni and Nobile. Another grazed the tent where Trojani lay, sick with gastric fever.
The men on the ice hugged each other and danced a grotesque jig.
Then, as one hydroplane swooped low, they saw a man leaning out
the window grinding a movie camera.

Instantly the men stopped dancing. They felt embarrassed.

Nobile's brother, Amadeo, had bitterly fought with Captain
Montagna about the cameraman a few hours earlier. The extra passenger meant a large case of chocolate had to be left behind.

At 11:10 A.M. Maddalena, with a wave, headed for King's Bay.
Penzo swooped down as if to land. The men on the floe feared he
had engine trouble. But as Penzo passed overhead, he leaned out
and shouted, "Au revoir!" Then he, too, flew back home.

The fourteen drops, each of which had been carefully marked this
time by Nobile with compass readings, contained enough provisions
for twenty days and many woolen clothes that, because the temperature was now only zero, Centigrade were not needed. And there
was medicine, a rifle, a carton of cigarettes, and two huge pairs of
shoes that fit Viglieri perfectly.

During the frantic rush for packages Biagi knocked against Behounek's right arm. The scientist cried out in pain. Only then was it learned that his arm had been severely wrenched in the crash of the dirigible. Behounek explained that he hadn't wanted to bother them with his personal problems.

The men sat in the brilliant sun, smoking and reading letters and newspapers in luxurious contentment. But Biagi and Nobile had noticed that the *City of Milan* had cut off communications with them, as if there were now nothing at all to be worried about.

The next evening at seven thirty two Swedish seaplanes located the floe by smoke signals. Five packages of well-chosen provisions, including two bottles of whisky were dropped on the floe in red parachutes. One bottle survived the drop.

"These Swedes are practical people!" said Nobile as he made an inventory. The men heartily agreed. People who could think of whisky knew what it meant to be stuck on an ice floe that was liable to disintegrate at any moment.

Attached to one of the packages was a message from Tornberg, the leader of the Swedish expedition. "If you can find a landing ground for airplanes fitted with skis," it read in the language of the North, English, "arrange the red parachutes in T shape on the leeward side."

Such a landing field—wide, surprisingly flat, and almost 350 yards long—had already been noted not far from the tent. Nobile dictated a radiogram to the Swedes in English, thanking them for their excellent supplies and telling about the landing field. But the message could not be sent: the *City of Milan* didn't answer Biagi's persistent calls.

That night the men groused, recriminated, and criticized. Their main theme was that their countrymen at King's Bay didn't realize how desperate their situation was. At any moment the unusually clear weather might end and the dense summer fogs begin. And as the weather grew warmer, the breakup of ice was accelerating and becoming more dangerous.

On June 23 Nobile sent a long message begging the *City of Milan* to speed operations. He told them that Cecioni and Behounek were both unfit for marching and should be taken off immediately before their ice floe broke up completely. He asked them to transmit his message about the landing field to the Swedes. Just at that point in the message the radio went dead. The men wondered if the Swedes, hearing nothing from them, would come back.

The next day, to keep the men's spirits up, Nobile held a conference to determine the order of leaving the floe. He told them he'd decided that Biagi should be last because he was the only one who could work the radio. The next-to-last would be Viglieri, the only man who could calculate the position of the drifting floe.

Because of his broken leg Cecioni would be the first to go. Then Behounek and Trojani would follow. Then Nobile himself.

The men agreed. Since the departure of Zappi it had not occurred to anyone to argue with the general.

It was their thirty-first day on the pack.

The men were glum as they sat down to dinner. No word had been received from the *City of Milan* at the regular time, 8:55 P.M. There was talk of taking to the boats when the pack broke up; they would steer through the ice for the nearest shore.

Abruptly Viglieri stopped eating. He said he thought he heard humming. Biagi heard it, too. In a moment everyone heard it. Viglieri ran outside.

"The airplanes are coming!" he shouted.

Behounek, Biagi, and Trojani ran out. Cecioni and Nobile dragged themselves to the ice.

"There they are!" cried Viglieri. Soon everyone could see two moving specks in the air.

"Make a smoke signal!" cried Nobile.

Smoke rose, dense and black, and floated northwestward in the light breeze. The two planes wheeled like hawks. They had seen the smoke.

"Viglieri and Biagi!" shouted Nobile, "Run to the field and lay down the landing signal. Hurry up! Run!"

The two men leaped across crevasses, scrambled up hummocks, ferried their way across wide channels using ice cakes as rafts. And now the planes were circling overhead.

"Get the sledge ready," Nobile told Cecioni.

The big man started wiring together pieces of the sledge.

"Trojani!" called Nobile impatiently. "Look in the box for wire. Quickly!"

Trojani, still weak and feverish, was lying in his sleeping bag. He grabbed several pieces of wire and staggered out onto the ice. Cecioni's clever hands worked desperately.

The hydroplane was still circling high above them. The second plane, equipped with skis, had disappeared from sight. Now it suddenly appeared, flying low. It skimmed over the ice and disappeared once again. Then it shot up in the air. The men wondered if it was having engine trouble.

When it repeated the maneuver again and again, the men realized that the pilot was looking the field over. Still again the plane swooped down. This time it seemed to touch the ice, and instead of being gunned skyward again, its skis bit into the snow. Particles of ice and snow flew up as the little plane skidded across the flat field. It rocked as it hit a small hummock, then stabilized and stopped.

Nobile let out his breath and whispered, "Thank God!"

Viglieri, Biagi, and Titina were racing across the ice toward the plane. They saw one man jump out and hold one wing while the pilot raced the motor and adroitly turned the plane into the wind.

Then a second man, the pilot, climbed out of the plane. The first was back in the cockpit keeping the motor running.

Viglieri reached the pilot first. He shouted in Italian. The blond, blue-eyed airman smiled and shook his head. The pilot tried a few words of Swedish. Viglieri shook his head. Biagi reached the plane. He embraced the pilot. Everyone was shouting and gesturing.

The pilot explained in English that he was a Swede, Lieutenant Einar Lundborg. He repeated the word "Nobile" several times. Viglieri pointed at the little tent 200 yards across the ice. The three men and the dog started on the dangerous trip, still laughing and shouting.

Nobile and Cecioni waited and waited for the group to reach them. The general was not an imposing figure in his gray sweater and knickers. On one foot he wore a leather shoe. His broken leg was covered with a stocking and *finsko*. He was bareheaded.

Lundborg, his arm extended and a broad grin on his face, walked up to Nobile.

"Here is the general," cried Viglieri in English.

Nobile took the Swede's hand in both of his. He tried to thank the airman but the words would not come out. He turned to Viglieri and Biagi and asked them to lift him up. They did. He flung his arms around Lundborg. A moment later he was laid back on the sledge.

Lundborg told them he'd be able to take all of them during the night. He reached down for Nobile. "You must come first, General."

Cecioni blanched.

"But that's impossible!" Nobile pointed to Cecioni. "Take him first. That's what I've decided."

Lundborg shook his head. "No. I must bring you first. We need your instructions to start looking for the others."

Cecioni began to cry.

"Please take him first!" begged Nobile. "Can't you see——"

Lundborg was embarrassed. He wished to oblige Nobile, but he had definite orders from Tornberg, the leader of the expedition. He wished he could comfort or apologize to Cecioni, but he couldn't speak Italian. He turned back to Nobile. "No, General," he said firmly. "We'll take you to our base. It's not far from here. Then I can come back quickly for the others."

Nobile started to protest again. This time Lundborg interrupted curtly, "I can't take him now, General. Can't you see he's too heavy?" He explained that if he took the giant he'd have to leave his mechanic behind. He refused to do that. "I'll come back and get him tonight. I promise." He anxiously looked at his plane. "Besides it'd take too long to carry him to the plane. We've got to hurry. Now please come quickly."

Nobile turned in despair to the others.

"Go," said Behounek.

Viglieri agreed.

"You go first," said Biagi. "It'll set our minds at rest." He knew that the general would make things hum at King's Bay.

Then Cecioni, tears still streaming down his face, nodded. "You go," he said. "Then whatever happens there'll be somebody to look after our families."

Nobile crawled into the tent to ask Trojani.

"Of course," growled Trojani, looking at the general as if he were crazy. "It's better that way. You go."

Lundborg was growing more and more impatient. Viglieri had brought out the bottle of whisky. Lundborg was touched but refused to accept a drink. Viglieri tried to force a pack of cigarettes on the Swede, but he shook his head violently. He took another glance at his idling plane and then, with a wave of his hand, turned and started across the ice. Titina, who had been making overtures to him from the first, tagged after him, almost tripping him up. She was leaving, no matter what happened.

Nobile came out of the tent. Lundborg turned and called back, "Hurry up, General!"

Nobile turned to Behounek. "Poor Behounek," he said, smiling sadly. The men embraced. Then Nobile put his arms around Cecioni, promising him that he'd soon be taken off the ice. The general left his reindeer boots, his woolen cap, his general's cap, and his heavy jersey. He took Maria's picture and two radio notebooks.

Viglieri and Biagi lifted Nobile, who now weighed only 125 pounds, and carried him out onto the pack. Halfway to the plane, the Swedish mechanic, Birger Schyberg, plodded through the snow to help. The three men finally slid Nobile aboard. Titina was already there, completely at home.

"Move Cecioni to the field at once so he's ready to start," said Nobile. He repeated the order in which the men would leave. "You, Viglieri, take command. Good-by until later. I'll be waiting for you." He shook Biagi and Viglieri warmly by the hand. "Don't forget to bring the little picture of the Madonna—good-by!"

The engine roared and the plane moved across the snow. Slowly, with difficulty, it lifted. Nobile sat up and looked out the cabin window. Below lay the terrible pack where he'd spent thirty-one days. He couldn't find the tent. Schyberg pointed it out. From above it was tiny, almost invisible, a scrap of dirty material against the variegated white. No wonder it had been so hard to find. A moment later Foyn Island lay below. The golden hope of their ice-bound days was a hilly mass covered with snow and studded with gray rocks.

The cold air swept back. Schyberg, seeing Nobile had no hat, took off his silk scarf and wound it around the general's head like a turban. Nobile lay back, holding Titina tightly so she wouldn't bother the fliers.

Half an hour later, when Nobile landed at the Swedish advanced base of operations, he was sure the saga of the ice floe was about over. Not long after Nobile and Titina were disembarked, Lundborg took off for another trip to the tent. This time the Swede left his mechanic behind so that he could take Cecioni.

But the ordeal on the ice would be long in ending. Lundborg's plane overturned on the snowfield almost at the feet of Cecioni, who was all prepared for the return flight. Once more there were six men stranded on the floe. And the Swedes had no other plane equipped with skis.

Tornberg wanted Nobile to wait for the *Quest* and sail back to the *City of Milan* in comfort; but the general, knowing his men would be disconsolate and embittered by the latest reverse, insisted that he be flown by hydroplane immediately.

Soon the plane landed at Virgo Bay, where Andrée had taken off in his balloon so many years before. The deck of the *City of Milan* was crowded with jubilant sailors. The crew cheered as he was carried to a cabin. Photographers and newsreel men begged the general to pose, but he waved them aside. He wanted to talk to Romagna. And he didn't want to be put on exhibit. He knew that he had a long bristly, grayish beard and his face was caked with grime. In the cabin he looked at himself in a mirror for the first time in thirty-two days. He looked worse than he'd imagined.

Romagna's greeting was shocking. "People might criticize you for coming first," he said curtly. "It would be well to give some explanation."

Nobile was puzzled. What explanations? Romagna said he knew

nothing of Lundborg's orders to take the general off first. Then
Nobile saw the newspapers. He was aghast to discover that he was
being pilloried for "deserting" his men. Bitter and disgusted, he
wanted to go back onto the ice. He became obsessed by the idea: he
had to escape from people who could believe such things of him. He
refused to see foreign correspondents, which served to renew their
attacks on him.

In his first meeting with Romagna he complained about the poor
radio communication. Romagna seemed surprised at his attitude.
"How was it you never heard our SOS?" asked Nobile angrily. "It
was picked up by Russians in Archangel!"

Romagna shrugged his shoulders. Was it, Nobile suggested, because he was too busy sending newspaper dispatches and as many as
400 personal radiograms a day? "Mariano, Zappi, and Malmgren
wouldn't have left us," accused Nobile, "if you'd been listening."

"But my dear General," said Romagna, "we were perfectly right
in imagining that you couldn't transmit—and so it was a waste
of time to listen for you." Then the captain blandly explained his
remarkable theory that Biagi's head had been chopped off by a
propeller.

Because Nobile insisted, the *City of Milan* operators now listened
in regularly. The general signed radiograms to his men, knowing his
name would assure them that he was watching over them. But after
a few days Romagna secretly had his own name substituted.

Nobile had a long talk with the Finnish flier, Sarko, urging him
to fit out the *Turku* with skis. When the interview was over Romagna burst into the cabin.

"I've heard, General," he said, "that you intend to go with the
Finns. I have orders from Rome to prevent you from taking part in
any rescue expedition." He glared at Nobile. "If you persist, I'll put
guards at the doors of your cabin!"

The general then called in Maddalena and Penzo and begged
them to keep searching for the dirigible and its six lost men. A moment later Nobile learned that Maddalena had told the Finns and
Swedes that the landing field at the floe was only 220 yards long
and very bumpy. In desperation, Nobile again called for Sarko. He
assured the Finn that the field was 350 yards long and extremely
smooth. Lundborg had tipped over because his engine had failed.
Sarko was convinced and left to make preparations for a landing.

The next day Nobile tried to convince Penzo to land a hydroplane on the wide channel. He begged Romagna to shift the
hydroplane base north, to save the fliers an extra 200 miles. But
the captain refused. He also refused to let the Italians use the
Swedish base.

On June 29 Viglieri sent a message asking them to hurry. The landing field was still in good condition but it would probably get worse. Lundborg added a message asking permission to start marching to Grosse Island.

Nobile knew that he had to say something to keep the men on the floe. He immediately wired that four planes, waiting only for good visibility, were ready to start for the "red tent."

Next day the Russian ice-cutter *Krassin* lay off Virgo Bay. Nobile asked Professor Samoilovich, leader of the expedition, if he could join the party. The Russian readily agreed. But Romagna insisted that Nobile was in poor physical condition and refused to let him leave the *City of Milan*. That same day Romagna, without telling Nobile, wired the tent that the *Krassin* was near Cape North and would probably reach them in two days.

When he learned of Romagna's wire, Nobile was furious. He knew how dangerous it was to raise the men's hopes falsely, and he wired his men the ice-breaker would not arrive for more than a week. He gave them detailed news of their families and words of advice and encouragement.

That afternoon, July 2, Riiser-Larsen landed at Virgo Bay. He had been ordered by the Norwegian government to return to the *Hobby* at King's Bay and look for Amundsen. But the Norwegian asked to see Nobile before his departure. When he came to Nobile's cabin, the general was in bed.

"How do you do, my dear Nobile?" he said. He went to the bed and flung his big arms around the Italian. Titina, who had recognized him, ran in between his legs, barking furiously. But Riiser-Larsen didn't recognize the dog—her black spots had been turned to brown by the month on the ice.

Nobile's eyes filled with tears. For a minute he could say nothing more than "Dear, dear Larsen." The others in the room, affected by the reunion, departed silently.

Nobile had so many things to say. He wanted to thank the Norwegian for his gallant aid. He wanted to say how unhappy he was about the trouble with Amundsen. He wanted to say how much he regretted the words he'd spoken belittling the great explorer.

"We must wait in faith," said Riiser-Larsen finally.

At last Nobile was able to talk. He told how much food the Malmgren party had taken.

"Oh, that's all right then!" cried Riiser-Larsen with relief. "They have enough for forty-five days!"

Nobile asked about Amundsen. Riiser-Larsen was confident he'd be found: The old man was too wily to be lost in the north. At that moment Lützow Holm, who had piloted the other Norwegian

rescue plane, came in. The three men chatted cordially. Then Nobile poured out a drink for each of them.

"Sholl!" said the Italian.

The Norwegians laughed and clinked glasses with him. "Skoll!"
they cried.

Arguments had sprung up on the floe. When the first messages
came through signed, "Your Nobile," the men were deeply moved.
They read them over and over again, and they knew at last that
everything was being done for them. Then curt messages signed
with Romagna's name were received. The men were stricken
by Nobile's silence. How could he have forgotten them so soon?

By the 5th of July, their forty-second day on the ice, the quarrels
were bitter. Lundborg, who was not content merely to sit on the
floe, told them they should march. Behounek sided with the Swede.
He said it was Viglieri's duty, as chief, to organize the march to
land.

"Your statements are unmilitary," Viglieri said stiffly.

"It's no place for military customs!" Behounek retorted.

The Italians were furious with Lundborg for the contradictory
reports he sent back on the state of the landing field. Biagi, who
was now ill with fever, made boisterous sport of the Swede's
fickle judgments. He would shout in English to Trojani, "Very good,
very bad, very good, very bad, very good, very bad!"

Each time the Swede, who refused to endanger the lives of other
Swedes, would walk off indignantly. And as soon as he did, a fresh
argument would spring up among the Italians on another subject.

Late in their forty-second afternoon a plane came over the floe.
It was a Swedish Hansa. Four packages, attached to red parachutes,
dropped out. An hour later another Swedish plane, a three-motored
Junker, roared over. It, too, dropped packages.

"Where the hell are the Italian planes?" grumbled Cecioni.

"Yes, where?" said Viglieri.

In the meantime Lundborg, remembering his Boy Scout signals,
was flashing a message to Lieutenant Karlsson in the Junker. "It is
possible to land here," he signaled.

Karlsson leaned out the window. "Understood," was his answer.

The men drank a toast to the Swedes in the Junker. Then Lundborg saw a message written on a rucksack: "We shall try to come
with the Moth tonight. Schyberg will fly it."

The Swede, whom all had agreed should leave first, was so happy
he took out his harmonica and played, "Old Man Noah."

The next morning at two o'clock Schyberg, accompanied by a

hydroplane, returned in a ski plane. Lundborg was taken off the floe. Now they were five again.

When Lundborg and Tornberg climbed aboard the *City of Milan,* soon after the rescue, Captain Romagna met them with a gloomy face.

"Why," he asked Lundborg testily, "did you have to take Nobile off first?"

The Swede was taken aback by the unfriendly greeting. "Because I believed he was the most exhausted of them all. Besides, he could give the rescue expedition invaluable information."

Romagna snorted. "Here he's only causing trouble!"

Nobile's greeting was much different. The general welcomed both Swedes warmly, thanking them for their great help. Lundborg then told of the unhappy conditions on the ice. Nobile was distressed. Although the Swedes had made up their minds to give up future rescue efforts, Nobile pleaded with them to keep up their work. Tornberg listened quietly. He thought for a minute and then said, "All right, General. We'll land again."

Nobile wrote a long letter to his men, scolding them like a father. To Cecioni he said, "You are strong in body. Let your spirit match it." He told them the Swedes were going to land as soon as the weather improved. "My dear Biagi," he concluded, "from now on you'll have a world-wide reputation. So you must get rid of the fever as soon as possible." Tornberg took the letter and promised to drop it with provisions in a few days.

That day Nobile learned that the *Krassin* was blocked by ice. Romagna then came into his cabin and told him that the Admiralty would probably order Viglieri to march for the coast, leaving Cecioni behind.

"You can't do that!" cried Nobile.

Romagna shrugged his shoulders as if the discussion was trivial, and went out.

The day was one of great discouragement. It was now almost certain that Amundsen was lost. The Russian aviator, Babushkin, had left the *Malygin* for exploration and failed to return. The alpinist Sora, and young Van Dongen, who had both left in dog teams for Foyn Island, hadn't been heard of for days. The tragedy was spreading.

News then came through that the *Krassin* was setting up an aircraft base. Romagna began to write out an answer telling the Russians that the *Braganza* was leaving for the north and the Swedes were about to make another flight.

"No! Not like that!" cried Nobile. "The Russians might think the Swedes and the *Braganza* have great chances of success." He wrote another message. "All our hopes are centered on the *Krassin*," it began.

The psychology worked. The Russian ice-breaker, in spite of a magnetic tempest that had cut off all communication with the ice floe for several days, headed north through the thickening ice.

On July 10 the Red flier, Chuknovsky, left the fogbound *Krassin* and headed for Charles XII Land. The fog increased, and those on the base ship built signal fires to guide him home. Then an electrifying word was flashed backed to the mother ship: "Malmgren!"

Chuknovsky radioed that he saw two men standing, and a third man lying down, on a tiny floe surrounded by water. He circled the men five times as one of them made a message in rags: "No Food." Chuknovsky took the position and then started back to the *Krassin*. A few minutes later he had to make a forced landing on the ice. Without hesitation he radioed the *Krassin* to forget him and his companions and pick up the Malmgren party first.

Tension rose aboard the Russian ship. Newspapermen put up a prize of 100 rubles for the first man who sighted the lost men. The ship's captain added another twenty-five rubles.

The *Krassin* plowed east in spite of a damaged helm and a broken propeller. At seven on the morning of July 12, First Mate Brennkopf, standing on the ship's bridge, saw two men on an ice floe about twenty feet by forty-five feet. With great shouts of joy the Russians headed toward the floe. A tall man was waving at them madly. A second man was lying on the ice.

Using ladders and planks the Russians reached the little floe. Brennkopf, seeing only two men, shouted in German, "Where's Malmgren?"

The tall man—it was Zappi—pointed vaguely in the distance. He was wearing two suits of clothing and parts of a third. On his wrists were three wrist watches and in his pocket three compasses. He wore two pair of shoes. The man lying on the floe was Mariano. He was almost dead. He had no shoes, only wet stockings. The Russians carried him to the ship. Zappi climbed up the *Krassin's* rope ladder like a monkey.

The Russians, knowing they were near the "red tent," pushed on as soon as Zappi and Mariano were aboard. Mariano refused to talk, but Zappi was voluble. He claimed he hadn't eaten for thirteen days, although the examining doctor said it was nearer three days. With nervous gestures the Italian naval officer explained that the third man Chuknovsky had spotted from the air, was just an extra flying suit.

"But where is Malmgren?" asked the Italian newsman, Giudici.
"He's at Broch Island."

"Then we'll go and search," said the *Krassin's* captain.

"Malmgren isn't there either," said Zappi almost hysterically. "He stayed on the ice." A minute later he elaborated on this story. Waving his arms wildly, he told the newsmen that Malmgren knew he was going to die and begged them to dig a grave in the ice. With their knives the Italians dug a shallow grave. Then—Zappi went on, the newsmen skeptically copying down the details—then Malmgren took off his clothes and lay in the grave. Quietly Malmgren stretched out his hand and bade them adieu. He gave Zappi his compass, asking that it be turned over to his mother. They left Malmgren and continued the march. Twenty-four hours later they had traveled only 100 yards. Looking back, Zappi said, they saw Malmgren raise his head from his ice grave.

"Go, go!" he cried. "At the price of my life you'll save all!"

After finishing this story Zappi bellowed, "Let me eat!"

Later he gave newsmen an even more fantastic story—one that was to revolt the world and stir up horrifying conjectures. In a braggadocio manner he said that only a few days before, when Mariano thought he was going to die, Mariano—like Malmgren— had taken off his clothes and lay on the ice. "When I die, you can eat me," cried Mariano. "But not before."

When this story was flashed back to Spitsbergen and on to the world it grew with every retelling. The fate of Malmgren now seemed obvious to millions: he'd been eaten.

That evening a lookout on the *Krassin* spotted an overturned plane next to a tiny tent on a far-off floe. A moment later the ship's whistle was blowing furiously. Five men on the floe could be seen jumping up and down and hugging each other.

Before long the five—castaways for forty-nine days—were on board the *Krassin*. Cecioni, tears streaming down his face, hobbled aboard on an improvised crutch. Then came Behounek, clasping several instruments tightly. Trojani, for a change, was beaming. Viglieri was weeping with joy. And last came Biagi. He had just sent a final message, signing off with a ". . . greeting to our beloved General Nobile!"

The general's cap was tilted cockily on Biagi's head. "When I get on board the *City of Milan*," he said, "I'll make them all stand at attention!"

Newsman Giudici talked with the young man as the Russians carefully packed every stick that was on the floe. "Would you come back to the Arctic again?" he asked.

"With the general, yes," said Biagi. Then he seized Giudici by the arm and looked across the ice. "Poor Pomella—" he said. Biagi knelt, bending his head in prayer.

Nobile was overjoyed when the news reached the *City of Milan.* He wired Samoilovich on the *Krassin,* suggesting that all efforts now be directed toward search of the lost dirigible. The professor wired back, "Please tell me if you are going to search for airship group with hydroplanes. In that case we will wait here by the tent." Nobile begged Romagna to get the Italian hydroplanes ready. But the captain refused. He saw no reason to risk the planes, and advised the *Krassin* to turn back. When Samoilovich got this message he was undecided. He asked Zappi's opinion.

"I consider the airship destroyed with all aboard," Zappi said with blunt certainty.

The Russians headed for Spitsbergen. Thus the search for the six in the dirigible was abandoned forever.

When the survivors came aboard the *City of Milan* the Italian sailors cheered and the ship's whistle blew. Cecioni hobbled up the gangway on his crutch. When he saw Nobile on deck he dropped the crutch, leaped forward, and embraced the general.

Behounek forced a smile. "Here I am back from my holiday," he said, wringing Nobile's hand.

Biagi, Viglieri, and Trojani hugged the general.

With Zappi, Nobile was distant, reserved.

"Why are you so cold, General?" asked Zappi.

Nobile looked angrily at the naval officer. "You shouldn't have told the Russians the men in the dirigible were surely dead!" He refused to shake Zappi's outstretched hand. "Why did you boast about going thirteen days without food?" he said. "Your party had food for forty-five days."

The general didn't see Mariano until a few days later, after the naval officer's frozen foot was amputated. Nobile was touched by his first officer's condition, but when Mariano asked that Nobile recommend Zappi and him for a gold medal for valor, the little general sadly shook his head.

Hostility toward Nobile grew stronger and stronger. He was being attacked from all parts of the world for his "cowardliness" in leaving the ice pack before his men. For some reason he was also blamed for leaving Malmgren on the ice to die. The Communist *Youth Pravda* bitterly called him "the Fascist general who took the Cross to the Pole but deserted his comrades."

"Why did he run away?" asked *Pravda.* "When they left Malm-

gren, was he dead or alive?" Thus the ugly charge of cannibalism
was laid at his door.

The American press, even the New York *Times,* joined the pack.
Papers and magazines printed hundreds of faked statements and
wild rumors. Behounek was falsely quoted as joining the attack on
the general. (He later wrote a book defending Nobile.) When
Lieutenant Lundborg tried to explain that he had insisted on Nobile leaving the floe first, few would listen. It wasn't a good
enough story.

On the 14th of July, Captain Sora and Van Dongen were rescued by Finnish and Swedish planes. Now the only ones unac-
counted for were the Amundsen party and the six on the dirigible.
To this day there have been no traces of either group.

On July 22, just before the *City of Milan* left King's Bay,
Penzo and Maddalena apologized to Nobile for not having done
more. They said they hadn't received the proper backing from
Romagna. The fliers asked Nobile to stay in King's Bay with them
and help continue the search for the dirigible. Nobile sent a telegram to Rome asking permission. He was told curtly to return to
Italy at once.

At Narvik the Italian survivors of the *Italia* were bundled into two
special railroad cars. They were ordered to stay in the cars and
speak to no one.

As the train moved across Norway, onlookers glared at them
with hatred.

At Vindelm, the first stop in Sweden, the atmosphere was notice-
ably different. A little blue-eyed girl, Ebba Haggstrom, came into
Nobile's car. She handed him a small bunch of flowers. The general stammered his thanks. And all through Sweden sympathetic
crowds stood quietly at each station and friendly notes were slipped
into Nobile's hands.

But in Germany the reception was again cold and threatening.
One of the mechanics sneaked off the train and bought a German
newspaper. An ugly cartoon was on the front page: it pictured
cannibals in a padlocked railroad car. As their train was leaving the
station at Halle a big man ran alongside, glaring at them and gnash-
ing his teeth. It was a memory none of them ever forgot.

As they approached Italy, the men worried about the reception
they would get in their own country. At the first Italian station
great cheering throngs descended on the train. When they got to
Rome on the evening of July 31, 200,000 swarmed over the big
station. The crowd welcomed Nobile and his men with wild affection and admiration and relief.

Like a ghost of himself, Nobile walked slowly through the crowd.
There was an abstracted gaze in his deep eyes. He looked years
older, but for the first time in many days he felt that he was surrounded by friends. His countrymen believed in him.

That was on July 31, 1928.

On March 3, 1929, his countrymen would present him with his
greatest humiliation of all.

12

THE MILLIONTH
CHANCE

In the early 1920's an American representative was discussing war reparations with Lloyd George. The British Prime Minister remarked half-jokingly that America might prefer a German-built airship to the money. The American official relayed the suggestion to Washington. Since President Harding had already been convinced of the potentialities of Zeppelins by a Yankee businessman, Harry Vissering, the facetious proposal by Lloyd George was accepted.

But the other Allies were not too enthusiastic. The French, in particular, wanted all German inventions suppressed. The Zeppelin, although it had actually killed few civilians in all its air raids, had been a terrifying war weapon. In order to discourage the United States, it was stipulated that such a ship could not be military or exceed 2,470,000 cubic feet—and that the Zeppelin Works at Friedrichshafen must be torn down after the dirigible's completion.

The United States not only agreed to these terms but offered 100,000 dollars to the Zeppelin Airship Construction Company if Dr. Hugo Eckener, the chairman of its board, would personally deliver the airship to the United States.

It was then unofficially suggested to Eckener by an American representative that the destruction of the Zeppelin Works and its technological knowledge would be a great loss. Since the Zeppelin Company was a private organization, what was to prevent another private organization from buying its patents? Eckener seized on the suggestion, and shortly thereafter a contract was made with the Goodyear Tire and Rubber Company. All the Zeppelin patents were turned over to the newly formed Goodyear-Zeppelin Company in 1924. It was also agreed that after the building of the ship, the *LZ-126*, Dr. Carl Arnstein, constructor of over seventy Zeppelins, would sail to the United States and become Vice-President and chief engineer of the young company.

The trip of the 670-foot *LZ-126* from Germany to Lakehurst was uneventful. At 4:15 A.M., on October 15, 1924—just seventy-five hours and forty minutes after leaving Friedrichshafen—the great ship flew over Boston. The noise of its engines soon awakened the city. As the dirigible's searchlights swept over the Common, ships in the harbor blasted their horns and blew their whistles. A few hours later New York gave an even greater reception. Already keyed up by the exploits of the *Shenandoah,* which was then tied up at a mast in California on her grand tour of the United States, the whole country went "Zeppelin mad."

Eckener and his men were feted continuously. President Coolidge proclaimed the flight "an event of world importance," and invited Eckener to Washington. The airshipmen were later given a ticker-tape welcome on Wall Street. They were taken on a boisterous drive through New York, ending at the Army-Notre Dame football game at the Polo Grounds; and the Germans were cheered more heartily than Crowley's winning touchdown. Two nights later they were guests of honor at the first showing of the Zeppelin movies at the Capitol Theatre—to the accompaniment of Wagnerian music. At the end of the feature, Buster Keaton in *The Navigator,* the applause for the German fliers was so persistent that Eckener had to arise and say a few words in his halting English. The orchestra then stood up and played the "Deutschlandlied." Eckener clenched his teeth, closed his eyes so he wouldn't cry. Germany, thanks to old Count Zeppelin's invention, was again honored among nations and, for the first time since the war, engaged in friendly intercourse with the United States.

Soon the *LZ-126,* designated the *ZR-3* by the U. S. Navy, was flown to Anacostia where "he"—the Germans still considered their dirigibles masculine—changed his sex. The wife of the President christened the ship the *Los Angeles,* using a bottle of water from the River Jordan. Doves of peace were released from inside the ship.

During the many years she remained in service the *Los Angeles* made scores of successful flights—all with happy endings. Unlike the stark, functional interior of the *Shenandoah,* her appointments were sumptuous. There were comfortable accommodations for twenty passengers under the forward end of the ship, including a spacious observation room. A modern kitchen, complete with a four-burner gas stove, portable ovens, and iceboxes, provided officers and men with hot meals such as the crew of the *Shenandoah* never dreamed of. The menu on a typical flying day, September 6, 1928:

BREAKFAST

Stewed Prunes   Fried Bacon and Eggs
Cocoa or Coffee   Bread and Butter

LUNCH
Fried Pork Chops   Buttered Rice
Apple Sauce   Baked Corn
Cocoa or Coffee   Oranges   Bread and Butter

DINNER
Cold sliced Ox Tongue   Baked Beans
Tomato and Cucumber Salad   Pickled Beets
Cocoa or Coffee   Pears   Bread, Butter and Jam

There were many other improvements over former dirigibles. Five Maybach engines of 525 horsepower each gave the *Los Angeles* a top speed of seventy-nine miles an hour. Since each of the motors could be reversed, the ship was easily maneuverable.

The dirigible's most famous captain was Lieutenant Commander Charles E. Rosendahl, who, since the fall of the *Shenandoah*, had become the most able and vocal of American supporters of the rigid dirigible. He took over the ship on May 10, 1926, succeeding Captain George W. Steele, Jr. For the next three years Rosendahl and the *Los Angeles* made air history.

Among her pioneering achievements the *Los Angeles* landed on the stern of the carrier, *Saratoga*, on a very gusty January day in 1927 without any special equipment. And on the 3rd of July, 1929, Lieutenant A. W. Gorton, in a standard Navy Vought observation plane, successfully hooked on to the belly of the big dirigible.

The "Pride of the Navy," as the *Los Angeles* was soon nicknamed, suffered a temporary reverse in 1926. The ship was moored at the high mast at Lakehurst. A light northwest wind of four miles an hour was blowing as the twenty-five men aboard prepared the ship for take-off. Suddenly a cold southeast breeze fought its way in from the ocean. It, too, was very light. But when the cold air hit the tail of the ship, giving it more buoyancy, the stern slowly started rising into the air.

The men inside the ship paid little attention to the slow rise. The four men going up the elevator inside the mooring mast were not disturbed by it, even though the tail had now climbed to 20 degrees.

Nick Garner, who was testing parachutes a half-mile away, stopped work in disbelief when the tail reached 45 degrees. Others on the great field stared thunderstruck as the big ship continued its slow, majestic rise. Now it was obvious something had gone wrong.

By this time the twenty-five men aboard were grabbing for support. In the control car the elevator man desperately yanked his wheel to drive the ship down, but the wind was too light to have any effect on the elevators. Officers in the car clung to tables and window ledges; instruments slid to the floor. Inside the hull, the riggers were hugging girders. Oil King Julius Malak, who thought he'd seen everything the night the *Shenandoah* crashed, skidded down the keel until he could wrap his arms around a girder. The contents of the cargo nets—spare carburetors, oil cans, tools—began falling past him, down the keel and finally out through the outer envelope.

Chief Rigger Frank Peckham, who with three others had now reached the top of the mast on the elevator, heard the crash and rattle as loose objects plummeted through the ship toward the nose. As the dirigible neared 80 degrees, he waited to hear the heavy ballast bags tear loose and come crashing through the delicate frame.

Everyone on the ground stared up, most of them sure that the *Los Angeles* was going to twist off the 158-foot mast and plunge to the earth. Yet there was nothing to do but watch her destroy herself.

At last the *Los Angeles* stood straight on her nose. Malak looked down. He was afraid the nose was going to collapse and the ship would be impaled on the mast. He closed his eyes, expecting the steel tower to rip up past him any second.

At the absolute perpendicular the *Los Angeles* paused like a circus performer waiting for applause. Then gracefully she twisted around and began to descend slowly on the other side of the mast, belly down. She continued floating downward until she was once more horizontal with the ground. At this point, having described a perfect arc of 180 degrees, she came to a stop parallel to the ground.

Jittery officers ordered the ship into the hangar; there she was minutely examined. Except for the holes made by falling objects, the ship was in perfect condition. The strange accident did prove one important point, at small cost: the high mast had to go. Designers were immediately put to work on a more practical "stub" mast.

During the next two years many successful flights were made, climaxed, late in April, 1928, with the first trip of any aircraft from New York to the Panama Canal. After a day's layover, the dirigible headed north for her home base. It was almost midnight of March 2, 1928, when the *Los Angeles* nosed in for a landing at Lakehurst. Gusts of over fifty miles an hour tossed up first the bow, then the stern. Three mooring wires were dropped and coupled to their mast wires by the ground crew of 250 men. A violent gust hit the ship and one wire snapped. Two sailors quickly knotted the broken ends and, in spite of the wind, the ship was drawn to the earth. The "Pride of the Navy" shivered as the force of the gale increased, and soon she was whipping around like a fish at the end of a line. A vicious gust shot the bow up. One of the main wires, nine-sixteenths of an inch with a strength of 25,000 pounds, snapped like a piece of string.

In the control car, Rosendahl ordered the other two wires cut. Without ballast—it had been dumped on the trip north—the *Los Angeles* shot rapidly to 1000 feet. The dangling wires were pulled in with difficulty. By this time the radio reported that the ground wind had slowed down to twelve miles an hour. So once more Rosendahl came in for a landing. When the control car drew near the ground a score of men reached up and grabbed its hand rail.

"Where'll we go when we get this thing in the barn?" Mechanic Nick Garner asked the man on the rail next to him—Coxswain Earl Kirkpatrick. Kirkpatrick didn't care as long as it was someplace interesting. Jackson, on his other side, made a suggestion and all three men laughed.

At that moment a blast swept in from the north. The ship attempted to rise just as a snow squall struck, driving the *Los Angeles* broadside across the field toward the pine trees.

"Hang on!" shouted Emil "Babe" Klaassen, in charge of one of the forward ground crews. Those on the long lines dug their feet into the sand but they were pulled relentlessly across the field. The men on the control car detail hung onto the hand rail as the ship tried to jerk away from them.

Rosendahl saw the *Los Angeles* couldn't be held down. "Let go everything!" he shouted.

The order was repeated by officers on the ground. All along the mooring lines the men let go. But for the men hanging onto the control car, the shrieking snow squall drowned out the commands. As soon as the mooring lines were released, the car, with a score of men still holding on the hand rail, shot up like a rocket. Fifteen feet above ground the men began dropping off. Garner landed, sitting down with a thump. Jackson almost fell on top of him. Apprentice Seaman Pitinsky sprawled nearby. He yelled in pain—he had sprained his ankle.

"Where's Kirk?" asked Jackson.

Garner looked up at the disappearing black hull of the ship. He knew Kirkpatrick was up there someplace.

As the ship soared up into the heart of the snow squall, Rosendahl ordered the engines started. Then an officer, seeing something move outside, went to the window. "My God, Captain!" he cried. "We've carried up a bunch of men on the hand rails! We've got to haul them in at once, sir!"

"Get lines and some more help!" ordered Rosendahl. "And tell those men to hold on just a moment more and we'll get them in!" Although he knew the force of the wind must be great he couldn't order the engines stopped until the ship was safely in the air.

Outside eight men were desperately clutching the cold rail. The snow whipped against their faces, blinding them. Kirkpatrick, his arms looped around the rail, was glad he couldn't see below. Otherwise he'd have been a lot more scared. Then he saw that Seaman Dils nearby was having trouble. "Hang on, sailor!" he called encouragingly.

At 500 feet Rosendahl ordered the engines cut. By now volunteers from the keel had dropped into the control car and were opening or kicking out windows so that lines could be passed around the men on the rails.

One of these volunteers was Seaman Donald Lipke, a newcomer to Lakehurst. When he heard the command, "Help forward!" he'd hurried into the control car. With his gloved hand he punched out a window. Then he climbed out of the car onto the rail. Holding onto the window frame with one hand he reached down and helped a man get a better grip. When this man was drawn into the car, Lipke edged along the rail to the next victim, grabbing him just as he was about to fall. The man, with Lipke's help, boosted himself up and wrapped a leg around the rail. A minute later a line was thrown around the ground crewman's waist and he was hauled, almost frozen, to safety. Lipke, his own hands white with cold, crawled back into the control car. It was only then he realized what he'd done. The blood drained from his face and he nearly fainted.

There were now two men left on the hand rails—Dils and Kirkpatrick. Dils' hands began slipping from the icy rail. "I can't hold on any longer!" he shouted.

"Don't be a fool!" commanded Radio man Cavadini, who was leaning out of his window barely out of reach. "Don't you dare let go!"

Kirkpatrick edged along the rail. Holding on with his right arm, he put his left around Dils' waist.

"I've got to let go!" cried the young apprentice.

"If you do," said Kirkpatrick angrily, "I'll punch you in the nose!" He kept talking to the terrified seaman as a line was lowered from the radio-room window. In a minute Dils was yanked into the *Los Angeles*. Kirkpatrick soon followed.

The airship now headed for the New Jersey coast. Rosendahl wired that eight men had been brought aboard. How many, he asked, were missing below?

There was an anxious wait of a few minutes. Then came the answer—"Eight."

That summer, on July 9, the day after the ninetieth birthday anniversary of Count Zeppelin, a great dirigible, the LZ-127, was christened at Friedrichshafen. The name, appropriately, was the *Graf Zeppelin*. This ship, the largest built to date, was a luxurious passenger craft 775 feet long, with a gas capacity of 3,700,000 feet. With it Dr. Hugo Eckener hoped to break down the prevailing distrust of airships and bring to fruition the old Count's fondest dream—a transatlantic passenger airline service.

In the fall of 1928 the *Graf Zeppelin*, carrying twenty passengers, a crew of forty, and 66,000 pieces of mail, started its first voyage to America. In mid-Atlantic the ship ran into a squall cloud. A current hit the dirigible's nose, driving it up sharply. Instead of lifting the tail the inexperienced elevator man brought up the nose. The watch officer quickly grabbed the wheel and leveled off the ship, but not before it shuddered as if it had hit a stone wall.

At that moment Lady Drummond Hay, the only woman passenger aboard, was eating her breakfast in the large dining room. Coffee flew into her face, and she fell into the lap of Dr. Ludwig Dittmann, an artist. She laughed; the other diners laughed.

It was no laughing matter: fabric had ripped off the port horizontal fin, and the ship was drifting helplessly.

In the control car, Eckener called for volunteers to make repairs in mid-flight. One of the volunteers was his own son, Knud. The engines were stopped while the men crawled out onto the huge tail. Even as they worked Eckener asked Lieutenant Commander Rosendahl, aboard as a passenger, to radio for help from the United States Navy. It was an embarrassing request, but Eckener preferred embarrassment to extra risk.

A shower suddenly hit the ship. Heavy from rain, it dropped toward the ocean. If the engines were started up, Eckener knew the workmen—including his son—would be swept overboard.

Eckener gave no command until the ship was down to 300 feet. Then he could wait no longer or the airship might be lost. "Set the telegraphs for engines three and four at full speed ahead," he ordered grimly.

But tragedy was avoided with a few seconds to spare. Just before the motors roared into action, the four men on the tail, noticing their dangerous proximity to the ocean, had crawled across the unprotected surface of the fin to take cover inside the structure.

Characteristically, the Americans were less sobered by the accident than stimulated by the successful handling of it. The *Graf* was wildly welcomed by every city it passed over—Washington, Baltimore, Philadelphia, Trenton, and finally New York. The din was so terrific in New York Harbor that the airship's engines could not be heard.

The reception of the *Los Angeles* crew had been predominantly a German-American affair, touched off by desire for friendly relations between two old war enemies. But the greeting of the *Graf Zeppelin* was both universal and impersonal. Hardheaded American financiers, influenced by the public enthusiasm, quickly set up the International Zeppelin Transport Company. An exciting era of world-wide air travel was about to begin.

In the spring of 1929 Eckener, always a master showman, announced that in addition to its Atlantic and Mediterranean flights, the *Graf* would that year make a round-the-world tour. Almost immediately all seats for the trip were snapped up. Amid a flood of publicity the Zeppelin left Lakehurst at 11:40 P.M., August 29, with an international passenger list of distinction. Twenty-one days, five hours, and fifty-four minutes later, the ship returned after circling the world at an average speed of 70.7 miles an hour. Colonel Charles Lindbergh was among the many thousands who greeted the airship at Lakehurst.

Eckener was lionized, invited to Washington to meet President Hoover, given a tumultuous ticker-tape welcome in New York City. Mayor Jimmy Walker called him "one of the greatest living men in the civilized world." Those who doubted the practicability of the dirigible were silenced.

Within a few months three countries were competing hotly for supremacy in the rigid-dirigible field. At Akron, Ohio, the Goodyear-Zeppelin Company had built the largest hangar in the world to house the two new Navy airships that would both be almost twice as big as the *Graf*. The hangar itself was a thing of wonder. Niagara Falls could have fit inside the colossal room. Strangely shaped like an egg cut in two, each of its great doors looked like a quarter of an orange. The two ships, the ZR-4 and ZR-5, would both have a capacity of 6,500,000 cubic feet and featured engine rooms inside the hull with propellers, on outriggers, that could be pitched from their regular position to drive the ship up or down.

Germany, naturally, was still ahead of the other countries. A vast new passenger ship was being designed with a lifting power of almost half a million pounds and an 8000-mile cruising radius.

England was also in the race. The two immense commercial airships, ordered built by the Air Ministry for service to the farthest reaches of the Empire, were nearing completion.

This English program had started in 1924. The contract for one dirigible, the *R-100*, was given to Vickers, and work was started at the deserted hangar in Howden. The second ship, the *R-101*, was to be built by the same team that designed the *R-38* (the *ZR-2*). Although the *R-38* had broken in two over the Humber River with the loss of many lives, and although the subsequent inquiry proved that little effort had been expended to resolve the aerodynamic problems peculiar to airship design, none of the designers was fired—or even censured.

From the first there was bitter rivalry between Lieutenant Colonel Victor Charles Richmond, designer of the *R-101*, and Mr. B. N. Wallis, designer of the *R-100*. During the five years of construction neither man visited the other, or even wrote each other about their common problems. The government-built ship, the *R-101*, which was in the works at Cardington, received most of the publicity. Vickers could hardly compete with the powerful public relations of the Air Ministry.

But the publicity backfired. Once a new device was designed and built, it had to be installed on the *R-101* whether it was suitable or not. At Howden the Vickers people discovered that the proposed diesel engines would make their ship too heavy, so they changed to Rolls-Royce gasoline engines. The *R-101* had the same weight problem. But because so many articles had been written about the safety features of their diesels, the change was disapproved by the Air Ministry—even though Colonel Richmond strongly urged it.

The *R-101* was finished first. Her maiden flight took place on October 14, 1929. The large crowd that came somewhat skeptically stayed to praise. For the government-built craft was beautiful to behold. But in the air she proved to be dangerously underpowered, with a useful lift of only thirty-five tons.

The Vickers ship was tried out the middle of December. The *R-100* was 709 feet long and 130 feet in diameter. Since she had fewer longitudinal girders, she lacked the outward beauty of her sister ship. But the *R-100* had one virtue—she could fly. Although she, too, was overheavy (her lift was fifty-seven tons instead of the estimated sixty-four tons), she reached eighty-one miles an hour—a remarkable speed for six Rolls-Royce Condor motors that had already seen service in the RAF since 1925.

Now the rivalry between the two staffs became even keener. The effects of the American depression were being felt in England, and it was obvious the entire airship program would have to be curtailed. This meant that the designers of the losing ship would lose their jobs.

In desperation the Cardington builders cut the *R-101* in two and inserted a new bay to give their ship more lift. On June 2, 1930, the rebuilt dirigible came out of her shed and went on the tower. Her entire cover began rippling from bow to stern, and within minutes a great tear ninety feet long appeared along the top of the ship. Riggers quickly repaired the damage with tapes. But the next day there was another split of forty feet.

The new troubles of the *R-101* were withheld from the public, and on June 28 the dirigible was pulled out of her hangar to be shown off at the Hendon Air Pageant. The ship rose easily enough from her home field and reached Hendon without trouble.

But on the return flight to Cardington a few hours later she went into a steep 500-foot dive. Height Coxswain "Mush" Oughton quickly brought the ship's nose up. After a long, slow climb the *R-101* was back to her flying height, 1200 feet. A few minutes later the ship dove again. Once more the coxswain, after a struggle, brought the ship to a safe altitude.

The officer on watch, Captain George Meager, was alarmed. Regularly assigned to the *R-100* as first officer, he had never before been in a dirigible that acted like the *R-101*. It was, he later admitted, the first time he'd "ever had the wind up in an airship."

"The ship seems to be heavy," he told Oughton.

Sweat was now streaming down the height coxswain's face. "It's as much as I can do to hold her up, sir," he said.

Suddenly the ship dove a third time. Meager grabbed the water-ballast toggles. Over a ton of water spilled out. The *R-101* nosed up.

"She's much easier now," said Oughton with relief.

A moment later Flight Lieutenant H. Carmichael Irwin, captain of the ship, came into the control car. He was annoyed by the release of the water ballast. Meager explained that the ship was heavy, but Irwin insisted that air bumps had caused the dives.

Half an hour later the ship landed safely at Cardington. On inspection, more than sixty small holes were found in the hydrogen cells. The *R-101*, unlike German and American airships, had no network dividing each gas bag. The single-ply cells not only had rubbed against each other but had chafed against girders as well.

The final test for each of the competing English dirigibles was to be a long, spectacular trip. The *R-100* was scheduled to fly to Canada and back and the *R-101* to India. The *R-101* designers, realizing that drastic action had to be taken to make their ship lighter, finally decided to rebuild the new bay. At this time they unofficially suggested to their rivals at Howden that it would be wiser to postpone both overseas trips until the next year.

The *R-100* builders at Howden, smarting over the many real and supposed indignities of the past five years, refused. Their ship was ready for the Canada flight and they intended to make it. Secretly, of course, they were delighted at their rivals' woes. On July 29, 1930, the *R-100* left England.

Although one of the secondhand engines went out of commission, the trip over the ocean was completed without mishap. But while the ship was cruising along the St. Lawrence River, a large section of fabric ripped off the fins. The accident was similar to the *Graf Zeppelin's* near-disaster in mid-ocean; and, as with the *Graf*, repairs were made in mid-air. Then, just after the *R-100* had passed over Quebec, a storm appeared dead ahead. Although Squadron Leader Booth was the ship's captain, Major G. H. Scott, an extremely able but overly daring man, ordered the helmsman to steer straight into the storm rather than skirt it in the Eckener manner. In the heavy weather more fabric ripped off. Even so the ship arrived safely at Montreal and was given a typical New World welcome. Posters of the *R-100* were plastered all over the city, and a song was written in Captain Booth's honor.

After repairs were made, the dirigible went on a twenty-four-hour tour of Canada, impressing the colonials with the technology of the mother country. Twelve days after its arrival in Montreal, the *R-100* started back across the Atlantic on five engines, touching down at Cardington after a speedy trip of fifty-seven and a half hours. Only a few hundred people were on hand to greet the triumphant fliers.

In spite of the skimpy reception, and not withstanding the ship's two casualties, it was quite evident that the *R-100's* round-trip crossing of the Atlantic had been a substantial success. It was a success that forced the designers of the *R-101* to make a difficult decision: to admit that their rivals had the better ship—and lose their jobs—or to fly to India. The choice was India.

At this point a complication arose to make the choice binding. Lord Thomson, the energetic Secretary of State for Air, announced that he would fly on the *R-101* so that he could keep several political engagements in India. These meetings were scheduled for September. "I must insist on the programme for the Indian flight being adhered to," he wrote the Cardington officials, "as I have made my plans accordingly."

The desperate *R-101* builders had to tell their chief that this would be impossible—the new bay would not be repaired until October 1. Impatiently Thomson laid out a new schedule. They would leave England on October 4, reach the Karachi mast on the 9th. They would leave Karachi on the 13th and arrive back in England on October 18. Such a rigid schedule for an experimental ship was more than impractical—it was foolhardy. But Thomson, who was slated to be the next Viceroy of India, held firm. He wanted to fly to his new empire in the most dramatic style.

Instead of protesting, the officials at Cardington rushed the repairs.

Late in September, a few days before the scheduled trip to India, one of the engineer-builders of the *R-100* visited Cardington to see his good friend, Squadron Leader Booth. The engineer was Nevil Shute Norway—later and better known as the novelist Nevil Shute. The captain of the *R-100* showed Norway a piece of outer-cover fabric. "What do you think of that?" he asked.

The fabric, which looked like scorched brown paper, crumpled into flakes when Norway squeezed it. He was horrified.

"That's off *R-101*," Booth told him. Rubber solution, applied to strengthen the fabric, had produced this strange and ominous reaction.

"I hope they've got all this stuff off the ship," said Norway.

"They *say* they have," replied Booth.

On October 1 the *R-101*, now 777 feet long, was brought out of the hangar for a trial. Soon after the ship took to the air the oil cooler of one engine failed. Although a flight of sixteen hours was logged, it was impossible to give the engines a full power trial.

Immediately the abbreviated test flight was over, Thomson ordered the trip started the next evening. The designers said the crew needed a rest. They compromised on the evening of October 4.

Then it was discovered that the ship lacked a certificate of aeronautics, a requirement for any flight over foreign land. Since there was no time for a thoroughgoing inspection, the ship received a quick once-over. The certificate was written out in the Air Ministry and handed to Captain Irwin as passengers and crew filed aboard.

On that Saturday evening the great majority of a large crowd stared in awe at the majestic dirigible as she parted from the mast. As for the few who were privy to the expediencies of the past five years, their awe was tempered with foreboding. In silence they watched the great ship, its fat sides scarred with the incisions of its recent operation, disappear slowly into the darkness.

The innocent majority cheered. Hadn't Lord Thomson told the world that "the *R-101* is as safe as a house, except for the millionth chance"?

The biggest airship in the world left Cardington at 6:36 P.M. with six passengers, including Lord Thomson; his valet, James Buck;

the Director of Airship Development, Wing Commander Colmore; six officials of the Royal Airship Works, headed by the ship's designer, Colonel Richmond; and a crew of forty-two.

Although nine and a half tons of water had been taken on, before the ship left the mast four tons were dumped to compensate for the heavy passenger and fuel load. All day the barometer had been falling threateningly.

Over Hitchin rain clouds loomed ahead, and strong, gusty winds made the R-101 roll and pitch heavily.

"I never knew her to roll so much," Squadron Leader Rope told Henry Leech, foreman engineer of the Royal Airship Works. "She's moving more like a seagoing ship than an aircraft."

A moment later the aft engine stopped. "It's the main oil pressure, sir," Engineer Arthur Bell told his chief engineer, W. R. Gent. Both men struggled unsuccessfully with the balky motor. Then civilian expert Leech was called. The three worked in the cramped gondola; they were working there at 8:08 P.M., as the ship sailed sluggishly over London. Rain began beating on top of the dirigible and dripped into the water recovery system.

A revised weather forecast now came over the radio: there would be winds of forty to fifty miles an hour over northern France. Major Scott, who was in charge of flying operations, glanced at the storm warning. But he didn't order the ship to return to Cardington. He headed the ship toward Paris—toward the heart of the brewing storm. He took the millionth chance.

The R-101, still flying with one motor out, crossed the English coast near Hastings at 9:35 P.M. No one in the control car was worried. A wire was sent to Cardington: "Ship is behaving well generally and we have already begun to recover water ballast."

In mid-channel the aft engine was finally repaired. As Leech wearily climbed the ladder into the belly of the ship, he looked down and saw whitecaps. He estimated, somewhat apprehensively, that they were only 700 feet above the water.

The first officer, Lieutenant Commander N. G. Atherstone, was worried. After looking at the altimeter he took the elevator wheel from Height Coxswain Oughton. In a minute the ship soared up to 1000 feet.

Atherstone handed the wheel back to the coxswain. "Don't let her go below one thousand feet," he warned. Perhaps the commander was thinking of an entry he'd made in his diary just the night before. "I feel that that thing called 'Luck,'" he'd written, "will figure conspicuously in our flight. Let's hope for good luck and do our best."

At eleven o'clock the watch was changed, and twenty-six minutes later the French coast was crossed at Pointe de St.-Quentin. The winds had increased to thirty-five miles an hour, and the dirigible was having trouble making headway.

But despite the buffeting Major Scott was well pleased with the R-101's performance. "After an excellent supper," the ship wired Cardington, "our distinguished passengers smoked a final cigar and, having sighted the French coast, have now gone to rest after the excitement of their leave-taking."

All was serene aboard the R-101, and the crew settled down for their long, tedious watch-keeping routine. By 1:00 A.M. only Chief Engineer Gent and civilian engineer Henry Leech were in the huge, luxurious smoking room. It was the first smoking room on any aircraft. It had been built in spite of the threat of hydrogen.

Captain Irwin, the ship's nominal skipper, dropped in for a cigarette a moment later. He told the two engineers that the aft engine had settled down and was running smoothly. Then he crushed out his butt and went forward to the control car. Gent yawned, said good night, and headed for the officers' quarters.

Leech, nervous and proud as a mother hen, now rose and began making the rounds of his engines. All five diesels were working as well as they had in extensive bench tests. But he still was a bit worried: no full-power test had been made since the insertion of the new bay. Unable to sleep, Leech went back to the smoking room. He mixed himself a drink, lit a cigarette, and then sat on a long, comfortable settee. He tried to relax but he couldn't.

The ship was just then passing over Poix Aerodrome, halfway between Abbéville and Beauvais. Louis Maillet, the resident in charge of the field, heard the dirigible's motors and looked out the window of his house. Although it was too cloudy to see the outline of the R-101, Maillet could distinguish a line of white lights moving slowly against the strong wind. The ship seemed only 100 yards above the field, which was on a plateau 200 yards high. Maillet wondered why the R-101 was flying less than half her own length from the ground.

In the control car the men noticed how close they were to the ground; yet the altimeter, which was set at sea level, recorded 1000 feet. The navigator was confused. He wrote out a message for Le Bourget airfield, forty miles away. "What is my true bearing?" he asked.

At 1:51 A.M. Le Bourget finally worked out the ship's position: five-eighths of a mile north of the field at Beauvais. A minute later the British dirigible acknowledged receipt of the information.

It was the last message from the R-101.

By this time the charge-hand, G. W. Short, was waking up the men for the two-o'clock watch. He shook engineer Alfred Cook. Yawning, Cook looked up at the gas bag above him—8 A, the new one. It was surging about him; he'd never seen it so pendulous before. But he thought little of it. He put on his shoes and started down the keel toward the port amidship engine. He knew his partner, Blake, must be getting tired.

Another engineer, Victor Savory, was out of his bunk instantly. He stopped up his ears with cotton wool and plasticene—the noise of the engine drove him crazy. In two minutes he had climbed down into the starboard amidship engine room.

His partner, Hastings, gave Savory the thumbs-up signal to show everything was fine.

"Get your carcass out quick!" called Savory cheerfully. "Get some sleep."

Short had a harder time rousing John Henry Binks, one of the aft engineers.

"How's my bloody engine behaving?" asked Binks wearily.

Short told him it was doing fine. "Now get a move on," he added impatiently.

Binks, who hadn't slept well because of the pitching and rolling, sauntered to the crew space and poured himself a cup of hot cocoa. Old Bell wouldn't mind a wait of a few extra minutes.

The first one in Beauvais to be awakened by the motors of the R-101 was Jules Patron, secretary of the Beauvais Police Station. He jumped out of bed, put on a pair of trousers and a jacket, and ran out into the rainy market place. He knew it was the great British airship. The papers had been full of news about its exciting trip to India by way of Ismailia. Even in the dark and storm he could see the outline of the dirigible. It was heading south. There were three green lights on the side. To get a better view Patron hurried home and climbed to the third story.

Julien Lechat, the jeweler, was waiting for the ship, too. He had worked in his shop until 1:00 A.M., for the next day was Saturday, market day. He was taking off his clothes when he heard the low drum of motors. He looked out his bedroom window and saw the ship "fighting the elements" just above the tower of St. Etienne. The dirigible was rolling and dipping. The wind blew in great squalls and the rain beat against Lechat's windowpanes like little bullets.

A few blocks away, Madame Julie Sostier, concierge at the Palais de Justice, awakened quickly. She saw a mass moving sideways slowly and with great difficulty. From her window she could see two white lights in front of the dirigible, a green light on the left, and a red one on the right. She was the only one in town who thought the ship was in trouble. It was so low she felt certain it was going to crash right in the center of her beloved town.

Lights began flashing on all over Beauvais. Everyone in the Woillez house was awake, and the children were wildly excited. The clock of St. Etienne struck two as the Bards, who lived across from the church, woke up. Madame Bard, knowing it was the *R-101*, threw open the window and peered out. She saw the ship just behind the tennis courts. It seemed to be about 200 yards above the ground.

In the port amidship gondola, Cook had already relieved Blake. Everything was all right, Blake had said, but Cook was the kind who liked to see for himself. He picked up his torch and flashed a beam of light along each side of his engine. Then he checked the instruments. Finally he looked at the log. The engine had been at cruising speed since seven o'clock. Everything *was* all right.

Binks was still drinking hot cocoa in the crew space. Then Short caught sight of him and told him to get cracking. The engineer started down the keel. After about 150 feet he reached the ladder leading down into the aft gondola. It was pitch black, and the violent wind tore at him as he climbed into the engine room.

"You're late!" Arthur Bell said good-naturedly.

"Only three minutes," replied Binks.

"Five!" Bell said, and they gossiped for a minute about the temperature and pressures.

Suddenly the ship went into a dive. Binks, who was leaning against the oil cooler, sat down with a thump. Bell, facing aft, fell against the starting engine.

"She's really got a nasty angle on!" thought Bell. But he didn't say anything—he just looked at Binks on the floor.

To Savory, in the port amidship engine room, the dip was "nothing to write home about." It wasn't even worth putting down in the log. In the starboard gondola, Alf Cook also thought it was just a "slight diving attitude."

But Electrician Arthur Disley, in his bunk just above the two amidship engines, was wakened out of a sound sleep by the dive. And in the smoking room forward, civilian engineer Leech's settee slid across the floor and banged against the forward bulkhead. A Sparklet Syphon and several glasses toppled off the table. As the ship leveled off somewhat, Leech staggered to his feet. He leaned over to pick up the debris.

Rigger Church, who a few minutes before had been relieved from his watch far forward, was walking back to the crew space when the ship dove. He grabbed a hand line for support.

"Release emergency ballast!" an officer shouted up from the control car to the passing rigger.

Church knew they were in trouble. He turned and ran forward along the keel to jettison the half-ton of water in the nose.

Leech by now had pulled the table from the wall and replaced the syphon and glasses. As he sat down on the settee again he could hear the telegraph bells in the control car ringing. Something was up.

The men in the control car already knew that the ship was doomed. Even though Height Coxswain Oughton had the wheel in a hard "up" position, the elevators weren't responding. Another dive was about to come. First Officer Atherstone ordered Chief Coxswain Hunt to go into the keel and rouse the sleeping crew to stand by for a crash.

The chief coxswain ran up into the ship and back toward the enlisted men's sleeping quarters. Arthur Disley was still in his bunk when Hunt shouted, "We are down, lads!"

Before Disley could ask him what was wrong, Hunt was running toward the tail of the dirigible, repeating his warning. Now Disley was aware of the jangle of telegraph bells in the control car.

Binks heard the aft engine telegraph ringing just as he got off the floor. The light was flashing a "slow" signal. His partner, Bell, instantly rang back an answer and then threw the motor into "slow."

Cook, in the port engine room, had received the unusual "slow" signal during the first dive, and his motor was already slowed down. He knew something serious had happened. As he peered out the gondola window, the ship went into another dive, steeper than the first. Hanging onto the door, Cook looked down but he could see only blackness below. He wondered how high up they were and what was wrong.

The second dive threw both Bell and Savory against their starting engines. Savory still didn't think much had happened. He looked up at his telegraph for an order. There was no blinking light. He figured that it was just the usual rough ride that followed a watch change. During sticky weather it usually took a few minutes for the new height coxswain to get the feel of the airship.

Few of those watching the dirigible noticed the first dive, but they all saw the second. From his window Louis Pettit, a wine merchant of Allonne, had been following the ship's shaky route for several minutes. As the R-101 passed between the villages of Allonne and Bongenoult he noticed that it "put out its fires." A moment later the lights came on again, and the dirigible started dipping toward the ground. Fernand Radel, a neighboring farmer, also saw the lights go off and on. Neither man realized the ship was only yawing in the heavy wind.

Louis Tellier, a shepherd of Bongenoult, was lying on his cot watching the dirigible fly over his little hut. The row of lights reminded him of a passing railroad train. Then the ship started to dive. Instinctively he turned his head to see if his sheep were safe.

Alfred Rabouille, who worked in a button factory by day and caught rabbits by night, was setting snares near the edge of a small woods when he heard the roar of engines. He looked up through the fine rain and saw a huge airship wobbling unsteadily. Suddenly it went into a dive. As he watched it headed straight for him. He stood rooted to the ground, not knowing what to do.

Electrician Disley, still drugged with sleep, swung his legs out of bed. Hunt's warning had told him the ship was going to crash. He knew he had to turn off the ship's electricity before it touched off an explosion of 5,500,000 cubic feet of hydrogen. With his left hand he punched a button that released one of the two field switches on the switchboard located at the head of his bed. But before he could push the second button he heard a "crushing" noise.

It was the underpart of the bow striking the earth. The dirigible hadn't hit with much impact and it pancaked gently along the ground for sixty feet. Rabouille, only 250 yards away, thought the fliers were in for no more than a little shaking up.

Then came a terrific, blinding explosion. Two smaller explosions followed. The rabbit catcher stared in horror as a huge flare lit up the sky. Then three rapid explosions knocked Rabouille off his feet.

In Beauvais those who were watching from the roof tops had seen the ship dive out of sight behind trees. Then they saw a great flash.

"What is that light?" asked Madame Bard, who was now sitting up in bed. Her husband looked sleepily out the window. A light like daybreak lit up the sky. Seven seconds later came a dull rumble that grew in intensity, shaking the house. Jules Patron, of the police station, could see bits of "flying paper" shoot up in the air in the distance.

The port amidship gondola didn't touch the ground at the first impact. Instinctively Cook turned off his ignition. Then he felt, rather than heard, an explosion. His car seemed to drop, with only a slight bump, onto the ground. He jumped out and ran.

On the starboard side, Engineer Savory had no idea what had happened. Before he could turn off his motor, a vivid flash shot through the gondola's open door, scorching his face and momentarily blinding him.

The aft gondola hit the earth lightly at first. It bounced along un-

til the bottom caved in. Water suddenly poured onto Binks and
Bell. They thought the ship had fallen into a river until they saw
water falling from a broken tank overhead. Waves of flame were
now rushing aft with a great rumble. The two men crouched in the
cabin a moment. Then they saw a path cut in the flames by the
water and leaped out of the gondola. Covering their faces with wet
handkerchiefs, they flopped on the dewy grass and rolled over and
over—away from the licking flames.

Civilian Leech was sitting on the smoking room settee when the
ship struck the ground. There was little shock. He merely slid
down the settee. The lights went out. Then there was an intense
flare in the doorway. The ceiling collapsed onto the settee. Leech
dropped to his knees and crawled aft. With his hands he tore a
path through a thin partition. Then he jumped through the flaming
envelope. He was the only civilian who had not been trapped in
bed.

Savory did not know how he had escaped from his burning engine room. He could still hear the crackling of flames as he was
led to safety by a French peasant.

The bow of the ship was now resting in the woods, the aft section in a meadow. Electrician Disley, dazed and shielding his eyes
from the blinding heat of the flames, looked at his ship. The envelope was still burning on some parts of the *R-101*, but there
seemed to be no cover at all on top of the dirigible. Apparently
great hunks of the top had ripped off in the two dives.

Cook was fascinated by the blaze. He walked a few yards
through the woods so he could look back at the tail. In the searing
light he could clearly see the huge elevators. They were jammed
in a severe "up" position. Height Coxswain Oughton had obviously
held tightly onto the wheel until the last minute in a vain effort to
keep the ship's nose up.

In a few minutes townspeople of Allonne and Bongenoult ran
onto the field. They did what they could, herding the eight who still
lived to safety. Two of these, riggers Church and Radcliffe, soon
died from their injuries. Only six survived: Leech, Disley, Cook,
Savory, Binks, and Bell.

The crash of the *R-101* stirred the British people more deeply
than any disaster since the war. In one stroke Secretary of State
for Air Thomson, the Director of Civil Aviation, and the elite of
Great Britain's airship service had been wiped out.

A great public funeral for the *R-101* dead was held in London.
The cortege of forty-eight coffins, stretching for many blocks, was
a grim spectacle. It marked the end of rigid dirigibles in England.

When Santos-Dumont learned of the tragedy, he declared that the deaths were his responsibility—for he had invented the airship. His sense of guilt, festering since the World War, drove him to hang himself with a necktie. His nephew cut him down just in time.

13

"QUEEN OF THE SKIES"

The explosion of the *R-101* cast a pall over the airship world.

The *Dixmude* had ended all chances of the rigid dirigible in France, and the mysterious disappearance of the *Italia* marked the finish of the semirigid in Italy. Now the enemies of lighter-than-air pointed out with satisfaction that they had long ago predicted the flaming end of the *R-101*.

At the British inquiry it was concluded that a large section of the envelope had torn, exposing the bow gas bags to the furious storm in north France. The cells had sprung leaks and the ship, losing buoyancy, had plunged to the ground. But other experts, led by Edward F. Spanner, were convinced that the fall was too sudden for a mere gas leakage. They maintained that the whole structure of the *R-101's* new bay had collapsed under the strain of the storm, and the ship had broken in two.

Whatever the cause, the two new masts at Ismailia and Karachi were never used; and the *R-100*, in spite of her successful trip to Canada, was never flown again. The Vickers airship, built at great cost over five years' work, was sold for junk. It brought 504 pounds.

At Akron 800 skilled men still worked on the two U.S. Navy dirigibles in spite of the growing legions of airship critics. But even before the first ship, the *ZR-4*, was completed another crisis arose. A Hungarian-born riveter, Paul F. Kassay, was accused of sabotaging its structural frame. Kassay was supposed to have told a friend that he had "spit on the rivets" and made them loose. A large, hysterical section of the press declared in headlines that it was a great Communist plot to wreck the ship. After a thorough Navy investigation had proved Kassay's work to be excellent, the rumors were found to be malicious. But the memory of the accusation lingered, and from that moment the ship seemed to be jinxed.

In the meantime the *Graf Zeppelin* continued its transatlantic and Mediterranean trips. To help counteract the rise of antidirigible propaganda, Dr. Eckener decided to make another spectacular flight. Back in 1929 the great Norwegian explorer, Nansen, and

the Australian, George Hubert Wilkins (who had flown with Ben
Eielson from Alaska to Spitsbergen) had interested Eckener in a
scientific polar trip in the *Graf.* But Nansen died, and the idea was
dropped. In 1930 the idea of Polar flight was again revived by
Eckener and Wilkins. The Australian conceived a sensational
scheme to raise money for the expedition. He would navigate a
submarine under the Polar ice field. At the North Pole he would cut
a hole in the ice with special equipment and have a rendezvous
with the *Graf Zeppelin.* Mail and passengers would be exchanged.
William Randolph Hearst was a natural sponsor for such an event.
He quickly promised 30,000 dollars for the exclusive story.

Wilkins, who by this time had been knighted, had dropped the
"George" and grown a dramatic goatee, borrowed the United States
Navy submarine *Nautilus,* made the necessary modifications, and
sailed to Norway. There it was found that extensive repairs would
have to be made in the submarine and the trip postponed until
the next year.

Eckener decided not to wait for Sir Hubert. Instead he arranged
a meeting with the Russian ice-breaker *Malygin* in the Franz
Josef Land area. On July 24, 1931, the *Graf* left its home base and
flew to Leningrad. There all luxuries were stripped from the dirigible and replaced with survival equipment and scientific instruments. Professor Samoilovich, who had led the *Krassin* expedition
to Nobile's "red tent," was taken aboard as scientific leader of the
large party, which included Lincoln Ellsworth and cub reporter
Arthur Koestler.

The *Graf* left Leningrad, followed the trail of the *Norge* and
Italia across the Barents Sea and, thirty-six hours later, at 8:45 P.M.
on July 27, sighted the *Malygin* in a bay on Hooker Island. The
airship slowly descended until the bumper bags of the control car
and the aft engine gondola floated on the open water.

The air was still and the surface of the water as smooth as a
mirror. A tiny boat, loaded with mail, left the *Malygin* and headed
toward the control car. Lincoln Ellsworth thought he recognized a
small man in the stern of the boat. Captain Ernst Lehmann, standing next to Ellsworth, fixed his binoculars on the man.

"It's Nobile!" he cried.

Eckener stuck his head out one of the front windows of the control car and directed the maneuvering of the mail boat. He called
out to Nobile and, as the boat drew alongside, caught his hand and
shook it heartily.

Ice floes now drifted dangerously close to the *Graf.* "Quick!
Quick!" shouted Eckener to those in the boat. Mail bags were
hastily exchanged.

Three old friends of Nobile's—Samoilovich, Molchanoff, and Bruns—leaned out of the control car. They all shook hands with Nobile as the mail boat drifted by. Then Ellsworth grasped Nobile's shoulders.

"Hello," Ellsworth said. "How do you do?"

The men were too moved to say anything more. They shook hands warmly.

Eckener now gave orders, and the ship slowly rose. As it did Ellsworth leaned far out the window as if trying to shake hands again with his old comrade. Nobile, on the little mail boat, extended his hand.

All the men on the *Graf* were moved by the strange meeting with the Italian who had been so roughly and unfairly treated by the world. His final indignity had come on March 3, 1929, when an inquiry in his own country had held him completely responsible for the crash of the *Italia*. He had been censured for planning the expedition poorly, choosing his personnel badly, and leaving the ice floe first. The same board exonerated Zappi and Mariano from all charges. In disgust Nobile had resigned his commission and accepted an invitation to become head of an airship project in Russia.

Lehmann noticed tears in Ellsworth's eyes as the *Malygin* became a dot. The American was undoubtedly thinking of the tragic fate of his co-leaders of the *Norge* expedition. Five years after their spectacular conquest of the Pole, Amundsen was lost somewhere in the frozen desert below, and Nobile lived in exile, a disgraced man in his own land.

The *Graf* now turned east, and the scientists aboard continued their observations. Contrary to popular belief, the airship did not fly over the Pole but explored the unknown region near Nicholas II Land. Then, ninety hours after leaving, it returned to Leningrad.

Before a crowd of 250,000 in the great Goodyear-Zeppelin hangar at Akron, Ohio, the ZR-4 was christened the *Akron* by Mrs. Herbert Hoover on August 8, 1931. Six weeks later the new dirigible, already dubbed "Queen of the Skies" by Navy publicists, made her first flight. Then, the jinx cropped up in January, 1932, when the *Akron* was torn loose from the mast on the tanker *Patoka*. It was an unimportant accident and caused no damage, but the House Naval Affairs Committee decided to conduct an investigation.

The Congressmen, whose principal interest seemed to be a ride in the new ship, arrived at Lakehurst on Washington's Birthday. The nose of the ship was attached to the new mobile "stub" mast— an ingenious structure mounted on two pairs of railroad tracks, forty feet apart. The Congressmen watched with schoolboy awe as the *Akron* was backed toward the mooring circle, far from the hangar.

Suddenly a freak gust of wind picked up the stern a few feet and dashed it down, crushing the lower vertical fin. The damage was more embarrassing than serious. Congress, of course, appointed a subcommittee to investigate the cause of the accident. After much deliberation the committeemen learned what everyone already knew—the wind had done it.

Many successful flights followed in the next few months. But rumors persisted that the *Akron* was poorly constructed. That May she was started on her first cross-country trip in the hope of silencing her critics. The 785-foot-long dirigible had no trouble during the first day of flight. All along the route thousands watched in amazement. It seemed impossible that a vehicle bigger than the *Leviathan* could float in the air.

On May 9 the *Akron* cruised majestically over Texas at 5500 feet, carrying her enormous load of 403,000 pounds with ease. Near El Paso at 8:00 P.M., the ground below was a dirty haze. Wind was whipping sand in great clouds.

Abruptly seized by fierce vertical air currents, the "Queen of the Skies" rose and fell faster than 1500 feet a minute. There was a short lull and then a second sandstorm struck. For twenty minutes the dirigible was tossed violently by the blasts of hot air. Sand was blown into the keels. At last the ship broke through into cool, smooth air. Riggers made quick inspection. Although several girders had buckled and there was an eight-inch hole in one of the gas cells, no serious damage could be found.

By the morning of May 11, as the ship approached San Diego, the crew was exhausted. The nonstop trip of seventy-seven hours had been a harrowing one, and everyone was looking forward to a rest before proceeding to the permanent base at Sunnyvale, near San Francisco.

A thick blanket of fog covered the emergency field, Camp Kearney. The big T-shaped door in the belly of the ship opened and a moment later a metal trapeze holding a fighter plane was slowly lowered. When the plane was about fifteen feet below the ship, the pilot, Lieutenant Ward Harrigan, released the catch on his upper wing and the fighter dropped through the fog.

The trapeze was pulled back into the hangar. Another plane, this one a two-place trainer, was attached to the trapeze. Two sailors stood on duralumin girders grasping the rings at each wing tip with duralumin steadying poles. The men wore no parachutes even though they stood only a few inches from the edge of a

4000-foot drop. An electric motor hummed and the trainer was lowered through the T opening. The sailors deftly guided the wing tips.

In this plane were the pilot, Lieutenant Howard Young, and Lieutenant Scotty Peck, who was going below to supervise the green landing crew.

At 9:30 A.M. the "Queen of the Skies" descended through the thick fog bank, coming into the clear at 1200 feet. Now the heat of the morning sun quickly expanded the helium, making the ship extremely buoyant. Four of the ship's propellers were inverted, like huge overhead fans, in an effort to pull the *Akron* toward the ground. The power fought the buoyancy, but the dirigible stayed aloft. Since Lieutenant Commander Rosendahl, the ship's skipper, did not want to valve precious helium, the battle against buoyancy lasted many minutes.

It wasn't until eleven o'clock that the 400-foot trail ropes were dropped from the port and starboard sides of the nose, falling neatly between the two landing parties. To the surprise of those in the control car the landing crew merely stood watching the ropes instead of picking them up. Rosendahl looked at Lieutenant George Campbell. Both men knew that they were in for a rough landing. The crew was more inexperienced than they had feared.

Rosendahl made two more passes over the sandy field before the trail ropes were finally grabbed and attached to "spiders," ground lines fitted with wooden toggles. Each of the ground crew men hung onto a wooden toggle, while Peck shouted instructions frantically. The seven-eighths-inch steel mooring cable spun out of the nose of the ship and hit the ground. It was coupled to a ground cable leading to the top of the mooring mast. The winch wound slowly, dragging the reluctant ship down.

The heat of the ground now made the *Akron* even more buoyant. The nose bobbed up. Those men on the forward spiders were lifted slightly from the ground. Then the tail leaped up, almost standing the "Queen of the Skies" on her stubby nose.

Engine Number 8 sputtered. Mechanic Sid Hooper struggled to keep it going but it soon stopped: the steep angle had cut off the fuel. Emil Klaassen had the same trouble in engine room Number 4.

Rosendahl instantly gave orders to valve helium, but it was too late. The angle had automatically tripped the ballast bags and 3000 pounds of water were dumped. All the engines had by this time rung up "stop." Rosendahl had to act quickly. "Cut the mooring cable!" he ordered. "Let everything go!"

The cable attached to the mast was released, and the two ground parties were told to let go. The *Akron* shot into the air with the long trail ropes dangling below.

From the hatch near Number 4 engine room, Mechanic Quinny Quernheim could see that the starboard trail rope was cleared. Then he noticed that there was a little cluster of men still clinging to the other rope. Fifty feet above ground a tiny figure dropped from the rope. At 100 feet, a second man slipped off the spiders even before the first one struck the ground.

Quernheim watched in horror as the second man hit and bounced. Shakily he went into the engine room. His face was pale. "My God!" he said to his partner, Klaassen. "That kid smoked when he hit the ground!"

Others in the ship were watching the third man on the spiders. He appeared to be tangled in the web of lines several hundred feet below the ship. Rosendahl knew that if he tried to land the buoyant ship he would probably dash the man to death. He told the rudder man to head for the ocean where the air was smoother.

Two crews, under Lieutenants Roland Mayer and George Campbell, began to improvise rigs to transfer the trail line to the mooring winch so the ground crew man could be reeled to safety.

The *Akron* was now flying 2000 feet above the Pacific. The stranded sailor, who was sitting astride a toggle, wrapped in a tangle of ropes, looked up, "Hey!" he called, "when the hell are you going to land me?"

An officer called encouragement through a megaphone, but the sailor below didn't seem to need it. He waved and then took off his white cap, stuffing it in his jumper. He didn't want to be read off for losing government property.

The men in the nose of the *Akron* were now trying to figure out a way to haul the sailor into the ship. The top twenty-five feet of the trail rope was one-inch cable—and wouldn't revolve around the drum of the mooring winch.

Boatswain's Mate Second Class Dick Deal volunteered to go down and tie a line below the steel cable section. Deal was slowly lowered out of the nose of the dirigible in a bosun's chair. As he swung dangerously, twenty-five feet below the bow platform, he grabbed at the swaying trail rope. Finally he reached it and, after fifteen minutes, tied a line to it. A few minutes later the steel cable section was cut off and the rope attached to the mooring winch. Then the sailor was hoisted up a few feet at a time.

After a tense hour and a half his head was level with the bow platform. Chief Arthur Carlson, a survivor of the *Shenandoah*, leaned down and grabbed the sailor. At last he was on the platform

—safe. He was a rugged, rawboned young man of twenty-one and he was far less excited than those on the platform. He looked around curiously. He had never seen a dirigible this close before.

Captain Rosendahl came up to the young man. "Son," he said, "what do you think of your ride?"

The sailor, whose name was Bud Cowart, grinned. "Captain, that was a lily dilly!"

Young Cowart escaped without a scratch, but two others had died. The "Queen of the Skies" was now more than a jinx, she was a killer.

14

THREE CAME BACK

Skies were overcast on the morning of April 3, 1933, at Lakehurst. Low clouds scudded across the field from the ocean. But despite the threat of bad weather, in Hangar Number 1 sailors and civilian workers were preparing the *Akron* for her fifty-ninth flight.

In the nearby Administration Building, just across Lansdowne Road, officers were anxiously looking out the windows of the commandant's office. One of the main missions of the flight was to calibrate radio direction-finding stations up in New England, the First Naval District. And work of this nature could not be accomplished unless the skies cleared.

A few minutes before eleven the phone in Commander Fred Berry's office rang. The commandant of the station talked a moment, and from the tone of his voice it was obvious that he was connected with Washington. Then he held out the phone to Commander Frank McCord, the *Akron's* new skipper. "The admiral wants to talk with you," said Berry.

McCord, a short, good-looking man, took the phone. He didn't have to be told who "the admiral" was. At Lakehurst there was only one admiral—William A. Moffett, Chief of the Bureau of Aeronautics and a staunch friend of the rigid dirigible.

While McCord was talking, his executive officer, Lieutenant Commander Herbert V. Wiley, went into the next room and called up the ship's aerologist. "What are the weather probabilities for the flight, Lieutenant?" he asked. Wiley was a big, solidly built man with a shock of shaggy gray hair and a ruddy face that was surprisingly young. With his deep, brooding eyes and broad, thoughtful forehead, he looked more like a philosopher than an airshipman—a philosopher with a barrel chest.

At the other end of the wire young Lieutenant Herbert Wescoat said the ship could be safely taken out of the hangar, but it would be definitely impossible to do any radio or compass work for at least another day.

Wiley quickly went back to the other room. In an undertone

he told McCord the bad news. The *Akron's* captain repeated it to Moffett, then hung up. "The admiral," he said, "is coming up from Washington. He wants to fly with us, in spite of the weather."

Late that afternoon the office was crowded with those scheduled to make the evening flight. Admiral Moffett, accompanied by Commander Harry Cecil, had arrived from Washington, where everyone was still buzzing from the new President's stirring "nothing to fear but fear itself" speech. Besides Commander Berry, others who were going along for the ride that evening were A. F. Masury, a reserve Army colonel from the International Motor Company; three junior officers from the station, who needed the flying time.

In spite of the threatening weather there was the usual preflight air of expectation and excitement, with a leavening of buffoonery and horseplay. For with Moffett present, the men knew the flight wouldn't be canceled unless a hurricane sprang up.

At 4:20 P.M. McCord and Wiley went to the station aerological office and examined the weather map made only twenty minutes before. The captain turned to his executive officer. "Cancel the airplane hook-on drill," he said. "But see if you can take aboard a training plane."

An hour and a half later the two men met again at the weather office. There was a light northeast wind and the temperature had fallen 20 degrees. Wiley phoned the hangar, ordered the Officer of the Deck to put 3500 pounds of water ballast aboard.

Wiley, a meticulous airshipman who never left a thing to chance, then went to the great hangar himself. Finding the inside temperature even higher than he'd expected, he ordered additional ballast put aboard to compensate for the difference of 16 degrees between the hangar and outside. He walked out on the field and looked up. Thick balls of fog were rapidly forming.

By six o'clock the hangar was alive. Most of the crew men making the flight had already put their gear on the *Akron*—toilet articles, sleeping-bag liners, and heavy flying clothes. Now they were standing under the ship or loafing in one of the adjoining shops.

Chief Machinist George Walsh looked in the big mechanic shop. "Hey," he called to Mechanic Sid Hooper, "You don't have to make the trip. It's only a short hop. Get Anderson."

Hooper didn't care. He had logged plenty of hours, and Vic Anderson, the third man in Number 8 engine room, needed a qualifying hop for watch-stander. Hooper found Anderson in the crowd. The youngster was nervous with excitement as Hooper handed over his heavy, fur-lined gabardine flight jacket, skull-cap flight helmet lined with fur, and big sheepskin-lined flying boots. Then Hooper went to the front of the hangar to wait for his wife. She was coming to watch the ship take off—the first time he'd allowed it. Now he wouldn't even be aboard.

A few late-comers were on their way, driving over the dark, lonely roads lined with scrubby pines and dwarf oaks. Robert Copeland, chief radio operator, was being chauffeured by his wife. The misty, overcast weather made her nervous. For the tenth time she asked him how dangerous lightning was. Copeland, who had originally studied to be a missionary, laughed at her fears. "Lightning will go right through the propellers and won't hurt us," he insisted.

Two veterans of the *Shenandoah* were on the back road from Lakewood. Henry Boswell still looked boyish and unsophisticated. The other man was Dick Deal, who had risked his life the year before to save Cowart in San Diego. He had been scheduled to make the last flight of the *Shenandoah,* but Ralph Joffray, who had relatives in St. Louis, had asked to take his place. Joffray had been at the wheel, next to Lansdowne, when the control car tore out of the *Shenandoah.* This last-minute change suggested to Dick's shipmates that he be called "Lucky" Deal. By a curious twist of fate, five years after the *Shenandoah* crash Deal had married Joffray's widow, the former Gertrude Matthews of Lakewood. At that moment she was at their home on 13th Street in Lakewood, worrying about their hound bitch who was about to have puppies.

Fog thickened as their car crawled through a hollow. Both men had made many stormy trips but neither liked the look of the weather. Boswell, usually a lighthearted fellow, became somber as they neared Lakehurst. "I hope," he said, "they've got sense enough to cancel this flight."

At 6:25 P.M. the heavy hangar doors opened slowly. Fog curled in like smoke. The ship was walked out of the hangar at six forty-one. Seven minutes later the mobile mast had carried its burden to the center of the mooring circle. The temperature was 41 degrees.

Every man was at his landing station. Captain McCord stood at the port side of the control car, giving commands to Lieutenant George Calnan, in charge of ballast. Wiley was at the captain's right, conning the rudder man. Boswell was at the elevator wheel just behind Captain McCord. Admiral Moffett stood back out of the way next to Navigator Harold MacLellan. The admiral watched the weighing-off operations with his usual absorption.

Copeland was in his radio shack, a tiny cabin above the control car. He looked out the window, trying to see his wife who was standing in front of Hangar Number 1. But it was so dark and foggy that the great shed was only a formless mass. At the bow stood Dick Deal, and at the other end of the ship, almost a sixth of a mile away,

Metalsmith Second Class Moody Irwin was at the emergency
control station, in the forward section of the huge lower fin. It was
a tiny room, just large enough for one man at the elevators and one
at the rudder wheel. Irwin leaned out the port window. It was his
job to release the X frames that supported the fin during handling
operations. Following the unfortunate accident in front of the
Congressmen, these X frames had been devised as insurance against
a freak gust of wind.

In all there were seventy-six aboard the *Akron* that evening, including the Navy's Air Chief; the commandant of Lakehurst; Lieutenant Calnan, a former world's champion fencer; Lieutenant Wil-
fred Bushnell, the copilot of the American balloon that had won the
Gordon Bennett Race over Switzerland the year before; five survivors of the *Shenandoah* crash, Boswell, Carlson, Quernheim,
Shevlowitz, and Russell; twenty-two-year-old John Weeks, who had
just married without telling his mother; and a young sailor, Paul
Hoover, who couldn't swim and had a morbid fear of water.

At seven twenty-eight the ship slowly left the ground, pushed up
by four inverted propellers. In front of the hangar, Mechanic Sid
Hooper, his wife, Mrs. Copeland, and others—wives, friends, civilian
workers—waved and shouted farewells that could not be heard.
They watched the great ship disappear into the dense fog at 300
feet. Now only the dull roar of its motors could be heard.

A moment later the roar was heard by Norman Walker, who was
driving his wife to Toms River. The veteran airshipman, the only
American to live through the ZR-2 (R-38) crash, tried to peer up
through the thick fog. "I hope," he said jokingly, "that thing holds
up."

Not a man aboard the *Akron* had the slightest feeling of apprehension. A few enlisted men did think it was damned foolishness to
be setting out on a calibrating mission in a pea-soup fog. But they
knew that Admiral Moffett would rather ride in a big rigid than
eat; and it was easy to sympathize with him, feeling almost the same
way themselves.

By now the ship was circling above the fog bank; the Naval Air
Station was a dim glow 1200 feet below. McCord realized that it
would be too dangerous to bring any planes aboard, and at 7:39 P.M.
he ordered Copeland to wire the station that planes weren't required. Since the fog extended over the ocean, McCord headed the
ship west with only six motors running. He had decided to cruise
inland where visibility was reported better. Then, when the coastal
regions cleared, the ship would turn north to arrive, at seven the
next morning, over Newport, Rhode Island.

"*Akron* flying Lakehurst to Philadelphia to Delaware Capes, thence along coast," wired Copeland at seven forty. It was the last clear message Lakehurst received from the ship.

Although the watch didn't change until eight o'clock, Metalsmith Moody Irwin decided to relieve his partner early. Irwin, a slender, thin-faced man of twenty-eight with a tiny mustache, walked up the port keel to frame 170 and took up his post in front of the telephone. Unlike the *Shenandoah,* the *Akron* had three keels, all V-shaped. One keel was near the top of the ship, running from bow to stern like a backbone. By means of this keel gas valves could now be inspected without going topside. The other two keels were near the bottom of the ship—one curving along the port side and the other along the starboard. Nine cross-walks connected the two lower keels, making the inside of the ship a complicated maze of tunnels.

The frames, like those of the *Shenandoah,* were numbered starting with the rudder. Engine Numbers 1 and 2 were at frame 57.5, 57.5 meters from the rudders; the airplane hangar ran from 123 to 147.5; the control car ladder was at 170; and the tip of the nose was 213.5. The frames aft of the rudder were given a minus designation: for example, the machine-gun nest at the extreme tail was —25.75. The cells were also numbered from the stern, running forward from cell o in the tail to cell 11 at the nose.

At eight o'clock Dick Deal took over the telephone watch on the starboard side of the ship. He hadn't been on duty more than ten minutes when a familiar, stocky figure came down the keel, heading for the officers' wardroom. It was Admiral Moffett. "Well, we're on our way!" said the admiral. He stopped and the two chatted for a few minutes. He and Deal had shared many flights and were old friends. Rank meant little to the Chief of the Bureau of Aeronautics. "These are my happiest hours," confided the admiral. "Nothing like being on board a dirigible!"

The admiral passed forward, and Deal looked out a window. Visibility had cleared; Philadelphia could be plainly seen. He looked at his watch. In forty-five minutes he was due to relieve Ralph Stine at the elevators.

In the blacked-out control car, Wiley decided to take a smoke. He walked back to the gun room, which also served as the officers' smoking room, in the after end of the car. Soon he noticed that the ship was moving faster. His curiosity aroused, he walked forward. He found that now eight engines were running at standard speed, and the ship had turned east.

In explanation McCord pointed to the south where lightning was flashing. At that moment Aerologist Wescoat reported that there had been thunderstorms over Washington at 7:00 P.M. Deal climbed into the car and took over the elevator wheel from Stine. McCord and Wiley stood by anxiously watching the lightning.

Wiley walked back to MacLellan's cubicle. "Where are we?" he asked.

"We'll cross the coast at Atlantic City, I think," said the navigator.

They were again shrouded in fog. McCord told Deal to bring the ship down to 1500 feet. Deal slowly lowered the *Akron*. At last the dull lights of a town could be seen through the mist. Lightning flashed again. It seemed to be only about twenty-five miles away. Rain began to strike the windows.

The captain ordered the course changed northeast.

"I think we'd better go west, sir," said Wiley tensely. Old airshipman had a theory that, with such a storm approaching, the dirigible should be headed toward shore. But McCord shook his head. "No," he said pointing to the west. "I saw two flashes of lightning there."

At least a dozen men aboard the *Akron* that night knew that the ship should have turned west. But the captain, although he'd passed the airship pilot's course, had spent almost all his Navy time at sea, learning to be a master mariner.

Deal began to have trouble with the elevators. The air was smooth, but the buoyancy of the ship kept changing capriciously as the *Akron* bobbed in and out of the fog. Stine was called back to the control car to stand by in case Deal needed help.

At ten o'clock Deal was exhausted and glad to be relieved by Rufus "Red" Johnson.

"The ship's one and one-half degrees light, sir," Deal told Lieutenant Clendening, the Officer of the Deck. "Can I go up into the ship now, sir?"

"Stand by Johnson," replied Clendening. He had just seen two thunderheads and was afraid the ship was in for some heavy weather.

MacLellan stuck his head out the navigator's cabin. "I think we're over Asbury Park, sir," he called to McCord.

The skipper nodded. Then he turned to Wiley, who was staring ahead at the turbulent skies. "I'm going up and take a look at the weather map," he said.

The lightning was now only a few miles off. Great, jagged bolts would strike horizontally and then be answered, a moment later, by vivid vertical flashes. But in spite of the lively electrical display the air was still calm and Johnson was having little trouble with the elevators.

Deal walked back to the navigator's room. Colonel Masury was seated at the port window, looking nervously out into the storm.

Suddenly thunder rumbled almost overhead. Long vertical bolts of lightning flashed on both sides of the ship, and the rain increased in force. The storm had caught up with them at last.

"It's pretty bad, isn't it?" the colonel said.

Deal tried to reassure Masury. "There's nothing to worry about, Colonel," he said. "We've been in worse electrical storms than this one." Lightning flashed, illuminating the colonel's drawn face. Deal wondered why older people, who had a lot less to live for, were always more frightened than the young. Deal peered forward. McCord, who had returned from the weather room, was anxiously looking out the starboard windows. Wiley looked out the port. Then the two officers silently changed positions.

"You should have been with us in the *Shenandoah*," said Deal to Masury. "The time we were coming from Buffalo back in nineteen twenty-four, the lightning was so bad over Wilkes-Barre that the control car seemed to be a ball of fire."

Masury found little reassurance in the story. "I'd just as soon not fly in a thunderstorm," he shouted above a resounding clap.

On the starboard side of the room MacLellan was dropping flares over the side to check his position. But the sea of fog below was too thick.

"Look!" cried Masury. He pointed down. "I can see lights on the ground!"

Deal looked out the port window. He saw the lights and called MacLellan. The navigator joined them. After a moment he began to laugh.

"That's just the reflection of the light from the officers' quarters on the fog."

In the radio room above them, Copeland, fearing that the antenna might be hit by the lightning, had hauled it in. Anyway the radio had been useless the past hour because of the static.

Copeland nodded in greeting as Admiral Moffett clambered past his room and down the ladder into the control car. The radio man figured that the admiral had been wakened by the lightning.

When Moffett reached the bottom of the ladder he looked forward. There Wiley and McCord were changing positions rapidly, like dancers in a peculiar ballet.

Thunder crashed, as if announcing the admiral's entrance. "It's almost as bad as one we struck in Alabama," he said to no one in particular. His feet apart, he rode the easy roll of the ship. There was no nervousness on his face. The admiral was enjoying himself.

McCord told Wiley to go up and have a look at the weather map. The executive officer went aloft and found out from Wescoat that only about two thirds of a map had been received before the radio went off. Wiley examined the map fragment, shook his head dolefully, and returned to the control car.

"What do you think, Commander?" McCord asked him.

"We certainly have a storm center down there, sir," answered Wiley. "It's something to play with."

"We'd better take her to sea," said McCord.

Again Wiley suggested heading west. But McCord had made up his mind. They would run east and then south to get ahead of the storm center.

The *Akron* headed out into the black skies over the Atlantic.

At 11:30 P.M. conditions were still normal in the ship. Deal was having coffee and a sandwich in the crew's mess hall above the airplane hangar, on the starboard side. He chatted with Chief Machinist Walsh for a few minutes. They agreed it was a sad night for flying. Then Walsh started on another inspection of his eight engines, and Deal strolled back to the starboard telephone at frame 170. Glancing out the window, he noticed lightning near the radio antenna. Copeland had just been given permission to lower one antenna fifteen feet, to the level of the bottom of the control car, so that he could try to get some weather information.

Lieutenant Calnan looked over Deal's shoulders. "Stand by the fire unit," he ordered, "in case anything catches fire."

Moody Irwin brushed by Calnan and started down the ladder to the control car. "I'm ready to relieve you, Red," he told elevator man Johnson a moment later.

"The ship's a little heavy," said Johnson, handing over the wheel. Because a "heavy" ship was inclined to climb, Irwin carried 5 degrees down elevator, which held the *Akron* at her given altitude, 1600 feet. Ralph Stine, an expert elevator man, stood behind Irwin in case of an emergency.

The lightning was now flashing all around the ship, blinding Irwin for several seconds at a time. He found he was having more and more difficulty holding the tail up.

"She's tail-heavy," he called to Lieutenant Calnan.

Calnan immediately sent for Henry Boswell, the most experienced elevator man on the ship. In a minute Boswell was at the controls.

"Check on the slack adjusters and counterbalance springs," said Calnan. Boswell nodded. He made the adjustments, then turned the wheel back to Irwin.

The storm seemed to get worse, and McCord finally ordered the dirigible headed back for the coast. But Navigator MacLellan had no idea where they were. Not only had the tricky, veering winds muddled their bearing, but also one of McCord's orders had been misunderstood: when the captain had called for a 15-degree change in course, the helmsmen thought he'd said 50 degrees.

Copeland was still doing his best to reach the home radio station. At 11:45 P.M. Radio man Third Class Robert Hill, the Lakehurst operator on duty, heard the *Akron's* call, but the static was too heavy to read the message. Five minutes later an amateur radio man, Arthur Hullfish of 224 East Montgomery Avenue, Wildwood, New Jersey, thought he could hear someone trying to establish communications on short wave. He distinctly heard the call letters "NAL," but then the message was broken up by static.

At a few minutes before twelve, Hill heard another call from the *Akron*. Again the Lakehurst operator couldn't make sense out of the message. It was just about this time that the men in the *Akron's* control car sighted the Jersey coastline. Neither MacLellan nor McCord had figured that they were so close to land.

"One hundred twenty degrees compass!" ordered McCord quickly. For all he knew they might be heading straight for the Empire State Building.

The *Akron* turned slowly and headed back over the Atlantic. In a few minutes she was submerged in fog.

At twelve the watch changed. Tony Swidersky and Joe Zimkus relieved Irwin and Stine at the elevators. Irwin started wearily toward the galley for sandwiches and coffee before turning in.

Dick Deal headed for the enlisted men's smoking room, which was above the plane hangar on the port side. Stine was there. So was Elmer Fink, an engineer and the ship's comedian. The thunder was now rumbling louder than ever.

"That's beer kegs being rolled around!" said Elmer.

It was a legitimate topical joke—3.2 beer was to be legalized the next day—and Stine and Deal laughed. And they smoked contentedly as little Elmer, in rare form despite the storm, continued to entertain them. After a pleasant ten minutes the two elevator men left the smoking room.

"Bad night for airships," remarked Deal. "Good night." The men separated, each heading for his bunk. Deal went into a tiny, canvas-walled room. He sat on his bunk and took off his shoes. He'd already removed his heavy flying trousers in the smoking room, and he flopped on the bunk with his head toward the keel walkway. On either side of him were two empty bunks. They belonged to men who'd just come off duty and were in the galley having a midnight lunch.

The keel lights shone dully over his head as he lay back and listened to the roar of Number 8 engine. It was a pleasant, comforting sound. He wasn't very tired. He never was tired on the first night of a flight. He flopped over on his stomach, leaning on his elbows with his face resting in his hands. There was no use corking off until his shipmates got back from the mess hall.

Irwin was lying on his bunk a few yards forward. He was too tired to take off anything except his shoes. It'd been a rough watch.

In Wildwood, the storm rose to such intensity that Arthur Hullfish decided to disconnect the radio belonging to the people who lived on the other side of his house. He ran out into the storm. Over the crackle of lightning and the crash of thunder, he could hear the heavy boom of the surf 1000 feet away. He looked out toward the Atlantic. It was blanketed with fog. Hullfish quickly unhooked the aerial and ran back into the house. He wanted to see if he could pick up those strange short wave calls again.

At twenty minutes past midnight Admiral Moffett again came down from his cabin above the control car. Even an old seadog couldn't sleep through a storm so wild. He stood in the darkened control car watching every maneuver intently.

Young Joe Zimkus was spelling Swidersky at the elevators. But Tony, by far the more experienced man, stood watchfully behind Joe. McCord and Wiley were still peering out the front windows, trying to find a break in the storm. The control car began to jerk spasmodically. Deafening peals of thunder were now following almost instantly after the rips of lightning. It seemed to Wiley that the sky above was cracking in two. The screaming wind told him that they must be near the center of the storm itself.

Suddenly young Zimkus cried, "We're falling!"

The elevator wheel tore out of Joe's hands and began spinning. Zimkus stood transfixed and watched the wheel whirl madly. Swidersky pushed Zimkus aside, threw himself on the wheel. It tried to tear itself from his hands. Wiley grabbed two of the wheel's spokes. Together the two powerful men yanked the nose of the ship up.

"I got it, sir," said Swidersky a moment later. He was in a sweat.

Wiley looked at the altimeter. It read 1100 feet and was sinking fast even though the ship was almost at an even keel.

"Should I drop ballast, Captain?" asked Wiley quietly.

"Yes," replied McCord, who had already rung up for more knots from the engines.

Wiley yanked at the toggles, emptying the service bags. The executive officer turned and looked at the altimeter again. They were down to 950 feet. But he knew that instrument was unreliable and could be off as much as several hundred feet. He reached up and pulled at the emergency toggles. 1600 pounds of water dumped out of frame 187. The needle on the altimeter wavered, stopped at 800 feet, and then began to shoot up almost as fast as it had fallen.

Wiley stood behind Swidersky, conning him cagily to reduce gradually the rate of rise. At 1300 feet the executive officer tensed. "All right," he said. A moment later he saw that Swidersky had good control of the ship. "Now bring her up to 1600 gradually, and then level off." Wiley stepped back a pace and began to breathe more normally. The crisis was over.

Inside the ship, Irwin had noticed the fall and rise. Several bunks aft, Deal had heard the telegraph ring in Number 8 engine room. Then he felt the ship surge forward with increased speed. After a few minutes he heard another ring in the engine room. The roar of Number 8 motor slacked off, and he knew they were back on standard speed.

Below them, the control car was swaying harder and faster than ever. Blinding flashes of lightning lit up the dark car, elongating the black figures of the men and distorting their faces weirdly. The ship was tossed up and down violently. Wiley knew they had finally hit the storm center.

"All hands to landing stations!" he called.

Although the rocking motion was less noticeable in the crew's sleeping quarters, which were near the ship's center of gravity, Deal wondered sleepily what the devil was going on. Leaning on one elbow he glanced up at Number 7 cell. It was surging and gasping like a creature in pain. It reminded him of one of those respiratory bladders attached to a patient during an operation. His drowsiness instantly disappeared. Something was happening. He rolled out of bed.

As Deal stood erect, the ship lurched sideways heavily, as if she had been hit by a big club. There was an alarming crackle overhead. He looked up. Girders 7 and 8 had snapped in two.

Irwin was half dozing when he heard a sound like the crack of a paper bag bursting. He looked up and saw that girder 7, the big longitudinal, had parted.

Up forward Chief Bosun's Mate Carl Dean was shouting, "All hands forward!"

The lurch almost knocked Wiley off his feet. The gust that had caused it was the most vicious he'd ever felt. As soon as he recovered his balance he saw that the lower rudder control rope had been carried away. He told the captain. Then he began unclutching the broken rudder control.

"She's falling," reported Elevator man Swidersky with no emotion in his voice.

Captain McCord looked at the altimeter. The ship was falling fast—faster than the first time.

"Full speed!" he ordered. The engineering officer instantly rang up the eight engine rooms.

Just as Wiley finished unclutching the lower control, the upper control snapped. He could hear a high, shrill whine inside the ship. It sounded to him likes sheaves carrying away. He knew the ship's structure had been damaged somewhere.

By this time Swidersky had the bow of the ship up almost 20 degrees in an effort to stop the fall. "Eight hundred feet!" he called monotonously.

There was no confusion in the control car as the ship plunged into blackness below. Lieutenant Calnan, who had appeared a moment after the landing station signal, was standing patiently by the ballast board. With both controls broken and useless, Wiley hung to the girder alongside the port window. He stared down fixedly, waiting for the water to loom into sight.

Arthur Hullfish was back at his short wave set. Once again he picked up faint staccato signals. Then he began to hear plain language instead of meaningless code. Hullfish knew he'd cut in on a distress signal of some kind. Frantically he began to copy words. "Two bays [or guys] control broken—ship bad condition—heavy storm strong wind—going up now—(something) broken." Then only isolated words and short phrases could be heard. "Out—700 feet—nose—nose up—breaking center—run into something—crashing [or cracking]."

There were a few more signals, then dead air. Hullfish looked at his watch. It was 12:26 A.M. He studied the gibberish he'd written. It made no sense whatever. He decided to forget the whole thing.

When Deal had seen the girders snap, he decided to call the control car. But when the ship began falling rapidly by the tail he knew he should drop fuel tanks first. Looking up the keel, he saw a tank, suspended above the walkway, start to break loose. He hurried forward so he wouldn't be crushed. The gangway was now so sharply angled that he had to pull himself up girder by girder.

Irwin was ten yards behind Deal. He, too, saw the gas tank tilting crazily, and he scrambled up the steep catwalk. Passing the tank, he heard a shriek of metal as the after-suspension gave way. The 120-gallon tank crashed to the keel. It missed Irwin by inches, but in his rush to get forward he never saw it. He climbed to the telephone at frame 170.

Deal, who hadn't had time to put on his shoes, was at frame 175 with half a dozen men. Chief Paul Jandick squeezed past him going aft. The others stood silently about, hanging onto girders for support. Girders were breaking and wires singing from strain. Though the lights were still glowing above the catwalk, everyone knew the ship was breaking up. Bill Russell, survivor of the *Shenandoah,* looked at Deal. Neither spoke. Chief Dean waited motionless.

Deal wondered whether they were over land or sea, and which would be worse for a crash. The men at 175 stared at each other and hoped for a little good luck.

Several miles away the German oil tanker, *Phoebus,* out of New York and bound for Tampico, was fighting the heavy seas. Thirty-four-year-old Captain Karl Dalldorf had taken the mate's watch because he wanted to be on the bridge all through the storm. Then a flashing of lights appeared in the air off his bow. He had no idea what the lights were, but he was sure they weren't the Barnegat Inlet Light: he had just passed it a few miles back.

Now the lights seemed to be on or near the water. Dalldorf, figuring it was a plane crashing into the sea, instantly changed his course. The 9226-ton, twin-screw motorship plowed through the twelve-foot waves full speed ahead.

Wiley, looking out the port window, could see nothing but fog below. Suddenly the choppy, wind-lashed sea appeared through a hole in the fog. "What's the altitude?" asked Wiley.

"Two hundred feet," answered Swidersky.

"Stand by to crash!" called Wiley. Since broken wires had ruined their regular telegraph system, he ordered the engineering officer to ring up the crash signal on the emergency bell-pull system. Just as the engine cars began repeating back the order, there was a heavy jolt. The tail, dragging far below the control car, had struck the ocean.

Lights went out all along both lower keels. Irwin jumped through the ship's outer covering. He plummeted through the criss-cross tangle of wires and out of the dirigible.

Ten yards forward, Deal felt icy water bursting through the keel at his feet. He had a horrible, panicky feeling. He and the others with him were caught inside a trap of metal and wires. There was still no sound from the men at frame 175. The *Akron* didn't carry life preservers. They all knew that it would soon be over.

Water flooded in over Deal's head. He felt his right leg being clutched and held by wires. He kicked frantically. He yanked at the wires. Somehow he got loose and shot to the surface of the water. The starboard side of the ship was drifting away from him.

Irwin struggled as the great hull of the *Akron* slowly rolled on top of him, pushing him below the waves. He jackknifed his legs until his feet were on the ship's structure. Then, his lungs bursting, he pushed off and dived as deep as he could. Moments later his head popped out of the water. He had barely cleared the sinking wreckage. He kicked off his low-cut crepe-soled shoes. It was easy because he had made a habit of leaving them untied when off duty. He took a deep breath and then, as he sank, started removing his bulky flying coat. Finally he got the coat off and shot to the surface again. Then he swam as hard as he could, away from the foundering ship and the undertow.

A few seconds after the crew's quarters were flooded, water rushed through the open port window of the control car, which was listing to starboard. The torrent picked up Wiley and carried him out the starboard window. He felt a mass of rubberized fabric on top of him and knew that he was being dragged down with the ship. He swam under water until his lungs seemed about to burst. Then he surfaced. Lightning flashed and, in the brief glow, he saw the dirigible, her bow pointed in the air, drifting away. He saw two lights on the stern section. Beyond were the lights of a vessel. Even farther off was a glare he thought came from Barnegat Lighthouse. Wiley swam toward the *Akron*.

Irwin was swimming away from the dirigible. He wasn't particularly afraid of drowning: he knew that they were near the Jersey coast, and he figured that if necessary he could swim to land. But he *was* afraid of sharks. He'd been afraid of them since he was a little boy. He kicked his feet frantically to scare them away. Looking around for something to help keep him afloat, he saw phosphorous flares blazing near the submerged control car. They had probably burst out of the locker in the navigator's room and ignited upon hitting the water. Finally he saw a fuel tank—perhaps the same one that had almost hit him a moment before the crash. It was bobbing like a giant cork twenty yards away. He struggled through the heavy seas toward it.

When at last he reached the 120-gallon tank, two men were already clinging to it. During the next flash of lightning he recognized Copeland, the radio operator, and Mechanic Lucius Rutan. Irwin grabbed onto the slippery tank with one hand and slowly took off everything but his underclothes. It wasn't until then that he realized how cold he was. Several hundred yards away he saw the "Queen of the Skies," her bow sticking out of the water like an inverted ice cream cone. A moment later, in another flash of lightning, he saw about a dozen men struggling in the water about fifty yards away. The sea was momentarily quiet, and the cries of the swimming men were faint and frightened. Irwin would never forget the sound of their cries.

Deal heard the cries for help all around him. But he couldn't help; he was hard put and lucky just to keep himself afloat. He figured that he'd been swimming about twenty minutes, and if he didn't find a piece of wood or floating debris he'd soon go under. A bolt of lightning lit up the great white-flecked swells. In the flash he saw several men floating by on a tank. Desperately he struck out for the tank, and he was tiring with each stroke. A few yards from it he reached the end of his endurance and started to go under. Then he felt himself being pulled. His hands hit metal. He hung onto the tank and took a deep breath.

"Who's here?" he asked.

"Irwin," said the man who had pulled him onto the tank.

Rutan didn't answer so Irwin added, "And Rutan."

The last man said, "This is Copeland."

Deal was hopeful for the first time since the crash. It was a good feeling to have company.

Wiley had heard the fading cries for help. He had found a board about three feet square, and when he saw a man struggling not far away he swam toward him. A wave tore the board from his frozen hands, and dragged him under. After he had fought his way to the surface again, he couldn't find the man who had cried out.

Wiley was now about 400 yards from the wallowing dirigible. The wind changed, and as the waves began hitting him squarely in the face, he realized that he didn't have a chance of swimming toward the ship. He wondered, without panic, how long a man could live in that icy, heaving sea. He knew he was in good condition; and if he budgeted his strength he had as good a chance for survival as anyone. So he swam easily, trying only to keep afloat.

The four men were having trouble hanging onto the bouncing fuel tank. Each big wave would sweep somebody off. Whenever Rutan was knocked off, he tried to climb on top of the tank; and each time the tank threatened to roll over. If it did, thought Deal, they'd all go under.

Then a wave tore Deal off the tank. As he swam back he noticed that the feed-pipe, which had connected with the main gas line, had snapped off.

"We've got to keep this feed-line above water!" he told the others. Should water flow into the broken pipe, the tank would fill up and sink. He clamped his hand over the jagged pipe to keep out the water.

"It's just a matter of time," said Deal encouragingly. "Somebody'll find us."

The men said nothing.

Irwin was no longer cold. In fact, he was beginning to feel pleasantly warm. His eyes started to close, and he realized with a start that he was freezing. Quickly he ducked his head under water to rouse himself. If he stopped fighting he'd be finished.

Deal was now at the other end of the tank. He reached across it with both hands. Irwin saw what he meant and clasped hands with him. The two men locked each other onto the bucking tank.

They'd been in the water over an hour.

Suddenly Deal shouted, "There's a ship!"

Irwin turned and looked. As the tank reached the crest of a wave, lightning ripped across the sky; and far away he saw the unreal outline of a ship.

Deal prayed that the ship would find them in the deep troughs and foaming water. He kept straining to follow the ship. One moment it would be riding high, the next it would plunge down and out of sight behind a great swell.

"It's just a matter of time," Deal kept repeating over and over.

A big wave smashed against the tank. Rutan slipped off. Slowly he sank. For a moment his hands writhed at the surface, then he was gone. No one could help him.

Now Deal could see a green light on the ship. He shouted. In a semidelirium Irwin saw two green lights, though vaguely he knew there should be only one. Perhaps the second was the reflection in the water. Then he began to shout, too. Copeland remained silent, his teeth clenched, a look of helpless strain and fatigue on his face.

The ship's deck lights flashed on. Deal felt a surge of hope. Then the ship's whistle began blowing. That must mean, he thought, that they'd spotted the tank.

A wave broke Irwin and Deal apart, and both floundered in the water. Irwin grabbed wearily at the tank. "I can't hold out any longer!" he gasped.

"Hold on!" Deal cried. "We'll be all right in five minutes."

Wiley saw the lights, too, and he heard the continuous, plaintive cries of the men on the fuel tank. He still had nothing to cling to, but he had been swimming with as little effort as possible, riding each giant wave cautiously. The rescue ship was floating toward him, almost broadsides. Wiley swam toward it with strong strokes. In a minute a circular life buoy was tossed near his head. Wiley reached out and caught the buoy. He was hauled aboard the *Phoebus.*

As if in a dream Irwin saw a life buoy scaling toward him from the darkness. It flopped in the water ten yards away. He left the tank and swam lazily to the buoy. His arms and legs were heavy, lifeless. He wished he could go to sleep. As he was dozing off he hooked his right arm through the buoy. He grabbed his chest with his right hand, locking himself to the preserver. Then he lost consciousness. When sailors pulled him onto the *Phoebus* at 2:00 A.M. his fingernails were dug into his bleeding chest, and his eyes were closed. He was in a deep sleep.

Deal, still holding onto the tank, saw a group of sailors hauling Irwin aboard and another group lowering a life boat from the ship. Dim figures were struggling with tackle lines, and Deal figured something must have fouled. It seemed an hour before the boat was finally over the side. At last it hit the water and speared toward the tank.

At that moment a big life raft floated serenely by. It was the fourteen-man raft kept in the airplane hangar—the only raft on the *Akron*. It was empty. A moment later he imagined he saw somebody grab Copeland. Then he felt himself being lifted. Then everything blacked out.

After the four men were picked up, the two lifeboats of the *Phoebus* continued searching in the forty-five-mile-an-hour gale. Several men sank just before they could be reached. Mattresses and bits of wreckage covered the sea. No more survivors were found.

When Deal came to, he was in a bunk in a pitching stateroom. Packed around his naked body were whisky bottles filled with hot water. German seamen were vigorously rubbing his legs.

Deal was shivering so violently that he couldn't talk. A fifth of whisky stood on a chair next to his bed. He sat up, his teeth chattering. He grabbed the bottle with numbed, fumbling hands. He took big gulps of the whisky. The German sailors laughed, encouraging him with broad gestures to drink more. He finished the entire fifth. But it had no effect on him—except to make him feel warm inside at last.

"What ship are we on?" he asked.

A young sailor who had lived in New York four years told him that it was the *Phoebus*. They'd left New York late that afternoon and luckily had been blown a little off their course. Then the door opened and Commander Wiley walked in.

"How do you feel?" he asked Deal. There were deep hollows under Wiley's dark, sad eyes, but he was in good condition.

"O.K.," said Deal. "How many survivors are there, sir?"

Wiley hesitated. Then he said, "Not many, Deal."

In the adjoining stateroom Irwin came awake and immediately felt warmth on his stomach. He didn't know it came from a bottle filled with hot water. As soon as he opened his eyes, the chief engineer of the *Phoebus* boosted him to a sitting position. The German started pouring a tumbler of whisky down his throat. Irwin thought he was still in the ocean, imagined he was swallowing salt water. He moaned and struck the glass out of the German's hand. He clutched at the chief engineer's hat, tearing it apart with violent jerks. Then he lost consciousness.

When he opened his eyes again there was no one in the room. He didn't know where he was or what had happened to him. He figured he'd been knocked out in an accident. He lay back on the bunk for a few minutes trying to make sense out of vague memories. A few minutes later he sat up. Seeing a bottle of 5 Star Hennessy on a table across the room, he slowly slung his legs out of the bunk. (Actually, it was 3 Star—there has never been a 5-Star Hennessy.) He wanted a good, long drink. He put his feet on the floor and took a step. But his numb legs crumpled under him. He lay on the floor unable to move.

The fourth man—Copeland, who had almost become a missionary —never regained consciousness. Before the Germans could lay him in a bunk his life faded away. Only three of the *Akron's* complement of seventy-six were now alive.

At five thirty on the morning of April 4, Mechanic Sid Hooper was awakened by a loud banging at the door of his Center Street apartment in Lakehurst. Sleepily he got up and padded into the front room. A pale, unhealthy light was just coming from the cloudy east. The banging continued. He figured that one of his friends was just getting in from an all-night party and wanted to give him a hard time. He opened the door.

Three women stood in the hallway: the wives of Donald Lipke and Pete Boelsen, and Mrs. Boelsen's sister. Their faces were distraught and tears were streaming down their cheeks.

"The *Akron* crashed off Barnegat Light!" cried Mrs. Boelsen.

Hooper was annoyed. "You shouldn't go around starting crazy rumors like that!" he said.

"They got word at the station!" insisted Mrs. Lipke, wife of the man who'd saved two from the hand rails of the *Los Angeles*.

The women were almost hysterical and it finally dawned on Hooper that there might be some substance in their story. At that moment his wife, wakened by the wailing, hurried into the room.

"Stay here with my wife," said Hooper. "I'll go over to the station and find out what really happened." He hurried into his clothes and in a quarter of an hour was at Hangar Number 1. A tense crowd was standing around one of the side doors. Now Hooper knew without being told that the *Akron* was down.

Lieutenant Commander Jess Kenworthy, Jr., acting commandant of the station in Commander Berry's absence, drove up. He gathered the off-duty section of the *Akron's* crew in a separate room in

the huge hangar. He told the men to stay there—he didn't want
wild stories to get out to the newspapers. Every few minutes another member of the idle section would check in. At first there
was lengthy and excited speculation. But after a while no one
wanted to talk. It was like a wake, thought Hooper.

At just about this time the English-speaking German sailor looked
out of the porthole of Deal's stateroom on the *Phoebus*. "Here
comes a Coast Guard destroyer!" he said.

Deal knew it was the *Tucker*, which was going to take the three
survivors to the Naval Hospital at Brooklyn. His hip was sore, and
the pharmacist's mate on the *Phoebus* had advised him to be transferred on a stretcher. Deal felt worse than he had in the water. His
body was covered with wire cuts and the little finger of his right
hand was broken. He figured he had broken it trying to stop up the
severed feed-line on the fuel tank. Deal exchanged addresses with
the many friends he had already made on the German tanker. Then
he was strapped in a stretcher.

Wiley and Irwin climbed down the ladder of the *Phoebus* into a
Navy cutter. Next Deal was lowered carefully. The crew of the
Phoebus looked peculiar to him, lined along the rail and waving
good-by. The sea was still heavy, with the wind almost forty-five
miles an hour, and the little Navy boat waiting below bobbed like
a chip of wood. Deal had a momentary feeling of terror as the lowered stretcher swayed. He didn't relish the idea of going back into
the sea with his arms and legs strapped down. If they dumped him
now he wouldn't have a chance.

After a rough trip the three men were brought safely aboard the
Tucker. Their first orders, telegraphed from the Chief of Naval Operations, were to talk to nobody about anything that had happened
during or after the disaster. They didn't feel like talking anyway.

At the same moment in Lakehurst, Mrs. Gertrude Deal's front
doorbell rang. She was still in bed. She'd had a long, tiring night
playing midwife to five puppies. As she was coming out of the
bedroom, her mother, her brother, and his wife burst into the house.
They asked if she'd heard about the *Akron*.

Dazedly she said she hadn't. Her brother told her it had been
wrecked somewhere off Barnegat. Mrs. Deal stood stock-still in
the middle of the room. Seven years before, she'd gone through the
same thing with Ralph Joffray. It suddenly occurred to her that
she'd been married to Ralph for just a year on the terrible morning
the news of the *Shenandoah* arrived. And now it was just a year
since she'd married Dick.

"Oh, Lord," she thought. "It's the same thing again."

Her brother was trying to tell her that Dick might possibly be safe. The story from Lakehurst was that four men had been picked up by a tanker. One of them was either Deal or Dean; Commander Kenworthy was trying to check on the proper spelling now.

Mrs. Deal was afraid to hope.

"I'm sure it was Dick who was saved," insisted her brother. "Carl Dean can't swim a stroke and Dick is like a fish in the water."

She nodded. It was true. She sat down in a stupor. She couldn't think. She couldn't do anything but wait for confirmation of the news. To this day she hasn't the slightest idea what she said or did for the harrowing nine hours that followed.

The crew of the *Akron's* sister ship, the ZR-5, which hadn't yet made her first trial flight, was that morning sleeping in Akron, Ohio. Most of them were on the same floor at the Anthony Wayne Hotel. A few, like Julius Malak, had brought their wives to Ohio. The Malaks lived in a little rented house.

Malak was lying in bed, wondering whether he should get up, when he heard the cry of a newsboy in the street. He wondered what the extra was all about. With the new President, Roosevelt, anything could happen. Maybe it was something to do with all the banks closing. The voice came closer. Now he got the words, *"AKRON* DOWN!"

Dressed only in his underwear he dashed into the street and bought a paper. The headlines made him sick: *"AKRON* CRASHES!!"

He walked slowly back to the house. Just a month earlier he'd had to make a choice among three assignments: Sunnyvale, the new ship, or the *Akron.*

"Stay on the *Akron* and then we won't have to leave Lakehurst," his wife had begged. Julius had agreed. But when he wrote down his first choice, he'd put down the new ship.

Mrs. Malak's face turned pale when she saw the headlines. She didn't say anything for a few minutes. She remembered how angry she'd been when Julius had crossed her up and they'd had to leave Lakehurst. Then she went up to Malak, who was staring silently out a window.

"From now on," she said, "you make all the decisions."

At the Anthony Wayne, the crew was still smarting from the reading off they'd had the night before from Commander Alger Dresel. A naked woman had been found wandering in the hallway of their floor. They'd taken the long lecture without a complaint, for they were well aware that sailors automatically get blamed for everything. There was no use telling Dresel that they were as inno-

cent as lambs. Actually, the woman had been a leftover from a convention.

Robert "Shaky" Davis, the new ship's leading chief, was an early
riser. Hearing the cries of newsboys, he went down to the lobby. A
moment later he was back upstairs. He burst into Chief Mechanic
Charlie Eckert's room.

"Hey, Charlie!" he said, "the *Akron* went down!"

Eckert was shocked. "Why the devil did she go down?"

The news spread fast all over the floor. There were a few
stunned, mumbled remarks, but mostly silence. The men thought of
three things: of their many old shipmates who'd never come back;
of the lucky chance that had made them choose the new ship; of
answers to the question—why did the *Akron* go down?

By mid-morning the Naval Air Station at Lakehurst was seething
with rumors and counter rumors. Wives, mothers, and children of
the *Akron's* crew crowded into the Welfare Building, anxiously
waiting for the latest news. Seven of the women—two officers'
wives, and five enlisted men's wives—had to be taken to the station
hospital for treatment. Others, like Mrs. Boswell and Mrs. Quernheim, were used to such ordeals. They were tight-lipped, dry-eyed.
Some of the younger women, like Mrs. Victor Anderson, wife of the
eager machinist who had taken Hooper's place at the last minute,
refused to believe their husbands were dead.

"Maybe he was picked up by a little boat without a radio," she
told a reporter. "Maybe he's safe. It might be days before we
hear——" She was going to have a baby in June. Four other wives
were also pregnant.

Every time the radio on the first floor of the Welfare Building was
turned on, the wives and mothers would rush to the top of the
stairs.

"It's this awful waiting," said one woman. "If I could only know
what's happened."

A moment later a sailor ran into the room. He shouted something. From the tone of his voice everyone knew he carried encouraging news. Those in the back of the room couldn't hear him
but the good word was soon passed. The British ship, *Panther*, had
just reported seeing 40 men drifting on wreckage off Barnegat
Light.

As soon as Lieutenant Commander Kenworthy got this report he
phoned Washington. All morning both heavier-than-air and lighter-
than-air pilots had been deviling him for permission to fly along
the coast to look for survivors. Kenworthy had refused: with a near-
gale-force wind blowing, another storm might break out any min-

ute. But the *Panther's* report changed the situation. Kenworthy conferred with Washington officials a few minutes. Then he called the officers of the two-engine blimp, the *J-3*, to the Administration Building.

At 10:30 A.M. Lieutenant Commander David E. Cummins, captain of the *J-3*, was briefed by Kenworthy. Cummins said the wind had increased and one of the *J-3's* motors was acting up. He wasn't as sanguine about the blimp's chances of survival as he had been earlier in the morning. But he volunteered to go.

Lieutenant Art Cockell, copilot, was also dubious but said he'd be willing to try it, too. So would Lieutenant Commander J. M. Thornton. Four enlisted men volunteered—Sprague, Manley, Meyers, and good-natured Pasquale Bettio, one of the heroes of the *Shenandoah's* breakaway from the mast.

Fifteen minutes later the rugged little *J-3* was ready for take-off. Rain was falling, and the wind was blowing in such violent gusts that the ground crew had trouble holding down the ship.

"Up ship!" called the ground chief through a megaphone. The men holding the gondola pushed up as hard as they could. The ship shot safely into the gloomy sky and headed for the ocean, with a strong tail wind pushing her along at record speed.

The rescuers cruised as low as 200 feet looking for wreckage from Barnegat to Atlantic City. Then they started back-tracking. A 45-knot wind hit the ship almost head on near Beach Haven. Cummins tried to return to Lakehurst, but even with a recorded speed of forty miles an hour the *J-3* was often held at a standstill.

The port engine began moving on its mountings. It was slowed down, and Bettio discovered that a plate was sheared through. The struts and outriggers were lashed as strongly as possible. With this engine going only half-speed, the blimp crawled toward the shore. Cummins, seeing a ship below, suggested an emergency landing; but Thornton thought they could reach the shore and save the *J-3*.

A large crowd was already lined along the boardwalk of Beach Haven. A retired Navy commander, R. E. P. Elmer, of Princeton, realized that the blimp was in trouble and guessed that they were trying to come in for a landing. Quickly he organized a ground party of men and boys.

Cummins, seeing the fifty people on the boardwalk, dropped drag lines. Elmer and his crew grabbed the ropes. The ship strained to escape. Art Cockell quickly pulled the emergency zipper rip cord that opened the big helium bag. Gas escaped, and the ship started to come down.

Just then, before the gas bag was completely deflated, a vicious gust hit it. The J-3 banged into the ground and rebounded 100 feet in the air. Another gust hit the limp bag. The lines were torn free from the amateur ground crew and the J-3 was carried like a giant kite over the ocean. One thousand feet offshore the undercarriage of the gondola smashed into the water. The derelict airship bounced into the air.

The men dropped ballast just as the ship struck again. The gondola was overthrown and the seven fliers dumped into the choppy ocean. Cummins was knocked out by the crash. Manley, Sprague, and Meyers took turns holding their captain's head above water. Thornton couldn't kick off his heavy flying boots. In spite of his struggles he began to sink. As he was disappearing Art Cockell grabbed for his collar. While Thornton got rid of one boot, Cockell pulled him to the surface. Again Thornton sank; again Cockell dragged him up.

There was little wreckage to cling to in the heavy seas. All seven men would probably have drowned, weighed down as they were by their heavy clothing, except for an odd chance. Sergeant Joe Forsythe, pilot of a New York City Police plane, had also been combing the coast for *Akron* wreckage. Patrolman Otto Kafka, his copilot, caught a glimpse of the J-3 as it crashed. Within minutes Forsythe, in spite of the rough water, landed his amphibian plane near the blimp. Thornton, who had just been pulled up for the third time by the exhausted Cockell, was brought aboard the police plane. So was Cockell. The police flyers ferried the two men to Beach Haven and returned for a second load. Three enlisted men and the unconscious skipper, Cummins, were flown ashore. Cummins was dead before he reached the Atlantic City Hospital.

One man was still missing—Pasquale Bettio. The police aviators flew back and forth but Bettio couldn't be found. An hour after the crash his body was washed ashore.

The toll of the *Akron* was now seventy-five.

The papers that evening were full of the double tragedy. The nation was stunned. President Roosevelt said, "The loss of the *Akron* with its crew of gallant officers and men is a national disaster." Billy Mitchell sprang to the defense of the rigid dirigible. "They were helping to develop a defensive arm that still will be invaluable in the future," he declared. "We should not let an accident of this kind hold up our airship development. We must go forward."

Red-bearded Anton Heinen was also heard from. "There should be no whitewash of the *Akron* disaster," he said, "as there was of the *Shenandoah* tragedy."

By the end of the day few believed anyone else had survived the deadliest crash in the history of aviation. But at Lakehurst the women still kept vigil. They still scanned the dark, empty skies as if expecting the big ship to return any moment. Although all the workmen had left Hangar Number 1 long before, half a dozen automobiles still stood inside the vast, tomblike building. They belonged to members of the *Akron's* crew. Outside the hangar half a dozen dogs sat waiting.

The day after the crash the three weary survivors were flown to Washington to see the Secretary of Navy. The next morning they were driven to the White House. Franklin D. Roosevelt insisted on taking time to talk with them.

"I'm thankful you're here," said the President. "Sit down and tell me all about it."

Wiley, in clipped tones, told of their crash and rescue. Deal, who wore tight-fitting civilian clothes, put in only a few words. Irwin said even less.

The President congratulated them on their narrow escape. Then, to relieve their tension, he told an amusing story of the inept congressional investigation of the *Titanic* sinking. The President told them that many of the Congressmen involved thought that starboard meant the left side of a ship.

The three men laughed a little.

When Wiley praised the seamanship of the *Phoebus* crew, Roosevelt turned to his Assistant Secretary of the Navy, Henry Latrobe Roosevelt. "I shall personally write a letter to the captain and crew of that ship," he said, "and thank them for their gallant work."

A few days later Deal returned to Lakehurst and his greatest ordeal. He didn't know what to say to the widows. It would be especially hard with the wives of his old mates of the *Shenandoah*.

Irwin also had a hard chore. He felt he had to go to Seaside Park, New Jersey, to see the wife of his dead friend, Red Johnson. She was on the beach when he arrived. After they talked a minute about Red she started like a sleepwalker across the sand, tears pouring down her cheeks. To Irwin's horror she walked into the ocean. Before he could kick off his shoes and take off his peajacket she had sunk out of sight.

Irwin dove in after her. He had a struggle bringing her back to the beach—she was bigger than he and she fought to stay in the sea.

That same day, not many miles away, the body of William Moffett, the airshipmen's favorite admiral, was washed ashore. The few who, like young Mrs. Anderson, still prayed for a miracle, knew at last it was the end of all hope.

15

THE HAPPIEST SHIP

All the big rigids in the United States Navy were "happy" ships. The hand-picked crews, like their commanders, regarded themselves as superior to heavier-than-air fliers. It took little finesse, they believed, to fly an airplane. But an airship was actually a flying battleship, and the airshipman, in addition to facing all the problems of flight, had to be an expert mariner as well—a sailor of the sky.

The new dirigible, the ZR-5, was the happiest of all the great rigids. Christened the *Macon* by Admiral Moffett's widow in 1933, she was flown by one of the most unusual and colorful crews ever assembled on one aircraft. Half of the men were tough veterans who had lived through crashes, narrow escapes, and free-wheeling experimentation; the other half were young, carefree, and completely oblivious of the constant hazards of their chosen profession.

This combination gave birth to a ship spirit unheard of in peacetime and rare during war. Only this spirit can explain the amazing mass reaction that took place when the *Macon* finally came to her sudden and strangely triumphant end.

After many routine flights the *Macon* was ordered to fly from her base at Sunnyvale, California—later called Moffett Field—to naval maneuvers in the Caribbean. She took off at 9:35 A.M. on April 20, 1934, and a day later was flying through the mountain pass between the Rio Grande Valley and the Pecos River Valley.

A few minutes before noon the sky was clear; there were scattered clouds, and the wind blew gently at about six knots from the southeast. It appeared to be perfect flying weather. But in the control car Commander Alger Dresel, the skipper, was prepared for any extremity. So were Gene Schellberg at the rudders and Pete Goode at the elevator wheel.

These men knew the rough ride that could be produced by the heat of the blistering sand below. Oldtimers in the crew dreaded the broiling flatland, the tortuous passes. Julius Malak, in engine room Number 5, remembered the harrowing trip the old *Shenandoah* had made back in 1924; and many others recalled the near-disaster on the *Akron's* Texas trip in 1932.

Leading Chief Robert "Shaky" Davis was wandering around near the fins. Shaky, who rarely slept on trips, had appointed himself personal guardian of the *Macon*. He was constantly on the move, tirelessly exploring the depths of the ship looking for trouble before it happened. Even from the rear anyone on the *Macon* would have recognized him by the jaunty swivel-hipped gait that had given him his name. Shaky was short, slender, and wore a small mustache. But his voice was big and gravelly, and when he spoke even the junior officers jumped.

At 11:55 A.M. Shaky crawled into the port horizontal fin. He felt a sharp shock. He knew the ship had been hit by a sudden blast of hot air from the sands below. Then he heard a peculiar grinding noise. A diagonal girder must have broken. He scrambled back to the crosswalk, shouted a warning, and then telephoned the control car.

Dresel himself picked up the ringing telephone.

"Slow down!" cried Shaky.

At once Dresel ordered the engines to "slow." Then he listened to Shaky's description of the damage. "All right," he said, "get it fixed." The captain hurried to his stateroom. He opened up a strongbox and put a wad of money in his pocket. If they crashed in Texas he didn't want his men to be broke.

Within minutes Shaky had everyone available, officers and men, carrying lumber from the forward part of the ship. Malak, who had just been relieved, saw a rigger heading aft on the starboard keel with a coil of lines. "What's wrong?" he asked.

"Nothing serious," said the rigger without stopping.

A moment later a pharmacist's mate went by toting a heavy load of six-by-eight planks. "I think we fractured a girder in the port side," he said.

Malak figured it was none of his business. He started for the crew space to play a little pinochle.

In engine room Number 4, on the port side, Mechanic Sid Hooper was puzzled by the sight of men running up the keel. A few minutes later the group was hurrying aft. They carried eight- and ten-foot-long boards, fitted with specially cut round blocks. Hooper figured that a box girder must have buckled. It was ship gossip that Shaky had had to put up a battle to carry these boards in case of an emergency.

Inside the port fin, both diagonals had buckled by now. Shaky was directing repair operations. The boards were clamped over the four

sides of the damaged girders, with the round blocks fitting neatly
into the lightening holes of the duralumin. Ropes were then tied
around the four boards, which acted like splints on a broken leg.
After being drawn tighter by a block and tackle, long three-eighths-
of-an-inch bolts were pushed through prepared holes in the planks
and secured.

The tail was bouncing roughly now, and the men knew they
were going through the narrowest and most dangerous part of the
pass. Shaky, sweat pouring down his face, turned to Rigger Charlie
Eckert. "It's a good thing we had those planks aboard, Charlie," he
said. He spoke loudly so the officer who had ridiculed the idea could
hear him plainly.

Back in the crew space, Malak and another mechanic were playing pinochle and drinking coffee from paper cups. After one severe
lurch the coffee cups rolled off the table. As Malak leaned down to
mop up the mess he noticed a young rigger clinging desperately to a
girder. It was the kid's first really tough trip, Malak told himself,
but he'd get used to it.

A chief came along the keel, told the rigger to go aft and help
Shaky Davis. The young man shook his head violently, clinging
tighter to the girder as the ship continued its wild rolling. "They
won't ever get me in another airship!" he kept saying over and over
again.

The chief looked at Malak. Both shrugged their shoulders. Then
the chief started aft, leaving the sailor on the girder. Hot air from
the desert hit the long ship another paralyzing blow. The cards
skidded off the table. Malak wondered if this was going to be another *Shenandoah*.

But a few minutes later they shot through the pass and into
smooth air. The danger was over. Shaky Davis had saved the ship.

The *Macon* reached Opa-Locka, Florida, without any more trouble. As soon as the ship was moored, the skipper stood the entire
crew to a long drink and then gave everyone liberty.

The next day civilian experts from the Goodyear-Zeppelin Company were flown in from Akron to repair the ship. Meanwhile some
of the mechanics had been called off liberty by an officious junior
officer, nicknamed "Slewfoot," and detailed to clean carbon from
the water-recovery system. When Dresel came out to inspect the
ship he saw the mechanics perched on the sides of the ship scrub-
bing diligently with Castile soap.

Dresel finally located the offending officer. "When I give liberty,
Lieutenant," he said in a voice quiet but shaking with rage, "I mean
liberty!"

Not only was Dresel an airshipman in the great tradition of Eckener, with an instinctive understanding of the whims of air currents, but he was also the kind of commander who made it his business to know the most personal details of his men's personal lives. One night, shortly after the start of a trip, he walked back along the keel on a tour of inspection. He found a rigger asleep at his post at frame 35. He leaned over and began shaking him.

The young sailor awoke to see the captain looming over him. He was terrified. He knew he had committed a court-martial offense.

"I hear your little girl was pretty sick last night," said Dresel.

"Y-yes, sir."

"Get any sleep yourself?"

"No, sir."

"Then you'd better cork off a few hours," said the Captain. "I'll stand your watch till you get someone to relieve me."

After temporary repairs the *Macon* took part in the Caribbean maneuvers. She was so successful as a lookout that the Navy enthusiastically ordered her west for the Pacific war games. The return trip was a quiet, uneventful one, and throughout Shaky Davis wandered about the ship in contented unease. Just as the ship was crossing into California late in the afternoon of May 17, he heard a loud splashing over his head from one of the ballast bags. Suspecting a major casualty, he climbed into the rigging. The splashing was louder. He opened the ballast bag and looked in. Swimming around excitedly was a two-foot alligator. The stowaway was never claimed.

Soon after landing at Moffett Field, Lieutenant Commander Herbert Wiley, the only officer to survive the *Akron*, took over the *Macon*. The men were sorry to lose Dresel, and sorrier when they discovered that Wiley was a strict disciplinarian who never hesitated to hand out extra duty. Since the terrible ordeal of the *Akron* crash he had developed a nervous idiosyncrasy: as he was about to discipline a man he would give a little giggle. The wits of the *Macon* tentatively christened him "Tee-hee," but when they saw the competent way he handled the ship the name was changed to "Pop."

As soon as he took over the *Macon*, Wiley began a personal investigation of the accident over Texas. He and Lieutenant Calvin Bolster, the ship's construction officer, inspected the damaged sector. Both men agreed that drastic permanent repairs should be made.

Bolster wrote a letter to the Navy's Bureau of Aeronautics, for the captain's signature, asking that the whole question of the damaged fin and its operational fitness be investigated. The Bureau decided that the fin should be reinforced but insisted that the repairs should not interfere with the *Macon's* operating schedule. The big dirigible had made such a favorable showing in the Caribbean that Washington wanted to show her off in other maneuvers. This meant that the ship would have to be repaired half the time and flown the other half.

In November the *Macon* left Sunnyvale to take part in the war games southwest of San Francisco. With her five planes she became the "eyes" of the Black Fleet, keeping enemy battleships and cruisers under constant surveillance without being observed. The airship's planes would warn her of approaching ships, and then she would hide in the clouds. From this cover an observation car, called the "angel basket" by the men, was lowered thousands of feet. Several times the hidden dirigible, directed by the man in the suspended car, dropped rolls of toilet paper that landed, ignominiously, on the decks of "enemy" cruisers, theoretically sinking them.

That year the *Macon* won many friends in Congress. In the Caribbean and on the Pacific she had proven that, with two scouting planes in operation at all times, she could cover as much as 172,000 square miles in a day—this in a craft that cost less than a destroyer and required a crew of only eighty men. President Roosevelt and Secretary of the Navy Swanson were so impressed that there was talk of sending the *Macon* or a new sister ship to Pearl Harbor for regular patrol duty. As 1934 ended it seemed that the dirigible was at last coming of age in America.

Early on the morning of February 11, 1935, the *Macon* was backed out of her huge elliptical hangar at Sunnyvale, a few miles south of San Francisco. The sky was overcast with high clouds, and a light rain was falling. The *Macon* was embarking on the highly publicized war games that were to take place off Los Angeles. These were the fleet maneuvers that were to prove to the last doubters that the rigid dirigible was a potent war weapon.

In spite of the inauspicious weather most of the eighty-three men aboard looked forward eagerly to the next two days. For it was a well-known fact that the air over an ocean was almost always smooth. It was the relative safety and stability of an oceangoing flight that had influenced the Bureau of Aeronautics to insist on the flight. The Bureau's decision took into consideration that, less than two years before, an identical airship, the *Akron,* had been destroyed over the Atlantic, and that the *Macon's* damaged tail had not yet been completely reinforced.

Each member of the full battle crew of eighty-one was at his station. There were also two guests aboard: Lieutenant Clinton Rounds and Commander Alfred Clay, who was slated to be the new commandant at Sunnyvale.

Coxswain Leo Gentile leaned his head out of a porthole at frame 35.

"Disconnect bridle!" shouted an officer from the ground. As the ship headed into the wind, Gentile slacked off his bridle. "Bridle's disconnected, station nine!" he shouted back. A wire fell to the ground.

A moment later the big ship slowly drifted up into the light rain. Since the dirigible had weighed off about 600 pounds light forward and only 300 pounds light aft, the bow was in an up attitude. The huge ship looked like a porpoise nosing lazily to the surface.

Wiley let the *Macon* free-balloon for 300 feet with the motors idling. Then he gave a crisp order and the engineering officer signaled his eight power cars. The ship lunged southward purposefully. Now she looked like a great shark on the attack. In a few moments five fighter planes trailed after her. One by one these "trapeze artists" hooked onto the belly of the ship and were drawn into the hangar, which lay amidships between the galley and the crew's quarters.

Shortly after passing San Jose the rain stopped. The ship continued south toward the maneuvering area. Wiley's orders were to search for and locate all fleet units. He was to operate secretly, maintaining radio silence until 6:00 P.M. the next day.

At three in the afternoon, just off Point Arguello, the planes were sent out to find the fleet. A blanket of heavy clouds now hung between the *Macon* and the sea. It was perfect weather for a dirigible.

All that afternoon the *Macon* cruised off the little islands strung out before Los Angeles like sea fortresses. Wiley kept the fleet under surveillance and the *Macon* hidden from sight below. The Captain received constant reports from his scouting planes and lowered Ernest Dailey, the chief radio man, in the angel basket. Dailey took a pounding from the wash of the ship and had to hang on firmly to keep from being pitched out of the tiny, bouncing car.

That night the dirigible cruised at fifty-two knots—about two-thirds speed—over the islands of Santa Cruz and Santa Catalina. The wind was about forty-five knots and the air turbulent. All the lights on the ship were blacked out. The men's flashlights were covered with dark blue cellophane so that the fleet below couldn't spot them.

About midnight Coxswain Arthur Oliver, the ship's leading comedian, and Seaman First Class Herbert "Monty" Rowe were gossiping on the dark port keel near frame 17.5. Oliver thought it was a boring trip. He wished something would happen to liven things up. At that moment the telephone rang.

"O.D. coming," was the friendly warning from a starboard station. The lieutenant known as "Sleepy" was on the prowl. This officer, like Shaky Davis, was constantly inspecting the ship, momentarily expecting disaster. He was constantly furious with the men for failing to acknowledge the constant danger.

"Let's try the Russell act on Sleepy," suggested Oliver. The "Russell act" was an institution. Every time a new man came aboard the oldtimers would warn him not to be surprised if he saw the ghost of Bill Russell, who went down with the *Akron,* wandering along the keel with seaweed in his hair. Rowe and Oliver agreed that Sleepy was fair game for the Russell act.

Oliver scrambled up a girder to the top of a cluster of gas tanks. A moment later the tall, stooped figure of Sleepy could be seen coming over the crosswalk from the port keel. As usual the lieutenant was clutching the guide ropes and edging along slowly, cautiously.

"Evening, sir," said Rowe politely as Sleepy approached. "It's real hairy back here tonight, sir."

"How come, Rowe?" asked Sleepy.

"The guys say Russell is wandering around again," said Rowe. "With seaweed in his hair."

"You don't believe that nonsense, do you?" scoffed Sleepy.

Just then a frightful moan came from above. The two men looked up. Above the gas tanks was a disembodied head. The face was ghastly blue. Matted hair covered the forehead. The eyes rolled. There was another moan.

Sleepy gasped. Then he turned and sprinted up the starboard keel. It was the first time he'd negotiated a keel without using the guide line.

After cruising west of Los Angeles early the next morning, the *Macon* started northwest at 10:30 A.M. She continued to scout the fleet without being observed, finally laying off Point Conception at noon. Just before two o'clock, when the exercises were completed, Radio man Ernest Dailey intercepted a message from the Commander-in-Chief of the Fleet directing the *Macon* to return to her base. Since it was now raining in San Francisco, Wiley set a course for Point Sur. He wanted to enter the Santa Clara Valley at Watsonville if the visibility was good.

At 3:55 P.M. Dailey sent his first message of the trip. "Am returning to base." A moment later Coxswain Leo Gentile came into the little radio room and found the tall, studious-looking operator taking down a message. He was smiling. The message over, Dailey took off his earphones. "I just heard I made Warrant," he told Gentile, peering through his glasses at the message.

The rigger shook his hand. Many of the men thought that Dailey was aloof, but Gentile liked him.

By now they had reached Point Buchon, and the planes had returned to roost. Everyone felt pleased with the Macon's performance in the games.

Except for Shaky Davis, it was a relaxed crew on the homeward journey. He was aft on the starboard keel with Pharmacist's Mate Third Class Vernon Moss. Shaky inspected the starboard fin. Then he beckoned Moss, and the two went over to the port fin. Shaky opened a flying hatch and crawled onto the big elevator. The fabric over the fin was "breathing" in the twenty-five-knot wind.

At four that afternoon the watch changed. Lieutenant Bolster, who took over the keel watch, climbed down into the control car. The air was bumpy, and he could see rain clouds to the north. A few minutes later, as Lieutenant George Campbell joined him, the ship was hit by a squall. But the men at the controls reported no trouble. The ship plowed steadily homeward at sixty-nine knots.

In the rear of the ship Mechanic Andy Galatian was sight-seeing in the lower fin. After several hours in a roaring engine room he liked the quiet of the little emergency control station. The ship was rising and falling quite abruptly, and Andy watched the altimeter and variometer register a 1200-foot rise, then an 1100-foot drop.

Point Piedras Blancas was now abeam to starboard. Campbell, seeing the visibility ahead closing down fast, quickly climbed up to Captain Wiley's cabin to warn him.

Back at frame 147 port, Shaky Davis was talking to the senior man on keel duty, Gene Schellberg.

"Do you want me to inspect topside and the fins?" asked Schellberg.

"No," said Shaky, "I'm going up there myself pretty soon. Give me a man to go along." Schellberg called across the ship for Steele.

By this time "Pop" Wiley was in the control car. At four fifteen he brought the ship down to 1700 feet to pass under a heavy cloud. Rain was falling in a solid sheet from the cloud to the surface of the ocean. When the ship hit the edge of the rain, she bounded jerkily.

Wilmer Conover, on the elevators, was having a rough time with the constant rises and falls. Coxswain Worther Hammond stood behind him, ready to grab the big wheel if he couldn't hold it alone.

On the top keel, Shaky Davis heard the rain pounding a few inches above his head. He made note of several leaks in the outer covering, and at frame 102 he noticed some broken cell netting. He told Steele to run forward and get some ramie cord to repair the netting.

At four thirty the *Macon* overhauled and passed a Luckenbach freighter heading north. Two minutes later she dove into fog. Cape San Martin now lay on the starboard beam—seven and a half miles away. Lieutenant Bolster, the construction and repair officer, decided to leave the control car and make a tour of the ship. He climbed up to the top keel and saw Shaky Davis and Steele finishing repairs on the cell netting.

"If you find any leaks in the drain bags," said Bolster, "just cut a hole in the bottom and let the water run into the walkway."

Shaky nodded and started aft looking for leaks. At frame 25.75 he noticed a bad one. Water was dripping onto the cell below. "Go forward to frame one hundred twenty-three," he told Steele, "and get a canvas bucket."

Wiley had now changed his course to pick up the coastline. Schellberg climbed down into the control car to take the wheel from Conover, who needed a rest after the bouncing they'd just gone through. Conover told him the altitude was 1400 feet, the ship was 5 degrees light, and the trim near-perfect. As soon as he took hold of the wheel, Schellberg found that the ship was behaving perfectly.

At four fifty a Union oil tanker was passed. The dirigible was flying smoothly and the sky ahead was brighter. "I think," said Lieutenant Campbell to Wiley, "we're out of the worst of it."

The captain nodded. He was looking out the starboard window at the coastline below. Then he moved to the port window. He saw a little flash of sunlight in the west. It was almost sunset. Seven heavy cruisers lay on the port side. Just then rain and clouds appeared in the north. Wiley wanted to stay in sight of land but not close enough to risk running afoul of the dangerous, fog-shrouded coastal mountains.

"Are we five miles off Point Sur?" Wiley asked the navigator.

"That's correct, sir. We'll be three miles off Point Sur at seventeen-o-five."

Conover took over the elevators again.

Schellberg went up to Lieutenant Campbell. "Can I go back and take a smoke, sir?" he asked, nodding at the officers' smoking room.

"Sure," said Campbell.

The rigger walked to the back of the control car and lit a cigarette. As he took his first puff, Wiley looked in from the navigating compartment.

"Do the enlisted men have a smoking room of their own?" he asked.

"Yes, sir."

"Well," replied the skipper with a warning tee-hee, "use it!" Schellberg decided he didn't want a cigarette after all. He walked self-consciously to the forward part of the control car.

In the rear of the ship Davis and Steele had just finished hanging a bucket under the leak in the covering. Shaky started toward the two triangular transverse girders near the top fin. Whenever the going was rough Shaky would put his hand between these two girders to see how far they bent under the strain. Below him, in the emergency control station, Galatian was still enjoying the sights. Andy counted the cruisers on the port side. There were seven.

At Point Sur the first assistant lighthouse-keeper, forty-six-year-old Harry Miller, saw the dirigible cruising majestically north with three men-of-war just to her south. Two of the Navy ships were closer to land than he had ever seen a big ship before. He hurried down the tower and into the little house next to the tower. "If you want to get a good look at those ships," he told his mates, "come on out." He grabbed his glasses and hurried back to the tower.

At five three Rigger Ted Brandes was under cell 1. Then he moved aft to look at cell 0. Below him, Mechanic Matthew Fraas had climbed into the emergency control station for a breather. Just as Galatian pointed out to him the Point Sur Lighthouse a gust dropped the tail down sharply.

The gust was the beginning of the end.

Moments before the gust hit, fifteen men were sitting amidships around the long table in the enlisted men's "chow hall." Messboy Florentino Edquiba gave Monty Rowe a big helping of roast beef, potatoes, and gravy. Nick Garner waited his turn. In the kitchen, just off the mess hall, Assistant Cook Max Cariaso (the ship's unofficial barber) expertly sliced thick slabs of rare roast beef.

Above the control car, Radio man Dailey was copying down a message from the Battle Force Commander. "Keep me informed of your movements," it read. "Considering unfavorable weather forecast, *Macon* proceed to base at discretion."

Below Dailey, in the rear of the control car, Emmett "Casey" Thurman, the chief machinist, and Lieutenant John Reppy were smoking cigarettes before getting ready for dinner.

A few yards forward, Captain Wiley peered toward Monterey Bay. It was obscured by a rain squall. The shoreline was a dark stretch three miles away. A heavy, drizzling mist set in, bringing an early darkness. Wiley decided that it would be wiser to avoid the storm.

"Left rudder," he ordered the helmsman.

Coxswain William Clarke turned the wheel half a revolution—a full turn displaced the rudder exactly 5 degrees.

"Bring it over again," ordered Wiley.

The air was smooth. Even though visibility was poor, no one in the control car felt a real concern.

Clarke completed his turn.

Then the gust hit them severally and in different ways.

Lieutenant Commander Jess Kenworthy, Jr., Wiley's executive officer and a former amateur heavyweight boxing champion, was resting his right arm on the starboard forward window, watching the approaching storm. Suddenly he felt a sharp gust from the starboard.

Lieutenant Campbell, standing behind Kenworthy, noticed papers fluttering in the control car. He felt the gust but thought it came from the port. So did Bolster. Wiley, aerologist Lieutenant Danis, and burly Lieutenant Scotty Peck felt no gust from either side.

In the officers' smoking room, Thurman was thrown to the starboard side. It was the worst shock he'd ever felt on a dirigible—even worse than those on the Texas trip. Lieutenant Reppy, although he too was thrown to the starboard side of the room, didn't think much of it. Without saying anything to Thurman he started topside to shave for dinner.

In the mess hall the sudden lurch knocked three men to the floor. Plates of meat, potatoes, and gravy fell on top of them. In the adjoining kitchen Assistant Cook Max Cariaso, knife in hand, was thrown to the floor. But none of the men thought that the mishap was serious. As those covered with food cleaned themselves, the others made jokes.

On the other side of the ship Sid Hooper, who was just coming out of the enlisted men's smoking room, had a premonition. He hurried aft to his engine room Number 4, to put on his life jacket.

The men in the tail already knew that the *Macon* had been badly hurt. Shaky Davis had put his hand between the two girders near the top fin just as the ship lurched. Then he heard a crash a few yards aft. There was a cold rush of helium, and he began to get dizzy. Looking up, he saw that the top of the fin had carried away.

After Ted Brandes, inspecting cell 0, had felt the lurch, he heard a snap like something striking the outer cover. He looked up, saw that cell 1 had deflated 60 per cent and that daylight was coming from above him. Then he saw control wires spinning wildly. He ran toward the phone at frame 35.

Galatian and Fraas in the lower fin heard a crashing noise above them. To Galatian it sounded like structure carrying away.

"There's something wrong!" cried Fraas. "I'm going up!"

"Wait a minute," said Galatian. "Don't get excited."

"Who the hell's excited?" shouted Fraas. "Something's carried away!"

Both looked up and saw deflating cells. They climbed up out of the control station to warn the riggers.

Just then the ship swung abruptly to the starboard and went down about 10 degrees at the nose. In the control car, Scotty Peck took a step toward Rudder man Clarke. The dirigible was heading straight for the hidden mountains.

Wiley guessed that Peck was going to tell Clarke to turn left. "Better wait a minute," he cautioned. "There seems to be something wrong."

Now the bow began to rise. Conover quickly applied down elevator. The big wheel suddenly jerked out of his hands with terrific force. Four spokes spun rapidly, painfully through his hands with a loud, cracking noise. Lieutenant Bolster and Schellberg threw themselves on the wheel.

At the same moment the rudder wheel was torn from Clarke's grasp. Captain Wiley, standing just behind the helmsman, jumped forward and grabbed it.

At the Point Sur Lighthouse, assistant keeper Miller figured that the *Macon,* was now about three miles away. Suddenly she began to behave strangely. Her tail dropped, and then the upper fin went to pieces like a paper sack blowing apart. Some of the pieces strung aft, and some were dangling.

The ship, flying at about 1500 feet, swung to the port. A moment later she dove, then raised a bit. Material that looked like ballast dropped from underneath the dirigible. Seconds later the material—whatever it was—hit the face of the ocean and seemed to explode.

Miller looked at his watch. It was exactly 5:06 P.M.

Miller's boss, head lighthouse-keeper Thomas Henderson, had come out to see the battleships. He, too, noticed the *Macon's* strange actions. Training his four-and-one-half power glasses on the airship, he saw the *Macon's* top fins go to pieces. A large section of outer covering ripped back. It hung for some time and then tore off, falling lazily into the ocean. He saw the dirigible turn left and disappear above the clouds. However he followed her course for two miles by tracking the line of splashes in the sea. Fifteen seconds after each splash he heard a dull explosion.

Captain Walter Woodson of the USS *Houston* (on whose deck the *Macon* had dropped newspapers and mail for President Roosevelt the summer before) saw the airship drop "blackish" ballast. To him it was just a routine maneuver. He thought nothing more of it.

From the port wing of the *Houston's* navigating bridge Ensign Terry Watkins saw the ballasting. At first it looked like smoke coming from the two after engines. Then he realized that a dark stream was dropping aft, a few seconds later making a large splash. At 5:12 P.M., just as the *Houston* completed a six turn, Watkins saw the big airship climb into the clouds and disappear. She didn't seem to be in any trouble.

But the *Macon* was mortally damaged. She was soon to start her last, uncontrollable dive to the sea.

16

DOWN TO THE SEA

"The wheel came loose in my hands," explained Helmsman Conover to Wiley.

"Do you have control now?" asked the skipper.

"I think I have control with the left rudder, sir." But even as Conover spoke the compass spun from 270 degrees to 225 degrees, and then all the way around to 110 degrees. The *Macon* was now bearing aimlessly southward toward the fleet. And Wiley knew he'd be lucky to save the rudderless ship. A minute later he was to learn that the situation was even worse.

The first rush of escaping helium almost knocked out Shaky Davis. He staggered dizzily forward along the top keel, knowing he had to reach a phone and report the casualty to Wiley. Ahead of him, young Steele was constantly slipping on the tilted keel.

"Take it easy!" called Shaky anxiously. "Watch out, or you'll fall down and go through cell 2!"

Far below them, four others were running to report damage. On the starboard keel, Connolly, after seeing the two turnbuckles forward of the emergency control clutch box spin crazily, ran to the phone at 35. On the port keel, just opposite Connolly, Ted Brandes was already talking to the control car. He reported that cell o was almost gone. As he hung up he heard Connolly, across the ship, reporting that the major controls had carried away on the starboard side.

Fraas and Galatian, who had scrambled up from the emergency control station, also ran for telephones—Fraas up the starboard keel and Galatian up the port. Fraas reached the phone at 35 just as Connolly was hanging up.

"You know about it, Joe?" he asked excitedly.

"Yes," answered Connolly. "The controls carried away and I got orders to drop the slip tanks."

On the port side, Galatian saw Brandes perched above the keel, cutting fuel tanks. Andy looked for a pair of pliers so that he could help.

The ship was rising fast with its nose up. As soon as Wiley learned of the severe casualties in the tail he ordered the front cells—8, 9, and 10—valved to bring the nose down. Bolster, with the captain's permission, was already dropping ballast and gasoline aft.

There was no excitement in the control car. Each man was doing his job quietly and efficiently. The ship was rising at the rate of 300 feet a minute, and Schellberg monotonously droned out the altitude. Wiley ordered the engineering officer to ring up slow speed; he didn't want to aggravate the torn tail. Then the skipper turned to Campbell, who was standing next to the voice tube leading up to the radio room. "Send out an SOS," said Wiley.

A minute later, at 5:15 P.M. Dailey calmly sent out one word: "Falling." Then he contacted CINCUS. "We have bad casualty," he informed them, giving the dirigible's position.

Below, in the control car, Scotty Peck asked Wiley if he didn't want all off-duty hands forward to bring the nose down. Wiley agreed. Schellberg was then detailed to go into the ship and pass the word.

At this moment Clarke said that he was having trouble with the elevators. Conover was still pulling in vain on the rudder wheel. "Can I go aft and shift control to the lower fin?" asked Lieutenant Bolster. "We can steer from back there."

The captain nodded and Bolster hurried up the ladder. Schellberg came down a moment later. As soon as he reported that the off-section men were coming forward, Wiley told him to go back up in the ship and drop the slip tanks at frame 125. Schellberg spun and climbed up the ladder.

In engine room Number 6, Babe Klaassen still didn't know that anything had happened. His partner Bill Baker, who had returned to the car a moment before, thought that Klaassen knew of the accident and hadn't bothered to tell him. But when an order came through to tilt the propeller and run full speed to take the ship up, Klaassen finally realized that they had a casualty. He looked over at Baker, who was stolidly watching the annunciator. Baker, he decided was the kind of a guy who'd walk, not run, out of a flaming building.

Then the engine began to run abnormally hot.

"Go ahead and decrease the speed," said Baker. "We'll only burn up the engine."

Without waiting to ask permission from the control car, Klaassen reduced to slow. Almost immediately the signal rang up, "stop." While Baker was replying at the annunciator, Chief Moe Miller stuck his head in the little room.

"Up forward, Babe," he ordered.

Klaassen, still wondering what it was all about, started up the keel toward the cargo hatch. Baker nonchalantly slid into the engineer's seat. He looked up at the annunciator, waiting for the next signal.

Lieutenant Reppy never got to shave that night. As he was heading for the officers' washroom he was stopped by Lieutenant Commander Kenworthy.

"Something's wrong back at Number one cell," said Kenworthy.

"Aye, aye, sir," said Reppy and started aft. Passing frame 170, he saw two enlisted men who had been ordered forward as ballast. "Come on with me," he said, "Something is wrong aft. Bring a cell repair kit."

"There's a kit back aft," replied one of the men. "We don't need to take one." The three, led by Reppy, ran downhill along the starboard keel as fast as they could; now the nose was tilted up so high that the engines began coughing and dying out. When Reppy got to frame 35 he looked toward the end of the gangway. Cell Number 1 was almost completely deflated. It was too late for a repair job.

"All hands at landing stations," announced Wiley. The word was quickly passed by phone and word of mouth. Wiley then ordered all the rubber rafts readied for lowering. (Benefited by the fatal lesson of the *Akron*, the *Macon* was equipped with a dozen rafts and a life preserver for each man.) "But hold them until I give the word to drop," he cautioned.

The men in the mess hall were arguing about what could have happened. There was a rumor from the tail that the top fin had carried away, and several of the more imaginative crew men swore that they could feel the breeze. Men were running up and down the keel, each with a different story.

"Go to your stations!" shouted an authoritative voice aft. The word was passed to the kitchen.

"It looks like the end of us all!" moaned Cook Bill Bucher comically. Max Cariaso laughed, but Messboy Edquiba was nervous.

"What's eating you?" asked Cariaso.

"I can't swim," said the little Filipino.

"Stay with me," advised Cariaso. "I'm a good swimmer and I'll help you." The three started for their station at 170.

Just about this time Lieutenant Bolster reached the emergency control station. His assistant, Chief Boatswain's mate Bill Buckley, a big, hulking man, was there with Coxswain Hammond.

"We're going to try and steer directionally from aft," shouted Bolster above the noise of the cracking girders.

"Aye, aye," said Buckley.

Bolster said he'd go back to the control car and shift the controls. Then he started up the tilting keel.

By this time the fleet below was preparing for rescue operations. "Serious casualty to *Macon* three miles off Point Sur," CINCUS radioed COMSCOFOR. "Proceed to assistance with utmost dispatch."

High above the converging fleet, hidden in thick clouds, the *Macon* continued its rise. Wiley battled to get his ship on an even keel, but most of the motors had been knocked out by the steep inclination. Mechanic Sid Hooper, who had run for his life jacket at the first lurch, went aft to his engine room, Number 4. He noticed that his partner, DeForest, who was answering the annunciators, was sweating freely. Since the thermometer read 105 degrees, Hooper opened up the engine room doors. The temperature quickly dropped 15 degrees. He removed a life jacket from the bulkhead and told DeForest to put it on.

The motor was now running again, and Hooper kerosened the valves and checked the cooling system expansion tank for indications of steam. The ship once more took a sharp up attitude, and DeForest had to use the aft bulkhead for a footrest while he operated the engine.

Hooper saw a rigger passing on the keel. "What's wrong?" he asked. "Number one cell is deflated," the rigger said.

Hooper stood in the doorway of the engine room and watched riggers drop all the slip tanks on the port side. He wasn't worried, for he knew that the ship could fly with one or even two cells completely deflated. Then he happened to look aft. He saw "Sue" Carroll come out on the walkway of adjoining Number 2 engine room, wiping the sweat from his neck and face. Sue wasn't wearing a life jacket. Sid started aft to warn him. There was no danger, but it was better to be on the safe side.

A half-dozen men were now at frame 187 on the starboard side. They had been told to go to their landing stations, but they had only a vague idea of what was going on. Rigger Monty Rowe was among them. He lifted up the phone. "Frame one hundred eighty-seven landing station manned," he said. A calm voice from the control car told him to stand by for instructions. One of the men began to grouse about the way things were being handled but he was soon shut up. Most of them were laughing and joking.

"All hands forward," shouted someone from near the galley. The word was passed. Those at 187 were joined by a dozen others.

"We're supposed to go as far forward as we can get," said Boatswain's Mate Second Class Francis "Doggy" Domian. The others followed the squat, powerful Doggy to the bow of the ship. In a few minutes almost thirty officers and enlisted men were crowded near the rope hatch doors, about twenty feet from the nose. Light came through the transparent panels; it wasn't dark, but still nobody knew what was going on. The talk veered from the casualty in the tail to the unsatisfactory promotion system to Oliver's latest gag. Then one rigger wondered if the new commandant coming to Sunnyvale was a good lighter-than-air man. Someone nudged the rigger. He looked up and saw, sitting next to Doggy Domian, Commander Clay, the man scheduled to be the station's next C.O.

At about 5:18 P.M. Schellberg heard Wiley order the planes dropped from the hangar. The senior rigger hurried up into the keel and passed the word. Then he continued aft to see if there was anything else he could throw out of the ship. When he reached frame 17.5 he looked up and saw that the last three cells were at least two-thirds deflated and that the whole top of the tail section was breaking up. He ran to the telephone at 35 and made a report to the control car.

Then he started forward, stopping at each engine room to tell the mechanics to throw out their tool boxes. When he opened the door of engine room Number 5, there was Malak, smiling as usual.

"Hey, what happened?" Malak asked.

"We're going to crash!" said Schellberg, staring at Malak as if he were crazy. Here the ship was canted at a steep angle, and still Malak was supremely unconcerned.

In the hangar, meanwhile, a dozen men were desperately trying to dump the planes. But the ship's severe nose-up attitude prevented Gentile and Lieutenant Reppy from budging the little Hawk fighter that hung on the trapeze. Shaky Davis, who had come down from the top keel with Steele, was directing the operations. Reppy tugged at the jammed transfer cable pulley but it wouldn't turn.

"Fellows," said Shaky, "we're not going to be able to do it." He hurried to a nearby phone, explained the difficulties they were having with the planes. "Do you still want us to go ahead with the planes?"

There was a slight pause. Then a voice from the control car answered tersely, "Belay it."

By now Schellberg was back in the control car. He heard Captain Wiley say that he wanted the deflated cells thrown from the ship if possible. Schellberg started aft with this in mind. But when he reached frame 17.5 Chief Buckley ordered him to man the port clutch box. In a moment Buckley called out that Hammond, in the emergency control station, had his rudder in neutral. Schellberg meshed his clutch collar. Below, in the lower fin, young Hammond grabbed the rudder wheel. The foundering *Macon* was at last being steered again.

By 5:25 P.M. the ship had shot up to 5000 feet. There it abruptly stopped rising, and Wiley, by valving the forward cells, at last managed to put the ship on an almost even keel. He ordered the engines to two-thirds speed. It was a touchy problem: he knew if he called for too much speed the entire tail section would collapse; and yet with too little speed the elevators had no effect and the ship couldn't be kept in trim.

Suddenly the ship began to drop. In the control car it felt like a runaway elevator. Wiley looked at the altimeter. They were plunging toward the sea at 300 feet a minute.

Amidship Lieutenant Reppy felt the sudden dive. Since the casualty was aft he decided to go back through the dizzying gas fumes and see if he could do anything at cell o to stop the fall. Cell o was three-quarters deflated. Cell 1 seemed to be hanging in the keel with a bubble of gas in its after end. Number 2 had a large bubble of gas in the forward end. Reppy looked up. Frame 17.5 at the top of the ship was completely severed. Both the inner and outer rings were gone. There was no trace of the upper keel which ended at that point.

Reppy did see part of the upper fin standing near frame O. He started forward and soon noticed water in the forward bag at frame 35.

"Valve the water out of the bag," Reppy told Gentile, who was standing nearby.

As Gentile went to work he saw the red-haired lieutenant head forward, looking for other things to do.

Hammond was still steering the ship from the little emergency station in the lower fin. His phone rang. The control car wanted to know if he had control.

"I have," he reported. He heard a screeching noise and looked up. The top of the rudder had ripped off completely, and rain beat in through the hole. He wondered how long he'd be able to steer.

In the control car, Wiley was discussing the possibilities of bringing the ship home. The *Macon* was now down to 3000 feet and still falling fast.

"Send word back to the engine rooms," he said, "that a backing order signal indicates, 'Back your engines and then abandon your stations.'" He looked at the altimeter. Then he said, "Pass word back through the keel to stand by to land on water."

Wiley had already ordered that all excess gear and movables be jettisoned. Kenworthy began throwing out everything he could lay hold of in the control car. His eye lit upon a radio homing device that weighed well over a hundred pounds. He yanked it out easily and shoved it overboard.

Word was passed to Shaky Davis and his crew to try again to free the jammed planes in the hangar. Reppy had now joined the men in the hangar. The key plane jammed the cable transfer pulley. Reppy put a jigger on the end of a forward plane. Just then one of the men, who was looking over the side, shouted, "Hey, we're getting damn close to the water!"

Mechanic Sid Hooper was watching the water from his engine room. The ship had just fallen out of a cloud bank, and it suddenly dawned on Hooper that Wiley was sitting the ship down by using the engines. He quickly removed the hatch doors to the outrigger and went back inside.

"We have to abandon ship," he told DeForest. "Let's get out on the outrigger and look the situation over." But as he stepped onto the walkway Galatian shouted to him, "Go forward!" Knowing they wanted to take as much weight as possible off the tail, Hooper ran forward along the port keel.

Across the ship, in engine room Number 5, Malak was sweating to keep up with the constantly changing orders from the control car. In the last half-hour he'd gone from standard to half to idle to reverse and back to standard. It was hard work, and the heat was brutal.

Aviation Machinist's Mate Second Class Jack F. Leonard, assigned to Number 3 car, just aft, came in.

"Malak," he called above the roar of the engine, "take off your overalls. We're going for a swim."

"Aw, get out," said Malak goodnaturedly. His annunciator rang, ordering him to stop his engine. Malak stopped the engine, then walked out onto the keel and took off his greasy overalls. The ship was now strangely quiet, for all but two of the engines had stopped. Just forward he could hear voices, but he couldn't make out what they were saying.

"Hey," he called, "what's this all about anyway?"

In the radio room at that moment—5:36 P.M.—Dailey was sending out his final message. "Will abandon ship," he radioed, "as soon as we land on the water somewhere within twenty miles of Point Sur, ten miles at sea."

At frame 187, trouble of a personal nature had broken out. For the past few months a big, heavy-set lieutenant had been making Monty Rowe's life miserable. It had started one afternoon when rigger Rowe was looking out the hangar window at a girl who'd just stepped out of a parked car. The girl bent over, with her back to Rowe, to pick up something.

Rowe whistled. The lieutenant came to the window in time to see a brisk wind blow the girl's skirt above her waist.

"Christ," said the big officer, "that babe's got a backside like a sea cow!"

The girl turned. It was the lieutenant's own wife.

Since that day the lieutenant, out of embarrassment, had assigned Rowe every unpleasant detail he could think of; and it appeared to Rowe that he was not going to let up merely because the *Macon* was about to crash.

"What the hell are you doing here without a life jacket?" the lieutenant asked.

"There was none at my landing station and then I was ordered forward."

"Go aft and find one," snapped the lieutenant.

Rowe bristled. He was tired of taking the lieutenant's guff. "I can't go aft. All hands were ordered forward."

"I'm telling you to go get a life jacket."

"It's abandon ship," retorted Rowe. "And you can't order me around."

"Well, I am!"

"Is that an order, *sir?*"

"That's an order," answered the lieutenant. "And when we get back to Sunnyvale I'm going to punch your nose!"

Rowe turned angrily and started aft. He almost bumped into Lieutenant Sempler, a heavier-than-air pilot, who was strolling forward, placidly eating a big piece of pie.

"Take it easy, boy," drawled Sempler in his broad Southern accent. "We've got all day."

In the control car, Wiley had just given the order to stand by to abandon ship. At 500 feet the emergency ballast forward, which had been saved to keep the nose down, was dropped by Lieutenant Campbell. There were now only two emergency ballast tanks left. He pulled them.

"Everyone out of the control car!" said Wiley calmly. He cautioned everyone to get into a window and hang on till the last possible second. At 300 feet he noticed that Clarke was still at the elevator wheel.

"Abandon it!" ordered Wiley sharply.

Clarke left the wheel, but instead of climbing into a window, he decided he'd have a better chance of saving himself in the keel. He scrambled up the ladder.

Back in the tail two men were still trying to save the ship. After throwing in the clutch so that Hammond could steer from the lower fin, Gene Schellberg tried to jettison one of the ruptured cells, Number 1. But he couldn't yank it free. Hearing the cry of "Abandon ship!" he decided he'd better think of a quick way to leave the dirigible. He went to frame 17.5 and with his sheath knife cut in the outer envelope a circular hole big enough to dive through. He pitched the knife out the hole and jumped. Too late, he remembered he'd forgotten to take off his glasses.

Hammond was still steering the ship from the lower fin, completely innocent of the impending crash.

"Hammond, for Christ's sake get out of the fin!" shouted Brandes from the port gangway above. Hammond looked down and saw that the tail was almost in the water. He scrambled up the ladder and started along the port gangway. Just as he reached frame 25 there was a crash underneath—the bottom of the fin had hit the ocean. He saw frame 35, just ahead, carrying away. Girders were crumbling on both sides of him. He ran back to 17.5. Water was now up to Girder 5, the one near the walkway. He kicked a hole in the cover of the dirigible. As he was about to jump, a girder fell on his left leg, trapping him. Water was rising fast. He finally heaved the girder from his leg and rolled out of the ship.

When Malak heard the cry "Abandon ship!" he was just reaching for a life jacket in the compartment above the door of his power car. He put it on and kicked off his shoes. Then he walked through a hatch onto the outrigger that supported the propeller of his motor. Looking back toward Number 3 car, he saw Jack Leonard standing on his outrigger.

"Let's go, Shellac!" yelled Leonard.

Then the tail hit the Pacific.

"You go first, Jack!" cried Malak.

Leonard dove head first from a height of about 30 feet. Malak, remembering that a jump with a fully inflated life jacket might break his neck, quickly let out most of the air. By the time he jumped, the bow of the Macon had bounced off the water and was rising again, and he went through the air for almost 50 feet. He hit the water and went so deep he thought he'd never come up.

Baker, in engine room Number 6 on the other side of the ship, still had his motor running at two-thirds speed. Just before the lower fin hit the water he received a "stop" signal from the control car. While he was answering the annunciator, the bottom of the control car slapped the water. At the same moment the scoop, which blew air into the engine room, was knocked off—probably by a wave. He looked down and saw a hole where the scoop had been. He walked out on the outrigger. His car had gone up again to about 50 feet. He returned to the engine room, closed the throttle of his motor, and turned off the ignition.

Unhurriedly he rolled up his flight log and stowed it in his pocket. Then he put on his life jacket, carefully deflated it to a safe pressure, and picked up his heavy flight coat. After finding a flashlight—it would soon be dark—he crawled back out on the tilting outrigger and looked down. The water was now several hundred feet below. He rolled up his coat, put it on the outrigger, and sat on it. He decided he'd take his time about jumping.

When, at exactly 5:40 P.M., the tail struck the ocean, the control car was still 250 feet in the air. Wiley threw binoculars and flares out of the window. Seeing the ship swerve slightly to port, he ran to the other side of the car and climbed into the starboard window. Gripping the ledge, he lowered his body and waited.

Kenworthy was hanging on the hand rail a few feet from the captain. They both jumped seconds before the control car hit. They were both underwater as the bow bounced back in the air.

In the airplane hangar, Lieutenant Reppy gave the order to abandon ship a minute before the tail struck. Leaving Shaky Davis to supervise the dumping of two four-man life rafts, Reppy ran forward up the port keel to see what else could be done.

As the tail hit, several men dropped from the hangar into the ocean. Gentile was anxious to jump, but Kirkpatrick was hanging indecisively onto a girder at the hatch opening. "What the hell you waiting for, Kirk?" shouted Gentile. "Get out of my way!"

Kirkpatrick waited another few seconds and then dropped. Gentile reached over, grabbed the girder recently vacated, hung on for a moment, and let go. He hit the water hard. As his head bobbed to the surface he saw one of the rafts they'd dropped a minute before. He swam toward it.

Just forward of the hangar, Monty Rowe was taking his time getting back to the bow of the ship. He had just torn off the sole of one shoe in the lightening hole of a girder, and was in his stocking feet. As the lieutenant had ordered, he had put on a life jacket. He carried two others for those up front who might need them. At frame 147.5 he saw Bill Herndon standing on the keel holding a hand to the side of his head and moaning. Herndon explained he had tried to dive through one of the slanting observation windows. He had thought the Plexiglas would break out, but it had merely bounced him back.

Rowe passed Herndon and climbed up the slanting keel until he reached the big cargo hatch at frame 187. Half a dozen men were lowering a life raft.

Nick Garner was laughing. "Hey, Babe," he called to Klaassen, "this'll be the last time I get a chance to do this." With relish Garner kicked a hole in the side of the dirigible. Then he took off his sneakers and jumped onto a pulley rope attached above the hatch for hauling heavy groceries. Still joking, he climbed down the rope several yards and jumped. Klaassen followed.

Rowe kept heading forward until he reached the large group at the very nose of the ship. He passed out the extra life jackets. Several of the men had cut holes in the nose and were looking down. The water was 250 feet below. Everyone decided to wait until the ship settled.

"Why doesn't someone go topside and tie off the gas valves?" suggested a rigger.

This sounded like a good idea to Rowe, for the ship was losing buoyancy. Besides, he didn't like to sit and wait. "I'd go if I had shoes," he volunteered.

"You can have my shoes," said Commander Clay affably.

Rowe tried to put on one of the commander's shoes. They were three sizes too small. "I'll go anyway," he said.

Doggy Domian stepped forward. "I'll go," he said.

Reppy, who was still looking for things to do, offered to take charge of the detail.

The three men poked a hole in the covering, and Rowe climbed up the outer nose of the ship. He slit the sealing strip and lacings so that he could crawl over a longitudinal girder. Doggy and Reppy followed as Rowe advanced step by step over the top of the dirigible toward the machine-gun nest above frame 187. Rowe's feet were cut at every step by the knife-sharp duralumin. He wondered why he'd ever volunteered for the detail in the first place.

As Gene Schellberg landed in the water, the force of the contact knocked off his glasses. His jacket was completely deflated, and he sank so deep an eardrum burst. When he finally came to the surface the starboard elevator fin was swinging down like a big trip hammer. He swam several furious strokes. The fin smashed into the water, just grazing his feet. Now that he was out of danger he kicked off his pants and shoes. A raft was bobbing a few yards away; he swam toward it. The raft was upside down, and Jack Leonard was trying to turn it over. With Schellberg's help, Leonard soon flipped the raft over. The two men climbed in.

Hammond had gone out of the tail on the port side. He tried

to swim away from the ship, but with each roll of the slowly sinking dirigible, the port elevator fin would push him under the water. Each time the fin lifted, Hammond desperately gained a few strokes. But soon, exhausted and groggy from swallowing water, he floundered. He knew he couldn't survive one more blow from the elevator fin. Just then the ship drifted to port, and he was free. He looked around, gasping for breath, but couldn't see any rafts. He wondered if this was going to be another *Akron*.

At the forward end of the wallowing wreck Lieutenant Campbell, who had dropped out of the control car, was having his troubles. As soon as he hit the water Campbell felt something fall on top of him. He tried to swim but his legs seemed paralyzed.

A few yards away Wiley was swimming along casually. "All right?" he called to Campbell.

"I can't make it," gasped Campbell, feeling himself being dragged under.

A few strong strokes and Wiley was at his side. He grabbed Campbell by the nape of the neck.

"Stay on your back," he said. Then the captain began towing the lieutenant toward the nearest raft. Campbell tried to kick his numbed legs to help. But Wiley didn't need any help.

More than half the men were still on the *Macon*, which was now sticking out of the water at a 45-degree angle. Clarke had climbed up out of the control car to the keel a few seconds before the crash. He almost bumped into Radio man Dailey, who had just left his radio shack. Clarke kept going forward and Dailey followed. When the elevator man reached longitudinal girder 9 he kicked a hole in the outer cover and looked out. Three girders above them, Mechanic Sid Hooper stood almost on top of the ship.

"Come on up here!" called Hooper. He told them they'd be trapped below if the ship settled fast. Dailey and Clarke climbed up. They saw that the mechanic had ripped off a large piece of the covering so that he'd have an escape hatch in an emergency.

The two newcomers had their jackets fully inflated; they planned to stay with the ship until they were level with the water. Dailey advised Hooper to inflate his jacket, but the mechanic said he didn't want to take a chance on breaking his neck in case he had to jump.

For a long moment the three stood silent, looking out at the big waves below.

"Well, Hoop," said Dailey finally. "We were lucky; we both missed the *Akron*. But here we are on the *Macon*."

"This is just like the crash in that movie, *Dirigible*," observed Clarke.

Dailey, who was standing between the others, reached over and ripped off a large section of the envelope. "Let's cut it into pieces for souvenirs," he suggested.

Hooper cut the strip in three parts, handing Dailey the center piece. "When we get back to shore," he said, "we can put them all back together."

Clarke pointed out the rainwater running off the ship's cover. They cupped their hands and drank deeply.

"This sure hits the spot," said Hooper.

Inside the ship at 170, Assistant Cook Cariaso was reassuring Messboy Edquiba. "Here's a tow rope," said Cariaso, reaching for a thick rope about twelve feet long. "When you jump in I'll follow with the rope. You hang on and I'll pull you to a raft." Cariaso bent down to coil up the rope. When he looked up Edquiba was gone.

The messboy had fled forward. At frame 187.5 he bumped into Leo Gentile. The rigger noticed that Edquiba's life jacket was fully inflated.

"Let most of the air out," Gentile advised.

But Edquiba didn't answer. He climbed past Gentile toward the nose. He was never seen again.

After the tail crashed in the water, Ted Brandes worked his way from the upper fin to amidships. With a rope tied to an overhead girder, he began lowering a raft. He thought he'd have a better chance of saving himself if he slid down the rope and landed right in the raft: he couldn't swim a stroke.

The moment the raft touched the water Brandes started down the line. Thirty feet above the Pacific he found himself at the end of frayed rope. He was stunned, panicked. The raft had somehow broken free. He hung as long as he could and then dropped. Water closed over his head. He hoped it didn't take too long to drown. Then, unexpectedly, he popped to the surface. As he was sinking a second time he felt something grabbing his shirt. A moment later he was on a raft.

By this time the three volunteers had reached the machine-gun nest on top of the ship. Rowe dropped onto the catwalk of the top keel. Gas hit his face, but he crept toward the nearest valve, a large disc about three feet in diameter.

From above on the machine-gun nest platform, Doggy and Reppy could feel the gas shooting up through the hatch.

"Hurry up, Rowe!" urged Reppy.

Inside the dim, gas-filled keel Rowe saw two pairs of shoes standing on the catwalk. He sat down and tried to put them on his bleeding feet. Both pairs were too small.

"For God's sake, come on out of there, Monty!" shouted Doggy.

"We came up to tie off those damn gas valves," Rowe said, "and I'm going to do it." He tugged at the big valve. It was wide open, and cold gas was pouring out with a shrill, steady whistle. He put all his weight on the dome of the valve, but he couldn't budge it. Then he began to get lightheaded. He pulled groggily at the curtain that protected the cell from the catwalk. Suddenly this sleeve broke loose. Gas poured onto the catwalk.

"Get the hell out fast!" ordered Reppy from above.

Rowe stumbled back toward the machine-gun nest. Finally he stuck his head into the fresh air.

"Are you O.K.?" asked Doggy.

"Sure," said Rowe in a high-pitched feminine voice. The helium had changed him to a soprano.

Far below at frame 102.5, Mechanic Bill Baker was still sitting serenely on the outrigger outside his engine room. He watched gasoline and oil tanks fall through the ship into the ocean. Underwater pressure exploded the tanks with the dull thud of a depth charge. Then great bubbles of gas and oil shot up, forming pools all around the settling airship. Baker saw some men slide down ropes into rafts without getting their feet wet. He saw others struggling in the sea, retching from the oily water. Just forward, he noticed Andy Galatian sitting on the outrigger of engine Number 8. Since the water had now risen level with Baker's propeller, he decided to crawl a little higher. He hoisted himself up the catwalk to Galatian's side. They talked for some time.

When they were about eight feet above water, Baker rolled up his flight coat, stuck the flashlight inside, and threw the bundle into the ocean. Then casually he jumped in. Galatian followed him. The two men paddled around. After a few minutes they saw a life raft being launched from the nose, which was still 200 feet above water. The raft was lowered to within fifty feet of the sea. Then a man slid down the rope. As he neared the raft he cut the rope above his hands. Raft and man plunged into the Pacific, out of sight.

Gentile and Galatian swam toward the bow but they still couldn't see the raft. Soon they heard someone calling, "Halloo! Halloo!"

The two mechanics shouted back. In a few minutes a man appeared, paddling a raft all by himself. It was the cook, Bill Bucher. His lands were bleeding from his fast trip down the rope. The two mechanics climbed into the raft.

The men still inside the nose of the ship realized that they were slowly being asphyxiated by escaping helium. They began punching more holes in the envelope. Then one by one they crawled on top of the ship. Most of the men had breathed in so much gas that their voices, like Rowe's, were shrill and feminine; and they were laughing hysterically, like a bevy of chorus girls. In fact they were so busy laughing at each other's squeaks and cackles that they did not follow Bucher down the rope that dangled from the nose.

Lieutenant Commander George Mills, who hadn't been aboard the *Macon* as long as the others, took the situation more seriously. "You men are damn fools!" he said in a high soprano.

The men shrieked with laughter.

"If you won't go down the rope, let me," said Mills angrily. He scrambled down the line.

Monty Rowe, seeing that Bucher had at last recovered his raft, decided to follow Mills. He started sliding down the rope. Before he'd gone down halfway, he felt someone's feet in his face. Then a pair of legs wrapped around his arms. Rowe dropped down the rope as fast as he could. He went so fast that his hands burned, and he had to let go when he was forty feet above water. He hit on his back and side. A flash of pain went through him. He had landed on a submerged antenna that stretched from the control car to the ship's nose.

The blow paralyzed him. For the first time he was frightened. He couldn't move his arms or legs. As he lay on his back in the half-inflated jacket, he could see into the submerging control car. Flight jackets were floating around inside, and he noticed binoculars swaying on the hooks.

As the ship sank deeper, the antenna receded from him until he was almost standing on the wire. Finding that he could at last move his arms, he dogpaddled away from the ship. Presently he noticed two heads in the water. One was his tormenter, the big lieutenant; the other was Mechanic Jimmy Todd. He saw that they were hanging over something that looked like a life raft. As he paddled closer he saw a paint splash that marked it as the life raft that had been stored in the starboard fin. It had just enough air in it to keep from sinking.

"Why don't you inflate it?" panted Rowe.

"There isn't any bottle on it," said Todd.

"The hell there isn't," replied Rowe. He'd been on watch the week before when one of the civilians, at work reinforcing the structure at frame 17.5, had tipped a small can of aluminum paint onto the raft. Rowe knew that this particular raft had a bottle attached on its top side.

While the lieutenant and Todd hung onto the life rope on one side of the upturned raft, Rowe snaked his arm through the lanyard on the opposite side. Then he ducked under the submerged raft. The bottle on the inside hit his face. He quickly found the valve; it was of the circular, faucet type. He turned the valve. Air rushed into the raft with a shriek.

Suddenly the raft flopped over. To Rowe's amazement he was inside it. He lay prostrate in the bottom for a moment, getting his breath. Then he dragged himself across the raft and put his arm over the side. He helped Todd, who was almost exhausted, into the raft. The two enlisted men dragged in the big lieutenant, then Rowe rolled over on his back, unable to move.

As the *Macon* settled foot by foot, Dailey, standing high in the girders above frame 170, was growing impatient. He took a last look over the side, removed his glasses, and crouched. Hooper, who had been talking with MacDonald on the next main frame forward, turned just as the radio man was poised to leap.

"Don't jump, Dailey!" he shouted. "We're too high!" He started toward Dailey, but the radio man leaped off in a head-first dive. Halfway to the water Dailey seemed to change his mind, to rearrange his body as if to hit water feet first. But before he could tuck his feet under him he landed on his back with a loud crack.

"Dailey!" shouted Hooper. "Dailey, are you all right?" Hooper leaned over the side, peered intently into the heaving water below. He didn't see his friend come to the surface.

Clarke sidled along the girder toward Hooper. "Do you think he's O.K., Hoop?" he asked.

"He probably came up under the ship," said Hooper, "and swam to the other side." But secretly he felt he'd never see Dailey again.

Then Hooper heard airplanes breaking loose from the hangar inside. He knew they'd have to abandon the *Macon* soon.

"I'm leaving the ship," he said.

"Don't jump!" warned Clarke. "We're still too far from the water."

"I'm not going to jump. I'm going to work my way down the side of the ship." Hooper took off his trousers and shoes. Then he yanked up the sealing strip that covered the lacings where the fabric panels were secured to the ship. He slowly lowered himself. Holding his weight with his left hand, he tore off another section of sealing strip with his right. It was a difficult descent, for the ship curved in. Looking up, Hooper saw that Clarke was coming down the forward side of the frame.

Suddenly Hooper felt the girder start to twist. He heard an

ominous, brittle crack. The pressure on his left hand increased unbearably, and he knew he'd have to let go soon.

"I have to let go!" he shouted to Clarke. He dropped feet first for
over fifty feet. When he came to the surface he swam clear of the
ship. Then he started to inflate his life jacket. But the water was
so rough that he kept swallowing salt water. He wished that the
officer who had warned about deflating jackets had also told how to
blow them up in rough water. The jacket kept slipping up to Hooper's neck, and he had to swim to keep it under him.

He looked around for Clarke and other survivors. In the dusk he
could barely make out the lighthouse at Point Sur. But except for the
sinking *Macon* nothing else was in sight. He wondered what had
happened to all the life rafts.

All but a group of fifteen men atop the nose were now in the
rafts, being hauled aboard, or struggling in the water. Some had
less trouble than they'd feared, others had more. Mechanic Eddie
Morris couldn't swim, and he thought his chances were slim of getting out of the mess alive. But when he found himself in the water
with a half-inflated preserver he was amazed to discover that swimming was easy after all. He paddled gaily toward a raft. He was so
intent on his new prowess that he swam right over Casey Thurman,
his boss.

"Pardon me, sir," said Eddie without stopping.

Engineer Malak had thought this crash would be child's play
after the long, harrowing breakup of the *Shenandoah*. But having
jumped nonchalantly into the water, he sank so alarmingly deep
that it seemed to take forever to rise to the surface. The airship had
drifted fifty yards and there didn't seem to be any life rafts. Then
he saw a young rigger floating easily in his fully inflated jacket.

"Can I put my hand on your shoulder?" gasped Malak.

"Yes," said the rigger.

Malak put his left hand on the rigger's shoulder and began blowing up his own empty preserver. But after several puffs a big wave
separated the men. When it had passed the rigger was ten feet away,
swimming in the opposite direction as fast as he could.

The salt water and gasoline Malak had swallowed was making
him sick, and he didn't have the energy to put more air into his limp
preserver. He rolled over on his back and floated for almost thirty
minutes, swallowing more and more water with each big wave. Just
as he was about to give up, he saw a life raft. Desperately he swam
toward it. His arms felt like lead. After a few strokes he was exhausted.

"Will someone help me?" he cried.

Pharmacist's Mate Vernon Moss dove off the raft. In a minute

he had pulled Malak to the side of the raft. Lt. Bolster leaned out
and hauled the water-logged mechanic aboard. Malak collapsed beside Bolster. "Can I lean against your shoulder?" he asked.

"Sure," said Bolster. Then he noticed that Malak's teeth were
chattering. He threw a wet jacket around the enlisted man's shoulders to protect him from the raw wind.

Wiley, Kenworthy, and Campbell were picked up by Nick
Garner's raft. The skipper immediately took charge, collecting all
the adjoining rafts and transferring men from the overcrowded
boats. During one transfer a lieutenant commander lost his hat. As
it floated away he remarked sadly, "There goes a twenty-seven-
dollar hat."

By now there were thirteen men in the eight-man raft that
Rowe had salvaged. Rowe himself was still lying in the bottom with
water up to his chin. Shaky Davis bailed with Commander Clay's
hat. But he had swallowed so much oil, gas, and salt water that he
had to stop every few minutes and vomit.

Fortunately the raft containing Baker and Galatian arrived just as
Rowe's craft was about to capsize. Among others they took aboard
Shaky, who immediately began rowing energetically. Across from
him was Andy Galatian, who was rowing just as energetically in the
opposite direction. The raft would go first one way then the opposite. Finally Shaky gave in and rowed in Galatian's direction.

Max Cariaso's raft was built for four and it held eight. A seam
on the side had torn, and Max was holding onto the ripped area with
his left hand as he pumped out the rising water with his right. The
others in the boat were laughing and joking, oblivious of Max's
problem.

"I'm tired," Max complained. "My hands are cramped." Nobody
paid him any attention. "All right, I'm giving it up," he said in disgust. "I can float." He let go the torn seam. Class, another cook,
grabbed it with both hands.

Only fifty feet of the *Macon* now protruded from the water.
Ten men still sat on top of the nose.

"Come on in and get your feet wet!" shouted a wag from one of
the rafts. "What the hell are you doing up there?"

"Wait for us!" shouted Doggy Domian in a piercing falsetto. His
mates on the bow roared with laughter. Then one by one they
dove or jumped, and swam to the nearby rafts. Finally there was
only one man left—Lieutenant Reppy. When the nose of the ship
was fifteen feet above water, the redhead climbed lazily to his feet,
as though reluctant to leave, and dove into the water. Less than a
minute later, at 6:20 P.M., forty minutes after the tail had first
struck the water, the last of the *Macon* disappeared with a slight

sucking noise. As it went under, fire broke out on the surface.
Phosphorus flares, ignited by water, had set afire the pools of gas
and oil that covered the sea. The men in the rafts paddled frantically to get away from the creeping flames.

Since Dailey's first SOS, all units of the fleet had been looking for
the *Macon*. The *F. J. Luckenbach* and the Standard Oil tanker,
J. A. Moffett, joined the search. But even though the stricken craft
remained with its bow out of water forty minutes, no one could
find her in the mist and gathering gloom.

The news soon spread all over Sunnyvale, and within an hour most
of the men's families had been informed of the disaster. Germaine,
on the off-duty section, was detailed to tell the wife of his friend,
Doc Safford. When he came to the Safford house in Mountain View
he brought along Mrs. Karpinsky, the wife of a veteran airshipman.

"The *Macon* made a forced landing," Germaine told Mrs. Safford.

"Well, everything's all right, isn't it?" Mrs. Safford asked. "They'll
bring it back, won't they?"

Germaine looked at her in solemn silence.

"No," said Mrs. Karpinsky gently. "They'll never bring that ship
back. It sank."

Mrs. Malak got the news differently. She was sick in bed, listening to the five-thirty broadcast in her bungalow on Ehrhorn Avenue, only a few blocks from the Saffords'. She jumped out of bed
and started dressing. "When I see him," she thought, "I'll believe he's
alive." Stories of the *Akron* kept going through her mind. It was
the same thing all over again.

The Malaks' six-and-a-half-year-old daughter, Anna, also heard the
broadcast. She burst into tears.

"If Daddy's saved," she promised, "I'll eat anything. Even beans
and corn meal!"

As the premature darkness of the stormy day set in, the men in
the rafts bailed out their foundering, overloaded boats and huddled
together for warmth. Although the water was not choppy, great
swells were running, and half of the rafts were shipping water
badly.

The men in the water were tiring after the long vigil. Friends
inside the rafts would sit on their arms so they wouldn't slip away
and go under the water.

"Where the hell is the damn fleet?" asked a shivering junior officer.

There was a shout from a distant raft. The top lights of some
vessel had been sighted in the distance. The men cheered lustily. In
a few minutes searchlights were sweeping the nearby waters, and

several dark, dim ships drew closer. For fifteen minutes the searchlights looked in vain. Then they began to move away.

"They can't see us for these big swells," said Bill Baker.

"Let's wet the oars and swing 'em," suggested Lieutenant
Mackey. "They might reflect the searchlights."

Oars were dipped in the water and waved high above the rafts.
Other men tied rags and shirts on oars and waved them.

At 7:18 P.M., a lookout on the USS *Richmond* saw a flash in the
distance. A moment later the ship's probing searchlights lit up two
life rafts. The half-frozen men waved and shouted. The long, cold
wait was over at last.

Of the seventy-six men on the *Akron*, only three survived. Of the
eighty-one men on the *Macon*, only two died. They were Radio man
Dailey and Messboy Edquiba. Their bodies were never found.

When Julius Malak came home the next day, his wife told him of
the promise little Anna had made. Malak decided to test her. That
evening he placed a heaping plate of beans and corn meal in front of
his daughter.

She pushed it away.

"But what about your promise?" reminded Mrs. Malak.

"Oh," said the child with disgust, "I can't eat dog food!"

A few hours after Monty Rowe's return to Sunnyvale he ran
into the big lieutenant who had been making his life difficult.
"Well, sir," said Rowe. "You said when we got back to Sunnyvale
you were going to punch my nose."

The lieutenant shrugged his shoulders. "Look, Rowe," he said,
"we were both damned lucky to get out of the *Macon* alive. Let's
forget it." The two men didn't shake hands, but their feud was ended.

Late that night a sailor noticed that the powerful beam atop the
Sunnyvale hangar had been automatically turned on. It was still
blinking faithfully, trying to guide home an airship that lay hundreds of feet beneath the Pacific. The sailor reported the mistake.
In a few minutes the big light went out. It was never again used to
home a rigid dirigible. The last dive of the *Macon* ended the great
ships of the sky in America.

Now Germany and Dr. Eckener stood alone.

17

TWILIGHT
OF THE GODS

On Thursday afternoon, May 6, 1937, the seventh-place Brooklyn
Dodgers were playing the leaders of the National League, the Pittsburgh Pirates, at Ebbets Field. And the Dodgers were winning. The
Brooklyn fans were so busy booing the umpires and cheering their
pitcher, Van Lingle Mungo, that little attention was paid a giant
airship that was floating lazily over Bedford Avenue. In fact, the
following morning not a single sports writer mentioned that the
luxury air-liner, the *Hindenburg*, had been briefly and remotely a
witness to the surprising 9-5 Dodger victory.

In less partisan sections of New York there was more interest.
Along Broadway automobiles, trucks, and rattle-trap trolley cars
stopped; passengers craned their necks to get a look at the flying
hotel—now nearing the end of its first transatlantic trip of the
year. Excited crowds in front of the Criterion Theatre, where
The Good Earth with Paul Muni was ending its fourteen-week run,
looked up and waved at the visitor from Germany. Taxis and busses
honked their horns in raucous greeting.

From the Battery to the Bronx faces were turned up. For although New Yorkers had seen the dirigible on many of its ten
round trips the year before, the *Hindenburg* was still a sight of
wonder and beauty. Even in that era of great new technological
triumphs it was awesome to look up and see, high in the sky, an object 146 feet high and 803 feet long—ninety-three feet longer than
the biggest battleship afloat.

At 3:32 P.M., just as the *Hindenburg* was turning gracefully
over the Empire State Building, the sun peered through the lowering, threatening clouds. Its rays glittered on the huge black Nazi
swastikas painted on the fins of the ship. On the *Hindenburg's*
promenade deck two authors, Mr. and Mrs. Leonhard Adelt, were
waving at the hundreds clustered on the observation platform of
the Empire State Building. The ship was now so close to the tower
that Adelt noticed sight-seers taking pictures. The city below
looked to him like a board of nails. The Statue of Liberty in New

York Harbor was so small that it reminded his wife of a porcelain figurine.

Then the *Hindenburg*, with ninety-seven passengers and crewmen aboard, headed south for its destination—Lakehurst, New Jersey. The planes that were following it looked ridiculously small. At last curious New Yorkers in the midtown area went back to work, believing they had seen the successful end of another routine passage of "the safest aircraft ever built"—a ship so safe that Lloyds of London had insured it for 500,000 pounds at the very low rate of 5 per cent.

On the bridge of the ship's control car, 175 feet from the bow, Captain Max Pruss, a blond, blue-eyed man, was giving quiet orders to the men at the two wheels. Kurt Schönherr, the rudder man, stared straight ahead, like the helmsman of any seagoing ship. Eduard Boetius, the elevator man, who was responsible for the ship's altitude, stood sideways with his right shoulder pointing ahead.

Watching Pruss was Captain Ernst Lehmann, commander of the dirigible on its last dramatic trip of the 1936 season. During this voyage over hurricane-tossed New England Lehmann had handled the great airship so skillfully that the passengers never realized they had gone through the worst storm of the year. In fact, not a passenger had been seasick; nor had a monogramed dish or a delicate wine glass, all unsecured since the dirigible was practically free of vibration, been broken.

Lehmann was a cordial, quietly forceful man of stocky build. Now, as an observer, he still felt the weight of duty—so deeply was a sense of duty impressed on every officer and crew man of the German Zeppelin Transport Company.

Just aft of the control car, passengers lined the slanting observation windows of the fifty-foot promenades on each side of the almost square A Deck. On the starboard side, just outboard of the modernistically decorated main salon, coat and suit manufacturer Philip Mangone was trying to find the building on Seventh Avenue that housed his large showrooms. In the adjoining reading-writing room, Mrs. Hermann Doehner was unconcernedly crocheting while her three children—Irene, ten, Walter, eight, and Werner, six—played games.

On the portside promenade, just outboard of the meticulously appointed forty-six-foot-by-sixteen-foot dining room, acrobat Joseph Spah, who made a good living taking comic falls under the stage name of Ben Dova, was straining his eyes to see his home town, Douglaston, Long Island. He had just finished a successful engagement at Berlin's Wintergarten Theatre and had flown on the

Hindenburg so that he could appear at the Radio City Music Hall on May 12.

A slender, energetic, balding man joined Spah. He was Birger Brink, the ace-reporter of the Stockholm *Tidningen*. Brink had never seen New York before, and Spah pointed out the big oceangoing ships tied up at the west-side piers.

Ferryboats and liners let loose a barrage of shrill whistles and deep moans as the *Hindenburg* passed over the Hudson River. Theodor Ritter, a young mechanic in the left forward gondola, waved excitedly. His mates in the three other engine gondolas were doing the same.

As the *Hindenburg* glided across New Jersey, some of the thirty-eight passengers hurried to their cabins, which were located in the middle of A Deck. Others, aware of the not uncommon delays in landing, sauntered down the wide, lavishly decorated staircase that led to B Deck. Because of the sharp curve of the ship B Deck was much narrower than A Deck; and the observation windows on each side were so deeply pitched that it was possible to look straight down.

On the starboard side, Rolf von Heidenstam, wealthy Swedish industrialist, stopped for a drink at the well-stocked bar. Then he rang a bell on the outside of the adjoining smoking room. The ring alerted Head Steward Howard Kubis, ensconced in a kind of sentry box. Kubis pressed a release; the industrialist was admitted into a "lock" and the door behind him closed. There was a wait of a moment, then a second door leading directly to the smoking room opened. Von Heidenstam joined other passengers who were smoking and discussing the Spanish Civil War and the coming marriage of the Duke of Windsor and Wally. When the stewards stepped out of hearing the latest Nazi jokes were exchanged.

Conversation later swung to the colorful murals depicting the history of airship travel on the washable leather walls. Then a German passenger proudly told of the million-mile safety record of the *Graf Zeppelin*. But the ship they were riding in, he concluded, was even safer—the safest dirigible ever built. It had only one drawback: its sixteen gas cells were loaded with over 7,000,000 cubic feet of highly flammable hydrogen.

On leaving the smoking room, Ferdinand Lammot Belin, Jr., called Peter by his family, was carefully searched for matches or a lighter by the chief steward. Belin, a graduate of Yale the year before, chided Kubis for enforcing regulations so stringently.

"We Germans," replied Kubis humorlessly, "don't fool with hydrogen."

Indeed they didn't, and they were proud of their precautions. Not only had all matches and lighters been confiscated when passengers boarded at Frankfort, but in addition the air inside the fireproofed room was kept at a higher pressure to repel any stray hydrogen.

As a further safety measure the three catwalks, including the main one which ran along the very bottom of the ship from bow to stern, were covered with rubber. Those treading the narrow "sidewalks" wore either sneakers or felt boots in order to prevent static or sparks. Crew men who went topside between the billowing, paunchy cells wore asbestos suits free of buttons or metal that could give off the smallest spark. Naturally, all ladders were rubber encased.

And the four 1100-horsepower motors that drove the ship at a dead air speed of 84.375 miles an hour required no ignition. They used a crude oil that wouldn't burn, it was claimed, even if a flaming match was tossed into the tank.

Between these precautions and their self-confident enforcement of them, the Germans had absolute faith in the safety of the *Hindenburg*.

Acrobat Spah had seen the German confidence close up on the second day of the trip. While walking along the main catwalk toward the tail to visit Ulla von Heidenstadt, the prize-winning Alsatian shepherd dog he was bringing home to his children, Spah had met Captain Lehmann.

"You know," the acrobat had said, "I'm a flying jinx." He explained that he had already been in three air crashes.

Lehmann had smiled good-naturedly, confidently. "You don't need to worry, my friend. Zeppelins never have accidents."

The Literary Digest, in its issue of October 17, 1936, shared the German view. "Nor need voyagers on the *Hindenburg* fear fire within the ship," the magazine stated flatly. It was the same issue that predicted, in its famous straw vote, that Landon would carry thirty-two states to sixteen for Roosevelt.

Meanwhile at the Naval Air Station on the flat, sandy scrubland a mile from Lakehurst, New Jersey, weary newsmen, photographers, and newsreel cameramen were lolling on the grass at the side of the airship hangar—a gigantic dome-shaped structure which rose dramatically to the height of a thirteen-story building. They were telling stories, trying to find out where they could get a drink, complaining about the ship's long delay and the head winds that had caused it. Many of them had been pulled out of bed at five that morning to catch the ferry to New Jersey. For the *Hindenburg* had been scheduled originally to land at about 8:00 A.M.

It was just another routine landing to these men. Although six newsreel companies were on hand, only two staffmen from the Metropolitan dailies had come down from New York to cover the story. Local correspondents, like Harry Kroh of Brielle, who represented eight New York, New Jersey, and Philadelphia papers, and Herb Rau of the Lakewood *Times,* who was also correspondent for the New York *Times,* and the Standard News Association, were relied upon to file the simple story. The Associated Press had Ed Okim to tap out the landing details on its direct wire to Newark.

The landing was considered so routine that Lieutenant George F. Watson, in charge of Public Information for the Naval Air Station, had set up only one telephone in the improvised press room at the northwest end of the hangar.

It had been a long day, too, for the families and friends of the incoming passengers. Many of them, like the large party on hand to greet Philip Mangone, had driven the twenty miles to the famed boardwalk at Asbury Park to get a decent lunch and help while away the dull hours. Mrs. Joseph Spah, after attending mass at Douglaston to celebrate the Feast of the Ascension, had made the long drive with her three children in the family's brand-new blue Ford sedan. After waiting since early morning, Gilbert, five, Marilyn, three, and Richard, two, were tired and cranky.

At 4:00 P.M. a newsreelman, standing atop a car with his long-legged camera, shouted, "There she is."

The newsmen got up from the grass, and the relatives edged closer to the restraining fence that ran west from the corner of the hanger. But 2200 feet away sailors and civilian workers, perched on the movable mooring mast in the center of the huge landing circle, made no move. Neither did Commander Charles Rosendahl, commandant of the station, who was in charge of the landing operations. For even though the *Hindenburg* was now coming in from the north, low and fast, Captain Pruss had already radioed Rosendahl that he didn't like the dark storm clouds that had been piling up. He was going to cruise around, Pruss said, until about 6:00 P.M.

Rosendahl wished that Pruss would come in for an immediate landing. In his opinion the weather was favorable enough. But he knew that Captain Pruss, like the other skippers of the Zeppelin Company, was a cautious operator. That was one reason the German airshipmen had won the confidence of the world—they never took a chance.

The *Hindenburg* passed over the flat, sandy field and dropped a tiny parachute with a message confirming the six-o'clock landing. As the ship rumbled overhead it was so low and huge that it reminded Mrs. Spah of a big black cloud.

Passengers waved from the windows of the observation lounges, and crew and officers shouted greetings from the control car and engine gondolas. The ship speeded over the mammoth hangar—it fitted into the hangar with only two feet of leeway on each end— and then headed south, its four diesel Daimler-Benz motors roaring deeply.

There was a groan from the crowd as it became obvious the landing would be delayed still longer. To make matters worse, a sudden shower came on, quickly making mud of the soft sand field. Reporters ran for the hangar. The newsreel men, who had cars parked just behind the mooring mast, dashed for cover.

An hour later, during a lull in the storm, the station siren blasted nine times. The big landing crew of 110 Navy men and 138 civilians marched onto the field. But before the men reached their positions near the railroad track that circled the mast, a new shower drenched them. Many ran for the doubtful shelter of the mast. Others, like civilian Charles Exel, didn't bother.

Some of the enlisted men began complaining about being deprived of liberty just to moor a German ship. They were quieted down by the authoritative bellows of Chief Fred "Bull" Tobin, the burly veteran of the *Shenandoah* disaster.

At six twelve, the ceiling was 200 feet and visibility five miles. The wind was west-northwest at eight knots, and the thunderstorms had about blown themselves out. Rosendahl sent off another message, "All clear and waiting."

From his cubicle in the rear of the control car Radio Officer Willy Speck relayed the message to Captain Pruss. The big ship, having cruised as far south as the mouth of the Delaware River, now headed back for Lakehurst.

The passengers were warned that a landing would be made soon. Those who hadn't packed hurried to do so. Some redeemed wine and postcard chits from Chief Steward Kubis; others checked their passports and customs declarations. Assistant stewards tore sheets off the beds of the twenty-five double cabins and made white mountains of linen at the ends of the corridors. Baggage was piled neatly in the hallways near the stairs. All the passengers felt that the trip was over and there was no longer the slightest danger. Even their cigarette lighters had been returned.

Captain Lehmann, who had been gossiping with the passengers in the lounge, came forward and climbed down into the control car. As he stood watching Pruss, his former first officer, navigate the ship, he ran over in his mind the many things he and Rosendahl had to discuss about the 1937 season. A heavy schedule of sixteen round-trip flights had been planned, and special arrangements had to be made. In addition, he hoped he and Leonhard Adelt could talk over revisions in their new book, *Zeppelin,* with their publishers, Longmans, Green and Company. Probably there wouldn't be time: while the *Hindenburg* usually stayed several days at Lakehurst before making the return trip, the ship was scheduled to leave that midnight to accommodate forty-five wealthy eastbound travelers—at that moment waiting at the Biltmore Hotel in New York—who wanted to attend the coronation of King George VI the next week. And Lehmann knew that if at all possible the departure would be on the minute: the German Zeppelin Transport Company prided itself on its prompt take-offs.

The airship's crew members were annoyed by the eleven-hour delay. Most of them had American friends at the Station and in the little town of Lakehurst, and were eager to renew old acquaintances—even if they shared only a few words in common. Then, too, there was always the possibility of dating one of the pretty American girls with the very short dresses.

In the gondolas and the crew's quarters in the stern section the men tried to figure out who would pull the refueling detail. Half would be given liberty for at least three or four hours.

Among the passengers put out by the delay was Birger Brink. He had been sent to America by his paper to write an article about the tercentennial celebration of the first landing of the Swedes in America. Brink was supposed to take a chartered plane to Harrisburg to interview Governor Earle. He had planned to fly back at once and be on board the *Hindenburg* for the take-off. Now it promised to be a hectic, if not impossible, trip. Other passengers had kindly offered to let him pass customs first.

A few seconds after 7:00 P.M. Rosendahl sent another message, recommending immediate landing. The ship, its two front lights on, came across the fast darkening skies from the south. As it passed the field at about 500 feet Pruss looked over the landing crew deployed below.

A mile and a half away, on the lawn in front of the Happy Landing Canteen, proprietress Mrs. James Galloway called inside to her waitress, Lenna Kirkpatrick, who was more interested in the dirigible than her customers. "My, it's certainly late this time," Mrs. Galloway announced. "It's just going to land now."

Her six-year-old son, Jerry, ran to her side. The Galloways were Navy people. The head of the family—he was just then swabbing down the bar inside—was a chief parachute rigger at the base. And Lenna's interest in the *Hindenburg* was more than curiosity: her husband Earl, a survior of the *Macon,* was in the landing party.

At the landing field the rain had slackened to a drizzle. There was a light variable surface wind southeast two knots, and a six-knot west wind at an altitude of 200 feet. The ceiling was now about 2500 feet. Everyone prepared for what appeared to be an easy landing.

The newsreel men were at their cameras, most of them on tops of cars. Photographers squinted through their view-finders and maneuvered for position. Jack Snyder of the Philadelphia *Record* shoved in a new plate. It was plate number 13. "Thirteen," he thought. "Something's bound to go wrong with this picture."

Moving forward with Commander Rosendahl was his wife and reporter Harry Kroh, who had covered many airship landings for his newspapers. Kroh wanted to ask Ernst Lehmann several questions, hoping the answers would make the routine story more interesting. Also in the little party were Commander Jess Kenworthy, Jr., who had been executive officer of the *Macon*, and the controversial Anton Heinen, now a lieutenant commander in the Naval Reserve.

William Craig, on his first assignment for the Standard Oil Company (New Jersey) magazine, *The Lamp*, walked to the mast. From there he would have a fine view of the new hydrogen-loading method that was to be tried out. If the method proved successful, two precious hours would be saved. Craig's wife and mother sat in the front seat of his Dodge in the parking area next to the airship hangar. They were both dry, but Craig's feet were soaked and his trenchcoat sodden.

Inside a little building attached to the west side of the heavier-than-air hangar, Herbert Morrison, an announcer from Station WLS, Chicago, checked over last-minute adjustments with his engineer, Charlie Nehlsen. They were to make a recording of the year's first transatlantic landing for the "Dinner Bell" program. They had flown in from Chicago only a few minutes before, and Nehlsen had just finished setting up his sixteen-inch portable Presto recorder, model 6N.

As the *Hindenburg* floated over Bachelor Officers Quarters, Morrison, a small, lantern-jawed man of about 120 pounds, called out, "Charlie, I'm going out for the recording." He left the building, which also housed the Navy's radio station, walked onto the field, and began talking into his hand microphone. He tried to bring as much color as possible into an essentially dull assignment. Usually there were such famous passengers aboard as Douglas Fairbanks and his wife, Lady Ashley, Max Schmeling, and Lady Grace Drummond Hay. Today's list was bare of celebrities.

Inside the radio building Nehlsen was worrying about the crosstalk he was getting from the naval signals. There was no time to change positions, and he was hurriedly trying to ground and filter out the disturbances.

On the tower at the helium plant, over half a mile east of the mooring mast, four civilian employees stood on a platform eighty feet in the air watching the big ship make what they thought was too sharp a turn.

Others thought the dirigible was coming in too fast. Mrs. Frank Peckham, wife of the veteran survivor of the *Shenandoah,* was standing outside the barracks for chief petty officers' families. She thought the Germans were being smart, trying "to show us up."

Reporter Harry Kroh thought the ship was going to pass over the field again—it was traveling fast at about 250 feet.

But Rosendahl thought Pruss had made a good, if slightly tight, turn, and was coming in handily.

In the control car, Pruss and his officers glanced at instruments and then adjusted the trim and buoyancy of the ship. At 7:19 P.M. hydrogen was valved and water ballast dumped as the ship leveled off under perfect control. At an altitude of 200 feet the *Hindenburg* headed into the wind toward the landing party. About 700 feet from the mooring mast, telegraphic orders were flashed by Pruss to all four engine gondolas. There was a sputter from each of the engines as the twenty-foot-long, four-bladed propellers reversed their direction. The ship's headway was quickly stopped.

The men on the helium tower shook their heads.

"That's not the way old Hugo sets them down," said riveter John C. Wainwright. The others agreed that Dr. Eckener, the canny old airshipman with the pouchy eyes, used to come in gently and land on a dime.

The reversing of the motors sounded to Mrs. Peckham like the screeching of boxcar wheels. From her vantage point north of Bachelor Officers Quarters the ship stopped so fast that it seemed to pivot as though attached to a mast.

But Rosendahl, who knew the surface winds were blowing southeast and those at ship level were driving west, thought Pruss had come in nicely under such conditions.

At seven-twenty tiny figures appeared on the platform at the indented nose of the dirigible. At seven twenty-one the first landing rope, over 400 feet long and two inches in diameter, spun down, hitting the wet sand inside the mooring circle. A moment later the second rope hit the ground. Sailors and civilians picked up the port line and pulled it toward one of the two little railway cars on the circular tracks. The starboard crew slowly pulled their line to the second car.

A light gust of wind from the port side moved the ship slowly to starboard, tightening the port rope. The old hands on the landing crew weren't worried. But Calvin Keck and William Brown, seniors at Lakewood High School, who were doing the job for the one-dollar fee and the excitement, became a little nervous at the strong tug.

In the control car both Pruss and Lehmann were pleased with the landing. A little aft of them Radio Officer Willy Speck was informing the *Graf Zeppelin*, then in passage over the South Atlantic, that the *Hindenburg* had just made a safe landing.

Back at the airship hangar Herb Rau hadn't felt like walking the 2200 feet to the mast with the other reporters. As soon as he saw the ropes drop from the *Hindenburg*, he started for the one phone in the press room. He quickly got through to Tom Kelly, the night editor of the Standard News, and began giving him the exact time of landing.

At the edge of the field, Morrison was continuing his picture of the scene. He had just announced that the ship was coming in "like some great feather"; and he remarked that this was Captain Pruss' first command—though actually it was the tenth time Pruss had captained the *Hindenburg* on a transatlantic flight. "Passengers are looking out the windows waving," Morrison went on. "The ship is standing still now."

Behind the spectators' restraining fence, Gilbert and Marilyn Spah were jumping about excitedly, trying to spot their father in the hovering ship. In the hubbub two-year-old Richard began to fuss, and his mother tried to soothe him. But she was as excited as the children.

Mr. and Mrs. Ferdinand Lammot Belin, Sr., on hand to greet their son Peter, edged forward expectantly.

Most of the passengers were in the main lounge, on the starboard side, lining up for customs inspection. But several, including Spah, were looking out the windows of the portside dining room. Spah thought he recognized his family and was focusing his Bell and Howell movie camera to shoot the last few feet of film.

Pat Dowling, the small, wiry major-domo of the American Zeppelin Transport Company (United States representatives for the German line), stood directly under the ship holding thirty-five pounds of dry ice for the perishable food kept in the all-electric kitchen on the portside of B Deck.

Sixteen customs men led by A. Raymond Raff, Collector of the Port of Philadelphia, started from the mooring mast toward the motionless ship. They were followed by immigration and public-health officials.

Among others moving toward the Zeppelin was Einar Thulin, New York correspondent for the Stockholm *Tidningen*. Thulin was in a car bouncing across the wet sand in second gear toward the mooring circle. He had made arrangements for Brink's flight to Harrisburg. Already a plane was being warmed up on one of the heavier-than-air runways west of the hangars. With Thulin were Dr. Amandus Johnson, head of the American-Swedish Historical Museum in Philadelphia, and "Duke" Krantz, chief pilot for the New York *Daily News*. Krantz, born in Sweden, wanted to say hello to his illustrious compatriot.

There was now a strange quiet. The *Hindenburg's* motors were turning over slowly, silently. The ship hung peacefully about seventy-five feet from the ground.

"The vast motors," Morrison said, "are just holding it, just enough to keep it from——" He stopped short.

It was exactly 7:25 P.M.

Suddenly a mushroom of flame burst from the top of the ship, just forward of the point where the front edge of the upper fin sloped into the hull.

Morrison's voice filled with horror. He gasped, "It's broken into flames! It's flashing—flashing! It's flashing terrible!"

When Mrs. Spah first saw the flash of light in the growing darkness she thought it was fireworks. She had never seen a landing before and figured the Germans were celebrating their long-delayed arrival.

Mrs. William Craig, wife of the Standard Oil magazine writer, who was now standing against the spectators' fence, thought the sun had finally burst through the storm clouds. A few feet away, sixteen-year-old Mrs. Matilda Smeling Randolph wasn't watching the airship. But when she heard her husband, Nathaniel, calmly say, "There she goes," she turned around. She saw a brilliant streak of light and screamed hysterically. Her husband slapped her face.

Chief Emil "Babe" Klaassen, a veteran of the *Macon* crash who had been assigned to the tail end of the ship, noticed the sky light up. Then he looked straight up and saw a burning mass. He had only one thought—to get away.

Civilian sheet-metal worker John Eitel had just helped attach the port landing line to one of the little railway cars. He was still holding onto the big line and looking up curiously at the port side of the dirigible. He saw flames race suddenly under the ship. He ran.

Electrician Leroy Comstock, a six-foot-four giant, was standing on a platform on the mooring mast, twelve feet from the ground, ready to plug an electric line into the *Hindenburg*. But when he saw the flash of light he dropped his line. Below him Rosendahl cried out, "My God, it's on fire!"

Chief David "Doc" Safford, another *Macon* survivor, had his back
to the ship's stern. He was watching the metal mooring cable
slowly unreel from the ship's snout and start toward the ground.
But before the cable could reach its destination, Safford felt a terrible blast of heat. He turned and saw the ship blazing above him.

Next to Safford was Monty Rowe, a shipmate on the *Macon*. He
saw the fins light up strangely. Only that afternoon at early supper,
when Rowe saw the approaching storm, he'd told his wife, "If that
thing is hit right she'll blow us right off the map." Now he thought,
"Here it is!"

"Run!" shouted a man on top of the mast through a megaphone.
It was First Class Boatswain Mate Bruce Herrington. He repeated
the warning half a dozen times. As for himself, all he could do was
cling, transfixed, watching the doomed men in the nearby nose of
the *Hindenburg*.

The explosion set off by the first burst of flame grew louder with
distance. To Rosendahl, wondering if he were having a horrible
dream, it was a muffled report. To fourteen-year-old Helen Disbrow,
a sight-seer who was in the parking area with a fellow Lakewood
schoolmate, Betty Zulker, it sounded like a big thump. To WLS
engineer Charlie Nehlsen, it was a startling "overcut" on his
sixteen-inch record. The thread tangled as flakes of whitewash dust,
shaken from the ceiling by the concussion, covered the whirling
disc. He desperately cleared the record and gave the O.K. signal
through the open window to Morrison.

Mrs. Nellie Gregg, a secretary who was just coming down the
stairs from the offices over the brick guardhouse behind the big
hangar, heard a noise like blasting. The concussion shook the
sturdy two-story building. In the opposite direction, at the petty
officers barracks, the first explosion reminded Mrs. Peckham of a
shotgun blast. Then she felt a strange suction.

"What's that?" asked a friend.

"That's the end," said Mrs. Peckham. "Let's get over to the Infirmary."

At the Happy Landing Canteen, Mrs. Galloway thought it
sounded like one of the big guns over at Fort Dix. The concussion
was so severe that it knocked young Jerry Galloway to the ground.

A mile and a half on the other side of the field, on the porch of her
home at 37 Pine Street in Lakehurst, Mrs. Margaret Runion, whose
son Everett was in the ground crew, heard a rumble like thunder.

And ten miles away in Toms River, startled townspeople saw the
sky flash briefly. Then they heard a heavy, dull thud.

Strangely, Herbert O'Laughlin, a businessman from Chicago, who
was in his cabin in the forward section of A Deck, heard nothing. He

felt only a slight tremor of the ship. Then, suddenly aware of running footsteps in the corridors, he walked out to the promenade deck on the port side to see what was wrong.

George Grant, a sixty-three-year-old Londoner distantly related to Ulysses Grant, was sitting with friends in the starboard observation salon. He was talking about the calm crossing and remarked that nobody had been seasick. Then he heard a crumbling sound.

A few feet away, Leonhard Adelt was standing beside his wife at an open window. Adelt was busy looking for his two brothers in the crowd below—brothers he hadn't seen for thirty years—when he noticed the crowd stiffen. He couldn't account for this strange reaction. Then he recalled having heard, a few seconds before, a light, dull detonation—something like a beer bottle being opened. He looked toward the stern and saw a rose glow, "like a sunrise." It was beautiful, but he knew the ship was on fire.

In the stern of the airship, walking along the main keel, Mechanic George Haupt saw a fire in gas cell Number 4. It spread to Number 3 and Number 5 making a loud pop like a gas range being lit too fast.

In the control car, Pruss felt a sudden shock. At first he thought one of the landing ropes had snapped. Then he heard a slight explosion, then the horrified cries of people on the field.

"What is it?" he asked. He looked out the gondola window but saw nothing unusual.

"The ship's burning!" cried Radio Officer Speck from his room in the rear of the gondola.

Suddenly the tail dipped. The captain's first instinct was to drop rear ballast to keep the ship level. But he realized that the ship would be a funeral pyre within a minute, and he made a quick decision that gave those in the stern at least a small chance for life. Instead of dropping the water ballast he let the burning stern fall fast to the ground.

The bow then shot up to a height of 500 feet, tumbling the passengers on both promenade decks like tenpins. Glassware, lined up with military precision in the pantry on the port side of B Deck, was smashed to bits.

Underneath the flaming Zeppelin the 248 men in the landing crew, the customs men, and Rosendahl's party were scattering wildly.

To announcer Morrison it looked as though everyone on the ship and most of the ground crew would be killed instantly. "It's bursting into flames and falling on the mooring mast!" he shouted desperately.

Tiny figures seemed to be catapulted from the dirigible, and fell.

"This is terrible!" Morrison cried. "This is one of the worst catastrophes in the world!" His agonized voice trailed off into incoherence. He turned desperately toward Nehlsen, who was watching him from the window.

The engineer gave the O.K. signal. "Keep going," he said in pantomime.

"Oh, the humanity and all the passengers!" Morrison broke into sobs. "I told you—it's a mass of smoking wreckage. Honest, I can hardly breathe." Again he looked at Nehlsen, again Nehlsen nodded encouragement.

"I'm going to step inside where I can't see it," Morrison said. "It's terrible. I—I—folks, I'm going to have to stop for a moment because I've lost my voice. This is the worst thing I've ever witnessed!"

Those under the ship had trouble running in the wet sand. Pat Dowling, still clutching his thirty-five pounds of dry ice, turned and struggled away from the ship. He stumbled, dropped the ice, righted himself, and kept running. The hair on the back of his head had been burned off. He still doesn't know how he got out alive.

As John Eitel fled he kept looking back over his shoulder. The dirigible appeared to be chasing him. His legs were leaden weights in the slippery sand. It was a nightmare.

Babe Klaassen, near the tail of the *Hindenburg*, thought the ship was chasing him too. It chased him for a block. As the cells ignited one by one, each explosion seeemed to shoot the dirigible forward in pursuit of him.

Everyone ran. Harry Bruno, press relations representative of the American Zeppelin Transport Company, was standing near Rosendahl. Both he and the commander, he says, turned and instinctively ran into the wind. The instinct saved their lives, for the airship eventually crashed where they'd been standing.

But Allen Hagaman, a civilian on the "dollar detail," stumbled on the circular track. The white-hot wreck fell directly on top of him. Although a reckless mate dragged him clear, Hagaman was to die a few hours later of third-degree burns.

Near him Charles Exel, another civilian ground crew member, found himself trapped by a falling circle of debris. He thought his number was up. But the heat-warped frame above him suddenly curved away at the center, and he jumped through an opening. Even so he probably would have been burned to death except for a fortunate misfortune—his clothes had been soaked by the afternoon's many showers.

In the press room Herb Rau saw a flash of fire reflected

on a windowpane, and he felt the telephone booth shake. "Hold it a minute," he told night editor Kelly. He ran to the open doors of the hangar and looked out. He doesn't remember how long he stood watching. Then he rushed back, in a daze, to the open telephone. "My God," he said, "the whole damn thing blew up!"

Kelly was so shocked that he couldn't answer. *I don't believe it,* he thought. Finally he said incredulously, "Take another look, Herb, and make sure."

Many were immobilized with horror. The Paramount newsreelman, together with the other five cameramen, had been getting good shots of the ground crew tugging on the long ropes. With his camera still pointing at ground level, he was staring at the fire as if hypnotized.

"For God's sake!" shouted his crew chief. "Turn it up!"

The stunned cameraman jerkily swung his camera up and began to take pictures.

Others, though stunned, did their jobs without thinking. Murray Becker, Associated Press photographer, had come forward to get an interesting angle shot from the tail side. Seconds after the first explosion he snapped his first picture. The ship was then still at an even keel. Dazed and frightened, he loaded his Speed Graphic automatically. His second picture—a shot that eventually won him a prize and became a classic—caught the *Hindenburg* as its stern crashed into the ground and a 100-foot tongue of flame leaped out the bow end. And Becker stumbled forward, saying, "Oh, my God! Oh, my God!" as he continued to load and shoot mechanically.

From the instant flames first appeared, exactly thirty-four seconds elapsed before the bow crashed to earth, with the ship almost completely enveloped in flames.

The men in the landing crew were so overwhelmed by the danger that they couldn't think of anything but getting out of the way. But the reporters standing in safety behind the mooring mast and the relatives still farther back near the hangar shared one horrible thought—no one aboard could possibly live. Only a miracle could save a human being in that mass of flaming hydrogen.

Manufacturer Philip Mangone's eighteen-year-old daughter, Katherine, kept saying over and over again, "Daddy died right away! Daddy died right away!"

Next to Katherine stood her sister Mrs. Florence Balish, silently clutching the hand of her five-year-old daughter, Joan. Nat Cohen, a business associate of Mangone, fell to the sand at Katherine's feet in a dead faint.

Mrs. Joseph Spah, the acrobat's wife, screamed hysterically. Two-year-old Richard, frightened by his mother's screams, screamed too. Marilyn just stared with open mouth. Five-year-old Gilbert dropped to his knees and said, "Please God, don't let my daddy die!"

To photographer Becker it was "a moment of spectacular madness." To Ferdinand Lammot Belin, Sr., ex-ambassador to Poland, the sight of the dirigible bursting into flames was a numbing blow. Dazed into false calmness, neither he nor his wife realized for some time that the ship carrying their son, Peter, had actually been destroyed. To Rosendahl it meant not only tragedy for many comrades but the probable death blow to his life's work—the rigid dirigible.

The thirty-four seconds were a lifetime to many on board the *Hindenburg.* Philip Mangone felt the ship jar. Then it tipped, and he rolled on the dining room promenade deck "like a log."

"Something's happened," he told himself with rare understatement. He tried to open one of the slanting observation windows. It was locked. He picked up a chair and knocked out the isinglass. He crawled onto the windowsill and then grabbed hold of the ledge. It burned his hands badly, and he dropped about thirty-five feet into sand. At first he was so stunned that he couldn't think of what to do. Then, looking up, he saw the flaming airship falling all around him like a giant cloak. A few seconds later, by a freak chance, he stood unharmed in the middle of molten wreckage. "How the hell am I going to get out of here?" he thought.

Young Peter Belin was standing near Mangone in the lounge, taking pictures. The first impact threw him to the deck. Then he got up and wrapped his arms around a girder for support. Two stewards opened a nearby window and jumped out. Belin started to follow but the window slammed shut. He couldn't open it, so he broke the glass—probably with a chair, he thinks—and jumped. As soon as he hit the ground, he began running.

In the left forward gondola, Theodor Ritter had just stopped the engines. Then there was a flash of flame, and his gondola seemed to be ripped from the ship. He lost consciousness. When he came to, the gondola was on the sand. His clothes were on fire, and he jumped out of the little cab and ran, scarcely realizing he'd been burned.

Eugene Schäuble, an assistant engineer who was in the stern port gondola, doesn't know to this day how he got out. He thinks he must have been blown out of the dirigible when a gas cell overhead exploded. He wasn't even bruised.

Herbert O'Laughlin, who hadn't heard the first explosion in his cabin, was climbing out a salon window on the port side when the sill buckled under his feet, catapulting him to the ground. Two sailors seized him and led him away.

Most of the passengers were in the main starboard salon. And the wind, unfortunately, was blowing to the starboard—so hard that blackened fragments of burned fabric were being scattered over many miles of scrubby pine and dwarf oak.

At first, when the ship dipped, George Grant was thrown to the salon floor. Then he scrambled to an open window and leaped. He was amazed to find himself on the ground unhurt. But as he was congratulating himself, a body struck him heavily in the back, injuring him. It was one of his friends who had jumped out after him.

A few yards away John Pannes, the genial, well-liked traffic manager of the Hamburg-American Line, was standing dazedly near a starboard window. A moment before the first explosion his wife had gone to their cabin to get her coat. Otto Clemens, the German photographer, staggered past the sixty-year-old official.

"Come on, Mr. Pannes!" said Clemens, climbing onto a window ledge. "Jump!"

Pannes shook his head. "Wait until I get my wife." He suddenly darted toward the cabins in the center of the dirigible. Clemens didn't wait. If he had paused even a few seconds, he would have been trapped. He jumped. As he fell he heard a chorus of screaming voices behind him.

In the same salon Leonhard Adelt knew he and his wife would have to jump. He thought of getting one of the piles of bed linen in the corridor to soften the leap. But at that moment the ship crashed on the edge of the mooring circle. The Adelts were thrown from the window to the staircase leading to B Deck. The bust of Hindenburg, which had presided on a pedestal at the head of the stairs, had already tumbled to the deck and lay in pieces. The aluminum piano, on which Captain Lehmann had often performed classical concerts, together with tables and chairs from the main lounge, crashed around them, forming a barricade.

Adelt pulled his wife to her feet. "Through the windows!" he shouted. Neither knows how they got to the ground. But Adelt does remember his feet touching the soft sand and grass. Hand in hand they rose from the sand. Enveloped in black oil clouds, they let go hands to thread their way through the molten wreckage. Several times Adelt pried open white-hot wires with his bare hands— and felt no pain.

Now they ran as if in a dream. Adelt suddenly realized that his wife wasn't with him. Turning, he saw her stretched motionless on the sand. He went back, jerked her upright, and gave her a push. She ran like a mechanical toy that had just been wound up. Adelt stumbled and lay on the ground, too tired to care what happened to him. But then his wife came back, took him by the hand, and led him away as if he were a child.

Mrs. Mathilde Doehner had been enjoying the landing operations from another starboard window. It was a thrilling sight. Then there was a blinding flash and the ship seemed to vibrate all over. She screamed for her husband, Hermann, who had been at the next window, but she couldn't find him. Her three children, the only children on board the *Hindenburg,* clung to her and she quickly decided there was only one way to save them—throw them out the window.

She first tried to get ten-year-old Irene onto the ledge, but the girl was too heavy to handle with the lounge tilting so crazily. Irene scrambled away, calling for her father. Mrs. Doehner picked up Werner, the youngest, and flung him through the window. A moment later she pushed Walter through the opening. She looked around again for Irene but the girl had disappeared. Mrs. Doehner jumped and the next she knew a sailor and a civilian were leading her to safety.

On the port side, Joseph Spah couldn't open a window. He smashed at the isinglass with his movie camera, loaded with films of the calm ocean crossing. The whole window fell out. As the ship tilted and rose he thrust his arm through the opening. Two men pushed against him.

"Get off!" shouted Spah above their screams of terror.

The two men climbed out the wide window. Spah followed them, his empty camera case slipping off his right shoulder and falling to the ground far below. The man on his right hung down facing the ship. Suddenly he shouted something unintelligible and fell.

Spah, who was holding onto the window ledge with one arm, facing outward, saw the man spread out like a dummy in mid-air. A moment later the man hit the sand and bounced. The other man gasped. Spah turned and saw him slipping. The man grabbed at Spah's coat, ripping off the lapel as he dropped. Spah watched as this man fell over a hundred feet, kicking wildly all the way down.

The ship rose even higher. Spah hung on with his right arm even though the ledge was hot. He thanked God that his best trick was holding onto a teetering lamp post with one arm. Finally he felt the ship falling slowly. Then, after what seemed hours, when he couldn't hold on any longer, he dropped. It was a fall of about forty feet and he knew he had to keep his feet under him. He remembers nothing of hitting the ground—just of crawling away from the terrible heat on all fours like an animal.

No one in the control car jumped while the dirigible was in the air. It never occurred to Pruss or Lehmann, First Officer Sammt, or the nine others to abandon their dying ship. The bow came down gently, even though the dirigible's envelope was by now almost consumed by fire. The big wheel under the control car hit the sand.

"Now," Pruss said, "now, jump!"

Seven men leaped out the windows. The rubber landing tire didn't explode under the great pressure but bounced the gondola back into the air. Five men were still in it: Pruss, Lehmann, Sammt, Herzog, and Speck.

The control car hung lazily in the air and then slowly descended. It landed again, this time settling in the sand.

The five men flung themselves out of the gondola. Seconds later red-hot girders crashed among them. Willy Speck sprawled out in front of Pruss, his head bleeding profusely. The captain, clothes and hair aflame, scooped up Speck and staggered through the twisted, glowing metal barrier.

He lay down the limp, smoldering body of Speck and began beating out the flames in his own clothes. Just then a civilian and a sailor ran forward to grab Speck. Pruss recognized the civilian as his old friend Andy Wickham, mayor of Seaside Park.

Mumbling incoherently, Pruss took off his rings and gave them to Wickham. Then he handed over his watch and wallet. "The passengers!" he cried suddenly. Turning away from Wickham, Pruss ran back into the sizzling ruins.

Above the control car, Assistant Radio Officer Herbert Dowe jumped out of his little radio room just as the gondola hit the sand a second time. The heat was so intense that he couldn't stand it. He fell to the ground, covering his face, hands, and head with wet sand. There he waited until the envelope of the ship had completely burned off. Then he got to his knees. Now he could breathe. Cautiously he picked his way through the glowing skeleton of the dirigible. He suffered only minor burns.

Just aft, on B Deck, Second Cook Alfred Groezinger, who had been polishing his electric stove, jumped out of an observation window near the hot and cold shower baths—the *badzimmer* of which the Germans were so proud. His leap, he guessed, was about sixteen meters. As he staggered across the sand, instead of marveling at his own escape, he was thinking how terrible it was that such a beautiful ship should be destroyed.

Probably the most unbelievable escape was that of fourteen-year-old Werner Franz, the cabin boy. Werner was in the belly of the dirigible, aft of the passengers' quarters, walking on the narrow keel catwalk, when he felt a hot blast. Stunned, unable to move, he waited as gas cells astern of him caught fire in rapid succession. Then he stumbled to an open hatch in the bottom of the ship and jumped through it. But the flaming dirigible was descending about him, and his breath was choked off by the scorching flame. He knew he was finished. But as he lost consciousness a water tank above him gave way—apparently exploded by the heat. Young Werner was soaked to the skin. The cold water revived him, and he was able to scramble free of the falling debris. Then he cautiously worked his way through the tangled mass. The boy escaped wringing wet— with only minor burns.

On the other side of the flaming ship, manufacturer Mangone found himself trapped by wreckage. Dropping to his knees, he dug a trench in the damp sand and burrowed his way out. When he emerged on the other side all his hair, except one small lock on his forehead, had been burned off. And the back of his coat was on fire.

Mangone's daughter Katherine ran onto the field. A reporter grabbed her, begged for her name and the name of the one she was looking for. She tried to break free but the reporter hung onto her.

"Go away!" she cried. "I have to find my father!"

"Tell me your father's name. If he's saved, I'll broadcast the name so your mother will know he's safe."

She gave him the information and hurried toward the wreck.

A hundred yards to the rear, Mrs. Spah was saying her rosary and trying to keep her hysterical children under control. Now she had a new fear: the field was a great snarl of cars, trucks, and ambulances rushing to the wreckage; sirens were shrieking and people shouting. Mrs. Spah was afraid the children would be run over. She was now saying out loud, "He's too good to die like that!"

As she repeated these words like a chant, she herded the children to the west side of the two small, connected airplane hangars next to the huge airship building. To quiet the children she showed them the airplanes parked outside the little hangars.

At first everyone near the mooring circle had run for his life. A moment later Navy and civilian workers automatically ran back to the wreckage to rescue survivors.

Those near Chief "Bull" Tobin heard his bellowing voice a few seconds after the first blast. "Stand fast!" he shouted.

One man, a junior officer, stopped—more afraid of Bull than of the fire.

There were many heroes. Heedless of their own safety, Navy men and civilians, with Rosendahl in command, carried rescue operations as close as they could to the sprawled wreck. Leroy Comstock, the huge electrician whose son Larry was somewhere in the landing crew, jumped from his perch on the mast and ran toward the flames. He saw acrobat Spah crawling slowly through the dense smoke as girders crashed nearby. Comstock, who looked like a distorted giant to Spah, put the acrobat under one arm and sprinted out of the searing heat. A moment later Comstock dumped Spah unceremoniously on the sand and ran back into the smoke for more survivors.

Most rescuers worked in twos. William Craig of Standard Oil, his camera banging unnoticed at his side, teamed up with a sailor in dungarees who carried a bottle of carbon dioxide. They saw a man strolling nonchalantly out of the wreck, completely—so it seemed —unharmed.

"I'm all right," said the survivor. They led him away from the furnacelike heat.

Next they found a girl lying in the sand. Her face and shoulders were untouched but the rest of her body was badly burned. She was mumbling in German as, one on each side of her, they dug their arms under the sand to make a cradle. But the sand was too hot. Craig grasped the girl by the arm but her flesh disintegrated to the bone. The girl didn't know he'd touched her. They had to carry her to an ambulance in a blanket.

As Craig and the sailor hurried back to the wreck they heard a man shouting repeatedly, "The fuel tanks are going to explode!"

No one paid any attention to the man at first. Then someone angrily cried, "Shut up, for God's sake!"

A man suddenly darted out of the wreck. It seemed impossible that a human being could live in that heat. A flame licked after the man, knocking him flat on his face. Rescuers couldn't advance because of the heat. Helplessly they watched the man get up, toss his hands in the air, stagger a few feet, and fall again. Again he tried, half rising in the blistering heat. Then he crawled desperately a few more feet, but finally wilted and lay still. Ten minutes later two sailors, shielding their faces, dragged him out. He was as black as a burned stump.

Another man, his clothes and hair burned off, came marching through the flames in a sort of goose step. Harry Kroh, the local reporter, took his arm.

"An ambulance is coming," said the newsman.

The man kept talking away in German. He was put in a truck. Then he abruptly keeled over, dead.

Tom Sleek, another of the sixteen survivors of the *Macon* present, saw a flaming man jump from the ship and fall on his head on the curving railroad track. He and Monty Rowe ran forward, beat out the man's burning clothes, and carried him toward safety. As they were leaving the skeleton of the *Hindenburg*, Rowe saw something he wishes he could forget—a transparent hand stuck to a white-hot girder like an empty glove.

Civilian metal worker John Eitel, who had won his race with the pursuing ship, ran to the mooring mast. He picked up a bottle of carbon dioxide but was so exhausted he couldn't return to the wreck. Like a relay runner, a sailor grabbed the bottle from his hand and disappeared in the black columns that were now billowing from the spilled diesel oil. Eitel got his breath and started toward the *Hindenburg* but he was ordered off the field by an officer.

Chief Julius Malak, a survivor of the *Shenandoah* and *Macon* wrecks, found himself running to help. As he ran, he thought, "I owe somebody a chance to live. They gave me a chance when I was in the same fix." He saw a woman jump out of the main lounge from a height of sixty feet. She landed on her face on the gravel inside the mooring circle. Malak saw that she was dead, and went to the bow of the dirigible. There in the nose stood the two German crew men who had been entrusted with lowering the landing lines. Both were grasping girders as if for dear life. They were burned to a crisp.

As though walking in her sleep, an elderly woman stepped out of the belly of the ship by the regular gangway. Two sailors pulled her free just as burning framework was about to crash on her.

Fifty feet from burning fuel tanks, two other sailors found a man, his clothes aflame, sitting on the sand. In a doped, lazy way he was idly slapping at the fire. The sailors threw sand on him and then led him away.

First Class Petty Officer John Iannacone, a member of the landing party, had stared with horror as passengers dropped like ants from the dirigible. He saw one man, waxy white in the glare, walking toward him wearing only shoes.

With a mate, Iannacone got to the lee side of the *Hindenburg*. Three elderly passengers were still inside the port lounge, standing stunned. The sailors had to pull them out by force.

Riveter John C. Wainwright had climbed down from the helium tower at the first explosion. He knew his seventeen-year-old son was in the landing crew, and started to look for him. When the elder Wainwright arrived near the wreck he saw a German officer, the back of his uniform burned out, being chased by three American sailors. Though severely burned the officer was trying to run back to the flames. He was finally caught and escorted, under protest, to an ambulance. It was Max Pruss. He had already made several trips into the center of the wreckage looking for survivors.

Within minutes fire engines, ambulances, and first-aid trucks from nearby towns and villages roared onto the field. A snow-white

Cadillac first-aid truck from Spring Lake speeded down Lansdowne Road at sixty miles an hour, wheeled left at the hangar, and turned onto the field without slowing. The driver headed straight for the wreck, unaware that there was another circular railroad track in front of the hanger—the track formerly used by the *Akron*. The Cadillac hit the rails, tearing off the front wheels. The driver and his assistant were slightly injured.

At Paul Kimball Hospital, ten miles away on the outskirts of Lakewood, Night Superintendent Lillian Walshe was on the second floor making her rounds when she was called downstairs to the phone.

A frantic voice shouted, "Get hold of all the doctors and nurses you can. Send them to Lakehurst Naval Station!"

Miss Walshe quickly notified Elizabeth Miller, the hospital's administrator. Together they went to the storeroom for bandages and supplies. Then they began transferring the few patients in the Male Ward to cots in another ward.

A second call came in a few minutes later. "'Don't send the doctors," said the same voice. "The *Hindenburg* exploded. But everybody's dead!"

"Guess we needn't bother any more," said Miss Walshe.

"We'll finish anyway," replied the administrator. Fortunately she remembered the frenzy that followed the *Morro Castle* fire.

Mrs. Clifton Alice Rhodes, a nurse from the same hospital, was home ironing. Boake Carter interrupted the radio program she was listening to. In his sepulchral voice he begged all nurses and doctors in the vicinity to rush to Lakehurst. In a minute Mrs. Rhodes and her husband were speeding in their car toward the naval station.

Meanwhile one of the first survivors, Herbert O'Laughlin, the Chicago businessman, was staggering toward the hangar, his face black from smoke. He ran up to James Macklin, an American Airlines pilot who was waiting to ferry passengers of the *Hindenburg* to Newark. The pilot was standing fascinated in the doorway of the hangar, watching the burning wreckage.

"Where's the telephone?" asked O'Laughlin. "I want to telephone my mother in Chicago!"

Macklin pointed inside the hangar.

Recovered from his breakdown, announcer Herb Morrison was again out on the field trying to find survivors to interview. He saw a man coming out of the flame and smoke with his hands raised high over his head as if in surrender. It was Mangone. Sailors were trying to lead the manufacturer to an ambulance.

"I won't go," said Mangone stolidly. "My daughters are here. They'll find me." He refused to budge.

At that moment Katherine Mangone was a few yards away questioning another survivor—a man sitting on something that looked to her like a stump.

"A lot of us are alive," said the man in a dazed voice.

A sailor told Miss Mangone that the man was an acrobat. Then the lights of a car bouncing across the dark field lit up her father, and she ran to him. His burned face was saffron-colored and skin hung down from his hands in long strips. But he seemed unperturbed, even good-natured. Morrison helped father and daughter into an improvised ambulance.

They were driven across the sandy field, then north along Lansdowne Road to the infirmary.

"Go telephone the family," insisted Mangone. Katherine, knowing her father was a stubborn man, left to find a phone.

Mrs. Spah was standing inside one of the small airplane hangars when a soldier from a Fort Dix sight-seeing party rushed in. He shouted a name that sounded like Spah.

"Over here!" she said, eager yet afraid.

The soldier said, "Your husband is alive." He sounded as though he could hardly believe it himself.

Holding the baby tightly, she followed the soldier into the nearby airship hangar. Her husband was sitting on a bench.

Mrs. Spah, without saying a word, felt him all over. She couldn't believe he was really unhurt.

"Are you all right?" she finally asked. He nodded dazedly. She repeated the question a dozen times, and he kept nodding. He told her he'd seen a new blue Ford next to the hangar. It was filled with baby clothes and the windows were covered with telltale finger and breath marks. Though he had never seen it before, he knew from descriptions in her letter that this was their car.

The soldier returned a moment later with Mrs. Spah's sister, Arlyene, and the other two children. Gilbert and Marilyn leaped all over their father.

Gilbert's first words were, "Where's Ulla?"

Spah didn't have the heart to tell his children that the dog was somewhere in the tail of the burning ship. Ulla's pedigree was still in his wallet.

"What's the matter with you?" asked Mrs. Spah, finally noticing that her husband was standing on his left leg like a crane.

It was only then that Spah realized his right leg pained him.

Now Morrison was recording an interview with another survivor in the little building next to the plane hangars. Otto Clemens was explaining excitedly in German how he'd escaped. A man holding Clemens' arm, a friend who'd come to meet him, translated the photographer's story into English. "He was on his way to his cabin when the explosion came. He jumped out." Then the friend exclaimed with wonder, "He's not hurt a bit!"

A note was handed to Morrison. A look of relief came on his face. He spoke into the microphone: "I have good news for you. It's just been announced that twenty-five to thirty people have been saved!"

Farther out on the field Harry Bruno, the press representative for the *Hindenburg's* owners, had gone toward the control car to see if he could find his old friend, Lehmann. A man, completely naked and burned a waxy white, staggered toward Bruno. He fell dying at the publicist's feet.

Then a short, stocky figure walked out of the flames. It was Lehmann. His clothes were burning. A sailor and Bruno ran toward him. They beat out the flames with their hands.

"Hello, again," said Lehmann. He was in shock but remarkably self-controlled. "I can't believe it. How many of my passengers and crew are saved?"

He stumbled. Bruno took one arm, the sailor the other. Lehmann's back was burned as if by an acetylene torch from his head to the base of his spine.

Then Chief Steward Kubis ran from the wreck clutching a tin box—the ship's "safe." He explained eagerly that he had remembered it only after he'd jumped out. He'd had to climb back into the ship to get it. Clutching his prize, he hurried to the headquarters of the American Zeppelin Transport Company in the hangar. When it was opened the box contained ashes.

By this time those in the parking area were sure there would be no more survivors. The Belins were convinced that their son, Peter, had been killed. Still in a state of shock, they were led to their car by Mrs. De Witt Clinton Poole of Princeton. Just as the three were about to drive away, they heard a peculiar whistle—like Peter's whistle. They all turned, shocked anew. And there he was, coming casually toward them.

Half a mile to the east, the dispensary was in a state of ordered chaos. At first there had been only one doctor and several corpsmen, but soon volunteers poured in. Navy wives and women civilian workers, who had stayed to see the landing, put gobs of Vaseline on gauze and helped shoot big doses of morphine into the survivors. Nurses and doctors, alerted by Night Superintendent Lillian Walshe, came from Paul Kimball Hospital within half an hour of the crash. Then nurses from Fitkin arrived.

Mrs. Doehner, the bun on her hair almost completely burned off, her fur collar singed badly, was brought in with her two little boys. Mrs. Nellie Gregg, a post secretary who had volunteered, was told to take them to the adjoining Family Hospital. Mrs. Gregg picked up the smaller boy, Werner. He was so frightened he couldn't speak. He didn't know his father was already dead and his sister Irene was dying.

Mrs. Peckham was another volunteer. She helped seat the glassy-eyed survivors on benches outside the infirmary while they waited for admittance. Hans Hugo Witt, a major in the Luftwaffe, asked in broken English if he could send a telegram to his wife.

"What do you want to say?" asked Mrs. Peckham after writing down his wife's address.

"I well," said the major, "I well!"

Spah, accompanied by his wife, hobbled into the dispensary. A doctor examined him. "I think your ankle is broken," the doctor said.

"All the falls I've taken," complained the acrobat, "and this is my first broken ankle!"

He was taped up and told to go home. Just then a nurse called, "Who speaks German?"

Spah, who was born in Alsace-Lorraine and spoke the language fluently, followed the nurse into a small room on the first floor. A young crew man, Erich Spehl, wanted to send a cable to his bride. Spah copied down the man's address.

"*Ich lebe*," [I live] said Spehl through swollen lips.

Spah wrote down the simple message. As he left the room to send the telegram, the young German died.

In the next room Captain Lehmann, bare from the waist up, was stretched out on a table on his stomach. Though he was so badly burned that he obviously couldn't survive, Lehmann was composed and thoughtful. Leonhard Adelt, passing by, saw his friend and collaborator and came into the room.

"What caused it?" asked Adelt.

"Lightning," answered Lehmann, his forehead wrinkling in a puzzled way. The two looked at each other a moment but said nothing more.

Down the hall Mrs. Gregg was cutting the coat and shirt from a German. She couldn't tell whether he was a crew man, officer, or passenger because his clothes were so badly burned. She tried to be as gentle as possible.

"*Sprechen Sie Deutsch?*" asked the man.

"No," she said, leaning close to him.

He put a charred hand on her cheek and tried to smile. "Sweet," he said.

Then he died.

The airship hangar was a madhouse. The first room on the east side had been set up as a temporary customs office. Next to it was a Western Union station for the convenience of passengers, and beyond, the press room. The newsmen, their ranks swelled by men like James Kilgallen of INS, who had rushed in from Brooklyn, were weary, high-strung, frantic: they were laboring through an incredibly dramatic story that was impossible to report adequately. Information came in bit by bit and was difficult to confirm. Nobody could interview the German-speaking survivors. Nobody from the Navy was available to give technical information on the probable cause of the disaster. Wild rumors, such as the death of Rosendahl, were passed. And to compound these difficulties, there was only one telephone, and it was in almost constant use for official business.

But all the newsmen cooperated that night. No one tried to beat the others out of the story. All the information was pooled.

Meanwhile Einar Thulin had looked all over the field in vain for journalist Birger Brink, whom he knew only by his photograph. Then he hurried to the Western Union station in the hangar. He was the only foreign correspondent on the spot and he knew he could scoop Europe. His was a double responsibility. He wired the bare details of the tragedy to the Stockholm *Tidningen* and added a postscript: "Shall I stay on story or find Brink?"

While Thulin was waiting for an answer, Katherine Mangone lined up at the telegraph desk behind a crowd of newsmen who had no other way of filing their stories. Katherine had tried to use a phone in one of the Navy buildings but was told it was restricted. A Navy truck had driven her to the hangar.

When the newsmen found out she wanted to send reassuring word about a survivor, they put her at the head of the line. She wrote two telegrams. The Western Union man promised that he would personally see they were given priority. Later she discovered that the two messages had been delivered in New York City within half an hour.

Before long an answer came to Thulin from Stockholm. It read, "Find Brink."

Since Thulin had already covered the infirmary, he drove quickly to the nearest hospital, Paul Kimball. In a corridor, buzzing with action, he saw a man sitting down, his face black.

"Are you Birger Brink?" asked Thulin.

"Why, no. Don't you recognize me?"

To his amazement Thulin realized it was his countryman, Rolf von Heidenstam, the industrialist.

"What happened to Brink?" asked Thulin.

"He and I were talking as the ship came in," said von Heidenstam. "We were looking out the main lounge window. That's a nice shot

for me,' said Brink. Then he went into his cabin to get his camera."
Brink was never seen again alive.

Thousands of miles away in Germany, a ringing telephone had
just awakened Dr. Hugo Eckener, director of the Zeppelin organization. It was the Berlin correspondent of the New York
Times.

"Yes, what do you want?" asked Dr. Eckener, sleepy and annoyed.

"I thought it my duty to report to you some bad news we have
just received from New York," said correspondent Weyer. "The
airship *Hindenburg* exploded over Lakehurst and crashed in flames."

Eckener was stunned. "Yes—no—no, it isn't possible," he stammered.

"Is there a possibility of sabotage, do you think?" asked Weyer.

"If it was in the air," said Eckener, hardly able to move his lips,
"then it might perhaps have been sabotage." Slowly he hung up
the phone.

By midnight the wild excitement at Lakehurst Naval Station had
abated. The last survivors had been taken in ambulances to Paul
Kimball, Fitkin, and Monmouth hospitals. Bodies of shipmates had
been carefully lined up inside the airship hangar. Funeral directors,
routed out of bed, were beginning to set up an improvised morgue
in the cavernous building.

And out on the edge of the mooring circle a guard had long before
been placed around the smoldering carcass of the *Hindenburg* with
orders from Rosendahl not to let anybody touch anything.

Weary volunteers were now leaving the dispensary. Civilian members of the landing crew dragged across the sand to their cars. All of
them went home and took off their filthy clothes, which smelled of
smoke, scorched hair, and burned flesh. Most of them threw these
clothes away.

Murray Becker, the AP photographer, walked slowly to the
front of the hangar. His first batch of plates had already been
flown by an American Airlines plane to Newark, and he wanted to
steal a few moments' rest before taking more pictures. Becker was
physically exhausted, emotionally washed out. He flopped to a sitting position with his back against one of the huge 1350-ton hangar
doors.

He looked out at the still-smoking wreck. Then he cried.

Never had a disaster hit with the impact of the *Hindenburg* explosion. Never before had photographers and newsreelmen been

present to record a major tragedy; and within hours shocking pictures of the fire were wired all over the world. By noon the next day newsreel extras of the catastrophe were being shown at the newsreel theaters along Broadway. Later in the day prints were rushed to thousands of theaters across the country. It was a rare showing that wasn't punctuated by screams from the audience.

At four thirty that afternoon NBC appalled its listeners with a fifteen-minute broadcast on the Blue Network of Herbert Morrison's harrowing recording. To this day thousands swear they heard an actual on-the-spot broadcast of the tragedy.

That same day a special search party found many curious objects in the wreckage of the *Hindenburg*. But of the many thousands of pounds of freight and luggage only a few handbags, pocketbooks, and brief cases were salvaged. Of the many sacks of mail, only 133 letters could be delivered. In addition to several pieces of silverware, ship's clocks, and assorted furnishings, a Luger pistol was found in the tangled mess. One shell had been fired and several newspapers luridly suggested that some officer or crew man had committed suicide. Joseph Spah's Bell and Howell movie camera was also discovered. It was in perfect running order. Even the roll of film inside was undamaged.

Reaction to the tragedy was, generally, first of disbelief and then of profound shock. For the world had been convinced of the safety of the commercial Zeppelins.

President Franklin D. Roosevelt, fishing for tarpon from the yacht *Potomac* in the Gulf of Mexico, sent a message of condolence to Chancellor Hitler. Ex-heavyweight boxing champion Max Schmeling, who had been forced to cancel his reservations on the fatal trip, said, "I just can't understand it. Only yesterday I was telling some friends in New York it was safer to travel on the *Hindenburg* than by boat."

Of the *Hindenburg's* forty-five eastbound passengers waiting in the Biltmore Hotel, the majority expressed a certain regret that they had lost their last chance of getting to England in time for the coronation the following week.

In Germany there was some bitterness because the United States had refused to sell the German Zeppelin Transport Company non-flammable helium. But the Führer wired his thanks to Roosevelt for his thoughtful message. Reichsmarschal Göring went even further. In an emotion-charged cable to the Secretary of Navy, Göring said, "The unreserved help of the American airmen coming to the rescue of their German comrades is a beautiful proof of the spirit which links the airmen of all nations." It was a spirit that was soon to come to a rude end.

The day after the tragedy, fatigued nurses and doctors were still on duty at Paul Kimball Hospital. Hans Luther, the Ambassador from Germany, visited the survivors. The pudgy little man was so upset that as he apologized to the American passengers he cried because they had been injured on a German airship.

One American passenger couldn't see Luther. Philip Mangone's face had swollen so badly that his eyes were tiny slits. A dapper, fastidious man, he kept asking his daughter Katherine how he looked.

"Fine," she always said.

Mangone asked to "see" his five-year-old granddaughter, Joan. Katherine went out and briefed her niece. "Granddaddy looks a little funny," she explained. "But if he asks how he looks, tell him fine."

The little girl was brought into the Male Ward.

"How do I look, dear?" asked Mangone.

Joan didn't hesitate. "You look awful, Grandpa."

Mangone burst out laughing. "Thank God somebody'll tell me the truth," he said. Although he lost small parts of both ears and his burned-off black hair came in snow-white, Mangone suffered no permanent injuries.

Lehmann was also at Paul Kimball. Although he told Nurse Walshe he was "in a lot of pain," he never complained or lost his astounding composure. He knew he was going to die soon; and he was pleased to learn that his comrade, Max Pruss, though badly burned in the face, would live.

Later in the day Lehmann was visited by Commander Rosendahl. The two friends went over every possible cause of the fire. But each possibility—from static electricity to a gas cell ruptured by a broken propeller blade—led into a blind alley.

"No, no," said Lehmann, slowly shaking his head. "It must have been an infernal machine." And then he added with the eternal optimism of all airshipmen, "But of course, regardless of the cause, the next ship must have helium."

Lehmann died late that afternoon, bringing the death toll to thirty-six—twenty-two crewmen, thirteen passengers, and one member of the ground crew, Allen Hagaman.

Collier's, fresh on the stands that day, carried a long article on the *Hindenburg*. In it W. B. Courtney stated, ". . . only a stroke of war or an unfathomable Act of God will ever mar this German dirigible passenger safety record."

On May 11, at Pier 86 at the foot of 46th Street, New York City, 10,000 mourners and thrill-seekers gathered to watch the Nazi rites for the twenty-eight European victims of the disaster. The swastika flew every few feet, and uniformed Storm Troopers stood at attention at the head of each coffin. Their right arms stiff and uplifted in the Nazi salute, children marched past the victims singing the Horst-wessel song. Then, with pomp and ceremony, the coffins were placed aboard the SS *Hamburg* for the journey home.

It was the end of the short but brilliant era of the giant dirigibles.

Although the Inquiry Board finally laid the disaster to St. Elmo's fire, the true cause remains unknown—and has become unimportant.*

Although the disaster could not have happened if helium had been used, the dirigible had proved its general unfitness to everyone but the most devout airshipmen.

Although the thirteen passengers who died in the holocaust were the first passenger casualties in airship history, not a single rigid dirigible—not even the reliable old *Graf Zeppelin*—carried another paying passenger since May 6, 1937.

---

*Several years after this book was first published, A. A. Hoehling gathered an amount of persuasive circumstantial evidence indicating that the *Hindenburg* had been destroyed by a time bomb planted in one of the gas cells by an anti-Nazi member of the ship's crew. This evidence was published in his well-researched book, *Who Destroyed the Hindenburg?* Even so, Hoehling admitted "incredible coincidence" and left the door, if not open, at least ajar. In 1972 Michael M. Mooney, using much of the same type of evidence, made a similar claim of sabotage in his book, *The Hindenburg*. Mooney, however, appeared to have no reservations.

In his review of *The Hindenburg* in *The New York Times Book Review* (March 19, 1972), former airship officer J. Gordon Vaeth points out that much of Mooney's evidence—including his detailed description of the supposed bomb—is offered without proof; that Dr. Hugo Eckener, an anti-Nazi himself, completely rejected the sabotage theory in his postwar memoirs even though such a theory would absolve his beloved zeppelin of blame in the disaster; and that the book contains more than forty factual mistakes. "The author's inattention to detail," concludes Vaeth, "evidenced by these errors, and his failure to report correctly easily verifiable historical fact raise doubts about the credibility of his sabotage findings."

I, too, have grave doubts and reaffirm my original statement that "the true cause remains unknown."

EPILOGUE

When the *Graf Zeppelin* arrived at Frankfort from Brazil, soon after the *Hindenburg* explosion, it was stored in its huge shed, never to be flown again. But in spite of the Lakehurst disaster and the retirement of the *Graf*, the newest ship of the Zeppelin Works, the *LZ-130*, was completed at Friedrichshafen. It was christened the *Graf Zeppelin*. The first test flight was made September 14, 1938. On November 1 the luxurious ship was flown to Frankfort. Other test flights were made from this base until August 22, 1939. Although the new *Graf* proved to be better than any dirigible ever made, Hitler would not allow the ship to make a single commercial flight. The Führer was paying back Eckener for refusing the use of the Friedrichshafen hangar for an early Nazi meeting.

In March, 1940, after a bitter argument between Captain Max Pruss, the *Hindenburg's* last captain, and Reichsmarschal Herman Göring, the original *Graf Zeppelin* and its namesake, the *LZ-130*, were dismantled. (Work on the super-Zeppelin, the *LZ-131*, had been stopped at the outbreak of war.) Then, two months later, the great airship hangars at Frankfort were blown up. The day was May 6, the third anniversary of the *Hindenburg* disaster.

But this was not the end of lighter-than-air travel. The phoenix that rose from the ashes of the *Hindenburg* was the blimp. Although ridiculed by many experts and nicknamed "rubber cow" and "poopy bag," the blimp was soon establishing impressive records of performance and safety.

In fourteen years the Goodyear Airship Fleet, operating from a bus that was both portable mast and mobile repair shop, carried 405,526 passengers 4,183,470 miles without a bump.

Goodyear and the U. S. Navy combined talents to make the blimp the safest and most rugged aircraft in the sky. In 1938 the Navy worked out a method of taking aboard ballast from the sea on the roughest days. A system was devised that enabled a blimp to refuel and change crews at sea. The hardy little ships—they never exceeded 385 feet in length—were so reliable that a trip in one was as devoid of excitement as a ride aboard a commuter train.

Strange proof of their maneuverability came in 1942. Early on the morning of August 16, Lieutenant Ernest "Bill" Cody and Ensign Hank Adams, a survivor of the *Macon*, left Moffett Field—formerly called Sunnyvale—on patrol in the *L-8*. The blimp was sighted several times along the coast, but about noon radio contact was lost. Late that afternoon the missing ship was sighted floating shoreward. She glided over Daly City, a few miles south of San Francisco, and then, with motors dead, gracefully landed in a suburb street. Women and children ran to the ship. The windows of the blimp were closed, all parachutes and life rafts were in place, and the ship was undamaged except for a few dents in the gondola. No one was aboard.

The mystery of the "Love" ship that landed herself added a new chapter to the Flying Dutchman story. To this day no trace of Cody and Adams has been found.

During World War II the blimp became a successful weapon of defense. They turned back the efforts of German submarines to raid shipping along the Atlantic coast; and not a single Allied ship was sunk on blimp-escorted convoys.

In 1944 the Navy airships were assigned their most important and difficult mission: to destroy or disperse German submarines threatening to block the Strait of Gibraltar. On May 28 the *K-123* and *K-130* took off from Weymouth, Massachusetts. After a flight of 58.7 hours the *K-123*, skippered by Commander Emmett Sullivan, landed near Gibraltar—the first Atlantic crossing by a nonrigid airship. Sullivan and his six blimps drove all submarines not only from the Gibraltar area but from the entire Mediterranean as well. Later the blimps cleaned out mines from the waters south of France in preparation for the Allied invasion.

Since the war these strange, anachronistic craft have become a vital link in our Early-Warning radar defense net. They have been so much improved that in May, 1954, a Goodyear *ZPG-2*, piloted by Navy men, cruised for more than 200 hours off the Atlantic coast without refueling.

While the blimp has been assured its specialized and glamorless function, until recently it seemed that the rigid dirigible had gone the way of the electric automobile. But in 1954 interest in the rigid dirigible was revived unexpectedly. It was suggested in Washington that a huge dirigible would be the best laboratory to test an atomic aircraft engine. Today staunch advocates of the rigid, like Admiral Rosendahl and Paul Litchfield, Chairman of the Board of the Goodyear Tire and Rubber Company, are still fighting for such a ship.

And in Germany, inspired by the so-called American "Atomic Dirigible," Captain Max Pruss and other Zeppelin enthusiasts have formed a committee to bring back the airship. Captain Pruss is now in Friedrichshafen holding conferences with the Luftschiffbau Zeppelin (Zeppelin Airship Works) to decide whether a great new commercial airship should be built.

"We can serve all the large routes of the world, as the ocean liner does, in much shorter time, to all continents," said Pruss just before the conferences. "This is our hope and the bright future we see. The mighty silvery ship will have its future and will dominate in a peaceful, happy world. This I believe, and so do all my airship friends as ever."

Such was the hope and bright future airshipmen had seen from the beginning. But General Maitland had insisted on taking out the *R-38;* Lansdowne's final request to postpone the last flight of the *Shenandoah* had been denied; McCord had turned the *Akron* east; and the reinforcement of the *Macon's* damaged fin had not been completed. These mischances had led to epic disasters; and the dirigible, an unsuccessful craft even in its own time, was outmoded by an age of spectacular progress in the air.

Now only the hope remains; the bright future is a thing of the past.

ACKNOWLEDGMENTS

This book had several hundred collaborators: airshipmen, their wives, and the witnesses of many of the events recorded. When I began the book, first tracing down the complicated story of the *Hindenburg*, I had no idea how lengthy and devious the path would be. In that story alone I interviewed a seemingly endless number of survivors and witnesses. Each person I talked with knew someone else connected with the last hour of the *Hindenburg*. When I had at last exhausted all leads, and myself, I found I had interviewed eighty-three people and corresponded with another fifty-one. While researching the stories of the *Macon* and *Shenandoah* I had the same experience.

Foreign sources proved to be equally productive. With the help of European newspapermen and foreign embassies I found airshipmen in Germany, Sweden, Norway, England, and Italy. Among others I discovered, in Rome, General Umberto Nobile, who kindly revealed many unpublished facts about his two flights to the North Pole.

Of the leading characters in the dirigible story, those still alive are today scattered all over the world. Charles Rosendahl, now a retired admiral, is Executive Director of the National Air Transport Coordinating Committee. His new book, *Airshipman*, will soon be published. Many old airmen like Julius Malak, Sid Hooper, Monty Rowe, Babe Klaassen, Nick Garner, and Moody Irwin are civilian employees at Lakehurst Naval Air Station. Bill Baker and Leo Gentile are lieutenant commanders assigned to duty at Lakehurst.

Many survivors of the *Macon* and *Shenandoah* still live close to the original base of the great Navy rigids. Chief Jack J. Leonard, who contributed many interesting facts, has a home in nearby Lakewood. So does "Red" Collier, who often plays cards with an old shipmate of the *Shenandoah*, John McCarthy. Collier and McCarthy still disagree about the cause of the accident. Frank Peckham runs a prosperous trailer camp within sight of the Lakehurst blimps and just a few hundred yards from the house of Norman Walker, only American survivor of the *R-38*.

Gene Schellberg resides a few miles away in Toms River, as does
Charlie Eckert. Dick Deal, one of the two living survivors of the
Akron, is a successful traveling salesman living in a Philadelphia
suburb.

Lester Coleman and Lou Allely, both of the *Shenandoah,* have
moved to Florida. Quite a few, including Bull Tobin and Roland
Mayer, have made Texas their home. Shaky Davis lives in San Diego,
California. Captain George Campbell, in the past twenty years a
regular contributor to major national magazines, has just retired
from the Navy to devote full time to free-lance writing. Lieutenant
Kivette, a heavier-than-air pilot from the *Macon,* is now Admiral
Kivette, Chief of Staff of the Pacific Fleet. Another *Macon* "trapeze
artist," H. B. ("Min") Miller—a retired admiral—is Director of the
American Petroleum Institute's Department of Information.

Across the Atlantic, Riiser-Larsen is stationed in Copenhagen,
and Birger Gottwaldt is a commodore in the Royal Norwegian Navy
in Oslo. Rudolph Sauter, chief engineering officer of the *Hindenburg,*
along with many other crew-member survivors, today lives in Frankfort on the Main. Titina, the only dog to fly over the North Pole—
and she did it twice—finished her long, illustrious career in Rome,
eleven years after the *Italia* disaster.

Zachary Lansdowne's widow is still vital and attractive. For years
after the *Shenandoah* crash, she worked on a New Jersey newspaper.
At present she lives in Washington, D. C. MacKinnon Lansdowne,
the only child to fly in a Navy rigid, is now a captain in the regular
Navy and the father of an eleven-year-old boy named Zachary.

William Craig, who had come to Lakehurst to write his first story
for the Standard Oil (New Jersey) magazine and stayed to see the
disaster, is still with Standard Oil. Charles Nehlsen, who waxed the
famous *Hindenburg* recording, is audio supervisor at WLS. Announcer Herb Morrison, contrary to the wide rumor that he left
radio after the disaster, is now associated with Station WJAS of
Pittsburgh.

Joseph Spah, the acrobat survivor of the *Hindenburg,* recently
returned to his home in Douglaston, Long Island, from another successful tour of European theaters and night clubs. This time he had
a partner—his son, Richard, who at two years old was probably
the youngest witness of the *Hindenburg* explosion.

Many people in Douglaston still remember all the facts of Spah's
remarkable escape. But the story is sometimes twisted by the passing years. Recently Spah was buying a newspaper at a local news-
stand. He noticed two twelve-year-old girls whispering and eying
him secretively. After a minute one of the girls got up courage and
approached him.

"Aren't you the man," she asked, "who fell off the top of the Empire State Building?"

To all these people who gave up so many hours to tell me their stories (Schellberg, for example, let me interview him from 10:30 A.M. to 6:10 P.M., February 29, 1956, on his day off) I owe the facts that make up this book. I also owe a debt of gratitude to the United States Navy. At Lakehurst, Lieutenant Bess Bryant lined up dozens of witnesses and former airshipmen for me to interview. In Washington, Lieutenant Herbert Hetu and his assistant, Miss Bing Piper, patiently dug up thousands of pages of testimony and tracked down the whereabouts of Mrs. Lansdowne and many others. The Navy made only one request of me—that I tell the truth.

To the best of my ability I have told the truth. Those facts that could be checked, I checked and rechecked. Those that couldn't, I left out. I was told many amusing, and some shocking, stories in confidence. All these stories (and some very regretfully) have been omitted. Other anecdotes and incidents were left out because they came from but one source. But in spite of precautions some mistakes may have slipped through. For these I apologize.

The scenes and dialogue are nonfiction. They were reconstructed painstakingly from court records, reports, and the memories of those involved. My hope was to show how men in crisis actually talk and act.

I am also grateful to Klaus Pruss for his long and illuminating letters about his father and other German airmen; Captain J. A. Sinclair, Great Britain's leading airship authority, for information about English dirigibles; the Goodyear Tire and Rubber Company for contributing many books and pictures; the Main Branch of the New York Public Library (and, in particular, Robert Hug of the Newspaper Section); the New York Geographical Society; the Brazilian and Italian embassies; the British and Norwegian Information Services; Miss Elizabeth Brown of the Institute of Aeronautical Sciences, Inc.; many European journalists (like Einar Thulin of the Stockholm *Aftonbladet*); and two gentlemen of Perth Amboy, New Jersey: Dr. William C. McGinnis, the city's historian, and antiquarian Louis P. Booz, who told me so much about America's forgotten genius, Dr. Solomon Andrews.

Books, magazines, official reports, flight records, and trial proceedings gave me additional valuable information. Of the more than hundred books I read the most useful were: General Umberto Nobile's *With the Italia to the North Pole*, translated by Frank Fleetwood; *Zeppelin* by Captain Ernst Lehmann and Leonhard Adelt; *Up Ship!; What About the Airship?* by Charles E. Rosendahl; *My Airships* by Alberto Santos-Dumont; *Santos-Dumont and the Con-*

quest of Air by Aluizio Napoleão; and *Airships in Peace and War* by Captain J. A. Sinclair. Of the countless articles I read, special mention should be made of "Seeing America from the *Shenandoah*" by Junius Wood in the January, 1925, *National Geographic;* "I Flew the Doomed Dirigibles" by Captain George L. Campbell in the June, 1955, *Cavalier;* and "The Flying Jerseyman," by Mary Kingsley in the July, 1954, *Proceedings of the New Jersey Historical Society.* The thousands of pages of official transcripts of the *Shenandoah, Akron, Macon* and *Hindenburg* trials also provided color, illumination, and confirmation of eye-witness stories.

Finally I would like to thank Rogers Terrill and Gerald Simons for their constant help and encouragement.

INDEX

Index

A CATALOGUE OF SELECTED DOVER BOOKS
IN ALL FIELDS OF INTEREST

A CATALOGUE OF SELECTED DOVER BOOKS
IN ALL FIELDS OF INTEREST

AMERICA'S OLD MASTERS, James T. Flexner. Four men emerged unexpectedly from provincial 18th century America to leadership in European art: Benjamin West, J. S. Copley, C. R. Peale, Gilbert Stuart. Brilliant coverage of lives and contributions. Revised, 1967 edition. 69 plates. 365pp. of text.
21806-6 Paperbound $3.00

FIRST FLOWERS OF OUR WILDERNESS: AMERICAN PAINTING, THE COLONIAL PERIOD, James T. Flexner. Painters, and regional painting traditions from earliest Colonial times up to the emergence of Copley, West and Peale Sr., Foster, Gustavus Hesselius, Feke, John Smibert and many anonymous painters in the primitive manner. Engaging presentation, with 162 illustrations. xxii + 368pp.
22180-6 Paperbound $3.50

THE LIGHT OF DISTANT SKIES: AMERICAN PAINTING, 1760-1835, James T. Flexner. The great generation of early American painters goes to Europe to learn and to teach: West, Copley, Gilbert Stuart and others. Allston, Trumbull, Morse; also contemporary American painters—primitives, derivatives, academics—who remained in America. 102 illustrations. xiii + 306pp.
22179-2 Paperbound $3.00

A HISTORY OF THE RISE AND PROGRESS OF THE ARTS OF DESIGN IN THE UNITED STATES, William Dunlap. Much the richest mine of information on early American painters, sculptors, architects, engravers, miniaturists, etc. The only source of information for scores of artists, the major primary source for many others. Unabridged reprint of rare original 1834 edition, with new introduction by James T. Flexner, and 394 new illustrations. Edited by Rita Weiss. 6⅝ x 9⅝.
21695-0, 21696-9, 21697-7 Three volumes, Paperbound $13.50

EPOCHS OF CHINESE AND JAPANESE ART, Ernest F. Fenollosa. From primitive Chinese art to the 20th century, thorough history, explanation of every important art period and form, including Japanese woodcuts; main stress on China and Japan, but Tibet, Korea also included. Still unexcelled for its detailed, rich coverage of cultural background, aesthetic elements, diffusion studies, particularly of the historical period. 2nd, 1913 edition. 242 illustrations. lii + 439pp. of text.
20364-6, 20365-4 Two volumes, Paperbound $6.00

THE GENTLE ART OF MAKING ENEMIES, James A. M. Whistler. Greatest wit of his day deflates Oscar Wilde, Ruskin, Swinburne; strikes back at inane critics, exhibitions, art journalism; aesthetics of impressionist revolution in most striking form. Highly readable classic by great painter. Reproduction of edition designed by Whistler. Introduction by Alfred Werner. xxxvi + 334pp.
21875-9 Paperbound $2.50

VISUAL ILLUSIONS: THEIR CAUSES, CHARACTERISTICS, AND APPLICATIONS, Matthew Luckiesh. Thorough description and discussion of optical illusion, geometric and perspective, particularly; size and shape distortions, illusions of color, of motion; natural illusions; use of illusion in art and magic, industry, etc. Most useful today with op art, also for classical art. Scores of effects illustrated. Introduction by William H. Ittleson. 100 illustrations. xxi + 252pp.

21530-X Paperbound $2.00

A HANDBOOK OF ANATOMY FOR ART STUDENTS, Arthur Thomson. Thorough, virtually exhaustive coverage of skeletal structure, musculature, etc. Full text, supplemented by anatomical diagrams and drawings and by photographs of undraped figures. Unique in its comparison of male and female forms, pointing out differences of contour, texture, form. 211 figures, 40 drawings, 86 photographs. xx + 459pp. 5⅜ x 8⅜.

21163-0 Paperbound $3.50

150 MASTERPIECES OF DRAWING, Selected by Anthony Toney. Full page reproductions of drawings from the early 16th to the end of the 18th century, all beautifully reproduced: Rembrandt, Michelangelo, Dürer, Fragonard, Urs, Graf, Wouwerman, many others. First-rate browsing book, model book for artists. xviii + 150pp. 8⅜ x 11¼.

21032-4 Paperbound $2.50

THE LATER WORK OF AUBREY BEARDSLEY, Aubrey Beardsley. Exotic, erotic, ironic masterpieces in full maturity: Comedy Ballet, Venus and Tannhauser, Pierrot, Lysistrata, Rape of the Lock, Savoy material, Ali Baba, Volpone, etc. This material revolutionized the art world, and is still powerful, fresh, brilliant. With *The Early Work*, all Beardsley's finest work. 174 plates, 2 in color. xiv + 176pp. 8⅛ x 11.

21817-1 Paperbound $3.00

DRAWINGS OF REMBRANDT, Rembrandt van Rijn. Complete reproduction of fabulously rare edition by Lippmann and Hofstede de Groot, completely reedited, updated, improved by Prof. Seymour Slive, Fogg Museum. Portraits, Biblical sketches, landscapes, Oriental types, nudes, episodes from classical mythology—All Rembrandt's fertile genius. Also selection of drawings by his pupils and followers. "Stunning volumes," *Saturday Review*. 550 illustrations. lxxviii + 552pp. 9⅛ x 12¼.

21485-0, 21486-9 Two volumes, Paperbound $10.00

THE DISASTERS OF WAR, Francisco Goya. One of the masterpieces of Western civilization—83 etchings that record Goya's shattering, bitter reaction to the Napoleonic war that swept through Spain after the insurrection of 1808 and to war in general. Reprint of the first edition, with three additional plates from Boston's Museum of Fine Arts. All plates facsimile size. Introduction by Philip Hofer, Fogg Museum. v + 97pp. 9⅜ x 8¼.

21872-4 Paperbound $2.00

GRAPHIC WORKS OF ODILON REDON. Largest collection of Redon's graphic works ever assembled: 172 lithographs, 28 etchings and engravings, 9 drawings. These include some of his most famous works. All the plates from *Odilon Redon: oeuvre graphique complet,* plus additional plates. New introduction and caption translations by Alfred Werner. 209 illustrations. xxvii + 209pp. 9⅛ x 12¼.

21966-8 Paperbound $4.00

A HISTORY OF COSTUME, Carl Köhler. Definitive history, based on surviving pieces of clothing primarily, and paintings, statues, etc. secondarily. Highly readable text, supplemented by 594 illustrations of costumes of the ancient Mediterranean peoples, Greece and Rome, the Teutonic prehistoric period; costumes of the Middle Ages, Renaissance, Baroque, 18th and 19th centuries. Clear, measured patterns are provided for many clothing articles. Approach is practical throughout. Enlarged by Emma von Sichart. 464pp. 21030-8 Paperbound $3.50

ORIENTAL RUGS, ANTIQUE AND MODERN, Walter A. Hawley. A complete and authoritative treatise on the Oriental rug—where they are made, by whom and how, designs and symbols, characteristics in detail of the six major groups, how to distinguish them and how to buy them. Detailed technical data is provided on periods, weaves, warps, wefts, textures, sides, ends and knots, although no technical background is required for an understanding. 11 color plates, 80 halftones, 4 maps. vi + 320pp. 6⅛ x 9⅛. 22366-3 Paperbound $5.00

TEN BOOKS ON ARCHITECTURE, Vitruvius. By any standards the most important book on architecture ever written. Early Roman discussion of aesthetics of building, construction methods, orders, sites, and every other aspect of architecture has inspired, instructed architecture for about 2,000 years. Stands behind Palladio, Michelangelo, Bramante, Wren, countless others. Definitive Morris H. Morgan translation. 68 illustrations. xii + 331pp. 20645-9 Paperbound $3.50

THE FOUR BOOKS OF ARCHITECTURE, Andrea Palladio. Translated into every major Western European language in the two centuries following its publication in 1570, this has been one of the most influential books in the history of architecture. Complete reprint of the 1738 Isaac Ware edition. New introduction by Adolf Placzek, Columbia Univ. 216 plates. xxii + 110pp. of text. 9½ x 12¾. 21308-0 Clothbound $10.00

STICKS AND STONES: A STUDY OF AMERICAN ARCHITECTURE AND CIVILIZATION, Lewis Mumford.One of the great classics of American cultural history. American architecture from the medieval-inspired earliest forms to the early 20th century; evolution of structure and style, and reciprocal influences on environment. 21 photographic illustrations. 238pp. 20202-X Paperbound $2.00

THE AMERICAN BUILDER'S COMPANION, Asher Benjamin. The most widely used early 19th century architectural style and source book, for colonial up into Greek Revival periods. Extensive development of geometry of carpentering, construction of sashes, frames, doors, stairs; plans and elevations of domestic and other buildings. Hundreds of thousands of houses were built according to this book, now invaluable to historians, architects, restorers, etc. 1827 edition. 59 plates. 114pp. 7⅞ x 10¾. 22236-5 Paperbound $3.50

DUTCH HOUSES IN THE HUDSON VALLEY BEFORE 1776, Helen Wilkinson Reynolds. The standard survey of the Dutch colonial house and outbuildings, with constructional features, decoration, and local history associated with individual homesteads. Introduction by Franklin D. Roosevelt. Map. 150 illustrations. 469pp. 6⅝ x 9¼. 21469-9 Paperbound $4.00

JOHANN SEBASTIAN BACH, Philipp Spitta. One of the great classics of musicology, this definitive analysis of Bach's music (and life) has never been surpassed. Lucid, nontechnical analyses of hundreds of pieces (30 pages devoted to St. Matthew Passion, 26 to B Minor Mass). Also includes major analysis of 18th-century music. 450 musical examples. 40-page musical supplement. Total of xx + 1799pp.

(EUK) 22278-0, 22279-9 Two volumes, Clothbound $15.00

MOZART AND HIS PIANO CONCERTOS, Cuthbert Girdlestone. The only full-length study of an important area of Mozart's creativity. Provides detailed analyses of all 23 concertos, traces inspirational sources. 417 musical examples. Second edition. 509pp.
(USO) 21271-8 Paperbound $3.50

THE PERFECT WAGNERITE: A COMMENTARY ON THE NIBLUNG'S RING, George Bernard Shaw. Brilliant and still relevant criticism in remarkable essays on Wagner's Ring cycle, Shaw's ideas on political and social ideology behind the plots, role of Leitmotifs, vocal requisites, etc. Prefaces. xxi + 136pp.
21707-8 Paperbound $1.50

DON GIOVANNI, W. A. Mozart. Complete libretto, modern English translation; biographies of composer and librettist; accounts of early performances and critical reaction. Lavishly illustrated. All the material you need to understand and appreciate this great work. Dover Opera Guide and Libretto Series; translated and introduced by Ellen Bleiler. 92 illustrations. 209pp.
21134-7 Paperbound $1.50

HIGH FIDELITY SYSTEMS: A LAYMAN'S GUIDE, Roy F. Allison. All the basic information you need for setting up your own audio system: high fidelity and stereo record players, tape records, F.M. Connections, adjusting tone arm, cartridge, checking needle alignment, positioning speakers, phasing speakers, adjusting hums, trouble-shooting, maintenance, and similar topics. Enlarged 1965 edition. More than 50 charts, diagrams, photos. iv + 91pp.
21514-8 Paperbound $1.25

REPRODUCTION OF SOUND, Edgar Villchur. Thorough coverage for laymen of high fidelity systems, reproducing systems in general, needles, amplifiers, preamps, loudspeakers, feedback, explaining physical background. "A rare talent for making technicalities vividly comprehensible," R. Darrell, *High Fidelity*. 69 figures. iv + 92pp.
21515-6 Paperbound $1.00

HEAR ME TALKIN' TO YA: THE STORY OF JAZZ AS TOLD BY THE MEN WHO MADE IT, Nat Shapiro and Nat Hentoff. Louis Armstrong, Fats Waller, Jo Jones, Clarence Williams, Billy Holiday, Duke Ellington, Jelly Roll Morton and dozens of other jazz greats tell how it was in Chicago's South Side, New Orleans, depression Harlem and the modern West Coast as jazz was born and grew. xvi + 429pp.
21726-4 Paperbound $2.50

FABLES OF AESOP, translated by Sir Roger L'Estrange. A reproduction of the very rare 1931 Paris edition; a selection of the most interesting fables, together with 50 imaginative drawings by Alexander Calder. v + 128pp. 6½x9¼.
21780-9 Paperbound $1.25

DESIGN BY ACCIDENT; A BOOK OF "ACCIDENTAL EFFECTS" FOR ARTISTS AND DESIGNERS, James F. O'Brien. Create your own unique, striking, imaginative effects by "controlled accident" interaction of materials: paints and lacquers, oil and water based paints, splatter, crackling materials, shatter, similar items. Everything you do will be different; first book on this limitless art, so useful to both fine artist and commercial artist. Full instructions. 192 plates showing "accidents," 8 in color. viii + 215pp. 8⅜ x 11¼.   21942-9 Paperbound $3.50

THE BOOK OF SIGNS, Rudolf Koch. Famed German type designer draws 493 beautiful symbols: religious, mystical, alchemical, imperial, property marks, runes, etc. Remarkable fusion of traditional and modern. Good for suggestions of timelessness, smartness, modernity. Text. vi + 104pp. 6⅛ x 9¼.
                                          20162-7 Paperbound $1.25

HISTORY OF INDIAN AND INDONESIAN ART, Ananda K. Coomaraswamy. An unabridged republication of one of the finest books by a great scholar in Eastern art. Rich in descriptive material, history, social backgrounds; Sunga reliefs, Rajput paintings, Gupta temples, Burmese frescoes, textiles, jewelry, sculpture, etc. 400 photos. viii + 423pp. 6⅜ x 9¾.   21436-2 Paperbound $4.00

PRIMITIVE ART, Franz Boas. America's foremost anthropologist surveys textiles, ceramics, woodcarving, basketry, metalwork, etc.; patterns, technology, creation of symbols, style origins. All areas of world, but very full on Northwest Coast Indians. More than 350 illustrations of baskets, boxes, totem poles, weapons, etc. 378 pp.
                                          20025-6 Paperbound $3.00

THE GENTLEMAN AND CABINET MAKER'S DIRECTOR, Thomas Chippendale. Full reprint (third edition, 1762) of most influential furniture book of all time, by master cabinetmaker. 200 plates, illustrating chairs, sofas, mirrors, tables, cabinets, plus 24 photographs of surviving pieces. Biographical introduction by N. Bienenstock. vi + 249pp. 9⅞ x 12¾.   21601-2 Paperbound $4.00

AMERICAN ANTIQUE FURNITURE, Edga G. Miller, Jr. The basic coverage of all American furniture before 1840. Individual chapters cover type of furniture—clocks, tables, sideboards, etc.—chronologically, with inexhaustible wealth of data. More than 2100 photographs, all identified, commented on. Essential to all early American collectors. Introduction by H. E. Keyes. vi + 1106pp. 7⅞ x 10¾.
                        21599-7, 21600-4 Two volumes, Paperbound $11.00

PENNSYLVANIA DUTCH AMERICAN FOLK ART, Henry J. Kauffman. 279 photos, 28 drawings of tulipware, Fraktur script, painted tinware, toys, flowered furniture, quilts, samplers, hex signs, house interiors, etc. Full descriptive text. Excellent for tourist, rewarding for designer, collector. Map. 146pp. 7⅞ x 10¾.
                                          21205-X Paperbound $2.50

EARLY NEW ENGLAND GRAVESTONE RUBBINGS, Edmund V. Gillon, Jr. 43 photographs, 226 carefully reproduced rubbings show heavily symbolic, sometimes macabre early gravestones, up to early 19th century. Remarkable early American primitive art, occasionally strikingly beautiful; always powerful. Text. xxvi + 207pp. 8⅜ x 11¼.   21380-3 Paperbound $3.50

ALPHABETS AND ORNAMENTS, Ernst Lehner. Well-known pictorial source for decorative alphabets, script examples, cartouches, frames, decorative title pages, calligraphic initials, borders, similar material. 14th to 19th century, mostly European. Useful in almost any graphic arts designing, varied styles. 750 illustrations. 256pp. 7 x 10.   21905-4 Paperbound $4.00

PAINTING: A CREATIVE APPROACH, Norman Colquhoun. For the beginner simple guide provides an instructive approach to painting: major stumbling blocks for beginner; overcoming them, technical points; paints and pigments; oil painting; watercolor and other media and color. New section on "plastic" paints. Glossary. Formerly Paint Your Own Pictures. 221pp.   22000-1 Paperbound $1.75

THE ENJOYMENT AND USE OF COLOR, Walter Sargent. Explanation of the relations between colors themselves and between colors in nature and art, including hundreds of little-known facts about color values, intensities, effects of high and low illumination, complementary colors. Many practical hints for painters, references to great masters. 7 color plates, 29 illustrations. x + 274pp.
20944-X Paperbound $2.75

THE NOTEBOOKS OF LEONARDO DA VINCI, compiled and edited by Jean Paul Richter. 1566 extracts from original manuscripts reveal the full range of Leonardo's versatile genius: all his writings on painting, sculpture, architecture, anatomy, astronomy, geography, topography, physiology, mining, music, etc., in both Italian and English, with 186 plates of manuscript pages and more than 500 additional drawings. Includes studies for the Last Supper, the lost Sforza monument, and other works. Total of xlvii + 866pp. 7⅞ x 10¾.
22572-0, 22573-9 Two volumes, Paperbound $10.00

MONTGOMERY WARD CATALOGUE OF 1895. Tea gowns, yards of flannel and pillow-case lace, stereoscopes, books of gospel hymns, the New Improved Singer Sewing Machine, side saddles, milk skimmers, straight-edged razors, high-button shoes, spittoons, and on and on ... listing some 25,000 items, practically all illustrated. Essential to the shoppers of the 1890's, it is our truest record of the spirit of the period. Unaltered reprint of Issue No. 57, Spring and Summer 1895. Introduction by Boris Emmet. Innumerable illustrations. xiii + 624pp. 8½ x 11⅝.
22377-9 Paperbound $6.95

THE CRYSTAL PALACE EXHIBITION ILLUSTRATED CATALOGUE (LONDON, 1851). One of the wonders of the modern world—the Crystal Palace Exhibition in which all the nations of the civilized world exhibited their achievements in the arts and sciences—presented in an equally important illustrated catalogue. More than 1700 items pictured with accompanying text—ceramics, textiles, cast-iron work, carpets, pianos, sleds, razors, wall-papers, billiard tables, beehives, silverware and hundreds of other artifacts—represent the focal point of Victorian culture in the Western World. Probably the largest collection of Victorian decorative art ever assembled—indispensable for antiquarians and designers. Unabridged republication of the Art-Journal Catalogue of the Great Exhibition of 1851, with all terminal essays. New introduction by John Gloag, F.S.A. xxxiv + 426pp. 9 x 12.
22503-8 Paperbound $4.50

THE RED FAIRY BOOK, Andrew Lang. Lang's color fairy books have long been children's favorites. This volume includes Rapunzel, Jack and the Bean-stalk and 35 other stories, familiar and unfamiliar. 4 plates, 93 illustrations x + 367pp.

21673-X Paperbound $2.50

THE BLUE FAIRY BOOK, Andrew Lang. Lang's tales come from all countries and all times. Here are 37 tales from Grimm, the Arabian Nights, Greek Mythology, and other fascinating sources. 8 plates, 130 illustrations. xi + 390pp.

21437-0 Paperbound $2.50

HOUSEHOLD STORIES BY THE BROTHERS GRIMM. Classic English-language edition of the well-known tales — Rumpelstiltskin, Snow White, Hansel and Gretel, The Twelve Brothers, Faithful John, Rapunzel, Tom Thumb (52 stories in all). Translated into simple, straightforward English by Lucy Crane. Ornamented with head-pieces, vignettes, elaborate decorative initials and a dozen full-page illustrations by Walter Crane. x + 269pp.

21080-4 Paperbound $2.50

THE MERRY ADVENTURES OF ROBIN HOOD, Howard Pyle. The finest modern versions of the traditional ballads and tales about the great English outlaw. Howard Pyle's complete prose version, with every word, every illustration of the first edition. Do not confuse this facsimile of the original (1883) with modern editions that change text or illustrations. 23 plates plus many page decorations. xxii + 296pp.

22043-5 Paperbound $2.50

THE STORY OF KING ARTHUR AND HIS KNIGHTS, Howard Pyle. The finest children's version of the life of King Arthur; brilliantly retold by Pyle, with 48 of his most imaginative illustrations. xviii + 313pp. 6⅛ x 9¼.

21445-1 Paperbound $2.50

THE WONDERFUL WIZARD OF OZ, L. Frank Baum. America's finest children's book in facsimile of first edition with all Denslow illustrations in full color. The edition a child should have. Introduction by Martin Gardner. 23 color plates, scores of drawings. iv + 267pp.

20691-2 Paperbound $2.50

THE MARVELOUS LAND OF OZ, L. Frank Baum. The second Oz book, every bit as imaginative as the Wizard. The hero is a boy named Tip, but the Scarecrow and the Tin Woodman are back, as is the Oz magic. 16 color plates, 120 drawings by John R. Neill. 287pp.

20692-0 Paperbound $2.50

THE MAGICAL MONARCH OF MO, L. Frank Baum. Remarkable adventures in a land even stranger than Oz. The best of Baum's books not in the Oz series. 15 color plates and dozens of drawings by Frank Verbeck. xviii + 237pp.

21892-9 Paperbound $2.25

THE BAD CHILD'S BOOK OF BEASTS, MORE BEASTS FOR WORSE CHILDREN, A MORAL ALPHABET, Hilaire Belloc. Three complete humor classics in one volume. Be kind to the frog, and do not call him names . . . and 28 other whimsical animals. Familiar favorites and some not so well known. Illustrated by Basil Blackwell. 156pp. (USO) 20749-8 Paperbound $1.50

CATALOGUE OF DOVER BOOKS

LAST AND FIRST MEN AND STAR MAKER, TWO SCIENCE FICTION NOVELS, Olaf Stapledon. Greatest future histories in science fiction. In the first, human intelligence is the "hero," through strange paths of evolution, interplanetary invasions, incredible technologies, near extinctions and reemergences. Star Maker describes the quest of a band of star rovers for intelligence itself, through time and space: weird inhuman civilizations, crustacean minds, symbiotic worlds, etc. Complete, unabridged. v + 438pp. 21962-3 Paperbound $2.50

THREE PROPHETIC NOVELS, H. G. WELLS. Stages of a consistently planned future for mankind. *When the Sleeper Wakes,* and *A Story of the Days to Come,* anticipate *Brave New World* and *1984,* in the 21st Century; *The Time Machine,* only complete version in print, shows farther future and the end of mankind. All .ow Wells's greatest gifts as storyteller and novelist. Edited by E. F. Bleiler. x + 335pp. (USO) 20605-X Paperbound $2.50

THE DEVIL'S DICTIONARY, Ambrose Bierce. America's own Oscar Wilde— Ambrose Bierce—offers his barbed iconoclastic wisdom in over 1,000 definitions hailed by H. L. Mencken as "some of the most gorgeous witticisms in the English language." 145pp. 20487-1 Paperbound $1.25

MAX AND MORITZ, Wilhelm Busch. Great children's classic, father of comic strip, of two bad boys, Max and Moritz. Also Ker and Plunk (Plisch und Plumm), Cat and Mouse, Deceitful Henry, Ice-Peter, The Boy and the Pipe, and five other pieces. Original German, with English translation. Edited by H. Arthur Klein; translations by various hands and H. Arthur Klein. vi + 216pp. 20181-3 Paperbound $2.00

PIGS IS PIGS AND OTHER FAVORITES, Ellis Parker Butler. The title story is one of the best humor short stories, as Mike Flannery obfuscates biology and English. Also included, That Pup of Murchison's, The Great American Pie Company, and Perkins of Portland. 14 illustrations. v + 109pp. 21532-6 Paperbound $1.25

THE PETERKIN PAPERS, Lucretia P. Hale. It takes genius to be as stupidly mad as the Peterkins, as they decide to become wise, celebrate the "Fourth," keep a cow, and otherwise strain the resources of the Lady from Philadelphia. Basic book of American humor. 153 illustrations. 219pp. 20794-3 Paperbound $1.50

PERRAULT'S FAIRY TALES, translated by A. E. Johnson and S. R. Littlewood, with 34 full-page illustrations by Gustave Doré. All the original Perrault stories— Cinderella, Sleeping Beauty, Bluebeard, Little Red Riding Hood, Puss in Boots, Tom Thumb, etc.—with their witty verse morals and the magnificent illustrations of Doré. One of the five or six great books of European fairy tales. viii + 117pp. 8⅛ x 11. 22311-6 Paperbound $2.00

OLD HUNGARIAN FAIRY TALES, Baroness Orczy. Favorites translated and adapted by author of the *Scarlet Pimpernel.* Eight fairy tales include "The Suitors of Princess Fire-Fly," "The Twin Hunchbacks," "Mr. Cuttlefish's Love Story," and "The Enchanted Cat." This little volume of magic and adventure will captivate children as it has for generations. 90 drawings by Montagu Barstow. 96pp. (USO) 22293-4 Paperbound $1.95

THE ARCHITECTURE OF COUNTRY HOUSES, Andrew J. Downing. Together with Vaux's *Villas and Cottages* this is the basic book for Hudson River Gothic architecture of the middle Victorian period. Full, sound discussions of general aspects of housing, architecture, style, decoration, furnishing, together with scores of detailed house plans, illustrations of specific buildings, accompanied by full text. Perhaps the most influential single American architectural book. 1850 edition. Introduction by J. Stewart Johnson. 321 figures, 34 architectural designs. xvi + 560pp.
22003-6 Paperbound $4.00

LOST EXAMPLES OF COLONIAL ARCHITECTURE, John Mead Howells. Full-page photographs of buildings that have disappeared or been so altered as to be denatured, including many designed by major early American architects. 245 plates. xvii + 248pp. 7⅞ x 10¾.
21143-6 Paperbound $3.50

DOMESTIC ARCHITECTURE OF THE AMERICAN COLONIES AND OF THE EARLY REPUBLIC, Fiske Kimball. Foremost architect and restorer of Williamsburg and Monticello covers nearly 200 homes between 1620-1825. Architectural details, construction, style features, special fixtures, floor plans, etc. Generally considered finest work in its area. 219 illustrations of houses, doorways, windows, capital mantels. xx + 314pp. 7⅞ x 10¾.
21743-4 Paperbound $4.00

EARLY AMERICAN ROOMS: 1650-1858, edited by Russell Hawes Kettell. Tour of 12 rooms, each representative of a different era in American history and each furnished, decorated, designed and occupied in the style of the era. 72 plans and elevations, 8-page color section, etc., show fabrics, wall papers, arrangements, etc. Full descriptive text. xvii + 200pp. of text. 8⅜ x 11¼.
21633-0 Paperbound $5.00

THE FITZWILLIAM VIRGINAL BOOK, edited by J. Fuller Maitland and W. B. Squire. Full modern printing of famous early 17th-century ms. volume of 300 works by Morley, Byrd, Bull, Gibbons, etc. For piano or other modern keyboard instrument; easy to read format. xxxvi + 938pp. 8⅜ x 11.
21068-5, 21069-3 Two volumes, Paperbound $10.00

KEYBOARD MUSIC, Johann Sebastian Bach. Bach Gesellschaft edition. A rich selection of Bach's masterpieces for the harpsichord: the six English Suites, six French Suites, the six Partitas (Clavierübung part I), the Goldberg Variations (Clavierübung part IV), the fifteen Two-Part Inventions and the fifteen Three-Part Sinfonias. Clearly reproduced on large sheets with ample margins; eminently playable. vi + 312pp. 8⅛ x 11.
22360-4 Paperbound $5.00

THE MUSIC OF BACH: AN INTRODUCTION, Charles Sanford Terry. A fine, nontechnical introduction to Bach's music, both instrumental and vocal. Covers organ music, chamber music, passion music, other types. Analyzes themes, developments, innovations. x + 114pp.
21075-8 Paperbound $1.25

BEETHOVEN AND HIS NINE SYMPHONIES, Sir George Grove. Noted British musicologist provides best history, analysis, commentary on symphonies. Very thorough, rigorously accurate; necessary to both advanced student and amateur music lover. 436 musical passages. vii + 407 pp.
20334-4 Paperbound $2.75

CATALOGUE OF DOVER BOOKS

AGAINST THE GRAIN (A REBOURS), Joris K. Huysmans. Filled with weird images, evidences of a bizarre imagination, exotic experiments with hallucinatory drugs, rich tastes and smells and the diversions of its sybarite hero Duc Jean des Esseintes, this classic novel pushed 19th-century literary decadence to its limits. Full unabridged edition. Do not confuse this with abridged editions generally sold. Introduction by Havelock Ellis. xlix + 206pp. 22190-3 Paperbound $2.00

VARIORUM SHAKESPEARE: HAMLET. Edited by Horace H. Furness; a landmark of American scholarship. Exhaustive footnotes and appendices treat all doubtful words and phrases, as well as suggested critical emendations throughout the play's history. First volume contains editor's own text, collated with all Quartos and Folios. Second volume contains full first Quarto, translations of Shakespeare's sources (Belleforest, and Saxo Grammaticus), Der Bestrafte Brudermord, and many essays on critical and historical points of interest by major authorities of past and present. Includes details of staging and costuming over the years. By far the best edition available for serious students of Shakespeare. Total of xx + 905pp. 21004-9, 21005-7, 2 volumes, Paperbound $7.00

A LIFE OF WILLIAM SHAKESPEARE, Sir Sidney Lee. This is the standard life of Shakespeare, summarizing everything known about Shakespeare and his plays. Incredibly rich in material, broad in coverage, clear and judicious, it has served thousands as the best introduction to Shakespeare. 1931 edition. 9 plates. xxix + 792pp. (USO) 21967-4 Paperbound $3.75

MASTERS OF THE DRAMA, John Gassner. Most comprehensive history of the drama in print, covering every tradition from Greeks to modern Europe and America, including India, Far East, etc. Covers more than 800 dramatists, 2000 plays, with biographical material, plot summaries, theatre history, criticism, etc. "Best of its kind in English," *New Republic*. 77 illustrations. xxii + 890pp. 20100-7 Clothbound $8.50

THE EVOLUTION OF THE ENGLISH LANGUAGE, George McKnight. The growth of English, from the 14th century to the present. Unusual, non-technical account presents basic information in very interesting form: sound shifts, change in grammar and syntax, vocabulary growth, similar topics. Abundantly illustrated with quotations. Formerly *Modern English in the Making*. xii + 590pp. 21932-1 Paperbound $3.50

AN ETYMOLOGICAL DICTIONARY OF MODERN ENGLISH, Ernest Weekley. Fullest, richest work of its sort, by foremost British lexicographer. Detailed word histories, including many colloquial and archaic words; extensive quotations. Do not confuse this with the Concise Etymological Dictionary, which is much abridged. Total of xxvii + 830pp. 6½ x 9¼. 21873-2, 21874-0 Two volumes, Paperbound $6.00

FLATLAND: A ROMANCE OF MANY DIMENSIONS, E. A. Abbott. Classic of science-fiction explores ramifications of life in a two-dimensional world, and what happens when a three-dimensional being intrudes. Amusing reading, but also useful as introduction to thought about hyperspace. Introduction by Banesh Hoffmann. 16 illustrations. xx + 103pp. 20001-9 Paperbound $1.00

POEMS OF ANNE BRADSTREET, edited with an introduction by Robert Hutchinson. A new selection of poems by America's first poet and perhaps the first significant woman poet in the English language. 48 poems display her development in works of considerable variety—love poems, domestic poems, religious meditations, formal elegies, "quaternions," etc. Notes, bibliography. viii + 222pp.

22160-1 Paperbound $2.00

THREE GOTHIC NOVELS: THE CASTLE OF OTRANTO BY HORACE WALPOLE; VATHEK BY WILLIAM BECKFORD; THE VAMPYRE BY JOHN POLIDORI, WITH FRAGMENT OF A NOVEL BY LORD BYRON, edited by E. F. Bleiler. The first Gothic novel, by Walpole; the finest Oriental tale in English, by Beckford; powerful Romantic supernatural story in versions by Polidori and Byron. All extremely important in history of literature; all still exciting, packed with supernatural thrills, ghosts, haunted castles, magic, etc. xl + 291pp.

21232-7 Paperbound $2.50

THE BEST TALES OF HOFFMANN, E. T. A. Hoffmann. 10 of Hoffmann's most important stories, in modern re-editings of standard translations: Nutcracker and the King of Mice, Signor Formica, Automata, The Sandman, Rath Krespel, The Golden Flowerpot, Master Martin the Cooper, The Mines of Falun, The King's Betrothed, A New Year's Eve Adventure. 7 illustrations by Hoffmann. Edited by E. F. Bleiler. xxxix + 419pp. 21793-0 Paperbound $3.00

GHOST AND HORROR STORIES OF AMBROSE BIERCE, Ambrose Bierce. 23 strikingly modern stories of the horrors latent in the human mind: The Eyes of the Panther, The Damned Thing, An Occurrence at Owl Creek Bridge, An Inhabitant of Carcosa, etc., plus the dream-essay, Visions of the Night. Edited by E. F. Bleiler. xxii + 199pp. 20767-6 Paperbound $1.50

BEST GHOST STORIES OF J. S. LEFANU, J. Sheridan LeFanu. Finest stories by Victorian master often considered greatest supernatural writer of all. Carmilla, Green Tea, The Haunted Baronet, The Familiar, and 12 others. Most never before available in the U. S. A. Edited by E. F. Bleiler. 8 illustrations from Victorian publications. xvii + 467pp. 20415-4 Paperbound $3.00

MATHEMATICAL FOUNDATIONS OF INFORMATION THEORY, A. I. Khinchin. Comprehensive introduction to work of Shannon, McMillan, Feinstein and Khinchin, placing these investigations on a rigorous mathematical basis. Covers entropy concept in probability theory, uniqueness theorem, Shannon's inequality, ergodic sources, the E property, martingale concept, noise, Feinstein's fundamental lemma, Shanon's first and second theorems. Translated by R. A. Silverman and M. D. Friedman. iii + 120pp. 60434-9 Paperbound $1.75

SEVEN SCIENCE FICTION NOVELS, H. G. Wells. The standard collection of the great novels. Complete, unabridged. *First Men in the Moon, Island of Dr. Moreau, War of the Worlds, Food of the Gods, Invisible Man, Time Machine, In the Days of the Comet.* Not only science fiction fans, but every educated person owes it to himself to read these novels. 1015pp 20264-X Clothbound $5.00

MATHEMATICAL PUZZLES FOR BEGINNERS AND ENTHUSIASTS, Geoffrey Mott-Smith. 189 puzzles from easy to difficult—involving arithmetic, logic, algebra, properties of digits, probability, etc.—for enjoyment and mental stimulus. Explanation of mathematical principles behind the puzzles. 135 illustrations. viii + 248pp.

20198-8 Paperbound $1.75

PAPER FOLDING FOR BEGINNERS, William D. Murray and Francis J. Rigney. Easiest book on the market, clearest instructions on making interesting, beautiful origami. Sail boats, cups, roosters, frogs that move legs, bonbon boxes, standing birds, etc. 40 projects; more than 275 diagrams and photographs. 94pp.

20713-7 Paperbound $1.00

TRICKS AND GAMES ON THE POOL TABLE, Fred Herrmann. 79 tricks and games— some solitaires, some for two or more players, some competitive games—to entertain you between formal games. Mystifying shots and throws, unusual caroms, tricks involving such props as cork, coins, a hat, etc. Formerly *Fun on the Pool Table*. 77 figures. 95pp.

21814-7 Paperbound $1.00

HAND SHADOWS TO BE THROWN UPON THE WALL: A SERIES OF NOVEL AND AMUSING FIGURES FORMED BY THE HAND, Henry Bursill. Delightful picturebook from great-grandfather's day shows how to make 18 different hand shadows: a bird that flies, duck that quacks, dog that wags his tail, camel, goose, deer, boy, turtle, etc. Only book of its sort. vi + 33pp. 6½ x 9¼. 21779-5 Paperbound $1.00

WHITTLING AND WOODCARVING, E. J. Tangerman. 18th printing of best book on market. "If you can cut a potato you can carve" toys and puzzles, chains, chessmen, caricatures, masks, frames, woodcut blocks, surface patterns, much more. Information on tools, woods, techniques. Also goes into serious wood sculpture from Middle Ages to present, East and West. 464 photos, figures. x + 293pp.

20965-2 Paperbound $2.00

HISTORY OF PHILOSOPHY, Julián Marías. Possibly the clearest, most easily followed, best planned, most useful one-volume history of philosophy on the market; neither skimpy nor overfull. Full details on system of every major philosopher and dozens of less important thinkers from pre-Socratics up to Existentialism and later. Strong on many European figures usually omitted. Has gone through dozens of editions in Europe. 1966 edition, translated by Stanley Appelbaum and Clarence Strowbridge. xviii + 505pp.

21739-6 Paperbound $3.00

YOGA: A SCIENTIFIC EVALUATION, Kovoor T. Behanan. Scientific but non-technical study of physiological results of yoga exercises; done under auspices of Yale U. Relations to Indian thought, to psychoanalysis, etc. 16 photos. xxiii + 270pp.

20505-3 Paperbound $2.50

Prices subject to change without notice.
Available at your book dealer or write for free catalogue to Dept. GI, Dover Publications, Inc., 180 Varick St., N. Y., N. Y. 10014. Dover publishes more than 150 books each year on science, elementary and advanced mathematics, biology, music, art, literary history, social sciences and other areas.